THE PSYCHOLOGY OF ENTERTAINMENT MEDIA

Blurring the Lines Between Entertainment and Persuasion

Second Edition

THE PSYCHOLOGY OF ENTERTAINMENT MEDIA

Blurring the Lines Between Entertainment and Persuasion

Second Edition

Edited by

L. J. Shrum

University of Texas at San Antonio

Routledge
Taylor & Francis Group
New York London

Routledge
Taylor & Francis Group
711 Third Avenue
New York, NY 10017

Routledge
Taylor & Francis Group
27 Church Road
Hove, East Sussex BN3 2FA

© 2012 by Taylor & Francis Group, LLC
Routledge is an imprint of Taylor & Francis Group, an Informa business

Printed in the United States of America on acid-free paper
Version Date: 20111130

International Standard Book Number: 978-1-84872-944-5 (Hardback)

Library of Congress Cataloging-in-Publication Data

The psychology of entertainment media : blurring the lines between
    entertainment and persuasion / editor, L.J. Shrum. -- 2nd ed.
        p. cm.
    Includes bibliographical references and index.
    ISBN 978-1-84872-944-5 (hardcover : alk. paper)
    1. Subliminal advertising. 2. Advertising--Psychological aspects. 3. Mass
media--Psychological aspects. 4. Persuasion (Psychology) 5. Manipulative
behavior. I. Shrum, L. J.

HF5827.9.P78 2012
659.101'9--dc23   2011046657

Visit the Taylor & Francis Web site at
http://www.taylorandfrancis.com

and the Psychology Press Web site at
http://www.psypress.com

I would like dedicate this book to my mother, Jean, and my late father, Joe, who always encouraged me to ask questions, and to Tina, who has provided so many answers.

Contents

SECTION II   The Programs Between the Ads: The Persuasive Power of Entertainment Media

Preface

It has been almost exactly nine years since the 21st Annual Advertising and Consumer Psychology Conference that launched the first edition of this book. As the chapters in this second edition attest, though a lot has changed in that short amount of time, a lot has stayed the same. One thing that has changed is the entertainment media landscape and the role of promotion practices within the different media vehicles. Product placement seems to be even more ubiquitous and also more blatant. Attitudes toward placement seem to be less negative and more tolerant of the practice. New entertainment vehicles are being developed whose sole purpose seems to be to serve as placement and sponsorship vehicles, a trend we first noted several years ago (Lowrey, Shrum, & McCarty, 2005). Another thing that has changed is the types of entertainment media being investigated. The first edition was almost exclusively devoted to television entertainment. In this edition, we also look at effects in the context of video and other digital games.

What has not changed, however, is the nature of the effects. Regardless of the medium or the message, the effects of entertainment media content on viewers—both intended and unintended—are remarkably consistent. The preceding nine years simply provided the opportunity to expand the evidence and narrow down the underlying processes in a more comprehensive manner. Thus, as with the previous volume, this edition explores how persuasion works in entertainment media contexts, and in doing so expands the notion of what constitutes persuasion, hopefully resulting in a more knowledgeable consumer and a better-informed public.

Acknowledgments

As part of the Society for Consumer Psychology's Advertising and Consumer Psychology Book Series, I want to thank SCP for all of their support for this as well as the prior edition. In particular, I would like to thank Steve Posavac, past SCP president, for urging me to consider doing a follow-up to the first book. I would also like to thank Anne Duffy of Taylor & Francis, who has worked closely with me on this book and who was also instrumental in convincing me to do this second edition. Thanks also to Andrea Zekus of Taylor & Francis for her assistance in the technical aspects of getting this book to press. And as always, thanks to Tina Lowrey, wife, colleague, and coauthor, for reading countless manuscripts and always providing good feedback.

L. J. Shrum

About the Authors

Susan Auty has recently retired from the marketing department at Lancaster University. Her research has been predominantly into the effects of product placement on children's choice of brands.

Vanessa M. Buote earned her PhD in social psychology in 2010 from Wilfrid Laurier University, Ontario, Canada. She is currently an instructor of psychology in the University Studies Department at Keyano College in Fort McMurray, Alberta. She is interested in the role of sociocultural norms for appearance on behaviors, feelings, and self-perceptions, and the role of self-appraisals of physical appearance in perceptions of relational value within various relationship contexts. Her secondary research investigates the role of attachment style in online and offline friendship characteristics.

Melinda C. R. Burgess is an associate professor of psychology at Southwestern Oklahoma State University. She earned her PhD in experimental psychology from Florida State University. Her research interests center on how media portrayals of women and minorities influence our attitudes about and treatment of women and minorities.

Jordan M. Carpenter is a doctoral candidate in the Department of Psychology at the University of North Carolina at Chapel Hill. His research focuses on mind reading and its effects on persuasion. Using his Mind Reading Motivation scale, he has examined the consequences of effortful perspective-taking on narrative transportation, political attitudes, prejudice, and other contexts.

George Comstock received his PhD from Stanford University. He is the S. I. Newhouse Professor at the Newhouse School of Public Communications at Syracuse University. He was science advisor to the Surgeon General's Scientific Advisory Committee on Television and Social Behavior that issued the federal report entitled *Television and Growing Up: The Impact of Televised Violence*. Dr. Comstock has previously served as chair of the Department of Journalism and Communication, Chinese University,

Hong Kong. His recent books (coauthored with Erica Scharrer) include *Media and the American Child* (2007) and *The Psychology of Media and Politics* (2005).

Elizabeth Cowley is a professor of marketing at the University of Sydney Business School. She received her PhD from the University of Toronto and her MBA from McGill University. Dr. Cowley's primary area of research investigates the construction and reconstruction of autobiographical memory. She is also interested in deception, both marketers misleading consumers with advertising and consumers lying to marketers. Her research has appeared in such journals as the *Journal of Consumer Research, Journal of Consumer Psychology, Journal of Advertising, International Journal of Research in Marketing, Academy of Marketing Science, Journal of Business Research,* and *Applied Cognitive Psychology.*

Karen E. Dill is the director of the Media Psychology Doctoral Program and Faculty at Fielding Graduate University. She earned her PhD in social psychology from the University of Missouri, Columbia. Her dissertation is one of the most cited studies examining video game violence. Her research investigates how media portrayals of violence, and more recently, of women and minorities, alter our thoughts and behaviors. Additionally, she is interested in how various media forms can be used to promote prosocial behaviors. Dr. Dill has presented her work worldwide, including testifying before the U.S. Congress in 2000 and 2007.

Douglas A. Gentile received his PhD from the University of Minnesota and is an associate professor of developmental psychology. He directs the Media Research Lab at Iowa State University. He is the editor of the book *Media Violence and Children* (Praeger Press, 2003), and coauthor of the book *Violent Video Game Effects on Children and Adolescents: Theory, Research, and Public Policy* (Oxford University Press, 2007). He has authored numerous peer-reviewed scientific journal articles, including studies on the positive and negative effects of video games on children in several countries, the validity of the American media ratings, how screen time contributes to youth obesity, and video game and Internet "addiction." His research has been supported by several grants, including grants from the National Institute of Child Health and Human Development and the Centers for Disease Control and Prevention. He is recipient of the 2010

Distinguished Contributions to Media Psychology award from Division 46 of the American Psychological Association.

Melanie C. Green is an assistant professor in the Department of Psychology at the University of North Carolina at Chapel Hill. She received her PhD from The Ohio State University. Dr. Green's theory of "transportation into a narrative world" focuses on immersion into a story as a mechanism of narrative influence. She has examined narrative persuasion in a variety of contexts, ranging from health communication to the influence of stories on beliefs about social issues. Her research has appeared in the *Journal of Personality and Social Psychology, Political Psychology, Journal of Social Issues, Media Psychology*, and other top journals. Her work has been funded by the National Institutes of Health, the Sage Foundation, and the American Psychological Association. Dr. Green has published two edited books, *Narrative Impact: Social and Cognitive Foundations* (Green, Strange, & Brock, 2002) and *Persuasion: Psychological Insights and Perspectives* (second edition; Brock & Green, 2006).

Haiming Hang is an assistant professor of marketing in the Henley Business School at the University of Reading, UK. He received his PhD in marketing from Lancaster University in the United Kingdom. His main research area is consumer psychology, with a particular focus on nonconscious processing, affect and decision-makings/judgments, and consumers' self-regulation. His recent projects explore children's responses to product placement in video games. His articles have appeared in the *Journal of Consumer Psychology.*

Jaehoon Lee is an assistant professor of marketing at the University of Houston–Clear Lake. He holds a PhD in marketing from the University of Texas at San Antonio, an MS in marketing from the University of Alabama, an MBA from Seoul National University, and a BA in business administration from Sogang University in Seoul, Korea. His current research interests focus on the motivations underlying conspicuous consumption and helping behavior. In particular, he is interested in the effects of social exclusion and social class on preferences for conspicuous consumption and helping. His research interests also include the antecedents and consequences of materialism and status pursuit. He has presented his research at several conferences, including the Association for Consumer Research, the Society for Consumer Psychology, and the Academy of Marketing Science. Dr. Lee has been published in *Human Communication Research.*

Charlie Lewis is a professor of family and developmental psychology at Lancaster University. His research focuses on the role of social processes on cognitive development.

Tina M. Lowrey is a professor of marketing at the University of Texas at San Antonio. She holds a PhD in communications from the Institute of Communications Research at the University of Illinois, an MS in advertising from the University of Illinois, and a BBA in finance from the University of Houston. She was previously a faculty member at Rider University, and has visited at Ecole Superieur de Commerce de Paris, the Stern School of Business at New York University, Tulane University, the University of Sydney, and the Wharton School of the University of Pennsylvania. She currently serves on the editorial review boards of the *Journal of Advertising, Journal of Consumer Psychology, Media Psychology,* and *Psychology & Marketing.* Her research interests include children's understanding of brand symbolism, gift-giving and ritual, and the application of psycholinguistic theory to marketing communications. Her research has been published in the *Journal of Consumer Research, Journal of Consumer Psychology, Journal of Advertising,* and other journals. Her two most recent edited books are *Brick & Mortar Shopping in the 21st Century* (Lawrence Erlbaum Associates, 2008) and *Psycholinguistic Phenomena in Marketing Communications* (Lawrence Erlbaum Associates, 2007).

Julia A. Maier received her PhD in psychology from Iowa State University. She is currently a visiting assistant professor of psychology at Saint Francis University in Loretto, Pennsylvania. Her research interests are particularly focused on integrating a psychological approach to understanding the experiences people have with various forms of the media. She has been involved in a number of projects exploring various relationships between the media and the viewer, including the effects of violent content in advertising on children; the relationship of psychological need, satisfaction, and pathological video game use; and the way portrayals of psychologists and clients in the media may influence a viewer's intention to seek mental health services.

John A. McCarty is an associate professor in the School of Business at the College of New Jersey in Ewing. Prior to taking this position, he taught at the University of Illinois at Urbana–Champaign, American University in Washington, DC, and George Mason University in Fairfax, Virginia. In the early 1980s, he was a research associate in the Chicago office of Needham Harper Worldwide (now DDB Chicago), an advertising agency. He has published in such journals as *Public Opinion Quarterly*, the *Journal of Advertising*, the *Journal of Public Policy* & *Marketing*, *Marketing Letters*, and the *Journal of Business Research*. He holds a PhD in social psychology from the University of Illinois at Urbana–Champaign.

Michelle R. Nelson received her PhD from the University of Illinois at Urbana–Champaign in 1997. She is an associate professor of advertising at the University of Illinois at Urbana–Champaign. Her research, professional marketing communication experience, and teaching focus primarily on international advertising and consumer behavior and media, including digital media and gaming. Dr. Nelson researched and worked in Denmark and England before assuming academic responsibilities in the United States. Dr. Nelson has published more than 30 book chapters and articles in journals such as the *Journal of Advertising, International Journal of Advertising, Journal of Advertising Research, Journal of Consumer Psychology,* and *Journal of Cross-Cultural Psychology*. During the dot-com era, she worked in marketing for a game technology company.

Laura Owen is a postdoctoral research assistant in the psychology department at the University of Reading, UK. Her research focuses on children's understanding of nontraditional forms of advertising and the implicit impact of exposure to product placement.

Jack Powers received his PhD from Syracuse University. He is an assistant professor in the Television–Radio Department at Roy H. Park School of Communications, Ithaca College, where he teaches research methods and mass media courses. His research interests include the influence of entertainment media in the socialization of children, the behavior of information users, and entertainment media processes.

Cristel Antonia Russell is a professor of marketing at American University in Washington, DC. She has published many articles on product placement and its impact in television series on audiences. Her research appears in the *Journal of Consumer Research, Journal of Advertising,* and *Journal of Advertising Research.* She is the principal investigator of NIH-funded research grants related specifically to the effects of alcohol placements in TV series.

Dale W. Russell is a research psychologist and assistant professor in the Department of Medical and Clinical Psychology at Uniformed Service University. His research focuses on health promotion and issues surrounding corporate social responsibility and consumer behavior. His work is published in *Marketing Letters,* the *International Journal of Research in Marketing,* and the *Journal of Advertising.*

L. J. Shrum is a professor and chair of marketing at the University of Texas at San Antonio College of Business. He received his PhD from the University of Illinois in communication and his MS in advertising. He is a past president of the Society for Consumer Psychology. His primary area of research investigates the psychological processes underlying consumer judgments, particularly the role of media information in the construction of values, attitudes, and beliefs. Dr. Shrum's recent research has investigated the antecedents and consequences of materialism. Other areas of research include psycholinguistics, impulsive and conspicuous consumption, and culture, and their relations to consumer behavior. His research has appeared in such journals as the *Journal of Consumer Research, Journal of Consumer Psychology, Journal of Personality and Social Psychology, Personality and Social Psychology Bulletin, Public Opinion Quarterly,* and *Journal of Advertising,* as well as numerous edited books.

Erin J. Strahan is an associate professor at the Brantford campus of Wilfrid Laurier University in Ontario, Canada. She received her PhD in social psychology from the University of Waterloo. Her research focuses on how sociocultural norms for ideal appearance influence contingencies of self-worth and eating behavior. She also studies how women's perceptions of their physical appearance influence their relational value and relationship standards. Dr. Strahan's work has appeared in journals such as *Personality and Social Psychology Bulletin* and *Journal of Experimental Social Psychology.*

Martin K. J. Waiguny received his PhD in business from the Alpen-Adria University at Klagenfurt, Austria, and is an assistant professor of international management at Alpen-Adria University. Dr. Waiguny's areas of research are advergaming, marketing for children, social networks, and Web 2.0, as well as advertising and communications in international contexts. Previously, he worked as a trainee at BMW, as a researcher and consultant at the eBusiness Institute (Biztec), and in several tourism-related companies.

Anne E. Wilson received her PhD at the University of Waterloo in 2000 and is currently an associate professor and a Tier II Canada Research Chair in social psychology at Wilfrid Laurier University in Ontario, Canada. Her research interests include identity over time, autobiographical memory and self-prediction, comparison processes, the psychology of time perception, collective memory, and sociocultural influences on the self. Dr. Wilson's work is supported by the Social Sciences and Humanities Research Council of Canada and the Natural Sciences and Engineering Research Council of Canada, and has appeared in journals such as the *Journal of Personality and Social Psychology* and *Personality and Social Psychology Bulletin*.

1

What's So Special About Entertainment Media and Why Do We Need a Psychology for It?: An Introduction to the Psychology of Entertainment Media

L. J. Shrum
University of Texas at San Antonio
San Antonio, Texas

I started with the same question in the first edition: Is there anything unique about entertainment media that warrants such close scrutiny and scientific interest? Why is persuasion through entertainment media different from any other forms of persuasion, both in terms of effects and processes? If current theories of persuasion can just as easily (and accurately) account for effects that occur *within* entertainment media (e.g., TV programs, films) as they can for effects that occur *between* entertainment media (e.g., advertisements), Occam's razor would lop off the unneeded new theory devoted to entertainment media.

Although there are a number of theoretical constructs that can account for certain effects of entertainment media (e.g., situation models, source-monitoring, story schemas; Johnson, 2002), current dual-processing models have a difficult time accounting for some types of media effects, particularly those occurring during the processing of narratives. In fact, there is ample evidence that people process entertainment (narrative) and promotional (rhetorical) information differently. Thus, it is likely that the ways in which entertainment and promotion exert effects on audiences are correspondingly different. The purpose of this book is to highlight these differences by documenting the effects that entertainment media have on audiences and to illuminate how these effects occur. Both components are critical in making for a better-informed consumer and public, and this is particularly important when the effects are often unintended but also unwanted (e.g., aggression, lower self-esteem, drug abuse, materialism, low impulse control).

The differences in processing between narrative and rhetoric are also what lead to *blurred lines* between what is entertainment and what is persuasion. In some instances, the lines are intentionally blurred by marketers who are interested in preventing some of the processes that may occur during the processing of rhetorical information (e.g., counterarguing). In other cases, the lines are unintentionally blurred because audience members do not understand the persuasive influence of entertainment media.

In sum, just as with the first edition, this volume attempts to understand (a) how is entertainment or narrative information processed? (b) is this fundamentally different from the processing of promotional or rhetorical information? and (c) if so, what are the consequences of these differences in processing on the persuasive impact of both the entertainment aspect and the promotional aspect?

ROADMAP FOR THE CHAPTERS

The chapters are divided into two parts. The first part pertains to intended effects of marketers, and focuses primarily on product placements embedded in entertainment programming, including television, film, and digital games. The second part pertains to unintended effects of the stories and games themselves.

PART I: EMBEDDING PROMOTIONS WITHIN ENTERTAINMENT MEDIA: PRODUCT PLACEMENT EFFECTS AND HOW THEY WORK

Part I focuses on what I think of as the epitome of blurred lines: product placement. Product placement generally refers to the deliberate inclusion of brands in stories, usually in television programs and films. However, as several authors note, other types of media, such as video games, are also fertile ground for product placements. McCarty and Lowrey (Chapter 2) kick off the first section with a comprehensive review of the marketing practice of product integration. Product integration refers to the mixing of commercial messages with noncommercial messages. Integration thus includes not only product placements, but also other marketing practices such as sponsorships of entire programs. McCarty and Lowrey differentiate the various types of product integration, discuss a number of prominent examples (some likely to be familiar to readers, some not), provide a broad review of research on product integration effects, and discuss the future of product integration research and practice.

Cowley (Chapter 3) delves into the psychological processes underlying product placement effects. She looks at how placements are processed as a function of such factors as placement characteristics (e.g., prominence, plot congruity), viewer characteristics (e.g., involvement, connection with characters), and program format (e.g., fiction, reality programs), and integrates these different characteristics into existing persuasion theories (e.g., priming, persuasion knowledge). She also discusses the implications for public policy, how current public policy addresses concerns about consumer welfare, and the implications of current psychological theories (e.g., memory, persuasion) for the success of practices aimed at better informing consumers of placement practices. She concludes by discussing what we still don't know about placement processes and effects and avenues for future research.

Owen, Hang, Lewis, and Auty (Chapter 4) continue with a focus on product placement processing, but with a specific look at the effects on children. They review the public policy and ethical debates about product placement, and then relate these specifically to the effects of such marketing practices on children. They note that children's limited cognitive and executive functioning skills may make them particularly vulnerable to product placement effects. Owen et al. then discuss previous research, including their own, on the psychological processes underlying product placement effects on children, with a particular focus on implicit influences of product placement and the role of conceptual fluency. They conclude with a discussion of how we might teach children to understand the practice of product placement and suggestions for future research.

In the concluding chapter of Part I, Nelson and Waiguny continue the discussion of psychological processes and effects in product integration practices, but move the focus from television and film to digital games (video, computer, etc.), a fast-developing area. They look at two types of integration: in-game advertising, which is similar to product placement, and what is termed *advergames*, which are games specifically designed by companies to promote their brands. Nelson and Waiguny provide a thorough discussion of the relationship between these forms of brand placement and cognitive processes such as activation and arousal, emotional responses, recall, attitude formation and change, and behavioral judgments. They review the emerging research in this area, including their own, and integrate this research into existing theories of persuasion.

PART II: THE PROGRAMS BETWEEN THE ADS: THE PERSUASIVE POWER OF ENTERTAINMENT MEDIA

Part II makes the shift from intended effects by marketers to unintended effects of the story creators. In Chapter 6, Shrum and Lee address the different types of effects that viewing of narrative entertainment fiction has on viewers. They look at two different types of effects. The first is the effects of program narratives on normative perceptions. They discuss how television influences viewers' perceptions of what others have and do, and how the world works in general. They detail research showing that the more people watch television, the more they tend to think the world portrayed on television is indicative of reality. The second effect Shrum and Lee examine pertains to the attitudes, values, and beliefs that are cultivated by the television messages. Here, they detail research that shows that the more people watch television, the more their beliefs correspond to the dominant messages in the programs. Finally, along with detailing these effects, they articulate separate psychological process models for each and discuss research that supports those models.

Carpenter and Green (Chapter 7) delve further into the persuasive power of fictional narratives. They discuss their own research as well as that of others on narrative persuasion and the effects of narrative transportation on persuasion. Narrative transportation refers to the process of becoming completely immersed (transported) into the world of the story. They discuss the processes associated with narrative transportation, such as reduction in counterarguing, increased emotion, and the creation of vivid thoughts, and how these influence beliefs. They discuss research showing that transportation can increase persuasion, even when the narrative is fictional. They conclude the chapter with a discussion of research on individual differences in narrative transportation and their associated effects.

In Chapter 8, Dill and Burgess continue with the focus on narrative (story) processing and persuasion, but look specifically at the persuasive power of social imagery and its powerful contribution to the narrative. They argue that social imagery in the media tells very powerful stories, ones that are in fact very persuasive, and that "seeing is believing," even if what is seen may be within the context of a fictional narrative. They review research to support their theorizing, and synthesize this research by proposing their theory of media imagery and social learning (MISL).

Beginning with Chapter 9, the focus shifts from general theoretical accounts of media effects to discussions of particular types of media effects. Russell and Russell (Chapter 9) address alcohol consumption portrayals in television series. They first review findings from content analyses. Using much of their own work as examples, they document the modalities of presentation and level of plot connection of alcohol messages, and distinguish between those messages that portray alcohol positively and those that portray alcohol negatively. Next, they provide a thorough review of the empirical evidence regarding how embedded alcohol messages are processed and the impact they have on audiences' alcohol beliefs and attitudes. A particularly intriguing finding is that audience connectedness moderates the cognitive processing and persuasive impact of messages about alcohol. Finally, they discuss the implications of this research for public health and public policy, particularly for younger audiences.

Strahan, Buote, and Wilson (Chapter 10) examine another unintended effect of both program and advertising portrayals: the effect of the media's idealized portrayals of women on women's feelings of self-esteem and self-worth. The authors note that the media's portrayal of women is very consistent: young, thin, and beautiful. Although the intended consequences of such portrayals are understandable (create audience liking, associate beauty characteristics with products and lifestyles), the unintended consequences resulting from the inability of audience members to attain those ideals are troubling. The authors provide a thorough discussion of research showing that exposure to idealized media images is linked to body dissatisfaction and the basing of self-worth on appearance, which in turn influences eating behavior and interpersonal relationships.

Finally, the last two chapters look at a long-debated effect of media exposure, its effect on viewer aggression. Maier and Gentile (Chapter 11) focus on theoretical issues of how viewers may learn from the media, and how these apply to the media exposure–aggression link. They first provide a theoretical examination of psychological theories of learning, and in particular the General Learning Model. They offer the General Learning Model as a metatheory that accounts for learning at multiple levels that may interact, and in doing so, incorporate both short- and long-term processes. They also discuss uses and gratifications theory and its focus on individual differences in motivations for media consumption, and its utility for understanding media effects research. They conclude by presenting the results of an experiment aimed at merging the psychological and communication theories to make predictions about media effects on aggression.

Comstock and Powers (Chapter 12) conclude the volume with a thorough review of the research on the link between exposure to television violence and aggression. In doing so, however, they make several important departures from most reviews of this type. First, they discuss a number of meta-analyses, including some of their own, that clearly show a positive correlation between media exposure (television, movies) and aggression or antisocial behavior. They address issues of causal direction, and suggest that the case for television viewing being the causal factor is quite strong, given that both correlational and experimental research yield very similar results. Comstock and Powers also make one additional point that is important. They argue that, from their analysis of past research, dispositions such as attitudes, norms, and values are not a necessary link between exposure to television violence and aggression. Although the link has been found in a number of studies, it is also the case that direct relations between exposure to television violence and aggression have been observed. They conclude with a discussion of the implications of this reformulation for the processes underlying media effects on aggressive behavior.

Entertainment Media Is Special

As with the first edition, the primary purpose of this volume is to address at least the first part of the question posed in the title to this introductory chapter: What is so special about entertainment media? All of the chapters in this book provide a perspective on the nature of entertainment media and how it often blends with overt persuasion attempts such as promotions. And virtually all in some manner speak to the issue of how entertainment media is processed, with the conclusion that media consumers do in fact tend to process entertainment (narrative) and promotional (rhetorical) information differently. This, if nothing else, is what makes entertainment media so special. And it is the premise of at least some of the chapters that this is also what makes entertainment media so potentially powerful. It should come as no surprise, then, that marketers would be interested in becoming part of that special processing, rather than separate from it.

Perhaps that is fine. This book does not take a position as to whether the blurring of the lines between entertainment and promotion is necessarily good or bad. But in the interest of the free flow of information and making informed decisions, hopefully the chapters in this book can at least contribute to more informed consumers who might then decide whether to provide their consent to be persuaded.

Section I

Embedding Promotions Within Entertainment Media: Product Placement Effects and How They Work

2

Product Integration: Current Practices and New Directions

John A. McCarty
The College of New Jersey
Ewing, New Jersey

Tina M. Lowrey
University of Texas at San Antonio
San Antonio, Texas

PRODUCT INTEGRATION: A DESCRIPTION OF THE PRACTICE

Product integration is the practice of incorporating a product or service into a movie, television show, or other medium in return for payment of money or other promotional consideration by a marketer (Gupta & Gould, 1997). Typically, product integration has been referred to loosely over the years as product placement; in fact, the version of this chapter in the previous edition of this volume (McCarty, 2004) used the term *product placement* to refer to this integration, regardless of the level of the incorporation. Much has changed in recent years with respect to product integration or placement, and far more is known, particularly about the complexity of the practice, than just a few years ago. Therefore, following Lowrey, Shrum, and McCarty (2005) and others, in the present chapter we use the term *product integration* to refer broadly to the practice of the incorporation of a product or service into a medium under some sort of an arrangement. Product placement is a subcategory of integration where a product is mentioned or merely seen, as when a character in a television show mentions a brand or is seen using a particular brand; *product* *immersion* is the term for integrations in which a product or service is an integral part of the story.* Having defined these two "levels" of product integration, in many ways, product placement and product immersion can be considered on a continuum (Russell, 1998). At one end, there are placements where a product is mentioned briefly or is visible for a moment (e.g., in the movie *The Firm*, the character played by Gene Hackman says to Tom Cruise's character, "Grab a Red Stripe out of the fridge"—this is the only mention of this beer brand in the movie, and the brand is not clearly visible in any frames of the movie). At the other end of this continuum is product immersion, where the brand is integral to the plot of the movie, as in *Harold and Kumar Go to White Castle*, where the main plot of the movie revolves around the two protagonists' search for a particular fast food restaurant—the brand is mentioned numerous times, the product is visible and is seen being consumed, product features are mentioned by the characters during the story (e.g., "In fact, just thinking about those tender little White Castle burgers and those grilled onions makes me want to burn this place to the ground and rebuild a White Castle in its place."). Somewhere in the middle on this continuum might be a placement/immersion where a product has some amount of airtime or is discussed, but is incidental to the main story, as when a Maserati is discussed by Tony Soprano and Johnny Sack in the HBO series *The Sopranos*.†

IMPORTANT DISTINCTIONS AND CONSIDERATIONS

An important aspect of this definition of product integration is that the product is placed in a medium in return for promotion consideration or

---

* The terminology used for these various practices over the years has not been consistent or always clear. For example, Patric Verrone of the Writer's Guild of America, the union representing writers in television and movie industries, stated to the *New York Times*, "Product placement is simply putting a branded box of cereal on the kitchen table in a show. ... Product integration is having the characters talk about the crunchy deliciousness of the cereal or provoking them to go out and tell their neighbors to buy that cereal" (Carvajal, 2006, p. 9). Thus, the distinction that Mr. Verrone makes is similar, but not the same, as the one we make here.
† Lowrey, Shrum, and McCarty (2005) discuss other practices that fall under the umbrella of product integration, specifically, placement-friendly program development, program sponsorship, and client-developed programming. These practices are all forms of product integration, as defined by Lowrey et al., but would not fall on the continuum between product placement and product immersion.

payment. Thus, the mere presence of a brand in a movie, television show, or other venue does not per se constitute product integration. There must be an arrangement between the owner of the brand and the media vehicle. We make this important distinction, which has not always been made when product integration has been discussed, because brands do appear in the stories when no such arrangements have been made. Authors of books routinely describe brands that a character uses to provide richness and realism to the character. There may not be any sort of arrangement between the author and the owner of the brands that are used in the story. Presumably, the author selected a particular brand to help paint the nature of a character, a location, and so on. For example, in Ian Fleming's novels about the famous British spy James Bond, he uses a number of different guns that are mentioned by brand name, and there is no indication that the mention of any of these weapons was a result of a relationship between the author and the brands.* Similarly, in the book *American Psycho*, a fictional story that documents the excesses of the 1980s, numerous brands are mentioned, including shirts by Ike Behar, suits by Ermenegildo Zegna, Fratelli Rossetti shoes, Panasonic, Tumi leather goods, among others. There is no evidence of these mentions being matters of arrangement; rather, they lend a sense of indulgence and materialism to the characters in the novel. Courvoisier cognac is in the title and lyrics of the rap song "Pass the Courvoisier" by Busta Rhymes. Although the sale of the cognac increased by double digits in the year of the release of the song, it was not a product placement in that there was not an arrangement made between the distiller and the artist before the release of the song (Roberts, 2002). Perhaps one of the "characters" in a recent movie that may have been assumed by many to be a paid product integration was not: Wilson in the Tom Hanks movie *Cast Away* (Maynard and Scala, 2006; Michael, 2000). A Wilson volleyball was selected for artistic reasons; the brand name needed to be one that would potentially be a name of a person in that the product becomes a character as the story progresses.

We make the point that when a brand is mentioned in a work of art when there was no arrangement between those creating the art and a brand, this does not constitute a "blurring of the lines"; the brand appearing in

---

* In fact, there is evidence that the Walther PPK (the handgun most associated with James Bond) was suggested to Ian Fleming by a gun expert who indicated to Fleming that the Beretta that Bond used in an early novel was a lady's gun and not one that a spy of Bond's stature would use (Rifkind, 2004).

the story, movie, television show, and so on is not encumbered by a commercial arrangement, and the creator of the art is putting a specific brand in his or her work because it "fits." Of course, from the perspective of a viewer, whether the exposure to the brand is a paid integration or not is immaterial to its potential effect.

A second important consideration with respect to our definition is that product integration can be in a variety of media and venues. Although for years integration was discussed in terms of being in the movies and in television, product integration is showing up in all sorts of places. This has been particularly apparent in the last decade or so. In recent years, arrangements for product integrations have been made such that brands have appeared in video and online games (Jones, 2002; Nelson, 2005), music videos and/or song lyrics (Fitzgerald, 2011; Helm, 2010), and novels (Murray, 2004), in addition to the traditional outlets of movies and television shows. The increase in the number of venues in which product integrations appear, as well as the total increase in number of integrations, is likely due to a number of factors. These include (1) the growing dissatisfaction among marketers with the performance of traditional advertising (de Gregorio & Sung, 2010); (2) a growth in the infrastructure that facilitates product integrations (Russell & Belch, 2005), such as the shift of product integrations from rather informal arrangements or one-time deals to a much more formalized endeavor where firms are engaged to actively seek out opportunities for a brand to be integrated into appropriate venues; (3) perceptions of the success of previous brand mentions in particular venues (e.g., the aforementioned Courvoisier in the lyrics and title of a song has been credited with increasing marketers' efforts to get their brands in songs (Wasserman, 2005)); and (4) an increase in the production costs of movies, television shows, music, and other artistic ventures, which has led producers of these efforts to seek methods of covering the production costs (Crisafulli, 1995; Darlin, 1995; de Gregorio & Sung, 2010; Russell & Belch, 2005). These four conditions have likely led to what might be described as a tipping point in product integration in the last decade.* What appears to be the situation is that marketers of branded products

---

* Although this explosion in product integrations has recently occurred, the practice has been around for a long time. The actual origin of product placement is unclear, but Newell, Salmon, and Chang (2006) indicate that it was as early as the 1890s in movies. In spite of this early use of it, it likely remained a matter of informal arrangements until the infrastructure developed to accommodate the level of activity that exists today.

and producers of entertainment are actively seeking mutually beneficial arrangements for what would occur whether or not money changed hands or other considerations took place—branded products appearing in entertainment media.* The double-digit growth in paid product integrations across all outlets for most of the years in the past decade point to this explosion of activity (Castillo, 2010); for example, in prime-time TV in the United States, there was a 9% growth in the first half of 2009 (Lowry and Helm, 2009). As new entertainment outlets develop, it is likely that marketers will creatively consider how they can integrate their brands into them as well.

A third consideration with respect to product integration is that it is often controversial. Controversies generally center around two interrelated issues: (1) the stealthy nature of the marketing communications; and (2) the extent to which the integrations affect the creative integrity of fictional or artistic material or, even of more concern, the integrity of journalistic endeavors. These concerns are interrelated in that both deal with the break in the wall that many believe should separate commercial communications from entertainment and editorial communications. Moreover, both of these issues relate to the extent to which consumers may not be receiving the communication that they expected, paid for, and so on.

With respect to the stealthy nature of the marketing communications, the concerns are that people are receiving commercial messages without being aware of their commercial nature. There have been long-standing rules and best practices regarding the identification of commercial messages as such. The payola rules of the FCC would cover product integrations for broadcast media (i.e., television and radio) and indicate that broadcast stations that "have accepted or agreed to receive payments, services, or other valuable consideration for airing material must disclose this

---

* A somewhat interesting variation on the typical arrangement is reverse product placement (Edery, 2006; Wasserman, 2007), where a previously fictional product from a movie, novel, etc., is later marketed as a real product. Examples of this phenomenon include Bubba Gump Shrimp Co. from the movie *Forrest Gump* and Potion, a beverage that appeared in the video game *Final Fantasy*. Probably the most unusual example of this is the restaurant chain Cheeburger Cheeburger. This chain most likely got its name from the *Saturday Night Live* skit about a diner where the grill cook yells "cheezborger cheezborger" when a patron orders a cheeseburger. This was a take-off on what a real grill cook at the Billy Goat Tavern in Chicago yelled when an order was placed. The tavern was frequented by several of the performers at Second City in Chicago who went on to star on *Saturday Night Live* (i.e., Don Novello, John Belushi, and Bill Murray) (Billy Goat Tavern, 2011), and there has been a lawsuit filed by the Billy Goat Tavern against the Cheeburger Cheeburger chain with the claim that the chain is using the tavern's slogan (Barcella, 2003).

fact" (FCC, 2011). In print media, the guidelines of the American Society of Magazine Editors (ASME) define the best practices for magazines and include a clear statement that advertising must be labeled as such (ASME, 2011). In recent years, there have been concerns raised as to the extent to which these policies have been followed or enforced with respect to product integrations (Newell, Blevins, & Bugeja, 2009).* Furthermore, the FTC, which has broad powers of regulation pertaining to advertising in all media (not just broadcast media as the FCC does), has generally declined to regulate product integrations in movies (Campbell, 2006).

Various consumer groups have pressed for explicit alerts to viewers as to the paid promotional nature of an appearance of a brand (Bennett, Pecotich, & Putrevu, 1999). Suggestions for alerts include text scrawls across the bottom of the screen when integrations are occurring or flashing red lights during integrations (Lowry & Helm, 2009).

The potential for the practice of product integration to affect the creative integrity of fictional stories or the editorial role of nonfictional programming (e.g., news) is very real. The perceived danger in fictional stories is that the nature of the plot, characters, and so on will be influenced by those who will pay rather than by artistic considerations. For example, the fictional character James Bond drove an Aston Martin in *Goldfinger* and some of the other early Bond movies. In some recent movies of this franchise, the character has driven automobiles by BMW, a company that engaged in integration arrangements with the producers of the movies. Although the use of a BMW may not bother most who see the movie, a James Bond "purist" may find it odd that a very British spy such as James Bond would drive a German automobile that, while expensive, is potentially within the grasp of a lot of people.† It has been noted that product

---

* Research has shown that consumers believe that the practice should be more heavily regulated (Hudson, Hudson, & Peloz, 2008), but there is also skepticism about the extent to which the government can regulate it (Newell, Blevins, & Bugeja, 2009). There may be some merit to this skepticism. The disclosure rules for television allow a show to take care of its disclosure obligation by scrolling at the end of a broadcast rather quickly the names of the brands that received consideration; a former commissioner at the FCC argued in 2005 that this scroll was not really enough, but little has changed in this regard (Schatz, 2005).

† Aston Martin is a high-end British automobile; until very recently, all of the models of the brand were very expensive, hand-built automobiles that few people could afford, but would be appropriate for the British spy, James Bond, who is known as uncompromising in his tastes across numerous product categories. Although a relatively expensive automobile, the German-manufactured BMW may seem to some in the movie audience that it is not an appropriate vehicle for James Bond in that it is a German automobile and is within their purchase capability.

integration deals put uncomfortable constraints on writers (George, 2005) and as the stakes get higher, it is likely that there will be more pressures to change the creative endeavors to fit the needs of the marketers. As Gary Elliott, a vice-president of Hewlett-Packard, has stated, "We absolutely expect to have input…. We have to look at the scripts. We have an agency that understands how our products are going to be treated and how we'd be viewed within the production" (George, 2005, p. 34). The concern over the control of the artistic aspects of the story is such that the Writer's Guild of America has denounced the practice of product integration and has pushed for a code of conduct with respect to it (Carvajal, 2006).

The potential for integrations to affect nonfictional programming is a concern as well. In fact, research indicates that the public accepts product integration in entertainment programming to a greater degree than integration in news via video news releases (Newell, Blevins, & Bugeja, 2009).* Legitimate news outlets have traditionally had extremely strong norms about the separation of commercial speech from editorial speech and concerns about advertisers influencing the nature of editorial speech. As an indication of these norms, David Brinkley was criticized by other journalists for his decision to become a spokesperson for Archer Daniels Midland after he had retired from news broadcasting (Lafayette, 1998). Recently, however, there are indications that products are showing up in interesting ways in news programming. Starbucks has made a deal with *Morning Joe*, a show with a news and editorial format featuring Joe Scarborough, to be featured during the show via graphics and mentions (Stelter, 2009). Although the brand is not contributing to the news or opinions expressed, there is an implicit indication that the particular brand of coffee is endorsed by the opinion leaders featured on the show.

PRODUCT INTEGRATION AS MARKETING COMMUNICATION

Given that product integrations can vary from a casual mention of a brand in a single scene of a movie to a brand being a major presence in the story,

---

* A video news release is a "fake" news story created by a marketer, public relations firm, etc., to appear as a regular news story.

supported by joint advertising and promotion of a movie and brand, it is perhaps inappropriate to characterize all of them as essentially the same thing. They can differ quite a bit and, most likely, the way and at what level viewers process them can vary as well. Having stated this caveat, product integrations can be compared to other forms of marketing communications in a number of ways, in that all product integrations share some common aspects with one another, but are different than other forms of marketing communications.

Balasubramanian (1994) considered product integrations as one type of a hybrid message, a combination of advertising and publicity. He considered hybrid messages as ones that are paid for in ways that are typically true of advertising (i.e., paid commercial messages in which the payer has much control over the message); however, they are *"communications that project a non-commercial character"* (italics in original) (p. 30). Balasubramanian reasoned that since these messages do not seem to the receiver to be a commercial message, they are likely processed differently from how commercial messages such as advertising would be processed.

As Balasubramanian noted, product integrations are generally paid for in some manner, just as with advertising, but integrations are not identified as paid persuasion efforts by sponsors, which makes them similar to publicity, such as news stories. Therefore, the sponsor gets the best of both of these traditional forms of communication, advertising and publicity. That is, the sponsor has some limited control over the communication (subject to editorial considerations of the movie, television show, or other venue), but the communication is not usually identified explicitly as a persuasion attempt; thus, the effort to persuade is not made salient to the audience.

In a similar discussion, Nebenzahl and Jaffe (1998) considered product integrations in their characterization of different kinds of marketing communications and how integrations might differ from other kinds of communications. They argued that different marketing communications can be considered along two dimensions: (a) the extent to which the sponsor of the message is disguised and the fact that the message is a paid advertisement is disguised, and (b) the extent to which the persuasive message is secondary to the main message of the communication. Product integrations can be contrasted to traditional advertising (and other marketing communications) along these dimensions. In the case of advertising, the sponsor of the product is not disguised, and the fact that it is a persuasive effort by that sponsor is generally clear to the audience. With respect to the second dimension, the advertising (persuasive) message is the salient part of the communication and not secondary to any other message. In contrast, a good product integration is different from an advertisement on both of these dimensions. The integration of the product in a scene in the movie, for example, is not connected with the company as an explicit attempt to persuade; the brand is presented in the context of a story. Considering the second dimension, the persuasive effort is generally secondary to the main communication of the movie or television show.* Although Nebenzahl and Jaffe's main interest related to the ethics of the communications as a function of how communications are presented to the audience in relation to these two dimensions (e.g., they argue that product integrations would be less ethical than advertising because integrations represent hidden, disguised persuasion attempts), these dimensions can illuminate the ways viewers might process the messages.

Therefore, the discussions of Balasubramanian (1994) and Nebenzahl and Jaffe (1998) indicate that the noncommercial and somewhat hidden, secondary nature of product integrations makes them inherently different from traditional advertising, and this suggests that viewers may not process them in the same way as they would an advertisement. Friestad and Wright's (1994) discussion of consumers' persuasion knowledge is relevant to considerations of how consumers might process product integrations differently from advertising, given the hidden and secondary nature of integrations. Friestad and Wright viewed persuasion knowledge as a set of interrelated beliefs consumers hold that relate to persuasion attempts by marketers. These beliefs focus on the perceived goals and tactics marketers use to persuade consumers, the perceived appropriateness and effectiveness of these tactics, as well as the consumers' perceptions of their own ability to cope with marketers' persuasion efforts. Friestad and Wright suggested that when consumers are confronted with a communication, a fundamental change of meaning occurs when the communication is recognized as an attempt to persuade. When consumers recognize a communication as a persuasion attempt, they will process the message differently than if no such recognition occurred. They may get distracted from the message, disengage from the communication, and develop assessments of the persuasion effort

---

* Product integrations are, in general, secondary to the main communication. However, in some extreme examples of product immersions where a brand is very central to the theme of the story, it could be argued that the integration is part of the main communication, as was the brand White Castle in the movie *Harold and Kumar Go to White Castle*.

and the company related to the communication. For example, when consumers view an advertisement featuring a spokesperson they admire, their evaluation of the message, the product, the spokesperson, and the company may be different than if they were unaware that the advertisement is a paid persuasive attempt. There is a change of meaning with respect to the message that the spokesperson is presenting. The message is interpreted in the context of this persuasion knowledge generated by the awareness that the advertisement is a persuasive communication. For a product integration in a movie, television show, or other outlet, however, a consumer's persuasion knowledge may not be activated, because there is a lack of identification of the integration as a persuasion attempt. Therefore, the hidden and secondary nature of product integrations may not activate the processes that typically put a consumer on guard in the case of advertising.

We suggest, therefore, that the stealthy nature of product integrations is one attribute that might be important in making them work as a promotional tool. However, although the promotional nature of product integrations is often disguised, this is not always the case. Alternatively, the connection between the product integration and the movie is sometimes made clear to consumers through joint advertising and promotion. The launch of the BMW Z3 roadster in the James Bond movie *Golden Eye* included TV and print advertising, a press launch in Central Park, a Neiman Marcus catalog offer, and publicity on the *Tonight Show with Jay Leno*; all of these clearly connected the Z3 to the movie *Golden Eye* (Fournier & Dolan, 1997), thus making it apparent that there was a tie-in between the product and the movie. In particular, the advertising campaign featured both the car and the movie. There are numerous other examples of product integrations in movies made public via tie-in advertising. Therefore, although it is typically not made salient to viewers that an integration is a promotional effort at the point in time the viewers see the integration, it is somewhat common that the connection between the product and movie is made in advertising and promotional materials. In fact, some professionals argue that promotional tie-ins are key to the success of product integrations. McCarthy (1994) reported that a product integration executive attributed the accompanying promotion to the success of Reese's Pieces in the movie *E.T.* in that "Hershey spent a lot of money at retail to let everyone know what E. T. was eating" (p. 32), since the bag and candy may not have been apparent in the frames of the movie.

Thus, at first glance it would seem that there is a contradiction between the assumption that product integrations derive their success from their disguised nature and the fact that many of the successful integrations are ones in which the consumer is made aware of their commercial nature via the accompanying advertising and promotion. It should be considered, however, that at the time that the consumer is seeing or hearing the product integration, its commercial nature is not emphasized, even if the connection has been made in other promotional activity. The product is placed in the context of a story; and it may be that this context is important for success.

To consider this apparent contradiction, it is instructive to note that product integrations are similar to one kind of advertisement in that they involve the presentation of the brand in the context of a story. Wells (1989) discussed two kinds of advertising formats: lectures and dramas. Lectures are advertisements that present outwardly to the audience, similar to what a speaker would do in a lecture hall. The television audience is spoken to and is presented with an argument and evidence. According to Wells, an effective lecture presents facts to be believed and should be credible in the presentation of these facts; it is generally clear that there is a persuasion attempt being made. In contrast, Wells suggested that a drama advertisement draws the audience into a story. Drama advertisements are like movies, novels, and other stories in that they can present a lesson about how the world works. An important aspect of a drama advertisement is that it works by allowing the audience to make an inference about the advertised brand from the story that is presented in the advertisement; this inference may provide a stronger impression than if the audience had been told the point through a lecture format. Wells indicated that an effective drama advertisement must engage the viewer and must be believable as a story. Part of the effectiveness of drama advertisements is that they draw the viewer into the story in such a way that the viewer forgets that the story is a persuasion attempt. With drama advertising, the normal skepticism that consumers may have with respect to advertisements is reduced when they see the product in the context of a story. This idea is consistent with the work of Deighton, Romer, and McQueen (1989) on the use of drama to persuade. They found that viewers "are less disposed to argue and believe the appeal to the extent that they accept the commercial's verisimilitude and respond to it emotionally" (p. 341) in the case of drama commercials, compared to argument commercials (i.e., lecture advertisements).

A product placement or immersion could therefore be considered as the ultimate form of drama advertising. The product is in the context of a story, but unlike the 30-second story typical of most television advertisements, the product is in a story that generally lasts over an hour in the case of movies and 30 minutes or more for a television show. Thinking of a product integration in this way may help explain why an integration may be successful, even when viewers are aware of the promotional tie-in between a movie and the product through the promotions and advertising. To the extent that the plot of the movie draws the viewer in, similar to a drama advertisement, the viewers will see the brand in context and will not think about it as a persuasion attempt.

Therefore, in the same way that a good story makes us forget that the main character is an actor we may know from other roles,* a good product integration may be one that fits with the story in such a way as to make us forget that it is there to persuade us. This idea of "fit" is critical and relates to the notion of seamlessness to which practitioners in product integration have often referred. According to Dean Ayers of the Entertainment Resources Marketing Association,

> The word that comes up a lot in our work is *seamless*. . . . We've found that most people do prefer to see a can of Pepsi or some other familiar brand rather than one that just says "Soda." But nobody wants to pay to see a commercial. (Crisafulli, 1995, p. 4)

When product integrations do not achieve a level of seamlessness, problems can arise. As stated by Gary Mezzatesta of Unique Product Placements, "When the audience snickers and says, 'I wonder how much they paid for that,' you know it's bad" (McCarthy, 1994, p. 32). Thus, when a product placement sticks out as an obvious commercial plug, it may activate viewers' persuasion knowledge, as well as distract them from the drama.

Although product integrations are likened to drama advertising, there is an important distinction that should be emphasized. A drama advertisement is designed from beginning to end as an advertisement. The purpose of the story is to sell the product. In the case of a product integration, the

---

* For example, when we see George Clooney play Danny Ocean in movies, we are not thinking about the protagonist as George Clooney, who we may know from other movies or from his political causes; rather, we are thinking of him as the slick and savvy person who outwits the owner of a casino. We are drawn into the story, and it is not salient to us that Clooney is an actor whom we have seen in a variety of other roles and has a personal life about which we know some things.

integration is often secondary to the main story. The story that unfolds is generally not designed as an advertisement for particular products.* Although it may not be specifically designed to do so, it may well be the case that the story incidentally presents a key selling point for a brand. For example, the performance characteristics of the Mini Cooper, a particularly small automobile featured in *The Italian Job*, were important to the storyline and were made apparent in several scenes of the movie. Although it was not a paid integration, in an episode of *Seinfeld*, Drake's coffee cake is mentioned as "the plain cake with the sweet brown crumbs on the top." Numerous examples come to mind of movies or television shows that present the luxurious life and suggest the kinds of brands that those who live such a life would use (e.g., *Sex in the City*), thus providing a clear, albeit subtle, selling point for a placed product.

THE MULTIDIMENSIONAL NATURE OF PRODUCT PLACEMENTS

Although all product integrations share some common characteristics, they can differ from one another in a number of ways. A brand can be visually present in a scene, or it can be mentioned and not seen. An integration can be a brief placement or the product can be an integral part of a character or the story. Therefore, it is likely that they can operate in very different ways, depending on the nature of the integration (see Chapter 3). Similar to how advertising can work at different levels (i.e., inform, persuade, remind, etc.), product integrations can operate at different levels depending on the extent to which and how the integration is woven into the movie, television show, or other venue.

Russell (1998) characterized product integrations in a three-dimensional framework. The first dimension she considered was the extent to which an integration is visual. An integration can be purely visual, such as a product placed in the background of a scene (e.g., a truck with the logo of the placed product on the side). The level of visual placement can

---

* This point could certainly be challenged in that some movies have so many product integrations in them that they appear to many as simply vehicles for brand communications. According to a *Marketing Week* article, the James Bond movie *Die Another Day* was referred to by many critics as "Buy Another Day" (Alarcon, 2008, p. 8).

also vary as a function of the number of times it is seen, or whether it is seen at all. Russell's second dimension was the auditory or verbal nature of the integration. The brand may not be mentioned at all in the dialogue of the story, can be mentioned several times, mentioned with emphasis, and so forth. The third dimension that Russell considered was the degree to which the integration is connected with the plot of the story. This dimension is really the same as the continuum we talked about at the beginning of this chapter: the continuum with a brief product placement at one end and a total product immersion at the other end. At one level, a brand can simply be one that is visible in a scene of a movie and not connected to the main part of the story. In this instance, it may only be a prop. For example, in movies we often see a billboard or the side of a truck with a brand name on it that is in the background of the action of the scene. At the other end of this dimension, an integration can be intimately tied to the plot, as in *You've Got Mail*, or closely connected to the nature of the character, such as the type of car that James Bond drives or the brand of wristwatch he wears.

PSYCHOLOGICAL PROCESSES AND PRODUCT INTEGRATIONS

The dimensions discussed by Russell (1998) illustrate the complexity of investigating how consumers may process product integrations. The multidimensional nature of product integrations, and how they can differ on each of these dimensions, suggests that a variety of psychological processes can be considered as operating when a viewer sees a brand in the context of a movie or television show.

At the most basic level, when product integrations involve brands that are merely seen or mentioned in a story, the process may be as simple as affective classical conditioning or mere exposure. As Baker (1999) explained, affective classical conditioning is a matter of pairing an unconditioned stimulus (e.g., a beautiful scene) with the conditioned stimulus (e.g., a brand of product) such that the good feelings associated with the scene are transferred to the brand. Although often discussed in the context of advertising, it is easy to see how such a psychological process is a potential way that product placements can work. Russell (1998) suggested that products in the background of a scene may often be processed by this nonconscious association between the brand and the movie. The conditioning process simply requires that a viewer make an association between the response to the scene or movie (i.e., the good feelings) and the brand that is placed.

If affective conditioning is indeed the process at work for simple and brief product placements, this poses a potential complication for the placement of a brand. When viewers are watching a movie or television show, they typically experience a variety of both positive and negative feelings during the course of the story, including joy, anger, fear, disbelief, hatred, and sadness. It may be difficult to predict which feeling will be associated with the brand. There is the possibility that a negative feeling will be linked to the brand. For example, in a scene of the movie *The Silence of the Lambs*, crumpled Arby's wrappers and cups were among the debris in the rather shabby house of the serial killer hunted by Jody Foster's character in the story. Focus group respondents reported a negative association between Arby's and the character in the movie, indicating that if they ate at Arby's, they would be reminded of the killer (Fournier & Dolan, 1997).

A second possibility is that the construct of mere exposure may explain simple product placements (Vollmers & Mizerski, 1994). Mere exposure suggests that a viewer will develop more favorable feelings toward a brand simply because of the repeated exposure to it (Baker 1999). Janiszewski's (1993) work showed that mere exposure may result in more favorable attitudes toward a brand, even though the person does not necessarily recall the exposure to the brand. It would seem that mere exposure may help explain some types of product placements, particularly ones involving brands presented as props in one or more scenes of a movie.

Clearly, many product integrations are more involved than a simple mention of the brand in the dialogue or the logo visible in the scene. As noted earlier, product integrations are often intimately tied to the character in the story or to the storyline. For example, the brands associated with James Bond are closely tied to the nature of the character; in fact, the brands that James Bond uses help define him as a character, they are part of his essence. Although conditioning or mere exposure may well be a part of why these work, there may be higher-order processing related to integrations in these circumstances. A transformational process has been suggested as such a possibility (Russell, 1998). Transformational advertising, as discussed by Puto and Wells (1984), is advertising that transforms or changes the experience of using a product such that it becomes more than it would otherwise be, making it "richer, warmer, more exciting, and/or more enjoyable" (p. 638). Numerous examples of transformational advertising come to mind for such products as jewelry, perfume, automobiles, and liquor.

In a similar way, a brand embedded in a movie can transform the experience of using it. The product is not just seen in its functional sense, but becomes the brand that is considered in the context of the story. It is, as Puto and Wells' discussion would suggest, endowed with the characteristics associated with the movie. A BMW is not just a well-made German automobile, but is the car that James Bond drives. AOL is not just a way to connect to the Internet, but the way that the trendy New Yorkers in *You've Got Mail* do so.

A similar notion is that of lifestyle advertising (Solomon & Englis, 1994). Solomon and Englis argued that lifestyle advertising associates a product with a way of life, perhaps presenting it in the context of a glamorous life or the good life. These ads can act as "models of living." Similarly, a product integrated in a movie can profit from the model of living that the story presents. An admirable character using a particular brand tells the audience that this is the brand of that product category that is "in" or "cool," or the way to the good life. It is likely that such a process may have been helpful to the success of Red Stripe's integration in the movie *The Firm*.* The two main characters who briefly discuss the brand of beer were wealthy lawyers visiting the Cayman Islands. The integration of Red Stripe in that context suggests that it was the "in" beer for such important professionals.

It would seem that the issue of the extent to which a brand is connected to the plot is indeed a very fundamental distinction between types of product integrations, as we and others (e.g., Russell, 1998) have argued. That is, whether the integration is connected to the plot or simply a prop would seem to be a basic qualitative difference in types of integrations. Connection to the plot makes an integration a different phenomenon and brings to bear a whole set of psychological processes that are likely absent for a simple prop placement. It is suggested, therefore, that product integration is a complex, multidimensional concept that may operate at different levels and affect viewers though a variety of psychological processes. The next section will consider some of the academic research on product integrations.

---

* The sales of Red Stripe increased by more than 50% shortly after the placement of the brand in the movie (Buss, 1998).

RESEARCH ON PRODUCT INTEGRATION

As the use of product integration has increased over the past three decades, there has been an increasing interest in it among academic researchers. Until rather recently, studies on product placement have generally related to three topic areas: the prevalence of product placement in movies and the nature of placements, the attitudes and beliefs regarding the practice of product placement, and the effects of placements in movies and television (DeLorme & Reid, 1999). Very recently, research has emerged that is attempting to understand the complexity of product placement. Rather than presenting an exhaustive review of the academic literature, this part of the chapter will consider some of what is known from research on product integration in order to give readers a feel for the nature of the research on the practice.*

STUDIES INVESTIGATING CONSUMERS' ATTITUDES AND PERCEPTIONS ABOUT PRODUCT INTEGRATION

Some of the academic research has focused on the attitudes and perceptions of consumers regarding the practice of product integration. Early studies in this area (e.g., Gupta & Gould, 1997; Nebenzahl & Secunda, 1993; Ong & Meri, 1994) were efforts to determine whether consumers find the practice objectionable, given the stealthy and "deceptive" nature of the product placement, as claimed by some consumer groups. These studies tended to find that, in general, the majority of people in the United States do not find the practice objectionable. In fact, the results of the Nebenzahl and Secunda study showed that the respondents preferred product integrations to traditional advertisements, and the authors of that study suggested that this preference relates to the notion that advertisements are perceived as intrusive and annoying, whereas the unobtrusive nature of product integrations make them more palatable to consumers. More recent research

---

* For a more in-depth discussion of the prior work on product integration, see DeLorme and Reid (1999) or Karrh (1998) for examinations of early work on the practice; for a discussion of more recent work on product integration, see Balasubramanian, Karrh, and Patwardhan (2006) or Van Reijmersdal, Neijens, and Smit (2009).

(e.g., Schmoll, Hafer, Hilt, & Reilly, 2006; Sung, de Gregorio, & Jung, 2009) confirms this general finding of an overall favorable view of product integration in the United States.* Furthermore, the studies by these two sets of authors suggest that consumers see product integrations as a means of providing realism to movies and television shows.

As is the case with consumers' attitudes toward most things, evaluations are often complex and nuanced. Recent research has attempted to consider the complexity of consumer evaluations of product integration. Although the practice of product integration tends to enjoy an overall positive evaluation, its acceptance varies as a function of a number of variables. The 1997 study by Gupta and Gould showed that attitudes about product integrations differ by product class. Specifically, integrations involving products that are controversial (e.g., tobacco products and alcohol) are perceived as less acceptable than noncontroversial products. Differences as a function of product class have been demonstrated in more recent research as well in that Sung, de Gregorio, & Jung (2009) found that the practice was perceived as less acceptable for products such as guns, cigarettes, alcohol, pharmaceuticals, and feminine hygiene items compared with relatively value-neutral products such as automobiles, electronics, and cameras. It should be noted, however, that consumers' views regarding the acceptability of advertising differ across product categories as well (Barnes & Dotson, 1990; Gupta & Gould, 1997); thus, it is likely that consumer attitudes about the use of product integration for controversial products would be similar to their beliefs about the use of any marketing communications for these products.

There is mounting evidence that consumers' attitudes regarding the acceptability of product integration differ as a function of the venue in which the integration resides. As noted previously in this chapter, product integrations are appearing in a number of different media, including novels, songs, music videos, and video games, as well as the traditional venues of movies and television shows. Some recent research has considered the acceptance of the practice in different media. A study by Nelson, Keum, and Yaros (2004) indicated that brand integrations in computer games were generally perceived positively by game players as such placements

---

* It should be noted that much of the academic research on product integration has been among samples of U.S. consumers. The acceptance of the practice has been shown to vary across counties (Eisend, 2009).

were considered to add realism to the games. Sung and de Gregorio (2008) found that consumers' attitudes regarding placements in video games and songs were generally positive, but more negative than for integrations in the traditional venues of television and movies. Furthermore, they showed that for each medium, consumers' attitudes about the appropriateness varied as a function of genre. In television, for example, product integrations were perceived as more appropriate for reality shows and situation comedies than for dramas and cartoons. Placements in hip-hop, pop, and country songs were perceived as more appropriate than in classical, Christian, or jazz genres.

STUDIES INVESTIGATING THE EFFECTIVENESS OF PRODUCT PLACEMENTS

The most active area of academic research on product integrations relates to the effects of placement on viewers. The effects have generally been considered in terms of memory (recognition and recall), evaluation of the brands, and purchase intention. A 1994 study by Ong and Meri found that recall of placed brands was weak for many of them. Babin and Carder (1996a) found that product integration was mixed with respect to making brands salient to viewers, and this study found no effect of the viewing of product placements on brand evaluations. In another study by Babin and Carder (1996b), the researchers investigated the ability of viewers to recognize brands they saw in a movie they just viewed, and to distinguish these from brands not in the film. Results showed that, in general, respondents were able to differentiate between brands that were in the movies they saw and brands not seen. Vollmers and Mizerski (1994) found that recall of brands in clips of a movie was very high, but there was no apparent effect of the integrations on the attitude toward the brands.

These early studies on the effects of product integration yielded mixed results with respect to the recall or recognition of brands placed in films; these studies generally showed weak or nonexistent effects of placements on brand evaluations. The mixed and weak results of these early studies on effectiveness are, in part, because these studies generally failed to recognize the multidimensional nature of product integrations. That is, they tended to treat all product integrations as similar, regardless of modality (visual or verbal), level of plot connection, context, and seamlessness. In any area of study, the nature of the inquiries become more sophisticated as the field matures. This appears to be true for investigations related to product integration in that more recent endeavors have attempted to consider these complexities of the practice.

Gupta and Lord (1998) conducted a study that compared the effectiveness of product placements of different modes (visual, audio) and prominence of the placement, using recall as the measure of effectiveness. The results showed that prominent product placements were remembered better than advertisements, but advertisements were remembered better than subtle placements. Explicit audio product placements were remembered better than subtle visual placements. Brennan, Dubas, and Babin (1999) investigated the relationship of type of placement (prop or more integral to the story) and exposure time with recognition of the integration. Their results showed that integrations more central to the story were remembered better. The effect of exposure time was a little less clear. Exposure time did not relate to recognition for background placements, but there was some indication that length of exposure was related to recognition for placements that were more central to the story.

Although recent research continues to suggest that differing levels of brand integration do lead to differences in levels of brand recognition and attitudes toward the brand (Yang & Roskos-Ewoldsen, 2007), some cautionary considerations are warranted. Homer (2009) found that repetition of prominent brand placements can impact brand attitudes negatively, but not so with more subtle placements. Van Reijmersdal (2009) found that more prominent placements have a positive impact on memory, but a negative impact on brand attitudes. Yoon, Choi, and Song (2010) showed that consumers' attitudes toward a brand are more positive when a placement is seamless than in instances when the placement appears more intrusively. Furthermore, recent research has shown that the context of the placement in terms of the information value of a program (van Reijmersdal, Smit, & Neijens, 2010) or the character that uses the product (Van der Waldt, Nunes, & Stroebel, 2008) can have effects on consumer attitudes. These findings point to the complex and nuanced nature of the practice of product integration. More exposure may, in general, be better for a brand, but it may depend on the extent to which it is done carefully and seamlessly.

In recent years, the research on product integration has continued to develop and take on new questions as the practice expands. For example, research is beginning to emerge on the effectiveness of product integrations in different media. MacKay, Ewing, Newton, and Windisch (2009), as well as Cauberghe and De Pelsmacker (2010), have investigated the effect of product integration in computer games. Delattre and Colovic (2009) considered brand placements in songs, and Brennan (2008) focused on the integration of brands in literature. Research has also continued with respect to important questions related to product integration, such as the ways in which these marketing communications are processed (see Chapter 4).

CONCLUSION

In recent decades, there has been an increase in the use of product integration as marketers attempt to find new ways to communicate with their customers. Moreover, there has been a proliferation of venues in which such integrations have appeared. In addition to the traditional media of movies and television, product integrations are now populating video games, novels, songs, and music videos. Although many marketing practitioners seem to have an intuitive understanding of how product integrations may work, until recently academic research had lagged behind in discovering how product integrations operate as a form of marketing communications. Studies conducted over the last 20 years or so are showing promise in terms of a systematic understanding of the practice. In particular, the most recent academic endeavors have acknowledged the complexity of the phenomena of product integration. Many of these studies have moved us further along in our understanding of the psychological processes relevant to the effectiveness of product integrations in a variety of circumstances.

REFERENCES

Alarcon, C. (2008, September 25). A quantum leap in product placement. *Marketing Week*, 8.

American Society of Magazine Editors (ASME). (2011). *ASME guidelines for editors and publishers*. Retrieved on April 3, 2011 from http://www.magazine.org/asme/asme_guidelines/guidelines.aspx

Babin, L. A., & Carder, S. T. (1996a). Advertising via the box office: Is product placement effective? *Journal of Promotion Management*, 3(1/2), 31–51.

Babin, L. A., & Carder, S. T. (1996b). Viewers' recognition of brands placed within a film. *International Journal of Advertising, 15*(2), 140–151.

Baker, W. E. (1999). When can affective conditioning and mere exposure directly influence brand choice? *Journal of Advertising, 28*(4), 31–46.

Balasubramanian, S. K. (1994). Beyond advertising and publicity: Hybrid messages and public policy issues. *Journal of Advertising, 23*(4), 29–46.

Balasubramanian, S. K., Karrh, J. A., & Patwardhan, H. (2006). Audience response to product placements: An integrative framework and future research agenda. *Journal of Advertising, 35*(3), 115–141.

Barcella, L. (2003, December 16). *Two restaurants battle over what's in a name.* Retrieved from http://www.cnn.com/2003/LAW/12/16/ctv.cheeseburger/

Barnes, J.H., & Dotson, M.J. (1990). An exploratory investigation into the nature of offensive television advertising. *Journal of Advertising, 19*(3), 61–69.

Bennett, M., Pecotich, A., & Putrevu, S. (1999). The influence of warnings on product placements. In B. Dubois, T. M. Lowrey, L. J. Shrum, & M. Vanhuele (Eds.), *European advances in consumer research* (Vol. 4, pp. 193–200). Provo, UT: Association for Consumer Research.

Billy Goat Tavern. (2011). *Our history.* Retrieved from http://www.billygoattavern.com/history.html.

Brennan, I. (2008). Brand placement in novels: A test of the generation effect. *International Journal of Advertising, 27*(4), 495–508.

Brennan, I., Dubas, K. M., & Babin, L. A. (1999). The influence of product-placement type & exposure time on product-placement recognition. *International Journal of Advertising, 18*(3), 323–337.

Buss, D. D. (1998, December). Making your mark in movies and TV. *Nation's Business, 86,* 28–32.

Campbell, A. J. (2006). Restricting the marketing of junk food to children by product placement and character selling. *Loyola of Los Angeles Law Review, 39*(1), 447–506.

Carvajal, D. (2006, January 17). Placing the product in the dialogue, too. *The New York Times*, p. B9.

Castillo, D. (2010, July 7). *New PQ Media report finds U.S. branded entertainment spending on consumer events & product placement dipped only 1.3% to $24.63 billion in 2009 & on pace to grow 5.3% in 2010, exceeding most advertising & marketing segments.* Retrieved from http://productplacement.biz/201007072619/branded-entertainment/new-pq-media-report-finds-u-s-branded-entertainment-spending-on-consumer-events-product-placement-dipped-only-1-3-to-24-63-billion-in-2009-on-pace-to-grow-5-3-in-2010-exceeding-most-advertising.html

Cauberghe, V., & De Pelsmacker, P. (2010). Advergames: The impact of brand prominence and game repetition on brand responses. *Journal of Advertising, 39*(1), 5–18.

Crisafulli, C. (1995, September 3). It's a wrap (but not plain): From Budweiser to BMW to Butterfinger, brand names are popping up more and more on screen, and it's usually not by chance. It's big business. *The Los Angeles Times*, p. 4.

Darlin, D. (1995, November 6). Junior Mints: I'm gonna make you a star. *Forbes, 156*(11), 90–94.

de Gregorio, F., & Sung, Y. (2010). Understanding attitudes toward and behaviors in response to product placement. *Journal of Advertising, 39*(1), 83–96.

Deighton, J., Romer, D., & McQueen, J. (1989). Using drama to persuade. *Journal of Consumer Research, 16*, 335–343.

Delattre, E., & Colovic, A. (2009). Memory and perception of brand mentions and placement of brands in songs. *International Journal of Advertising, 28*(5), 807–842.

DeLorme, D. E., & Reid, L. N. (1999). Moviegoers' experiences and interpretations of brands in films revisited. *Journal of Advertising, 28*(2), 71–95.

Edery, D. (2006). Reverse product placement in virtual worlds. *Harvard Business Review, 84*(12), 24.

Eisend, M. (2009). A cross-cultural generalizability study of consumers' acceptance of product placement in movies. *Journal of Current Issues and Research in Advertising, 31*(1), 15–25.

Federal Communications Commission (FCC). (2011). *The FCC's Payola rules*. Retrieved Aug. 2, 2011, from http://www.fcc.gov/guides/payola=rules

Fitzgerald, G. (2011, March 5). A time and a placement. *Music Week*, p. 18.

Fournier, S., & Dolan, R. J. (1997). *Launching the BMW Z3 roadster*. Case No N9-597-002. Boston: Harvard Business School.

Friestad, M., & Wright, P. (1994). The persuasion knowledge model: How people cope with persuasion attempts. *Journal of Consumer Research, 21*, 1–31.

George, L. (2005). Is Kiefer Sutherland trying to sell you something? *MacLean's, 118*(8), 30–35.

Gupta, P. B., & Gould, S. J. (1997). Consumers' perceptions of the ethics and acceptability of product placements in movies: Product category and individual differences. *Journal of Current Issues and Research in Advertising, 19*(1), 38–50.

Gupta, P. B., & Lord, K. R. (1998). Product placement in movies: The effect of prominence and mode on audience recall. *Journal of Current Issues and Research in Advertising, 20*(1), 47–59.

Helm, B. (2010, December 6). Singing songs of [Your Brand Here!]. *Bloomberg Businessweek, 4207*, 86–90.

Homer, P. M. (2009). Product placements: The impact of placement type and repetition on attitude. *Journal of Advertising, 38*(3), 21–31.

Hudson, S., Hudson, D., & Peloza, J. (2008). Meet the parents: A parents' perspective on product placement in children's films. *Journal of Business Ethics, 80*(2), 289–304.

Janiszewski, C. (1993). Preattentive mere exposure effects. *Journal of Consumer Research, 20*(3), 376–392.

Jones, M. C. (2002). The virtual gaming world finally gives way to Adland. *Brand Strategy, 165*, 10–11.

Karrh, J. A. (1998). Brand placement: A review. *Journal of Current Issues and Research in Advertising, 20*(2), 31–49.

Lafayette, J. (1998, January 12). Brinkley's ADM ads draw criticism—and shrugs. *Electronic Media, 17*(2), A1–A2.

Lowrey, T. M., Shrum, L. J., & McCarty, J. A. (2005). The future of television advertising. In A. J. Kimmel (Ed.), *Marketing communication: New approaches, technologies, and styles* (pp. 113–132). Oxford, UK: Oxford University Press.

Lowry, T., & Helm, B. (2009, October 26). Blasting away at product placement. *BusinessWeek, 4152*, p. 9.

MacKay, T., Ewing, M., Newton, F., & Windisch, L. (2009). The effect of product placement in computer games on brand attitude and recall. *International Journal of Advertising, 28*(3), 423–438.

Maynard, M. L., & Scala, M. (2006). Unpaid advertising: A case of Wilson the volleyball in *Cast Away*. *The Journal of Popular Culture, 39*(4), 622–638.

McCarthy, M. (1994, March 28). Studios place, show and win: Product placement grows up. *Brandweek, 35*, p. 30, 32.

McCarty, J. A. (2004). Product placement: The nature of the practice and potential avenues of inquiry. In L. J. Shrum (Ed.), *The psychology of entertainment media: Blurring the lines between entertainment and persuasion* (pp. 45–61). Mahwah, NJ: Lawrence Erlbaum.

Michael, D. (2000, December 20). *Tom Hanks casts a new role in latest film*. Retrieved from http://articles.cnn.com/2000-12-20/entertainment/tom.hanks_1_cnn-word -processor-interview/2?_s=PM:SHOWBIZ

Murray, I. (2004, March 11). Product placement is the oldest trick in the book. *Marketing Week, 27*(11), 70.

Nebenzahl, I. D., & Jaffe, E. D. (1998). Ethical dimensions of advertising executions. *Journal of Business Ethics, 17*(7), 805–815.

Nebenzahl, I. D., & Secunda, E. (1993). Consumers' attitudes toward product placement in movies. *International Journal of Advertising, 12*(1), 1–11.

Nelson, M. R. (2005). Exploring consumer response to "advergaming." In C. Haugtvedt, K. Machleit, & R. Yalch (Eds.), *Online consumer psychology: Understanding and influencing consumer behavior in the virtual world* (pp. 167–194). Mahwah, NJ: Erlbaum.

Nelson, M. R., Keum, H., & Yaros, R. A. (2004). Advertaiment or adcreep? Game players' attitudes toward advertising and product placements in computer games. *Journal of Interactive Advertising, 5*(1), 3–21.

Newell, J., Blevins, J. L., & Bugeja, M. (2009). Tragedies of the broadcast commons: Consumer perspectives on the ethics of product placement and video news releases. *Journal of Mass Media Ethics, 24*(4), 201–219.

Newell, J., Salmon, C. T., & Chang, S. (2006). The hidden history of product placement. *Journal of Broadcasting & Electronic Media, 50*(4), 575–594.

Ong, B. S., & Meri, D. (1994). Should product placement in movies be banned? *Journal of Promotion Management, 2*(3/4), 159–175.

Puto, C. P., & Wells, W. D. (1984). Informational and transformational advertising: The differential effects of time. In T. C. Kinnear (Ed.), *Advances in consumer research* (Vol. 15, pp. 638–343). Provo, UT: Association for Consumer Research.

Rifkind, H. (2004, October 24). Man who made Bond give up his girlie gun. *The Sunday Times*, p. Ecosse 3.

Roberts, J. (2002, September 2). The rap of luxury. *Newsweek, 140*, 42–44.

Russell, C. A. (1998). Toward a framework of product placement: Theoretical propositions. In J. W. Alba & J. W. Hutchinson (Eds.), *Advances in consumer research* (Vol. 25, pp. 357–362). Provo, UT: Association for Consumer Research.

Russell, C. A., & Belch, M. (2005). A managerial investigation into the product placement industry. *Journal of Advertising Research, 45*(1), 73–92.

Schatz, A. (2005). FCC watchdog presses case for enforcement of payola laws. *Wall Street Journal*, 1.

Schmoll, N. M., Hafer, J., Hilt, M., & Reilly, H. (2006). Baby boomers' attitudes towards product placements. *Journal of Current Issues and Research in Advertising, 28*(2), 33–53.

Solomon, M. R., & Englis, B. G. (1994). Reality engineering: Blurring the boundaries between commercial signification and popular culture. *Journal of Current Issues and Research in Advertising, 16*(2), 1–17.

Stelter, B. (2009, June 1). Starbucks is now the official Joe of "Morning Joe." *The New York Times*, p. B6.

Sung, Y., & de Gregorio, F. (2008). New brand worlds: College student consumer attitudes toward brand placement in films, television shows, songs, and video games. *Journal of Promotion Management, 14*(1/2), 85–101.

Sung, Y., de Gregorio, F., & Jung, J.-H. (2009). Non-student consumer attitudes towards product placement: Implications for public policy and advertisers. *International Journal of Advertising, 28*(2), 257–285.

van der Waldt, D. L. R., Nunes, V., & Stroebel, J. (2008). Product placement: Exploring effects of product usage by principal actors. *African Journal of Business Management, 2*(6), 111–118.

van Reijmersdal, E. (2009). Brand placement prominence: Good for memory! Bad for attitudes? *Journal of Advertising Research, 49*(2), 151–153.

van Reijmersdal, E., Neijens, P., & Smit, E. G. (2009). A new branch of advertising: Reviewing factors that influence reactions to product placement. *Journal of Advertising Research, 49*(4), 429–449.

van Reijmersdal, E., Smit, E., & Neijens, P. (2010). How media factors affect audience responses to brand placement. *International Journal of Advertising, 29*(2), 279–302.

Vollmers, S., & Mizerski, R. W. (1994). A review and investigation into the effectiveness of product placements in films. In K. W. King (Ed.), *Proceedings of the 1994 conference of the American Academy of Advertising* (pp. 97–102). Athens, GA: American Academy of Advertising.

Wasserman, T. (2005, July 25). Playing the hip-hop name drop. *Brandweek, 46*(28), 24–27.

Wasserman, T. (2007, January 29). Forward thinkers push reverse product placement. *Brandweek, 48*(5), 5.

Wells, W. D. (1989). Lectures and dramas. In P. Cafferata and A. M. Tybout (Eds.), *Cognitive and affective responses to advertising* (pp. 13–20). Lexington, MA: Lexington Books.

Yang, M., & Roskos-Ewoldsen, D. R. (2007). The effectiveness of brand placements in the movies: Levels of placements, explicit and implicit memory, and brand-choice behavior. *Journal of Communication, 57*(3), 469–489.

Yoon, S., Choi, Y. K., & Song, S. (2010). Not all products are placed equal: A quasi-experimental approach to the integration effects of conspicuous product placement on affective brand attitude. In M. C. Campbell, J. Inman, & R. Pieters (Eds.), *Advances in consumer research* (Vol. 37, p. 600). Duluth, MN: Association for Consumer Research.

3

As a Backdrop, Part of the Plot, or a Goal in a Game: The Ubiquitous Product Placement

Elizabeth Cowley
The University of Sydney
Sydney, Australia

INTRODUCTION

Originally used in films, subsequently appearing in television programs, and more recently emerging in video games, product placement has moved from enhancing the realistic nature of a scene in a movie to playing an intricate role in the entertainment value of a video game. Early in the last century, branded gasoline stations materialized as part of the landscape in films. The brand was a nonessential element of the backdrop, as opposed to a critical component of the audience's cinematic experience. In fact, consumers were relatively unaware of the brand inclusion. By the mid-1990s, product placement was a comparatively common occurrence in movies and on television, garnering a mixed reception by consumers (Gould & Gupta, 2000) and policymakers alike. The aim of the brand placements was to combat the seemingly successful strategies of viewers to avoid advertisements with remote control converters, in the hope of improving consumers' awareness of the brand and their brand attitude. Many studies have found product placement to positively influence memory (Gupta & Lord, 1998; Law & Braun, 2000; Roehm, Roehm, & Boone, 2004; Russell, 2002) and choice (Law & Braun, 2000). Other studies, however, have found conditions where viewers feel less positively toward the brand after exposure to a product placement (Cowley & Barron, 2008). More recently, brand inclusions have surfaced in video games. The placements can be as innocuous as the appearance of a logo or brand name on the landscape (called *billboarding*) in an automobile racing game or as fundamental to the experience as earning points to make different choices between brands in a snowboarding game. The choices entail selecting a jacket, a snow-board, or a pair of sunglasses from an increasingly expensive set of brands to "buy" with points earned from previous games for use in future games. The presence of the placed brands, and their prestige factor, play a crucial role in the gaming event. For placements in video games, the inclusion of brands is definitely noticed by the player, and welcomed by some gamers (Nelson, 2002).

The ever-increasing variety of environments for placements poses important questions for consumer researchers, marketing practitioners, and policymakers. Consumer researchers need to know how exposure to different types of brand placements causes a shift in brand attitude, and whether the effect is positive or negative. Marketing practitioners want to identify conditions under which placements are most effective. Social policymakers question whether consumers need to be protected from, or at least warned of, brand inclusions; and if viewers do need to be alerted, how this can be done successfully.

Four general issues are discussed in this chapter to address these ques-tions. First, to understand the ramifications of product placement for memory and brand attitude, it is essential to review the means by which product placement influences consumers' thoughts and feelings about brands. In this section, research on mere exposure, conditioning, and inference generation is discussed. Second, it is necessary to consider the context of the placement in order to predict when product placements will be successful. In this section, research on the characteristics of the place-ment itself, the likelihood of activating persuasion knowledge, and the viewers' relationship with the brand is examined to identify situations in which brand attitudes are more positive after exposure to product place-ments versus situations in which brand attitudes are more negative after exposure to a placement. The possible consequences of viewer reactions are also discussed. And environments in which consumers might wel-come the use of brands in entertaining activities are considered. Third, the strategies policymakers are using to guard the consumer against the "under the radar" approach to influencing consumers' thoughts and feel-ings about brands are critiqued in order to evaluate whether viewers can, in fact, be protected from the effects of product placement. Finally, some thoughts on what we currently do not know about the moderating factors of program format are presented, and ideas about the longer-term consequences of product placements are offered.

HOW PLACEMENTS AFFECT MEMORY AND BRAND ATTITUDE

Placements come in all shapes and sizes. Some are very subtle, such as the appearance of a Jack Daniels bottle on the table in *Two and a Half Men* or a Dos Equis beer sign in *Fantastic Four*. Other placements are more prominent, such as the pivotal role of the McDonald's McFlurry in the dialogue between Jack Donaghy and his spicy Latina lover, Elisa, in an episode of *30 Rock*. The underlying process by which product placement can impact brand attitudes differs depending on the attention paid to the placement by the viewer. With very subtle placements, the brand appears on the screen without the viewer noticing. In this case, the placement could influence the viewers' attitude because the exposure creates processing fluency: a mere exposure effect. The subtle placement could also influence the viewer through evaluative conditioning. If the program makes viewers feel good, then they may feel more positively toward the brand simply due to the temporal co-occurrence of the humor, romance, or sentimentality that generates positive feelings in general, and the exposure to the brand inclusion specifically. With more noticeable placements, the viewer may accumulate knowledge or generate inferences about the brand on the basis of how the placement is incorporated into the plot of the program. The processing of the information will create new, or reinforce old, brand associations that have the potential to alter brand attitude.

Mere Exposure

In the subtlest form of a brand inclusion, the appearance of a logo or brand name in a program, the placement may cause the viewer's attitude toward a brand to be more favorable simply due to the exposure itself: the mere exposure effect (Zajonc, 1968). Though there have been various explanations of how the mere exposure effect works, current thinking proposes that exposure to a stimulus causes perceptual fluency. Perceptual fluency refers to the ease and effortlessness of processing following increased exposure to a stimulus (Tulving & Schacter, 1990). The perceptual fluency automatically engenders a positive affective response that is psychologically detectable (Harmon-Jones & Allen, 1998; Winkielman & Cacioppo, 2001) and is transferred to the evaluative judgments of the stimuli (Monahan, Murphy, & Zajonc, 2000). In the case of product placement, the positive affect is transferred to the brand name or logo. The perceptual fluency associated with the mere exposure effect is greater for less familiar stimuli; therefore, less familiar brands may derive more significant benefits from subtle placements compared to better-known brands.

The mere exposure effect is also facilitated by repetition. Therefore, the effect may have a limited role to play in one-time-only placements, but could have a substantial impact on viewer attitudes when they see Coca-Cola glasses on the table in front of the judges in every episode of *American Idol*. It is important to note that the program itself does not need to elicit any feelings in the viewer before or during the product placement for the mere exposure effect to improve brand attitudes. But, research does show that the effects of subtle placements are moderated by an awareness of the manipulation (Warth, 2008). Specifically, the effect is stronger if the viewers do not pay attention to the presence of the brand. Although viewers cannot stop the mere exposure effect itself, they can discount brand attitudes in response to the perceived fluency effect if they are made aware of the placement. However, the discounting reaction requires viewers to (a) explicitly notice the exposure, (b) retrieve a sophisticated and informed set of lay beliefs about the potential influence of brand exposure on brand attitude, and (c) discount their brand attitudes accordingly. The question is whether this is likely to occur while viewers are engaged in an activity for entertainment or educational purposes.

Conditioning

Placements can also have an effect on brand attitude through evaluative conditioning. The same way Pavlov's dog came to salivate at the sound of a bell ringing, viewers' attitudes can be formed or changed when they are exposed to the temporal co-occurrence of something that elicits a feeling and the brand itself. For Pavlov's dog, the repeated pairing of a conditioned stimulus (a bell) and an unconditioned stimulus (his food) eventually caused the dog to salivate at the sound of the bell even when the food was not presented. Evaluative conditioning works the same way as Pavlov's classical conditioning (Martin & Levey, 1978, 1994). If a brand is paired with an evaluatively valenced stimulus, then the brand may take on the valence of the unconditioned stimulus. Therefore, after a placement, consumers may respond more favorably toward a brand if the logo or brand name was seen (or heard) with a positively affect-laden stimulus (De Houwer, Thomas, & Baeyens, 2001; Stuart, Shimp, & Engle, 1987). In the case of product placement, the affect-laden stimulus may be a character or a situation in the program that elicits a positive feeling in the viewer. The positive feeling toward the brand is the result of spatiotemporal contiguity with the elicited affective response (Martin & Levey, 1978, 1994; Walther, Nagengast, & Trasselli, 2005) that can occur without any intention to evaluate the brand (Cunningham, Raye, & Johnson, 2004). For example, just seeing a can of Diet Coke or part of the logo in a *Seinfeld* episode may cause viewers to feel more positively toward the brand if the show has made them laugh or feel good before or during the brand inclusion. No explicit thoughts about Diet Coke are required on the part of the viewer. The effect is particularly relevant if the members of the target group for the placement are card-carrying fans of the program.

For relatively well-known brands, the process is slightly different. With a preexisting network of associations in memory formed over frequent previous exposures to the brand, seeing the Diet Coke can in Jerry Seinfeld's hand may activate a subset of the associations that are consistent with the emotion elicited by the program, therefore, shifting attitude more in a positive direction (Gibson, 2008). For lesser-known brands, seeing the brand with a well-liked character or during a funny scene in the program results in a new mental representation (Strick, van Baaren, Holland, & van Knippenberg, 2009), which in this case would be positively valenced.

One critical difference between the mere exposure effect and evaluative conditioning is that the brand attitude will always be positively affected if the mere exposure effect is at work, but brand attitude can potentially be damaged by evaluative conditioning. How might this happen? During the process of evaluative conditioning, the circumstances in the plot or setting of the program could elicit a negative feeling in the viewer such as fear, anxiety, or sadness. If this elicitation is temporally contiguous with the brand placement, it may ultimately result in the reactivation or creation of a negative brand association. If this occurs, then the brand may elicit a more negative feeling when the consumer is next presented with the brand name or logo. Although the consequences can differ for mere exposure effects versus evaluative conditioning, one of the antecedents is the same. In both cases, the viewer does not need to pay explicit attention to the brand or its placement in the program.

Generating Inferences and Learning

As the prominence of the placement increases, the effect of the placement is more likely to be cognitively mediated. In other words, viewers may have thoughts or form inferences on the basis of the placement that will lead to a change in attitude or behavior. Viewers may feel more positive toward a brand if they assume the brand is liked by a favored character. For example, after seeing Edward drive a Volvo in the movie *Twilight*, the viewer may have a stronger affinity for Volvo because he or she associates the brand with Edward. Alternatively, viewers may report a stronger preference for a brand if they see an aspirational character using the brand. For example, after seeing Edward drive the Volvo, the viewer may think "I'll be more like Edward from *Twilight* if I drove a Volvo." Finally, consumers may believe that the brand is a better-quality brand after exposure to a placement in which the brand is implicitly endorsed by experts in an "allegedly" nonfictional show. For instance, viewers might think "Brita water filters must be great because Bob and Julian from *The Biggest Loser* use them." They could even think "Maybe using Brita water filters will help me lose weight."

In addition to the varied affective implications of product placement (whether they are cognitively mediated or not), viewers may also be encouraged to think about products or brands in new or different ways. In terms of new uses, a viewer watching *Masterchef* might learn that Bounty paper towels can be used under a cutting board to make the board more stable when slicing or chopping during meal preparation. In terms of new brands, viewers may learn about a new product or line extension even before its launch. This tactic is called *reverse product placement*, a term that describes the practice of introducing a product or brand in a book (e.g., Bertie Bott's Every Flavor Beans in *Harry Potter*), or a movie (e.g., Bubba Gump Shrimp Co. in *Forrest Gump*), before actually introducing it to the marketplace (Edery, 2006). Therefore, instead of placing a product to alter memory or attitude for a brand consumers already know something about, the placement occurs before the brand actually exists. Thus, the order is reversed. Reverse placement has not only been used in traditional media, but it also been used to generate interest in a virtual world for a new offering before its launch into the "real" world (Gutnik, Huang, Lin, & Schmidt 2007). For example, American Apparel test-marketed and later launched their first line of jeans in *Second Life* before eventually bringing it onto the market. In contexts such as *Second Life*, the tactic allows for the collection of consumer reactions as well.

WHAT AFFECTS THE SUCCESS OF A PLACEMENT?

Like any promotional tactic, it is important for marketers to understand the conditions under which the desired effect will occur. Research in product placement has focused on the characteristics of the placement itself: the prominence of the placement, the modality, and plot connection, in particular. To a lesser extent, research has investigated the relationship the viewer has with the characters in the program and the show itself. And to an even more minor degree, research has considered the format of the program. This section briefly reviews what we know about when placements are or are not successful at altering memory, brand attitude, and purchase intention.

The Characteristics of the Placement

A common focus for research investigating the persuasive impact of placement has been on the characteristics of the placement itself. Specifically, aspects such as modality (Law & Braun, 2000; Russell 2002), congruity with the plot (Russell, 2002), type of program (d'Astous & Seguin, 1999; Roehm, Roehm, & Boone, 2004), and, in particular, placement prominence have been identified as important determinants of the success of a placement. Although prominence is generally considered to describe the degree to which a placement moves out of the "ground" and into the "figure" of the viewing experience, it has been discussed and/or operationalized in a variety of ways including the size of the product or logo, centrality in the screen, integration into the plot, centrality to the plot, number of mentions, duration on screen, amount of movement, strength of the placement, and/or modality (Auty & Lewis, 2004; Babin & Carder, 1996; Bhatnagar, Aksoy, & Malkoc, 2004; Cauberghe & De Pelsmacker, 2010; Cowley & Barron, 2008; Gupta & Lord, 1998; Homer, 2009; Law & Braun, 2000; Russell, 2002; Van Reijmersdal, 2009). It is interesting to note that the same variables used to manipulate prominence are the variables used to determine the amount of money a marketer is willing to pay for the placement (Bhatnagar, Aksoy, & Malkoc, 2004; Karrh, McKee, & Pardun, 2003). In general, marketing decision makers pay substantially more for prominent placements.

Regardless of the operationalization, prominence has consistently been found to influence memory performance, with more prominent brands better remembered than less prominent brands (Babin & Carder, 1996; Cauberghe & De Pelsmacker, 2010; Gupta & Lord, 1998; Law & Braun, 2000). However, an improvement in explicit memory for the placement does not necessarily guarantee an improvement in brand attitude (Cowley & Barron, 2008; Gupta & Lord, 1998; Homer, 2009). In fact, the consumer's lack of awareness of a brand inclusion is central to the effectiveness of the placement (Bhatnagar, Aksoy, & Malkoc, 2004). Why? Increased prominence can cause an increase in counterarguing (Friestad & Wright, 1994; Wright, 1974) because persuasion knowledge has been activated. According to the Persuasion Knowledge Model (Friestad & Wright, 1994), people develop knowledge about how, why, and when a message is intended to influence them. This knowledge helps them "cope" with persuasive episodes. A prominent placement encourages questions about why the brand is present in the film or show and the objectives of the producers of the film or television program. The subsequent thoughts may not always be positive. The activation of persuasion knowledge is discussed further in the next section.

In addition, or alternatively, increased prominence can interrupt the consumer's viewing experience, thus causing irritation (Aaker & Bruzzone, 1985; Ha, 1996). For example, if the placement is pulled from the background, where it merely creates a context upon which drama or humor emerges, and into the foreground, where the humor is created as a vehicle to highlight the product, then prominent placements may interrupt the "suspension of disbelief." At this point, even without the activation of persuasion knowledge, the persuasive intent interrupts the editorial content, which may cause irritation in the viewer (Ha, 1996).

Placements and Priming Persuasion or
Activating Persuasion Knowledge

Research has considered the activation of persuasion knowledge and its role on the effectiveness of placements. Previous research using the Persuasion Knowledge Model has investigated situations in which consumers must contend with a sales agent (Campbell, 1995; Campbell & Kirmani, 2000) or an advertising message (Ahluwalia & Burnkrant, 2004). The very presence of a sales agent or an advertisement is sufficient for persuasion knowledge to be activated. However, exposure to product placements is different. The consumer is viewing a movie or a television show as a form of entertainment, and because product placements are present in a limited number of television shows, there is no reason for the activation of persuasion knowledge on every television viewing occasion. In fact, one of the perceived advantages of product placement is that when consumers are presented with a stimulus in a context that is construed to be an entertaining experience, they will not activate "their marketplace-related social intelligence, however deeply developed, ... leaving their performance unguided by that domain-specific knowledge" (Wright 2002, p. 680). That is, the advantage that product placements have over traditional television advertising is ascribed to the placement's hidden motive of persuasion (Bhatnagar, Aksoy, & Malkoc, 2004). Marketing practitioners perceive product placements as vehicles by which brand promotion occurs under consumers' radar. However, the assumption may be too general in its application. When will a product placement be "over" the radar?

Persuasion knowledge is not typically chronically activated after its acquisition. Instead, it is available for activation when the consumer believes a message is intended to persuade. When a tactic is perceived to have persuasive intent, the message will be affected by the *change of meaning principle* that has implications for how consumers interpret the actions of persuasive agents. When a change of meaning occurs, viewers may "disengage somewhat from the ongoing interaction, draw inferences of some sort, get distracted from the message, ... or discount what the spokesperson says" (Friestad & Wright, 1994, p. 13). If a viewer notices that a placement is pulled from the background to the foreground, it may cause a change in meaning for that viewer.

The Persuasion Knowledge Model predicts that as soon as an ulterior motivate is perceived, persuasion knowledge will be activated (Friestad &

Wright, 1994, 1995). Campbell and Kirmani (2000) investigate the accessibility of an ulterior motive as an antecedent to the activation of persuasion knowledge. Using an ulterior motive as a contextual prime, they found that when an ulterior motive is highly accessible, activation of persuasion knowledge is more likely. The activation of persuasion knowledge has also been shown to occur through exposure to an advertisement before seeing a prominent product placement for the same brand (Cowley and Barron, 2008). They found that previously positive effects on attitude after exposure to a placement became damaging to brand attitude if the placement was preceded by an advertisement for the same brand. The advertisement activated persuasion knowledge, which in turn encouraged skepticism in the viewer. This skepticism resulted in the increased detection of placements that were not simply part of the scenery, but clearly placed for commercial purposes. Reactance ensued.

The Viewers' Relationship With the Characters and the Program

An important factor in the success of a placement is the relationship the viewer has with the characters in the program or the program in general. Although involvement in the program (Anand & Sternthal, 1992; Lord & Burnkrant, 1993; Soldow & Principe, 1981), the mood created by the plot of the program (Goldberg & Gorn, 1987), and the advertisement–program consistency (Feltham & Arnold, 1994) have been investigated with respect to a traditional advertising format, we know relatively little about how the viewer's relationship with the program will impact the effectiveness of a placement (the exceptions are discussed in the following text). Although there may be similarities in the effects found between placements and traditional advertising, there is potential for differences given that the program does not only set the mood and attention paid to the brand as it might in advertising studies, but the brand can be incorporated into the plot of the program when viewing a placement.

We do know that when the viewer feels a strong attachment to a character in a program, the character's (dis)liking of the placed brand will influence the viewer's (dis)liking of the brand (Russell & Stern, 2006). In this research, Russell and Stern (2006) looked at placements in situation comedies, in particular, because of the potential for long relationships with characters. They found that the strength of the relationship, caused by the longevity of the viewer's involvement with the show and the characters, was further bolstered by the standardization of the characters which, in situation comedies, are designed to be accessible by the nature of their familiar and recognizable roles (Russell & Stern, 2006). In addition, the intimacy of most settings in the situation comedy genre (i.e., the living rooms, bedrooms, and workplaces of the characters) offers an opportunity for the viewer to form a strong connection to the personalities portrayed in the programs. Using a tricomponent approach to understanding attitude formation and change, Russell and Stern (2006) demonstrated that the relationship the viewer has with the characters in the program influences the effectiveness of the placements.

We also know that taking the perspective of characters perceived to be dissimilar to one's self requires effort on the part of the viewer, resulting in fewer cognitive resources to question the purpose of the product placement (Bhatnagar & Wan, 2008, 2011). These researchers reasoned that fewer available mental resources may cause the viewer to be more susceptible to the persuasive effects of placements because the viewer is less able to question the motivation behind the brand inclusion. They found that when consumers were immersed in the narrative of a story concerning a dissimilar character, they were more favorable toward the brand after exposure to a placement (Bhatnagar & Wan, 2011).

Viewers not only become attached to specific characters or types of characters in a program, but they can, more generally, feel favorably toward a program. Instead of considering the characters in the program, Cowley and Barron (2008) demonstrate the importance of program liking as a moderating factor on a placement characteristic, specifically placement prominence. They hypothesized that a viewer who reports high program liking will be more likely to notice placements and will be more sensitive to their prominence because the high program viewer looks forward to watching a program to satisfy his or her entertainment goals. They proposed that the increased attention to the program could result in a greater chance of realizing that a brand is placed in the program for commercial reasons, which disengages the viewer from the reality created by the program. It "makes one conscious, or more conscious than otherwise, that the other party sees you as someone on whom they think persuasion tactics can be or need to be used" (Friestad & Wright, 1994, p. 13). This realization is particularly off-putting for an involved viewer as he or she is wrapped up in the plot and may be concentrating on the longer-term implications of the exchanges among the characters in the program.

Cowley and Barron (2008) conducted an experiment to test this proposition. They used episodes of the *Seinfeld* television program varying in the prominence of the target placements from Jerry holding a can of Diet Coke with an obstructed logo (low prominence) to Kramer becoming enamored with a woman that smelled like Pantene shampoo (high prominence). They found that higher program-liking viewers reported more positive brand attitudes after exposure to subtle placements and more negative attitudes toward prominently paced brands. As expected, viewers who were lower in program liking were less attentive while watching a television program because they are less reliant on the program to satisfy their entertainment goals. The lower level of attention was evidenced by low levels of explicit memory for a placement. Lower levels of attention were not expected to be accompanied by perceptions that a placement is intrusive. In any case, the lower program-liking viewers were less able to explicitly remember the placements and did not react negatively toward them (Cowley & Barron, 2008).

Why would people watch a program they feel less liking for, or may even be neutral about? According to the Nielsen Company, Americans watched a daily average of 4 hours and 51 minutes of television in 2010, up from the 4 hours and 25 minutes reported by Eurodata TV in 2003. The global average is not much lower. Given this incredible volume of viewing, it is difficult to believe that only highly liked programs are watched. There are other reasons why people watch television programs: Viewers may watch the program to pass time, because they feel like watching television, perhaps the program is the best program on at the moment, and/or because the viewer in question is watching television with a high program-liking viewer.

The Format of the Program

Research investigating the effectiveness of product placements has typically been studied in the context of fiction, both on television (i.e., *Seinfeld, Friends,* or *Frasier*) *and* in film (i.e., *Big, Ferris Bueller's Day Off,* or *Raising Arizona*). However, placements are also commonly used in reality television shows (i.e., *Survivor, Big Brother,* or *Masterchef*). In the 2008 season, reality shows topped the placement frequency chart with 6,248 instances of product placements on *The Biggest Loser*, 4,636 on *American Idol*, and 3,371 on *Extreme Makeover*.

There are three reasons why consumers may react differently to the inclusion of a placement in reality programming. First, given that consumers believe that critically acclaimed films and shows should be kept sacred or protected from the profane persuasive tactics of marketers (Wiles & Danielova, 2009), consumers may react less negatively to prominent placements in a reality show as some critics allege reality programs themselves may be bordering on profane (Hill, 2005). Second, the suspension of disbelief, an essential requirement when consuming fiction, may not be as necessary when watching reality television. The gritty realism or authenticity manufactured by the reality television program producers with an "unproduced" quality of the show (Rose & Wood, 2005), and the purportedly unscripted dialogue, does not require a suspension of disbelief. Instead, there may be an argument for the benefit of a "nonsuspension" or continuation of belief: The more the program keeps the viewer in what they perceive to be reality, the better. Third, one of the objectives for some of the competition-based shows such as *Masterchef, Trading Places,* or *The Biggest Loser* is to acquire skills about cooking, renovating, or losing weight. In this case, product placements may be welcomed as they are consistent with the goal of accumulating knowledge, new strategies, and refined tactics for the achievement of the goal. In this case, placements do not detract from the viewer's goal but actually contribute to the viewing experience. As mentioned earlier, the viewer may also believe that the experts, commonly judges or coaches of the contestants on the show, would not use or implicitly promote products or services that were not of premium quality. At this point, there is little research comparing different genres of television programming (with the exception of La Ferle & Edwards, 2006). Clearly, there may be lessons learned from exploring various programming formats, as the viewers' expectations and goals when consuming the programs could attenuate, amplify, or moderate the effectiveness of various types of product placements.

Placements in Active Entertainment Activities

As marketers discovered new spaces to include their brands, and entertainment creators found new methods of funding the development of their products, brand placements have made their way into video games

(Hang & Auty, 2011; Lee & Faber, 2007; Nelson, 2002; Nelson & Waiguny, Chapter 5, this volume). The migration to video games moves placement from the relatively passive activity of watching television or a movie to a more active entertainment pursuit. The interactivity associated with the gaming introduces the potential for conceptual fluency, in addition to perceptual fluency, to arise (Hang & Auty, 2011). While perceptual fluency has been shown to affect attitudes or liking (Anand & Sternthal, 1992; Bornstein, 1989), conceptual fluency is more prone to affect consideration-set membership and brand choice (Lee, 2002; Nedungadi, 1990; Shapiro, 1999). The latter consequences are of particular interest to marketing practitioners.

Video games not only introduce interactivity to the mix, but their design also allows placements to play a role in the satisfaction of the entertainment goals of the consumer. As in television and film, placements in video games provide the opportunity to use brands as a backdrop to create a natural environment for the gaming challenge and offer a chance to manufacture a brand inclusion in the plotline of the game. However, placements in video games also furnish a chance to present a brand as an intricate ingredient in the achievement of the entertainment goal of the player. For example, consumers playing Ubisoft's *Shaun White Snowboarding* game earn points to "buy" equipment (i.e., Forum, Nitro, or Capita snowboards), accessories (i.e., Oakley, Anon, or Spy goggles), and snowboarding outfits (i.e., Burton, Special Blend, or Foursquare jackets) to improve their performance in future games or just look cooler on the virtual slope. The brand inclusions allow the consumer to compare brands and actively form or use brand preferences in the game that may be used in nonvirtual purchase decisions, assuming, of course, that the player actually participates in the "real" version of the sport or activity.

One additional and important advantage for placements in games is that the negative reaction to prominent placements found in a television or film context does not appear to be an issue for video game placements. Cauberghe and De Pelsmacker (2010) used an existing video game to measure the effect of the prominence of placements. They found an effect for memory but not for brand attitude. One explanation is that the gamers did not feel the prominent placements detracted from the gaming experience. Some support for the explanation is offered by the findings of a study focused on automobile placements in a racing game, *Gran Turismo 2*. Based on interviews with gamers, Nelson (2002) found that not only were product placements not considered to be deceptive or interruptive of the gaming experience, the placements actually enhanced the gaming experience.

Although there are many benefits of in-game placements, such as more positive attitudes without irritation or feelings of interrupted play, there may be drawbacks to including brand choice in video games. One possibility is that consumers will become confused about the brand's offering. Given that consumers believe they are "learning" about or trying out brands, they may judge or form inferences about the brand's performance while using the brand even though their score during the game is completely independent of the brand of equipment they have selected for use. Consumers may also make price and quality inferences on the basis of the points necessary for the acquisition of certain brands relative to other in-game choices that may or may not be correlated to the real quality of the brands. These are speculations, however, which require testing.

PLACEMENTS AND PUBLIC POLICY

Whereas academic researchers consider the contexts under which placements affect memory, attitudes, and purchase behavior, public policymakers worry that the under-the-radar advertising strategy is a tactic that may alter the behavior of viewers, and thus, policy may be required to protect consumers. Countries such as the United Kingdom have gone to the extent of prohibiting the inclusion of product placements in local productions (although the policy was relaxed dramatically in 2010), but not in foreign television programs or foreign movies. Other European countries, under an EU Audiovisual Media Service Directive, have taken a more moderate approach to protecting viewers from the persuasive impact of placements. Their approach is to allow brand inclusions (excluding product categories such as cigarettes, tobacco, alcohol, infant baby milk, and the national lottery) in shows that were not aimed at children. They do, however, require the insertion of a warning at the beginning and end of locally produced programs notifying viewers that there are (or were) placements included in the show. Examples of the product placement warning, or the PP symbol, for Belgium and the United Kingdom are provided as follows (Figures 3.1 and 3.2).

FIGURE 3.1
Product placement warning symbol in Belgium.

FIGURE 3.2
Proposed product placement warning symbols in the United Kingdom.

Both academic- and private industry–sponsored research have called the efficacy of the cautionary alert into question. For example, IP Deutschland tested the effectiveness of the insertion of the PP symbol before and after shows. They found that the presence of the label actually enhanced memory for the placed brands (unaided recall increased by a staggering 80% and aided recall increased by a still impressive 23%!), presumably because the warning drew attention to the placements. They also found no evidence supporting a negative effect on brand attitudes. In fact, they found no effect at all. These findings are consistent with an earlier study conducted by academic researchers. Bennett, Pecotich, and Putrevu (1999) had participants view a film with placements included and manipulated whether or not the placement warning was inserted. Instead of a symbol, the warning was verbal and included a list of the placed products before a full-length screening of the film *Reality Bites*. They found that those who were exposed to the warning were more likely to remember seeing the placements than those who did not receive a warning. However, the two groups did not differ in their reported brand attitudes. One possibility is that the increase in memory for the placed brands was the result of increased activation of the brands caused by the additional exposure when reading the list of brands in the warning.

However, not all studies have found enhanced memory for a brand following exposure to a placement. Preliminary academic research among Belgian researchers did not reveal a boost in memory after exposure to the warnings. Instead, Tessitore, Geuens, and Adams (2011) found no effect for memory or brand attitude when the PP symbol was included. In their studies, which were conducted in Belgium where the PP symbol had been used for some 7 or 8 months, participants were equally likely to remember the brands placed in the programs regardless of whether there was a PP symbol inserted. Participants in the warning and no-warning conditions were also equivalent in terms of their attitudes toward the brands. Therefore, the results differ from the results reported by IP Deutschland. Perhaps the memory results in Germany were partially caused by a novelty factor as the symbols were not familiar to their sample. The same novelty factor would not have existed in Belgium. Therefore, the warning may have been ignored. Also consistent with the novelty factor as a possible means of reconciling the divergent results, Tessitore, Geuens, and Adams (2011) found increased memory and reduced purchase intentions after exposure to a text-based warning that was not used in Belgium at the time of the studies.

The issue of protecting consumers against the persuasive effects of placements is thus a paradox of sorts. Ironically, if the objective of the marketer is to build brand awareness or increase the accessibility of a brand in memory and a notification of a placement improves memory for the brand, then the warning benefits their commercial objectives. If the goal of the policymakers is to deter the achievement of the commercial goal, then it appears the policymaker has more work to do in order to find a satisfactory solution to reducing the effects of the brand inclusions. If the consumer's goal is to reduce program interruptions and a warning serves to draw their attention to placements, then a placement notification will not assist the viewer in meeting his or her entertainment goal. The interruption will be particularly intrusive if the consumer must make a conscious effort to identify the feelings or emotions associated with the character to try to discount or negate any unwanted transfer of affect to the brand from a character or setting.

Based on evidence to date, warnings do not appear to be helpful in protecting the consumer from persuasive influence of brand inclusions. On the brighter side for policy makers, if the warning draws attention to the brand, then the PP symbol may alter the effects from implicit mere exposure effects

(Zajonc, 1980), which are difficult for the consumer to combat, to more manageable explicit effects. Specifically, without the warning the viewers simply see the brand, resulting in an increase in processing fluency, which can be misattributed as positive affect. With the warning, the viewers may have explicit memory for the placement, which potentially allows them a better chance of limiting the effects.

SOME OF THE THINGS WE DON'T KNOW ABOUT THE EFFECTIVENESS OF PLACEMENTS

Although a significant number of papers have been published on the topic of product placement, there are many things we still do not understand about how placements affect memory and when placements influence consumer attitudes and purchase intentions. The challenge is exacerbated by the continually evolving use of placements. Here are a small sample of the questions yet unanswered. How long will the reported recall and brand attitude effects persist? When will saturation levels occur? What will the reaction of viewers be if saturation does transpire? How does the format of the program matter and what will the interactions of program format with explicit and implicit memory effects tell us?

Placement Effects on Attitude and Memory Over Time

One of the critical and relatively under-researched aspects of product placement is the longer-term (versus shorter-term) effects for the attitude toward brand. If marketers and placement specialists can successfully determine how to place brands such that viewers' attitudes are positively affected by the brand inclusion, will the attitude change persist?

Decades of research have established when attitude change will endure. However, the conditions are not consistent with the circumstances surrounding a product placement. Attitude change persists when the message is deeply processed. For instance, persistence is more likely when the change is based on extensive issue-relevant cognitive activity during message exposure (Mackie, 1987; Petty, Haugtvedt, & Smith, 1995), if the message is repeated (Johnson & Watkins, 1971), if there is time to think about the message (Mitnick & McGinnies, 1958), or if there is little distraction around the message (Watts & Holt, 1979). Attitude change also persists if there is a chance that the changed attitude will have to be justified to others (Boninger, Brock, Cook, Gruder, & Romer, 1990; Chaiken, 1980).

Given that placements in a situation comedy or television drama are generally not intended to garner the attention of a great proportion of the viewers' cognitive resources nor will viewers believe that any shift in attitude will be questioned later, previous research considering the persistence of attitude change resulting from a persuasive message suggests a short-lived attitude effect after exposure to a brand inclusion. One exception is if the placement caused an interruption to the viewing experience or the activation of persuasion knowledge resulting in skeptical thoughts regarding the purpose of the placement. In such cases, there may be extensive cognitive activity accompanying the negative attitude change. What is ironic about this occurrence is that the initially negative attitude change may actually become positive over time, if sleeper effects follow. A sleeper effect (Cook, Gruder, Hennigan, & Flay, 1979) takes place when memory for an initially negative cue, such as the irritation caused by an intrusive placement, fades more quickly than the actual message, which must be positive, leaving the residue from the positive message without the discounting effect of the negative cue. In other words, the viewer forgets that the placement was irritating. This may be one of the few occasions in which all of the ducks are in a line. Both a strong negative cue and a strong argument are present, which is an unusual combination (Petty and Wegener, 1997), and the negative cue occurs after the message, which has been shown to be critical for obtaining a sleeper effect (Pratkanis, Greenwald, Lieppe, & Baumgardner, 1988). Importantly, the sleeper effect has been shown to positively shift brand attitudes over time (Moore & Hutchinson, 1983).

Attitude change persistence after exposure to placements in nonfictional programs may enjoy a more substantial longevity than the "nonsleeper affected" placement in a fictional context because of differential participation objectives. For instance, attitude change from a reality show placement based on a competition, in which the viewer's objective is to learn something from the program, may result in stronger persistence because the placement may cause more message-relevant thoughts, particularly if the viewer takes explicit note of the brand and its use. Video game placement, when it is incorporated into the competitive goals of the game, may also enjoy a relatively improved longevity in terms of attitude change, not due to the objective of engaging in the activity, but because of the repeated exposure during play and the autobiographical nature of the thoughts about the brand generated by the player (Lydon, Zanna, & Ross, 1988).

Finally, the underlying processes responsible for the initial attitude change may also affect the longevity of the shift. Attitude change after exposure to a product placement may occur via an increase in implicit memory (accessibility) for a brand without necessarily improving explicit memory. If so, the consumer may misattribute the increase in accessibility for a brand as liking of the brand, resulting in the mere exposure effect (Zajonc, 1968). Hence, the consumer may not explicitly remember seeing the brand as a placement but may report a more positive brand attitude as a result of the exposure. The mere exposure effect has been used to explain the increase in brand choice after exposure to product placements found by Law and Braun (2000), and could also be used to explain the positive attitude shift for visual placements that were low in plot connection in Russell's (2002) study. Given that the longevity of mere exposure effects is still in question (Zajonc, 2001), the reported attitude change may or may not endure beyond the short duration tested in experimental settings.

Moderating Effect of Program Format

Although the research on placements to date has focused on brand inclusions in television programs and movies, we know very little about the moderating effects of program format. For instance, on television alone there are dramas, comedies, documentaries, news shows, game shows, and reality shows. Even within the reality show format, there are subgenres that create different opportunities for the inclusion of a brand. Television viewers watch people at home, both celebrities (e.g., *The Osbournes*) and noncelebrities (e.g., *Big Brother*), where they see the products and brands consumed in what should be a relatively private setting. In this home setting, viewers see how the products are used by people they admire (i.e., celebrities) or people who they may believe are similar to them (i.e., noncelebrities). Viewers also watch people do their jobs (e.g., *Cops*), where they may witness what is consumed in that context. Reality shows also present people talking about their problems and embarrassing moments (e.g., *The Jerry Springer Show*) that may result in negative associations with brands and products. Other situations included in reality shows are noncelebrities competing for employment (e.g., *The Apprentice*), love (e.g., *The Bachelor*), or money (e.g., *Survivor*), and celebrities competing for accolades (e.g., *Dancing With the Stars*). Each subgenre may be watched to fulfill different viewer objectives, may be associated with various expectations for brand inclusions, and may rely on more or less of a suspension of viewers' disbelief, among other variables.

Placements have even found their way into comic books. For example, Nike logos have appeared on the clothing of the characters in Marvel Comics' *New X-Men* and in DC Comics' *Rush City* where the hero drives a Pontiac Solstice with the spokespeople for DC claiming it will be "as essential to the character as the Aston Martin was to James Bond" (Steinberg, 2006). In this context, the placed brand logos and products are presented as cartoons and the reader controls the timing of the exposure to the placement. Both of these factors may have implications for the memory, brand attitude, and purchase behavior of the reader of the comic book.

Perhaps it is more surprising than the emergence of brand placements in comic books that placements have been introduced into popular music lyrics and music videos. It is surprising because the decision to blatantly include brands seems to contravene the creative integrity of the artist. Lady GaGa and Beyonce released a video for their song *Telephone* that contained obvious placements for Miracle Whip, Virgin Mobile, Diet Coke (with a new use for the product container: cans as hair ornaments), Plenty of Fish, and Wonder Bread. Brands have also been incorporated into lyrics, such as *Pass the Courvoisier Part Two* by Busta Rhymes and Puff Daddy. Schemer, Matthes, Wirth, and Textor (2008) question the merit of placing brands in lyrics or music videos. They argue that there is a risk of negative conditioning, particularly in certain genres of music, as the imagery is not always positive. Certainly, the frequency of exposure lends itself to the conditioning process more than most formats for placements. An important assumption of their concern about negative conditioning, however, is that the evaluative conditioning is specific to a precise aspect of the imagery in the video or a particular line in the lyrics of the song, and not to the general mood or feeling generated by listening to the music. In addition, what others might find offensive or negative, the fan may not find to be quite so negative.

Finally, and as mentioned in earlier sections, virtual placements have appeared in video games. The interactivity and immersion into the games adds new dimensions to the understanding of the influences of brand inclusion. In direct opposition to the passiveness of watching television or a movie, gamers actively think about the brands and can make choices between them.

They may behave as though they have had direct experience with the brand that has many implications for consumption behaviors, including a potential strengthening of the correlation between attitude and behavior because of greater memory accessibility (Fazio, Powell, & Herr, 1983). Placements are also a ubiquitous element of virtual spaces such as *Second Life*, an experience in which immersed consumers report going to check out Harvard Business School or calm down by flying around Bora Bora Island (Mahyari, Drennan, & Luck, 2009). How will these objectively virtual, but subjectively direct, experiences shape affect, cognition, and conation?

CONCLUSION

A recent forecast published in *Advertising Age* suggested that revenue from brand inclusion would double between the years 2010 and 2014. The breadth of the proliferation of brand inclusions, from movies and television to video games, comic books, music lyrics, and videos, signifies the importance of the promotional tactic. Each of these contexts introduces different issues for understanding how consumers will be affected by the placements. In addition to the moderating effects of prominence, modality, and plot connectedness researched in television and movie placements, comic books include cartoon versions of the logos, lyrics and music videos are associated with the potential for unprecedented repetition effects, and video games involve immersion and interactivity. The challenge for researchers is to provide an understanding of how these different contexts alter the effectiveness of placements, how they interact with traditional a forms of advertising and promotion, and what the longer-term effects of placement are for memory, attitude, and behavior. A tall order. We'd better sit down in our Philippe Starck chairs, have a tall Grey Goose, and think about it.

REFERENCES

Aaker, D. A., & Bruzzone, D. E. (1985). Causes of irritation in advertising. *Journal of Marketing, 49* (Spring), 47–57.

Ahluwalia, R., & Burnkrant, R. E. (2004). Answering questions about questions: A persuasion knowledge perspective for understanding the effects of rhetorical questions. *Journal of Consumer Research, 31*(June), 26–42.

Anand, P., & Sternthal, B. (1992). The effects of program involvement and ease of message counterarguing on advertising persuasiveness. *Journal of Consumer Psychology, 1*(3), 225–238.

Auty, S., & Lewis, C. (2004). Exploring children's choice: The reminder effect of product placement. *Psychology & Marketing, 21*(September), 697–713.

Babin, L. A., & Carder, S. T. (1996). Viewers' recognition of brands placed within a film. *International Journal of Advertising, 15*, 140–151.

Balasubramanian, S. K. (1994). Beyond advertising and publicity: Hybrid messages and public policy issues. *Journal of Advertising, 23*(4), 29–46.

Balasubramanian, S. K., Karrh, J. A., & Patwardhan, H. (2006). Audience response to product placements: An integrative framework and future research agenda. *Journal of Advertising, 35*(Fall), 115–141.

Bennett, M., Pecotich, A., & Putrevu, S. (1999). The influence of warnings on product placements. In B. Dubois, T. M. Lowrey, L. J. Shrum, & M. Vanhuele (Eds.), *European advances in consumer research* (Vol. 4, pp. 193–200). Provo, UT: Association for Consumer Research.

Bhatnagar, N., Aksoy, L., & Malkoc, S. A. (2004). Embedding brands within media content: The impact of message, media, and consumer characteristics on placement efficacy. In L. J. Shrum (Ed.), *The psychology of entertainment media: Blurring the lines between entertainment and persuasion* (pp. 99–116). Mahwah, NJ: Lawrence Erlbaum Associates.

Bhatnagar, N., & Wan, F. (2008). The impact of narrative immersion and perceived self-character similarity on evaluations of product placements. In A. Y. Lee & D. Soman (Eds.), *Advances in consumer research* (Vol. 35, pp. 728–729). Provo, UT: Association of Consumer Research.

Bhatnagar, N., & Wan, F. (2011). Is self-character similarity always beneficial? The moderating role of immersion in product placement effects. *Journal of Advertising, 40*(2), 39–51.

Boninger, D. S., Brock, T. C., Cook, T. D., Gruder, C. L., & Romer, D. (1990). Discovery of reliable attitude change persistence resulting from a transmitter tuning set. *Psychological Science, 1*, 268–271.

Bornstein, M. H. (1989). Exposure and affect: Overview and meta analysis of research, 1968–1987. *Psychological Bulletin, 106*, 265–289.

Campbell, M. C. (1995). When attention-getting advertising tactics elicit consumer inferences of manipulative intent: The importance of balancing benefits and investments. *Journal of Consumer Psychology, 4*(3), 225–254.

Campbell, M. C., & Kirmani, A. (2000). Consumers' use of persuasion knowledge: The effects of accessibility and cognitive capacity on perceptions of an influence agent. *Journal of Consumer Research, 27*(June), 69–83.

Cauberghe, V., & De Pelsmacker, P. (2010). Advergames: The impact of brand prominence and game repetition on brand responses. *Journal of Advertising, 39*(1), 5–18.

Chaiken, S. (1980). Heuristic versus systematic information processing in the use of source versus message cues in persuasion. *Journal of Personality and Social Psychology, 39*, 752–766.

Cook, T. D., Gruder, C. L., Hennigan, K. M., & Flay, B. R. (1979). History of the sleeper effect: Some logical pitfalls in accepting the null hypothesis. *Psychological Bulletin, 86*, 662–679.

Cowley, E., & Barron, C. (2008). When product placement goes wrong: The effects of program liking and placement prominence. *Journal of Advertising, 37*(1), 89–98.

Cunningham, W. A., Raye, C. L., & Johnson, M. K. (2004). Implicit and explicit evaluation: fMRI correlates of valence, emotional intensity, and control in the processing of attitudes. *Journal of Cognitive Neuroscience, 16*, 1717–1729.

d'Astous, A., & Seguin, N. (1999). Consumer reactions to product placement strategies in television sponsorship. *European Journal of Marketing, 33*(9–10), 896–910.

De Houwer, J., Thomas, S., & Baeyens, F. (2001). Associative learning of likes and dislikes: A review of 25 years of research on human evaluative conditioning. *Psychological Bulletin, 127*, 853–869.

Edery, D. (2006). *Changing the game: How video games are transforming the future of business.* Upper Saddle River, NJ: Pearson.

Edwards, S. M., Li, H., & Lee, J. H. (2002). Forced exposure and psychological reactance: Antecedents and consequences of the perceived intrusiveness of pop-up ads. *Journal of Advertising, 31*(Fall), 83–95.

Fazio, R. H., Powell, M. C., & Herr, P. M. (1983). Toward a process model of the attitude-behavior relation: Assessing one's attitude upon mere observation of the attitude object. *Journal of Personality and Social Psychology,·44*, 723–735.

Feltham, T. S., & Arnold, S. J. (1994). Program involvement and ad/program consistency as moderators of program context effects. *Journal of Consumer Psychology, 3*(1), 51–77.

Friestad, M., & Wright, P. (1994). The persuasion knowledge model: How people cope with persuasion attempts. *Journal of Consumer Research, 21*(June), 1–31.

Friestad, M., & Wright, P. (1995). Persuasion knowledge: Lay people's and researchers' beliefs about the psychology of advertising. *Journal of Consumer Research, 22*(June), 62–74.

Gibson, B. (2008). Can evaluative conditioning change attitudes toward mature brands? New evidence from the Implicit Association Test. *Journal of Consumer Research, 35*, 178–188.

Goldberg, M. E., & Gorn, G. J. (1987). Happy and sad TV programs: How they affect reactions to commercials. *Journal of Consumer Research, 14*(3), 387–403.

Gould, S. J., & Gupta, P. B. (2000). Product placement in movies: A cross-cultural analysis of Austrian, French, and American consumers' attitude toward this emerging international promotional medium, *Journal of Advertising, 29*(4), 41–58.

Gupta, P. B., & Lord, K. L. (1998). Product placement in movies: The effect of prominence and mode on audience recall. *Journal of Current Issues and Research in Advertising, 20*(1), 47–59.

Gutnik, L., Huang, T., Lin, J. B., & Schmidt, T. (2007). New trends in product placement. *Strategic Computing and Communication Technology*, Spring, 1–22.

Ha, L. (1996). Advertising clutter in consumer magazines: Dimensions and effects. *Journal of Advertising Research, 36* (July/August), 76–83.

Hang, H., & Auty, S. (2011). Children playing branded video games: The impact of interactivity on product placement effectiveness. *Journal of Consumer Psychology, 21*(1), 65–72.

Harmon-Jones, E., & Allen, J. B. (1998). The role of affect in the mere exposure effect: Evidence from psychophysiological and industrial difference approaches. *Personality and Social Psychology Bulletin, 27*(7), 889–898.

Hill, A. (2005). *Reality TV: Audiences and popular factual television.* New York: Routledge.

Homer, P. (2009). Product placements: The impact of placement type and repetition on attitude. *Journal of Advertising, 38*(3), 21–31.

Johnson, H. H., & Watkins, T. A. (1971). The effects of message repetitions on immediate and delayed attitude change. *Psychonomic Science, 22*, 101–103.

Karrh, J. A., McKee, K. B., & Pardun, C. J. (2003). Practitioners' evolving views on product placement effectiveness. *Journal of Advertising Research, 43*, 138–149.

La Ferle, C., & Edwards, S. M. (2006). Product placement: How brands appear on television. *Journal of Advertising, 35*(4), 65–86.

Law, S., & Braun, K. A. (2000). I'll have what she's having: Gauging the impact of product placements on viewers. *Psychology and Marketing, 17*(12), 1059–1075.

Lee, A. Y. (2002). Effects of implicit memory on memory-based versus stimulus-based brand choice. *Journal of Marketing Research, 39*(November), 440–454.

Lee, M., & Faber, R. J. (2007). Effects of product placement in on-line games on brand memory: A perspective of the limited-capacity model of attention. *Journal of Advertising, 36*(4), 75–90.

Lord, K. R., & Burnkrant, R. E. (1993). Attention versus distraction: The interactive effect of program involvement and attentional devices on commercial processing. *Journal of Advertising, 22*(1), 47–60.

Lydon, J., Zanna, M. P., & Ross, M. (1988). Bolstering attitudes by autobiographical recall: Attitude persistence and selective memory. *Personality and Social Psychology Bulletin, 14*, 78–86.

Mackie, D. M. (1987). Systematic and non-systematic processing of majority and minority persuasive communications. *Journal of Personality and Social Psychology, 53*, 41–52.

Mahyari, P., Drennan, J., & Luck, E. M. (2009). The effectiveness of product placement within the immersive environment. In: *Proceedings of the 38th annual European Marketing Academy conference*, May 2009, Nantes, France.

Martin, I., & Levey, A. B. (1978). Evaluative conditioning. *Advances in Behaviour Research and Therapy, 1*, 57–102.

Martin, I., & Levey, A. B. (1994). The evaluative response: Primitive but necessary. *Behaviour Research and Therapy, 32*, 301–305.

Mitnick, L., & McGinnies, E. (1958). Influencing ethnocentrism in small discussion groups through a film communication. *Journal of Abnormal and Social Psychology, 56*, 82–90.

Monahan, J. L., Murphy, S. T., & Zajonc, R. B. (2000). Subliminal mere exposure: Specific, general, and diffuse effects. *Psychological Science, 11*, 462–466.

Moore, D. L., & Hutchinson, J. W. (1983). The effects of ad affect on advertising effectiveness. In R. P. Bagozzi & A. M. Tybout (Eds.), *Advances in consumer research* (Vol. 10, 526–531). Ann Arbor, MI: Association for Consumer Research.

Nedungadi, P. (1990). Recall and consumer consideration sets: Influencing choice without altering brand evaluations. *Journal of Consumer Research, 17*(December), 263–276.

Nelson, M. R. (2002). Recall of brand placements in computer/video games. *Journal of Advertising Research, 42*, 80–92.

Petty, R. E., Haugtvedt, C. P., & Smith, S. M. (1995). Elaboration as a determinant of attitude strength. In R. E. Petty and J. A. Krosnick (Eds.), *Attitude strength: Antecedents and consequences* (pp. 93–130). Mahwah, NJ: Erlbaum.

Petty, R. E., & Wegener, D. T. (1997). Attitude change: Multiple roles for persuasion variables. In D. T. Gilbert, S. T. Fiske, & G. Lindzey (Eds.), *The handbook of social psychology* (4th ed., volume 1, pp. 323–390). New York: Oxford University Press.

Pratkanis, A. R., Greenwald, A. G., Lieppe, M. R., & Baumgardner, M. H. (1988). In search of reliable persuasion effects: III: The sleeper effect is dead. Long live the sleeper effect. *Journal of Personality and Social Psychology, 54*, 203–218.

Roehm, M. L., Roehm Jr., H. A., & Boone, D. S. (2004). Plugs versus placements: A comparison of alternatives for within-program brand exposure. *Psychology & Marketing, 21*(1), 17–28.

Rose, R., & Wood, S. (2005). Paradox and the consumption of authenticity through reality television. *Journal of Consumer Research, 32*(September), 284–296.

Russell, C. A. (2002). Investigating the effectiveness of product placements in television shows: The role of modality and plot connection congruence on brand memory and attitude. *Journal of Consumer Research, 29*(December), 306–318.

Russell, C. A., & Stern. B. (2006). Consumers, characteristics, and products: A balance model of sitcom product placement effects. *Journal of Advertising, 35*(1), 7–21.

Schemer, C., Matthes, J., Wirth, W., & Textor, S. (2008). Does "Passing the Courvoisier" always pay off? Positive and negative evaluative conditioning effects of brand placements in music videos. *Psychology and Marketing, 25*(10), 923–943.

Shapiro, S. (1999). When an ad's influence is beyond our conscious control: Perceptual and conceptual fluency effects caused by incidental ad exposure. *Journal of Consumer Research, 26*(1), 16–36.

Soldow, G. F., & Principe, V. (1981). Response to commercials as a function of program context. *Journal of Advertising Research, 21,* 59–65.

Steinberg, B. (2006). Look—Up in the sky! Product placement! *Wall Street Journal.* April 18, 2006.

Strick, M., Holland, R. W., & Van Knippenberg, A. (2008). Seductive eyes: Attractiveness and direct gaze increase desire for associated objects. *Cognition, 106,* 1487–1496.

Strick, M., van Baaren, R. B., Holland, R. W., & van Kaippenberg, A. (2009). Humor in advertisements enhances product liking by mere association. *Journal of Experimental Psychology: Applied, 15*(1), 35–45.

Stuart, E. W., Shimp, T. A., & Engle, R. W. (1987). Classical conditioning of consumer attitudes: Four experiments in an advertising context. *Journal of Consumer Research, 14,* 334–349.

Tessitore, T., Geuens, M., & Adams, L. (2011). *Warning consumers against product placement: What does and does not work?* Conference Proceedings of the Society for Consumer Psychology, Atlanta.

Tulving, E., & Schacter, D. L. (1990). Priming and human memory systems. *Science, 247,* 301–306.

Van Reijmersdal, E. (2009). Brand placement prominence: Good for memory! Bad for attitudes? *Journal of Advertising Research, 49*(2), 151–153.

Walther, E., Nagengast, B., & Trasselli, C. (2005). Evaluative conditioning in social psychology: Facts and speculations. *Cognition & Emotion, 19,* 175–196.

Warth, M. (2008). *Beiläufige Werbewirkung als Anwendungsbeispiel des Fluency-Konzepts: Meta-Analyse und Kosten-Nutzen_Analyse.* Unpublished master's thesis, University of Mannheim, Germany.

Watts, W. A., & Holt, L. E. (1979). Persistence of opinion change induced under conditions of forewarning and distraction. *Journal of Personality and Social Psychology, 37,* 787–789.

Wiles, M. A., & Danielova, A. (2009). The worth of product placement in successful films: An event study analysis. *Journal of Marketing, 73*(4), 44–63.

Winkielman, P., & Cacioppo, J. T. (2001). Mind at ease puts a smile on the face: Psychophysiological evidence that processing facilitation elicits positive affect. *Journal of Personality and Social Psychology, 81,* 989–1000.

Wright, P. (1974). The harassed decision maker: Time pressures, distractions, and the use of evidence. *Journal of Applied Psychology, 59*(October), 555–561.

Wright, P. (2002). Marketplace metacognition and social intelligence. *Journal of Consumer Research, 28*(March), 677–682.

Zajonc, R. B. (1968). Attitudinal effects of mere exposure. *Journal of Personality and Social Psychology, 9,* 1–27.

Zajonc, R. B. (1980). Feeling and thinking: Preferences need no inferences. *American Psychologist, 35*(2), 151–175.

Zajonc, R. B. (2001). Mere exposure: A gateway to the subliminal. *Current Directions in Psychological Science, 10,* 224–228.

4

Children's Processing of Embedded Brand Messages: Product Placement and the Role of Conceptual Fluency

Laura Owen
University of Reading
Reading, United Kingdom

Haiming Hang
University of Reading
Reading, United Kingdom

Charlie Lewis
Lancaster University
Lancaster, United Kingdom

Susan Auty
Lancaster University
Lancaster, United Kingdom

With its huge economic potential, the children's market has become increasingly important to advertisers (McNeal, 1999). In the United Kingdom, it is estimated that children spend £12 billion per year (Nairn, 2009), and statistics from many other countries show this same pattern of high spending (Gunter, Oates, & Blades, 2005). Millions of dollars are consequently being invested worldwide in targeting this growing consumer segment. For example, food and beverage companies currently spend around $1.6 billion per year marketing their products to children (FTC, 2008; Marr, 2008).

Children are thus exposed to countless commercial messages on a daily basis, with a considerable proportion of these messages embedded in non-commercial contexts (La Ferle & Edwards, 2006; Moore, 2004; Moore & Rideout, 2007; Wright, Friestad, & Boush, 2005).

Product placement is one such example of embedded advertising, and as such has received research attention over the past 20 years. It comprises paid messages intended to influence audiences via the unobtrusive use of branded products within a variety of media presentations (Balasubramanian, 1991; McCarty, 2004). As a result, it blurs the boundaries between advertising, entertainment, and information (Mallinckrodt & Mizerski, 2007; Wright et al., 2005). As they are typically embedded, brands are not necessarily perceived consciously. The persuasive intent of product placement may thus not be immediately apparent, particularly to children (Moore & Rideout, 2007; Owen, Lewis, Auty, & Buijzen, 2011). As a consequence, skepticism and rejection of the commercial message become less likely (Calvert, 2008; Nairn & Fine, 2008). The effectiveness of product placement is therefore based largely on subtle, implicit rather than explicit, persuasion processes (Law & Braun, 2000; Law & Braun, 2004; Nairn & Fine, 2008; van Reijmersdal, Neijens & Smit, 2007). Thus, this form of message may operate under our radar of consciousness and, as a result, the phenomenon has generated heated ethical and public policy debate worldwide (Balasubramanian, 1994; d'Astous & Seguin, 1999; Hackley, Tiwsakul, & Preuss, 2008; Hudson, Hudson, & Peloza, 2008; Nebenzahl & Jaffe, 1998).

PUBLIC POLICY AND ETHICAL DEBATES ABOUT PRODUCT PLACEMENT

Central to current policy debates is the notion that product placement blurs the line between advertising and entertainment because its persuasive intent is not disclosed to consumers. Therefore, some argue that product placement is deceptive (Balasubramanian, 1994; Balasubramanian, Karrh, & Patwardhan, 2006; Petty & Andrews, 2008), as consumers may not perceive it as a marketing effort, and therefore may be less skeptical about its presence (Darke & Ritchie, 2007). Organizations and consumers holding this view urge public policy makers to intervene to protect consumers' interests. In contrast, others argue that product placement is not covert marketing but freedom of speech and artistic expression, which are protected in the United States by the First Amendment. For example, Kuhn, Hume, and Love (2010) claim that product placement is used to enhance the verisimilitude of programs, and consumers are more likely to be offended if generic products rather than branded products are used.

This impassioned debate is accompanied by inconsistent worldwide public policies on product placement. For example, in the United Kingdom, the Office of Communications (OFCOM) initially banned product placement in TV and radio for breaching its broadcast code of clear separation of advertising from programming (OFCOM, 2006). However, at the time of writing, OFCOM has revised its policy, and on February 28, 2011, allowed product placement to appear in both TV and radio programs (although a symbol marking the appearance of placements will be required at both the start and end of programs and at ad breaks)*, as long as these were not current affairs, news, or programs specifically for children. Nonetheless, it must be acknowledged that children are also highly likely to be exposed to programming that is aimed at adults (e.g., in the U.K. soaps such as *Coronation Street* and talent shows like the *X Factor* are watched by children). OFCOM has defended its U-turn by insisting that broadcasters face great difficulty in subsidizing their high production costs in a challenging economic climate (OFCOM, 2010). Consumer Focus, the United Kingdom's independent consumer watchdog, is strongly opposed to such a move, arguing that the evidence that product placement generates a significant income for broadcasters is still absent (Consumer Focus, 2010).

Different strands of moral philosophy, namely utilitarianism, deontology, and virtue ethics, are used in the extant literature to evaluate the ethics of product placement. However, Hackley et al. (2008) argue that consumer autonomy should be the primary focus of the debate. True freedom of choice and action should be available to all, and any marketing activities depriving consumers of autonomy thus lack humanity and are unethical (Robin & Reidenbach, 1987). From this point of view, the ethics of product placement is doubtful, as its hybrid nature may lead consumers to fail to realize its inherent commercial intent, thus jeopardizing their ability to make an informed choice. This inability to distinguish

---

* The OFCOM ruling further disallows product placement of foods high in fat, salt, or sugar (HFSS foods), alcohol, cigarettes, infant baby milk, and over-the-counter medicines.

commercial activity from programming is particularly evident among children owing to their limited cognitive abilities.

Children's Vulnerability to Product Placement

The literature suggests that, compared with adults, children's limited cognitive and executive functioning skills may make them especially vulnerable to commercial messages (Moore, 2004; Moses & Baldwin, 2005). A report of the Task Force on Children and Advertising of the American Psychological Association, for example, emphasizes that young children lack the necessary cognitive skills possessed by older children and adults to comprehend commercial messages effectively (Kunkel et al., 2004). The APA report suggests that for consumers to resist the persuasive intent of advertising, they are initially required, at a perceptual level, to discriminate between commercial and noncommercial content, and second, to attribute persuasive intent to the advertisement. Others propose a requirement of not only grasping advertisers' motives but also utilizing this understanding to counteract the influence of advertising (Friestad & Wright, 1994; Wright et al., 2005). Persuasive intent is thus assumed to be a necessary prerequisite to evaluate advertising messages critically (Lindstrom & Seybold, 2003).

The embedded nature of product placement may thus pose particular problems for children, especially with regard to understanding its inherent persuasive intent. However, limited academic research exists into children's grasp of this advertising technique. Owen, Lewis, Auty, and Buijzen (2011) compared 7 to 10-year-old children's understanding of TV advertising with various examples of nontraditional advertising, including product placement in films, in-game brand placement, program sponsorship, licensed products, and advergames. They noted that compared to TV messages, children's comprehension of less transparent nontraditional advertising was considerably lower and less well developed. Moreover, children's appreciation of the more embedded examples of nontraditional practices (i.e., product placement in films and in-game brand placement) was significantly poorer than it was for the less embedded examples (i.e., program sponsorship, product licensing, and advergames). The escalating use of product placement thus raises substantial concern among a number of academics and policymakers. Many critics argue that targeting children with these covert messages when they demonstrate a limited ability to understand advertising is both deceptive and unfair.

How Does Product Placement Influence Children?

The unobtrusive nature of product placement may bypass children's cognitive defenses completely, thus rendering them unable to resist its persuasive intent (Auty & Lewis, 2004a; Balasubramanian, 1994; Nairn & Fine, 2008). However, the majority of empirical studies exploring product placement effectiveness use only explicit recall or recognition measures to gauge its impact (for reviews, see Balasubramanian et al., 2006; Shrum, Lowrey, & Liu, 2009; van Reijmersdal, Neijens, & Smit, 2009). As product placement typically embeds products and brands within the context of a story (either as a background prop or an integral feature of the storyline), the focus of attention is directed toward the plotline of the program or control of the video game. Fewer cognitive resources thus remain available to consciously process the placed brand. This means that embedded brands are much more likely to be processed on an implicit or preconscious level (Law & Braun, 2000; Nairn & Fine, 2008; van Reijmersdal et al., 2007). Recent investigations among adults have suggested that product placement exposure typically induces implicit priming in the form of a positive bias toward the brand, without explicit awareness of brand exposure (van Reijmersdal et al., 2007; Yang, Roskos-Ewoldsen, Dinu, & Arpan, 2006). The practice of product placement thus demands a greater regard for the "implicit" effects of exposure, in which preferences and behavior are subject to change outside conscious awareness.

Implicit processing is likely to be particularly evident when consumers (especially children) lack the cognitive capacities or the motivations to process stimuli in sufficient detail to perceive a message. Indeed, in order to be alert to persuasive intent, children must utilize cognitive resources concerning their existing knowledge of the intent of advertising, which requires deliberate, effortful processing (Livingstone & Helsper, 2006). As product placement is typically processed at a preconscious level, sufficient conscious elaboration is highly unlikely.

A number of studies have found that exposure to product placement may influence children's brand preference and even brand choice (e.g., Auty & Lewis, 2004a, 2004b; Hang & Auty, 2010, 2011; Mallinckrodt &

Mizerski, 2007). For example, Mallinckrodt and Mizerski (2007) noted that playing an advergame containing Froot Loops cereal increased 5–8-year-old children's preference for the brand. Interestingly, they found that this effect was stronger for the older children than the younger ones despite the fact that nearly half the children in the treatment group understood that the purpose of the advergame was to encourage them to eat Froot Loops.

One of the few studies to compare children's implicit versus explicit memory for product placement noted that exposure to Pepsi in a film clip significantly increased children's likelihood of selecting Pepsi over Coca-Cola when given a choice (Auty & Lewis, 2004a, 2004b). The children were unable to recall seeing Pepsi, confirming the adult literature noting an increase in positive affect toward brands without a corresponding increase in conscious recognition. Prior exposure to the film further enhanced these effects, suggesting that repeated viewings can increase the implicit influence of product placement. It is this issue that we focus our attention on next.

THE IMPLICIT INFLUENCE OF PRODUCT PLACEMENT: UNDERLYING PROCESSING MECHANISMS

According to widely accepted terminology in cognitive psychology, explicit memory denotes a deliberate act of recollection of the source and context of the information encoded, whereas implicit memory reflects the nonintentional, nonconscious retrieval of previously acquired information (Lee, 2002; Shapiro & Krishnan, 2001). Furthermore, research evidence suggests that explicit memory may be diluted or even absent in conditions of divided attention (Debner & Jacoby, 1994), whereas implicit memory may remain intact (Shapiro & Krishnan, 2001). In other words, performing different tasks concurrently has no effect on implicit memory but has adverse effects on explicit memory (Lee, 2002). In addition, numerous studies have suggested that whereas explicit memory improves during childhood, reaches a peak during young adulthood, and then declines during later life (Law & Braun, 2000), implicit memory appears insensitive to age differences, with children demonstrating comparable implicit memory capacity to adults (Naito, 1990).

This dissociation between explicit and implicit memory indicates that an individual's performance on an explicit memory task may not predict his or her performance on an implicit memory task, and vice versa (Law & Braun, 2000; Lee, 2002). Thus, different methods are necessary to measure explicit versus implicit memory, with the former typically gauged via recall or recognition tasks and the latter typically determined via task improvement without conscious reference to previously acquired information (Roediger, 1990). As consumers (and children in particular) are likely to process product placements under low attention conditions, the use of explicit memory tasks to measure their effectiveness is likely to be misleading (Law & Braun, 2000). Instead, a combination of both implicit and explicit memory tasks may provide the most complete picture of product placement effectiveness (e.g., Auty & Lewis, 2004b; Shapiro & Krishnan 2001; Yang et al., 2006).

How Does Implicit Memory Work?

Traditional theories of implicit memory focused largely on the role of perceptual fluency, in which stimulus analysis occurs purely in terms of its physical features. This feature-level analysis facilitates feature-level processing during a subsequent exposure to the same stimuli (e.g., Bornstein & D'Agostino, 1992, 1994; Tulving & Schacter, 1990). As the fluency with which this stimulus is processed becomes enhanced, individuals frequently experience feelings of familiarity that may, in turn, be misinterpreted as a beneficial quality, leading to feelings of positive affect toward the exposed stimulus (Jacoby, Kelley, & Dywan, 1989; Janiszewski, 1993). Such an approach shares many conceptual similarities with the mere exposure effect in which prior exposure to a stimulus is sufficient to induce positive affect (Zajonc, 1968, 1980).

However, brand logos provide a very different stimulus from that commonly used to ascertain the effects of mere exposure (e.g., novel abstract shapes and symbols; Zajonc, 1968). Instead, logos are symbolic representations, capable of conjuring up an array of connotations, emotions, and experiences for each individual. Even preschool children attach meanings to logos and demonstrate distinct brand preferences (Hite & Hite, 1995; Pine & Nash, 2003; Robinson, Borzekowski, Matheson, & Kraemer, 2007). The processing of product placement is therefore likely to be based on more than just the perceptual features of the product or logo and is thus more complex than can be captured by existing perceptual fluency approaches. Instead, product placement processing appears likely to incorporate a conceptual fluency component in which the implicit effects are primed by conceptual, semantic links, such as preexisting knowledge and experience.

Recent research suggests that perceptual and conceptual fluency are independent (Cabeza & Ohta, 1993), with differing antecedents and consequences (Lee, 2002; Lee & Labroo, 2004). For example, nonconscious elaboration at the time of exposure may benefit conceptual fluency but not perceptual fluency (Hamann, 1990). In addition, perceptual fluency is modality sensitive, and will be strongest when the physical features of the stimuli are identical at both encoding and retrieval. In contrast, conceptual fluency is frequently still found following modality changes between exposure and test (e.g., Jacoby & Dallas, 1981). Lee (2002) also suggests that perceptual fluency is more evident in tasks requiring a stimulus-based choice (e. g., picking a brand off a shelf), whereas conceptual fluency is more evident in tasks relying upon memory-based choice (devising a shopping list of brands).

Indeed, recently academics have begun to argue against the notion of mere exposure and have acknowledged the role of conceptual fluency in implicit memory (e.g., Braun-LaTour & Zaltman, 2006; Hourihan & MacLeod, 2007; Mantonakis, Whittlesea, & Yoon, 2008; Winkielman, Schwarz, Fazendeiro, & Reber, 2003). Braun-LaTour and Zaltman (2006), for example, put forward a "memory integration paradigm" that affirms that existing attitudes and values, prior knowledge, relevance, semantics, and the advertising context all play a role when advertising messages are processed by adults. Such a paradigm requires further testing among children, especially in the context of covert messages such as product placement.

MEASURING IMPLICIT EFFECTS OF PRODUCT PLACEMENT ON CHILDREN

The vast majority of advertising research depends upon explicit recall or recognition measures, and product placement is no exception (e.g., Babin & Carder, 1996; Bressoud, Lehu, & Russell, 2010; Gupta & Lord, 1998; Nelson, Yaros, & Keum, 2006). However, heightened interest in the implicit influence of advertising has been matched with a need to develop new tools to accurately tap such "under the radar" effects. The Implicit Association Test, or IAT, provides one such methodology (for recent reviews of IAT see Dimofte, 2010; Perkins, Forehand, Greenwald, & Maison, 2008). Developed by Greenwald, McGhee, and Schwartz (1998), the IAT is a categorization task measuring the relative strength of associations among different concepts in memory. It does not require the conscious retrieval of information from memory. Rather, association strength is gauged via the ease or difficulty with which participants are able to assign the same response to different concepts (Dimofte, 2010; Perkins et al., 2008). Association strength is measured via participants' response speed. An important application of IAT in product placement research is to provide a tool to gauge children's implicit attitudes toward the placed brands following exposure (for a recent example of how the IAT can be used to measure implicit attitudes, see Horcajo, Briñol, & Petty, 2010).

An alternative tool used frequently to measure implicit effects is fragmented word completion. In a fragmented word completion task, participants are typically provided with incomplete word stems and are asked to complete these stems as quickly as possible. Implicit memory is measured by the increased probability that participants will complete the stems using target words to which they were recently exposed (e.g., Krishnan & Chakravarti, 1999). By comparing participants' task performance with a baseline performance (without prior target word exposure), implicit memory may be identified as improved performance in terms of ease of word completion on account of the previously exposed words coming to mind more quickly and effortlessly (Krishnan & Chakravarti, 1999). Applying this tool to product placement research, one would anticipate an increased probability that participants would complete word stems using brand names to which they had been subjected during placement exposure.

Of specific relevance to a marketing context, the consumer choice task provides a commonly utilized measure of implicit effects. Within this task, participants are exposed initially to an advertising stimulus and are then presented (typically incidentally) with a choice scenario. However, hypothetical choice tasks have been subject to criticism as they are likely to draw upon nonimplicit factors such as social desirability or the influence of explicit memory (e.g. Butler & Berry, 2001). Thus, Hang and Auty (2010, 2011) followed Shapiro (1999) by using a recollection–exclude

procedure to separate the conscious impact of product placement exposure on children's choice from the unconscious impact (based on Curran
& Hintzman's 1995 procedures). In their research, children were first
asked to write down any brands that they remembered being exposed to—
the recollection procedure. Then, in the exclude procedure, children were
asked to choose a preferred brand but, crucially, this brand could not be
one that they had written down during the recollection procedure (Hang
& Auty, 2010, 2011). The implicit effect of product placement is gauged
via the increased probability of children choosing the exposed (but not
recollected) brand when compared to the choices of children who had not
been exposed to product placement. The validity and reliability of similar
procedures with children have been supported by previous research. For
example, Holliday and Hayes (2001) used the process dissociation procedure, an alternative form of the recollect–exclude procedure, to separate
children's autonomic and intentional memory processes.

A New Measure of Implicit Memory

Owen, Lewis, and Auty (2011) developed a new measure of implicit memory with the specific purpose of assessing children's implicit processing
of product placement—the "Fragmented Logo Implicit Recognition Task"
(FLIRT)—adapted from Snodgrass, Smith, Feenan, and Corwin (1987).
Within the FLIRT, children are shown a picture of a highly degraded
brand logo, with seven-eighths of the original pixels removed randomly
across a grid overlaying the logo, and asked to identify the image (e.g., tell
the researcher the brand name). Following this first image, the children
are presented with a series of seven increasingly more complete images
of the same logo (each with one-eighth more of the total pixels added)
through to the complete image of the brand logo (see Figure 4.1). In terms
of scoring, if the child is able to identify the brand logo on the first picture,
it receives eight points. If the child correctly identifies the brand on the
second picture, it receives seven points, and so on. If the child is unable
to name the final complete brand image, it receives a score of zero and is
excluded from further analysis. Ease of recognition is the dependent measure, with brand identification from a more degraded image indicative of
greater implicit memory.

Following the FLIRT, the children perform an explicit brand recognition
task to tap their conscious memory for product placement. In this explicit

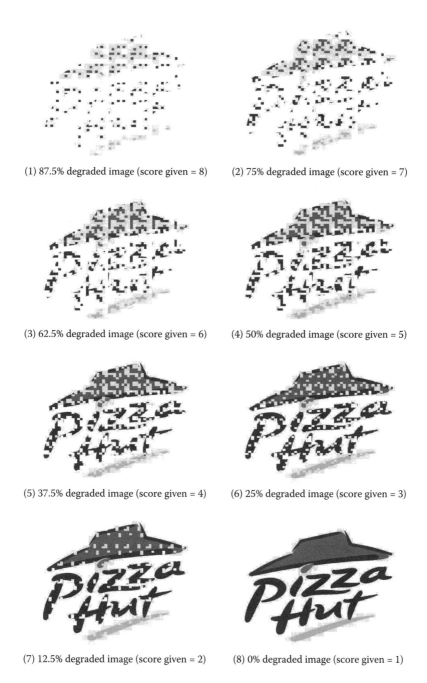

(1) 87.5% degraded image (score given = 8)   (2) 75% degraded image (score given = 7)

(3) 62.5% degraded image (score given = 6)   (4) 50% degraded image (score given = 5)

(5) 37.5% degraded image (score given = 4)   (6) 25% degraded image (score given = 3)

(7) 12.5% degraded image (score given = 2)   (8) 0% degraded image (score given = 1)

FIGURE 4.1

An example of the FLIRT test: Children are shown each image until they can identify the logo.

task, the children are shown an array of brand logos and are asked to select any brands that they remember seeing in the movie clip. This combination of tasks allows a direct comparison between implicit and explicit recognition of product placements. The FLIRT has been used across a number of contexts (Owen, Lewis, & Auty, 2011, under review) and provides a sensitive priming measure of implicit memory that enables us to ascertain the preconscious effects of various advertising techniques across a diverse age range of participants.

The basic premise of the aforementioned tools is that performance is facilitated by past experiences without the participants' intention or awareness that they are relying on these experiences. According to Sheldon and Moscovitch (2010), there is a two-stage process by which an exposure associated with a prior event becomes available to all memory systems in the brain, including explicit storage functions. In the first stage, the interaction between the stored information and its output occurs automatically and without conscious awareness. Only in the second stage might there be explicit awareness, but this explicit recollection does not always occur. They provide evidence for the role of nonconscious recollection in priming tasks, and their findings lend support to the importance of prior knowledge and repetition for the effectiveness of product placement. Thus, it is in the advertisers' interests to expose children early and often to relevant brands.

PRODUCT PLACEMENT IN DIFFERENT MEDIA AND CONTEXTS

It has been argued that advertising effectiveness is determined partly by the context in which it appears (Malthouse, Calder, & Tamhane, 2007). Product placement is no exception. Surprisingly, therefore, there has been only scant exploration of contextual influences on the impact of product placement on children, despite the fact that children are rarely exposed to product placement under controlled laboratory conditions. What is the role of contextual factors such as the personal salience of the placed brand, the emotional context of the placement, and the child's engagement with the media? The following section reviews the existing theoretical and empirical evidence to provide support for the importance of conceptual fluency in children's implicit processing of product placement and considers a variety of contextual factors.

Personal Salience

Salience has been used previously to refer to the prominence or level of activation of a brand in memory (e.g., Alba & Chattopadhyay, 1986; Miller & Berry, 1998). We conceptualize personal salience here as a brand's relevance to an individual, incorporating both brand awareness (as an essential first stage) and also personal interest in the brand or product category as a whole. Research has noted that even preschool children are capable of demonstrating defined brand preferences and attaching meanings to logos (Hite & Hite, 1995; Pine & Nash, 2003; Robinson et al., 2007). Given the nonconscious interaction between implicit and explicit memory functions as suggested by Sheldon and Moscovitch (2010), personal salience is likely to encourage such interaction in the following manner.

Enhanced explicit memory for familiar over unfamiliar product placements has reliably been noted among adults (Brennan, Dubas, & Babin, 1999; Nelson et al., 2006). This finding may be attributable to familiar items being more accessible to attitudes, thus commanding superior use of memory resources and systematic processing (Roskos-Ewoldsen & Fazio, 1992). Comparable results for personally relevant over less relevant product placements have also been obtained (Nelson, 2002).

So, how might personal salience enhance implicit memory? Preexisting knowledge and experience is likely to influence implicit memory in much the same way as it influences explicit memory, for example, via facilitating a richer encoding at exposure and thus a greater number of retrieval routes at test (Murphy, McKone, & Slee, 2003). Exposure to personally salient brands is thus anticipated to unconsciously activate existing, conceptually related, semantic information in memory that will enhance the fluency with which these brands are processed implicitly (Lee & Labroo, 2004).

In a study by Owen, Lewis, Auty, & Buijzen (2011), 143 6- to 10-year-old children were randomly allocated to one of two groups. Group one viewed a test film clip containing two familiar brand placements varying in personal salience. The first was a visual-only Pizza Hut placement, in which the main character was portrayed working in a Pizza Hut restaurant. The second was a visual-only Nike placement, in which the main character took part in a soccer match and his team uniform displayed the Nike logo. Group two viewed the control clip, which was taken from the same movie, considered by two independent judges to be of comparable pace and interest, but containing no brands.

With regard to personal salience, Pizza Hut represents a child-oriented fast-food brand and was thus deemed highly salient among 6- to 10-year-old children. In contrast, as sports brands increase in salience among older children and adolescents (Pine & Nash, 2003; Walshe & Brown, 2000), Nike represented a less salient brand. Indeed, when shown the logo and asked what it represented, almost all of the children knew Pizza Hut, while only 75% (significantly less) knew Nike.

Utilizing the FLIRT methodology described in the preceding section, Owen, Lewis, Auty, & Buijzen noted that ease of recognition of Pizza Hut was significantly greater among children in the test condition compared to the controls. However, ease of recognition of Nike did not differ significantly between the two conditions. This suggests that the children's implicit memory was enhanced significantly following exposure to the personally salient brand (Pizza Hut) but not following exposure to the less salient brand (Nike). Basic brand familiarity may thus be insufficient to enhance implicit memory. Instead, the personal salience of the brand may enhance the implicit effects following product placement exposure. With reference to Lee and Labroo (2004), such an effect is likely to operate via the unconscious activation of conceptually related information in memory that serves to enhance the fluency with which personally salient brands are processed implicitly. That comparable findings were not observed for both Pizza Hut and Nike suggests that much more than the mere physical features of the brand logo are at play when product placements are processed by children.

Owen et al. further noted that explicit memory for both brands was poor and did not account for success on the implicit task. This frequently observed dichotomy in product placement research findings (van Reijmersdal et al., 2007; Yang et al., 2006) is in keeping with Sheldon and Moscovitch's (2010) theory. An increase in affect without an increase in recall has also been observed among children. Auty & Lewis (2004a, 2004b) noted that exposure to an audiovisual Pepsi placement significantly enhanced children's probability of selecting Pepsi over Coca-Cola in a choice task, compared to a control group who had seen no brands. However, the children were unable to consciously recall seeing Pepsi.

In that experiment, the effect of repetition was also supported, with children who had been exposed to the film on an earlier occasion being more likely than first-time viewers to select the exposed brand. An earlier exposure may increase the *specific* perceptual and conceptual associations, and be one of the reasons why earlier exposure to actual placements has a stronger priming effect than exposure from experience. Repetition becomes an especially important factor in the context of product placement in video games, where it naturally occurs within the game and also from the tendency for players to over-learn routines. Moreover, repeated game play may alter the processing of information in games never attempted before. In the sections below, we consider the role of interactivity in games and differences between frequent and occasional game players with regard to the effectiveness of product placement.

Interactivity

With the advance of interactive media such as video games and the Internet, children now spend more time playing video/Internet games than they do watching TV (Gentile, 2009). This change has caused many corporations to shift their marketing investments from traditional television advertising to in-game product placements and advergames (Yang et al., 2006). Indeed, the prevalence of advergames targeted at children has become a key feature of the current marketplace (Moore & Rideout, 2007).

Existing literature suggests that one of the key advantages of product placement in games lies in their interactive nature. The longer shelf life of games over films, the increased sensory immersion (e.g. Grodal, 2000; Vorderer, 2000), and bidirectional information flow between players and games (Liu & Shrum, 2002, 2009; Nelson, 2002) can subsequently increase players' exposure to, and involvement with, the product placement (Nelson, 2002; Schneider & Cornwell, 2005) and may lead to the formation of stronger, positive attitudes toward the placed brands (Roehm & Haugtvedt, 1999). All of these may contribute to the increased impact exerted by product placement within this media context.

The role of interactivity in product placement effectiveness was explored by Hang and Auty (2011). They found that when children were able to interact with product placements in a game, the enhanced elaboration at the time of exposure appeared to strengthen their implicit processing of product placement, an effect that they attributed to conceptual fluency. Whereas perceptual fluency is modality sensitive and may disappear when the modality of the stimulus between exposure and test has been changed (Jacoby & Dallas, 1981), conceptual fluency goes beyond the physical features of the stimulus, and may still be evident when the modality changes between exposure and test (Lee, 2002; Lee & Labroo, 2004). In Hang and Auty (2011), exposure to the Nike logo in the video game made children more likely to write Nike in a shopping list test than children who were not exposed, suggesting that children were able to implicitly process conceptual information and not just the physical features of the brand.

Repetition/Frequency of Play

Owen (2008) explored frequency of game play as a factor in the effectiveness of product placement within games. One hundred 6–10-year-old children played one of two video games, matched for pace and interest, either containing a brand (Cool Spot, which is sponsored by and heavily features the 7 Up brand) or containing no brands (Sonic the Hedgehog). Following game play, the children were told that they could choose a drink from a selection of 7 Up and Sprite cans while they were asked some questions. Owen assessed each child's frequency of game play and utilized a brand logo recognition task to establish whether the children were able to recognize explicitly any brand names from the video game they had just played.

Owen noted that children who played video games more frequently were more likely to select the 7 Up brand when offered a drink, suggesting that video game playing experience may play a role in the implicit processing of product placements. More experienced players may be required to focus lesser amounts of attentional resources on control of the game and are therefore able to absorb (albeit preconsciously) more peripheral features, including the 7 Up logo. Indeed, a series of studies by Green and Bavelier (2003) suggest that frequent video game play enhances both visual attentional capacity and also the allocation of spatial attention over the visual field. In line with these findings, the frequent video game players in Owen's study may have found gameplay easy, thus freeing up spare resources that enable processing of extraneous stimuli, including the 7 Up product placement. Green and Bavelier propose that this increased information processing ability is likely to result from speeded perceptual processes and better management of several tasks at the central executive level among experienced video game players.

A factor that has not yet been explored in this interactive context is mood. Perhaps the frustrations of playing an advergame might inhibit the nonconscious interaction between implicit and explicit memory found by Sheldon and Moscovitch (2010). Thus, another question of interest is the effect of mood during exposure to product placement, both in a resource-intensive activity such as video games and more generally in other media.

Mood

In nonlaboratory viewing conditions, children are necessarily exposed to product placement within some sort of mood context. For example, some placements may appear in a happy movie or during a particularly positive, uplifting scene while others may appear in a sad movie or during a scene with negative connotations. Research has advocated repeatedly that mood may reliably influence consumers' processing of advertising, specifically, by rendering viewers more likely to evaluate advertising in a mood-congruent way (e.g. Aylesworth & MacKenzie, 1998; Goldberg & Gorn, 1987; Mathur & Chattopadhyay, 1991).

Focusing on traditional TV advertising that is separate from programs, previous studies have noted that consumers in a positive mood are more likely to process advertising in detail than those in a negative mood (Aylesworth & MacKenzie, 1998; Mathur & Chattopadhyay, 1991). The explanation for this effect is that in order to alter their problematic situations, people in a negative mood are motivated to process the source of their problems—the TV programs—centrally, and thus fewer cognitive resources remain available to process the advertising messages appearing during breaks in the program. In contrast, in order to maintain their current favorable state, people in a positive mood tend to avoid cognitive effort. As they are thus devoting fewer cognitive resources to processing the TV programs, more resources remain available to process the advertising messages (Aylesworth & MacKenzie, 1998). However, as discussed earlier, product placement differs from traditional television advertising in several ways, especially by being embedded within the entertainment. In a research project designed to test the influence of mood in an interactive entertainment, Hang and Auty (2010) found that mood states affect children's choices following exposure to product placement in a mood-congruent way. That is, children in a positive mood were more likely to choose a brand to which they had been exposed at test than those in a negative mood. However, this held true only for product placements that were linked to a specific negative or positive mood stimulus (e.g., playing for either the best or worst team with the Nike brand logo displayed in both cases on the team's T-shirt). When a placement was linked to a mood-neutral stimulus (e.g., the Adidas logo prominently displayed on the boundary wall), children's brand choices did not differ. Hang and Auty hypothesize that moods may not influence children's judgments in a general way. Rather, they may influence children's choice judgments only when the mood is linked specifically to the placed brand. Further research is needed to find out if mood-related motives for playing the game in the first place (e.g., being scolded by a parent or celebrating a good mark) will also affect choice of a placed brand.

Turning now to mood influences on product placement in general, Owen, Lewis, & Auty (2011) explored the impact of the mood context of product placement in movies on children. In their study, 128 10-year-old children were exposed to a movie clip containing a Nike product placement presented in either a positive context (in which the main character puts his Nike trainers on and wins an important basketball game to rapturous applause from the audience), a negative context (in which the main character is bullied and his Nike trainers are stolen and thrown onto a telephone cable), or to a control movie clip that was matched for pace and appeal yet contained no brand placements. Utilizing the FLIRT methodology, Owen et al. noted that ease of recognition of Nike was significantly enhanced among children who had viewed the positive movie clip but was not enhanced among children who had viewed the negative movie clip. Indeed, recognition levels among the latter group were comparable to the controls. This suggests that a positive mood context within the entertainment enhances children's implicit processing of product placement. Again, supporting the dissociated relationship between implicit and explicit memory noted in several product placement studies (e.g., Auty & Lewis, 2004a, 2004b), Owen et al. noted that explicit memory for the placed brand was poor and did not account for success on the implicit task.

One explanation for this kind of mood-congruency effect is that a positive context may activate positive links in the semantic network, leading to enhanced processing fluency and, thus, positive affect (Lee & Labroo, 2004). In a typical viewing situation, the context of exposure to product placement (i.e., playing video games and watching films) is likely to be a positive one, particularly for children. As such, cognitive effort is likely to be avoided and conscious, systematic processing thus appears unlikely. As a consequence, implicit, affective processing of product placements will, on the whole, be greater than explicit, detailed processing.

The aforementioned series of studies regarding contextual influences on the impact of product placement support the premise that product placement exerts a powerful implicit influence on children's identification of, preferences for, and consumer behavior toward brands, typically without children's explicit awareness that they have been exposed to advertising. The research suggests that these implicit effects appear to be primed by conceptual links. Explicit memories of brand concepts are likely to interact automatically and nonconsciously with a priming stimulus to affect implicit memory tasks (Sheldon & Moscovitch, 2010) and by implication, choice tasks and preference. Crucially, if a product placement is for a personally salient brand, if it is presented in a positive way, and in an interactive, familiar, or relevant medium, then children are more likely to respond implicitly and favorably to it.

CAN WE TEACH CHILDREN TO UNDERSTAND THE PRACTICE OF PRODUCT PLACEMENT?

How can we best protect children from the implicit influence of product placement? One view is that forewarning children that product placements are contained within the specific portion of entertainment (e.g., a TV program or video game) may "inoculate" them against the stealthy effects of this form of advertising. Wei, Fischer, and Main (2008) provide evidence that if adult consumers are notified prior to exposure, then their persuasion knowledge becomes activated, which may thus lead to more skeptical placement evaluations. However, unlike adults, young children are likely to lack the relevant persuasion knowledge (Wright et al., 2005), particularly regarding nontraditional forms of advertising (Owen, Lewis, Auty, & Buijzen, 2011). Thus, even when provided with a warning or alert, it is likely that children still lack the necessary cognitive abilities to evaluate and deal with product placement. Nairn and Fine (2008) propose that implicit media literacy is necessary to cope with nontraditional advertising on account of the implicit processing component involved. Thus, instead of being taught only about how advertising tries to get them to buy certain goods, children should also be shown how product placement, celebrity endorsement, and cartoon character merchandising serve the same purpose as advertising.

There have been some steps recently to increase children's understanding of these kinds of alternative advertising techniques. In the United Kingdom, for example, a website entitled "Chew on This" (www.chewonthis.org.uk) run by the Food Commission includes informative sections for children on the use of celebrity endorsements, product placements, and advertising online. The Media Smart Program, developed and funded by the advertising industry in conjunction with OFCOM, now also includes a section on children's media literacy. However, it is important to acknowledge that a sophisticated understanding of advertising and the associated consumer defenses may still fail to safeguard children from the impact of commercial messages that operate on a largely preconscious level (Chernin, 2008; Livingstone & Helsper, 2006; Mallinckrodt & Mizerski, 2007; Moses & Baldwin, 2005; Rozendaal, Buijzen, & Valkenburg, 2009).

Two lessons can be drawn from the research on product placement for researchers and policymakers who attempt to use implicit effects to convey healthy messages or to protect children from exposure to placements of which they are unaware. First, the very repetition of a name or logo can establish some brand familiarity. Second, and more importantly, the effects of prior brand knowledge underline the importance of conceptual implicit memory to the effectiveness of product placement. If a placed category is not relevant, there is simply no effect, either in terms of implicit recognition or choice, or in terms of explicit recall. Children have fewer relevant categories, but are highly attuned to specific categories of brand and differences within relevant categories.

Future Research

We suggest that a full range of possible ways to educate children about product placement has not yet been identified and tested. In the United Kingdom, programs that now include product placement are required to display a prominent "P" logo for three seconds at the beginning and end of programs, and after ad breaks (see, e.g., http://media.ofcom.org.uk/2011/02/14/product-placement-logo-to-be-shown-on-tv-screens/). It is much too early to evaluate this legislation, but longitudinal studies could provide some crucial answers to cross-national researchers and policymakers who are considering the same issue.

As noted earlier, more work is needed on mood contexts, specifically how a child's processing of product placement is affected by negative external mood influences, for example, parental problems, which might override the normally positive mood induced by entertainment. Such investigations, however, are difficult to design because researchers do not wish to subject children to upsetting external conditions that may not easily be overcome.

Another area that awaits future research is gender differences in the processing of product placements in video games, films, television programs, and music videos. The study by Owen (2008) suggests that there are gender differences in the impact exerted by a brand in a video game. The higher involvement among males engaged with this type of medium may explain these differences, but research is needed to clarify the role of gender as well as the proposition that the relevance of the particular advertising medium to a child also affects how product placement is received.

The possibility of cross-cultural differences follows from research that has found that auditory and visual advertising elements may interact with Chinese and English words differently, because reading alphabetic words relies more on sound-based processes while reading logographs relies more on visual processes (Tavassoli & Lee, 2003). Thus far, in the research we have reported on earlier—where Chinese children comprised the participant pool in some of the experiments—there is little evidence of any divergent effects. However, the underlying mechanisms of information processing might usefully be explored in cross-cultural research projects.

CONCLUSION

A common finding of research to date is that exposure to product placement can have a clear impact on children's brand preference and choice. These studies further suggest that owing to the unobtrusive nature of product placement, its impact is mainly driven by subtle, implicit rather than explicit, processes, leading to very limited brand recall. However, low recall does not mean no influence, as prior incidental exposure to advertising (Baker, 1999) and product placement in particular (Law & Braun, 2000; Yang et al., 2006) are sufficient to influence consumers' judgments and decision making without any cognitive processing. Prior exposure may automatically activate the stimuli's representations in memory, enhancing the ease of processing (or processing fluency) on subsequent encounters. Since brands are symbolic representations, the ease of processing product placement is likely to reflect conceptual fluency; that is, the ease of processing the meaning of the brand. As the experience of fluency is positively valenced (Reber, Winkielman, & Schwarz, 1998), children may misattribute the positive evaluative response elicited by the conceptual fluency as brand preference and choose accordingly (e.g., Lee & Labroo, 2004; Shapiro, 1999). Brand salience, interactivity of media, repetition and frequency (especially relevant to video games), and mood appear to affect how product placements are processed and thus how effective they are in changing children's attitudes and, more importantly, their behavior.

REFERENCES

Alba, J. W., & Chattopadhyay, A. (1986). Salience effects in brand recall. *Journal of Marketing Research, 23*, 363–369.

Auty, S., & Lewis, C. (2004a). Exploring children's choice: The reminder effect of product placement. *Psychology & Marketing, 21,* 697–713.

Auty, S., & Lewis, C. (2004b). The "delicious paradox": Preconscious processing of product placements by children. In, L. J. Shrum (Ed.), *The psychology of entertainment media: Blurring the lines between entertainment and persuasion* (pp. 117–133). Mahwah, NJ: Lawrence Erlbaum Associates.

Aylesworth, A. B., & MacKenzie, S. B. (1998). Context is key: The effect of program-induced mood on thoughts about the ad. *Journal of Advertising, 27*(2), 17–31.

Babin, L., & Carder, S. (1996). Viewers' recognition of brands placed within a film. *International Journal of Advertising, 15*(2), 140–151.

Baker, W. E. (1999). When can affective conditioning and mere exposure directly influence brand choice? *Journal of Advertising, 28*(4), 31–46.

Balasubramanian, S. K. (1991). *Beyond advertising and publicity: The domain of the hybrid messages.* Cambridge, MA: Marketing Science Institute.

Balasubramanian, S. K. (1994). Beyond advertising and publicity: Hybrid messages and public policy issues. *Journal of Advertising, 23*(4), 29–46.

Balasubramanian, S. K., Karrh, J. A., & Patwardhan, H. (2006). Audience response to product placements. *Journal of Advertising, 35*(3), 115–141.

Bornstein, R., & D'Agostino, P. (1992). Stimulus recognition and the mere exposure effect. *Journal of Personality & Social Psychology, 63*(4), 545–552.

Bornstein, R., & D'Agostino, P. (1994). The attribution and discounting of perceptual fluency: Preliminary tests of a perceptual fluency/attributional model of the mere exposure effect. *Social Cognition, 12,* 103–128.

Braun-LaTour, K.A., & Zaltman, G. (2006). Memory change: An intimate measure of persuasion. *Journal of Advertising Research, 46*(1), 57–72.

Brennan, I., Dubas, K., & Babin, L. (1999). The influence of product placement type and exposure time on product placement recognition. *International Journal of Advertising, 18,* 323–336.

Bressoud, E., Lehu, J., & Russell, C. R. (2010). The product well placed: The relative impact of placement and audience characteristics on placement recall. *Journal of Advertising Research, 50*(4), 374–385.

Butler, L., & Berry, D. (2001). Implicit memory: Intention and awareness revisited. *Trends in Cognitive Sciences, 5*(5), 192–197.

Cabeza, R., & Ohta, N. (1993). Dissociating conceptual priming, perceptual priming and explicit memory. *European Journal of Cognitive Psychology, 5*(1), 35–53.

Calvert, S. (2008). Children as consumers: Advertising and marketing. *The Future of Children, 18,* 205–234.

Chernin, A. (2008). The effects of food marketing on children's preferences: Testing the moderating roles of age and gender. *The Annals of the American Academy of Political & Social Science, 615,* 101–118.

Consumer Focus. (2010). *Consumer Focus response to DCMS consultation on product placement on UK television.* http://www.consumerfocus.org.uk/assets/1/files/2009/06/Consumer-Focus-response-to-Product-placement-consultation.pdf (accessed on 15 January 2011).

Curran, T., & Hintzman, D. T. (1995). Violations of the independence assumption in process dissociation. *Journal of Experimental Psychology: Learning, Memory, & Cognition, 21*(3), 531–547.

Darke, P.R., & Ritchie, R.B. (2007). The defensive consumer: Advertising deception, defensive processing, and distrust. *Journal of Marketing Research, 44*(Feb), 114–127.

d'Astous, A., & Seguin, N. (1999). Consumer reactions to product placement strategies in television sponsorship. *European Journal of Marketing, 33*(9/10), 896–910.

Debner, J., & Jacoby, L. (1994). Unconscious perception: Attention, awareness and control. *Journal of Experimental Psychology: Learning, Memory, & Cognition, 20,* 304–317.

Dimofte, C.V. (2010). Implicit measures of consumer cognition: A review. *Psychology & Marketing, 27*(10), 921–937.

Federal Trade Commission (FTC). (2008). *Marketing food to children and adolescents: A review of industry expenditures, activities, and self-regulation.* http://www.ftc.gov/os/2008/07/P064504foodmktingreportappendices.pdf (accessed on 27 August 2010).

Friestad, M., & Wright, P. (1994). The persuasion knowledge model: How people cope with persuasion attempts. *Journal of Consumer Research, 21*(June), 1–31.

Gentile, D. A. (2009). Pathological video game use among youth 8 to 18: A national study. *Psychological Science, 20*(5), 594–602.

Goldberg, M. E., & Gorn, G. J. (1987). Happy and sad TV programs: How they affect reactions to commercials. *Journal of Consumer Research, 14*(3), 387–402.

Green, C., & Bavelier, D. (2003). Action video game modifies visual selective attention. *Nature, 423,* 534–537.

Greenwald, A. G., McGhee, D. E., & Schwartz, J. L. K. (1998). Measuring individual differences in implicit cognition: The implicit association test. *Journal of Personality & Social Psychology, 74*(6), 1464–1480.

Grodal, T. (2000). Video games and the pleasure of control. In D. Zillmann & P. Vorderer (Eds.), *Media entertainment: The psychology of its appeal* (pp. 197–214). Mahwah, NJ: Lawrence Erlbaum Associates.

Gunter, B., Oates, C., & Blades, M. (2005*). Advertising to children on TV: Content, impact and regulation*. Mahwah, NJ: Lawrence Erlbaum Associates.

Gupta, P., & Lord, K. (1998). Product placement in movies: The effect of prominence and mode on audience recall. *Journal of Current Issues & Research in Advertising, 20*(1), 47–60.

Hackley, C., Tiwsakul, R. A., & Preuss, L. (2008). An ethical evaluation of product placement: A deceptive practice? *Business Ethics: A European Review, 17*(2), 109–120.

Hamann, S.B. (1990). Level-of-processing effects in conceptually driven implicit tasks. *Journal of Experimental Psychology: Learning, Memory, & Cognition, 16*(6), 970–977.

Hang, H., & Auty, S. (2010). Children's moods and brand placement effectiveness: The disassociation between brand recall and brand choice. Paper under review.

Hang, H., & Auty, S. (2011). Children playing branded video games: The impact of interactivity on product placement effectiveness. *Journal of Consumer Psychology, 21*(1), 65–72.

Hite, C. F., & Hite, R. E. (1995). Reliance on brand by young children. *Journal of the Market Research Society, 37,* 185–193.

Holliday, R. E., & Hayes, B. K. (2001). Automatic and intentional processes in children's eyewitness suggestibility. *Cognitive Development, 16*(1), 617–636.

Horcajo, J., Briñol, P., & Petty, R. E. (2010). Consumer persuasion: Indirect change and implicit balance. *Psychology & Marketing, 27,* 938–963.

Hourihan, K. L., & MacLeod, C. M. (2007). Capturing conceptual implicit memory: The time it takes to produce an association. *Memory & Cognition, 35,* 1187–1196.

Hudson, S., Hudson, D., & Peloza, J. (2008). Meet the parents: A parents' perspective on product placement in children's films. *Journal of Business Ethics, 80,* 289–304.

Jacoby, L. L., & Dallas, M. (1981). On the relationship between autobiographical memory and perceptual learning. *Journal of Experimental Psychology: General, 110*(3), 306–340.

Jacoby, L.L., Kelley, C. M., & Dywan, J. (1989). Memory attributions. In H. Roediger & F. Craik (Eds.), *Varieties of memory and consciousness: Essays in honour of Endel Tulving* (pp. 391–422). Hillsdale, NJ: Lawrence Erlbaum Associates.

Janiszewski, C. (1993). Preattentive mere exposure effects. *Journal of Consumer Research, 20*(3), 376–393.

Krishnan, H., & Chakravarti, D. (1999). Memory measures for pretesting advertisements: An integrative conceptual framework and a diagnostic template. *Journal of Consumer Psychology, 8*(1), 1–37.

Kuhn, K., Hume, M., & Love, A. (2010). Examining the covert nature of product placement: Implications for public policy. *Journal of Promotion Management, 16*(1), 59–79.

Kunkel, D., Wilcox, B. L., Cantor, J., Palmer, E., Linn, S., & Dowrick, P. (2004). *Report of the APA task force on advertising and children.* http://www.apa.org/releases/childrenads.pdf (accessed on 14 January 2009).

La Ferle, C., & Edwards, S. M. (2006). Product placement: How brands appear on television. *Journal of Advertising, 35*(4), 65–86.

Law, S., & Braun, K. (2000). I'll have what she's having: Gauging the impact of product placements on viewers. *Psychology & Marketing, 17*(12), 1059–1075.

Law, S., & Braun, K. (2004). Product placements: How to measure their impact. In L. J. Shrum (Ed.), *The psychology of entertainment media: Blurring the lines between entertainment and persuasion* (pp. 63–78). Mahwah, NJ: Lawrence Erlbaum Associates.

Lee, A. Y. (2002). Effects of implicit memory on memory-based versus stimulus-based brand choice. *Journal of Marketing Research, 39*(November), 440–454.

Lee, A. Y., & Labroo, A. A. (2004). The effect of conceptual and perceptual fluency on brand evaluation. *Journal of Marketing Research, 41*(May), 151–165.

Lindstrom, M., & Seybold, P. B. (2003). *Brand child.* London: Kogan Page.

Liu, Y., & Shrum, L. J. (2002). What is interactivity and is it always such a good thing? Implications of definition, person, and situation for the influence of interactivity on advertising effectiveness. *Journal of Advertising, 31*(4), 53–64.

Liu, Y., & Shrum, L. J. (2009). A dual-process model of interactivity effects. *Journal of Advertising, 38*(2), 53–68.

Livingstone, S., & Helsper, E. (2006). Does advertising literacy mediate the effects of advertising on children? A critical examination of two linked research literatures in relation to obesity and food choice. *Journal of Communication, 56*(3), 560–584.

Mallinckrodt, V., & Mizerski, D. (2007). The effects of playing an advergame on young children's perceptions, preferences and requests. *Journal of Advertising, 36*(2), 87–100.

Malthouse, E., Calder, B., & Tamhane, A. (2007). The effects of media context experiences on advertising effectiveness. *Journal of Advertising, 36*(3), 7–18.

Mantonakis, A., Whittlesea, B. W. A, & Yoon, C. (2008). Consumer memory, fluency, and familiarity. In C. P. Haugtvedt, P.M. Herr, & F. R. Kardes (Eds.), *Handbook of consumer psychology* (pp. 77–102). Mahwah, NJ: Lawrence Erlbaum Associates.

Marr, K. (2008). Children targets of $1.6 billion in food ads. *Wall Street Journal*, 30 July, p. D01.

Mathur, M., & Chattopadhyay, A. (1991). The impact of moods generated by television programs on responses to advertising. *Psychology & Marketing, 8*(1), 59–77.

McCarty, J. (2004). Product placement: The nature of the practice and potential avenues of inquiry. In, L. J. Shrum (Ed.), *The psychology of entertainment media: Blurring the lines between entertainment and persuasion* (pp. 45–62). Mahwah, NJ: Lawrence Erlbaum Associates.

McNeal, J. (1999). *The kids market: Myths and realities.* Ithaca, NY: Paramount Market Publishing.

Miller, S., & Berry, L. (1998). Brand salience versus brand image: Two theories of advertising effectiveness. *Journal of Advertising Research. 38*(5), 77–83.

Moore, E. (2004). Children and the changing world of advertising. *Journal of Business Ethics, 52*(2), 161–167.

Moore, E. & Rideout, V. (2007). The online marketing of food to children: Is it just fun and games? *Journal of Public Policy & Marketing, 26*(2), 202–220.

Moses, L. & Baldwin, D. (2005). What can the study of cognitive development reveal about children's ability to appreciate and cope with advertising? *Journal of Public Policy & Marketing, 24*(2), 186–201.

Murphy, K., McKone, E., & Slee, J. (2003). Dissociations between implicit and explicit memory in children: The role of strategic processing and the knowledge base. *Journal of Experimental Child Psychology, 84*, 124–165.

Nairn, A. (2009). *Business thinks family*. http://www.agnesnairn.co.uk/policy_reports/business_thinks_family_final_report_january_2009.pdf (accessed on 20 January 2011).

Nairn, A., & Fine, C. (2008). Who's messing with my mind? The implications of dual-process models for the ethics of advertising to children. *International Journal of Advertising, 27*(3), 447–470.

Naito, M. (1990). Repetition priming in children and adults: Age-related dissociation between implicit and explicit memory. *Journal of Experimental Child Psychology, 50*(3), 462–484.

Nebenzahl, I., & Jaffe, E. (1998). Ethical dimensions of advertising executions. *Journal of Business Ethics, 17,* 805–815.

Nelson, M. R. (2002). Recall of brand placements in computer/video games. *Journal of Advertising Research, 42*(2), 80–92.

Nelson, M., Yaros, R., & Keum, H. (2006). Examining the influence of telepresence on spectator and player processing of real and fictitious brands in a computer game. *Journal of Advertising, 35*(4), 87–99.

Office of Communications (OFCOM). (2006). *Product placement: Summary of responses to consultation on issues relating to product placement*. http://stakeholders.ofcom.org.uk/binaries/consultations/product_placement/statement/statement.pdf (accessed 20 January 2011).

Office of Communications (OFCOM). (2010). *Rules for product placement on TV and paid-for references to brands and products on radio*. http://media.ofcom.org.uk/2010/12/20/rules-for-product-placement/ (accessed 24 January 2011).

Owen, L. H. (2008). *The role of conceptual fluency in children's processing of incidental forms of advertising*. PhD thesis, Lancaster, UK: Lancaster University.

Owen, L. H., Lewis, C., & Auty, S. (2011). *Children's implicit processing of brand placements in movies: General developmental changes versus personal salience, prominence and modality*. Paper under review.

Owen, L. H., Lewis, C., Auty, S., & Buijzen, M. (2011). *Is children's understanding of non–traditional advertising comparable to their understanding of television advertising?* Paper under review.

Perkins, A., Forehand, M., Greenwald, A., & Maison, D. (2008). Measuring the nonconscious: Implicit social cognition in consumer behavior. In C. P. Haugtvedt, P.M. Herr, & F. R. Kardes (Eds.), *Handbook of consumer psychology* (pp. 461–475). Mahwah, NJ: Lawrence Erlbaum Associates.

Petty, R., & Andrews, C. (2008). Covert marketing unmasked: A legal and regulatory guide for practices that mask marketing messages. *Journal of Public Policy & Marketing, 27*(1), 7–18.

Pine, K. J., & Nash, A. S. (2003). Barbie or Betty? Pre-school children's preference for branded products and evidence for gender-linked differences. *Journal of Developmental & Behavioral Pediatrics, 24*(4), 219–224.

Reber, R., Winkielman, P., & Schwarz, N. (1998). Effects of perceptual fluency on affective judgments. *Psychological Science, 9*(1), 45–48.

Robin, D. P., & Reidenbach, E. R. (1987). Social responsibility, ethics, and marketing strategy: Closing the gap between concept and application. *Journal of Marketing, 51*(January), 44–58.

Robinson, T., Borzekowski, D., Matheson, D., & Kraemer, H. (2007). Effects of fast food branding on young children's taste preferences. *Archives of Pediatrics & Adolescent Medicine, 161*(8), 792–797.

Roediger, H.L. (1990). Implicit memory: Retention without remembering. *American Psychologist, 45,* 1043–1056.

Roehm, H.A., & Haugtvedt, C.P. (1999). Understanding of interactivity of cyberspace advertising. In D. W. Schumann & E. Thorson (Eds.), *Advertising and the World Wide Web* (pp. 27–40). Mahwah, NJ: Lawrence Erlbaum Associates.

Roskos-Ewoldsen, D. R., & Fazio, R. H. (1992). On the orienting value of attitudes: Attitude accessibility as a determinant of an object's attraction of visual attention. *Journal of Personality & Social Psychology, 63,* 198–211.

Rozendaal, E., Buijzen, M., & Valkenburg, P. M. (2009). Do children's cognitive advertising defenses reduce their desire for advertised products? *Communications, 34,* 287–303.

Schneider, L., & Cornwell, T. (2005). Cashing in on crashes via brand placement in computer games. *International Journal of Advertising, 24*(3), 321–343.

Shapiro, S. (1999). When an ad's influence is beyond our conscious control: Perceptual and conceptual fluency effects caused by incidental ad exposure. *Journal of Consumer Research, 26*(June), 16–36.

Shapiro, S., & Krishnan, S. (2001). Memory-based measures for assessing advertising effects: A comparison of explicit and implicit memory effects. *Journal of Advertising, 30*(Fall), 1–14.

Sheldon, S. A. M., & Moscovitch, M. (2010). Recollective performance advantages for implicit memory tasks. *Memory, 18*(7), 681–697.

Shrum, L. J., Lowrey, T. M., & Liu, Y. (2009). Emerging issues in advertising research. In M. B. Oliver & R. Nabi (Eds.), *The SAGE handbook of media processes and effects* (pp. 299–312). Thousand Oaks, CA: Sage.

Snodgrass, J. G., Smith, B., Keenan, K., & Corwin, J. (1987). Fragmenting pictures on the Apple MacIntosh computer for experimental and clinical applications. *Behavior Research Methods, Instruments and Computers, 19,* 270–274.

Tavassoli, N. T., & Lee, Y. H. (2003). The differential interaction of auditory and visual advertising elements with Chinese and English. *Journal of Marketing Research, 40*(4), 468–480.

Tulving, E., & Schacter, D. L. (1990). Priming and human memory systems. *Science, 247*(January), 301–306.

van Reijmersdal, E. A., Neijens, P. C., & Smit, E. G. (2007). Effects of television brand placement on brand image. *Psychology & Marketing, 24*(5), 403–420.

van Reijmersdal, E. A., Neijens, P. C., & Smit, E. G. (2009). A new branch of advertising: Reviewing factors that influence reactions to product placement. *Journal of Advertising Research, 49*(4), 429–449.

Vorderer, P. (2000). Interactive entertainment and beyond. In D. Zillmann & P. Vorderer (Eds.), *Media entertainment: The psychology of its appeal* (pp. 21–36). Mahwah, NJ: Lawrence Erlbaum Associates.

Walshe P., & Brown, M. (2000). Getting to know you: Children and their brand relationships. *Admap, January,* 21–23.

Wei, M., Fischer, E., & Main, K. J. (2008). An examination of the effects of activating persuasion knowledge on consumer response to brands engaging in covert marketing. *Journal of Public Policy & Marketing, 27*(1), 34–44.

Winkielman, P., Schwarz, N., Fazendeiro, T. A., & Reber, R. (2003). The hedonic marking of processing fluency: Implications for evaluative judgment. In J. Musch & K. C. Klauer (Eds.), *The psychology of evaluation: Affective processes in cognition and emotion* (pp. 189–217). Mahwah, NJ: Lawrence Erlbaum Associates.

Wright, P., Friestad, M., & Boush, D. M. (2005). The development of marketplace persuasion knowledge in children, adolescents, and young adults. *Journal of Public Policy and Marketing, 24*(2), 222–233.

Yang, M., Roskos-Ewoldsen, D. R., Dinu, L., & Arpan, L. M. (2006). The effectiveness of "in-game" advertising: Comparing college students' explicit and implicit memory for brand names. *Journal of Advertising, 35*(4), 143–152.

Zajonc, R. (1968). Attitudinal effects of mere exposure. *Journal of Personality & Social Psychology Monographs, 9*(2), 1–27.

Zajonc, R. (1980). Feeling and thinking: Preferences need no inferences. *American Psychologist, 35*, 151–175.

5

Psychological Processing of In-Game Advertising and Advergaming: Branded Entertainment or Entertaining Persuasion?

Michelle R. Nelson
University of Illinois at Urbana–Champaign
Urbana and Champaign, Illinois

Martin K. J. Waiguny
Alpen-Adria University of Klagenfurt
Klagenfurt, Austria

Cool Spot. Kool-Aid Man. Candystand.com. FarmVille. Angry Birds. 2010 FIFA. Although the content, form, and platform of digital games have changed since the earliest commercial games of *Galaxy Game* and *Pong* in the 1970s, the motivations to play have not. Games are played for entertainment and fun. Games provide "a distraction, a challenge, compelling characters, and storytelling experiences" that often allow players to try out or do things they cannot in the real world as they explore new and interesting virtual spaces (Gartenberg & Horwitz, 2004). In this respect, games are like other entertainment media discussed in this book, offering the gratifications of escape and diversion to the audience (Severin & Tankard, 1997). What is different from other media is the audience's active control (interactivity) of the entertainment process and outcomes, and the resultant variability in experience every time the game is played. In this way, the content of the game (including branded content) can also be experienced and processed differently for every engagement.

Although brands have been included in digital games since the 1970s (Vedrashko, 2006), they are now placed as a persuasion tactic. From background billboards in racing games to branded avatars and virtual cheeseburgers on social network games, brands are playing a more central role in the game. The effectiveness and effects of those brands and the ways in which those brands are psychologically processed is the focus of our chapter. We first discuss the definitions and forms of branded content in games; we then outline the possible distinctions and ramifications for psychological processing and effects, focusing on research that relates to memory-based effects and persuasion. In addition, we present some important mediating and moderating variables such as game–brand congruence, brand familiarity, and game player experience. Finally, given what we know about possible psychological effects, we discuss ethical issues associated with these techniques.

DEFINITIONS, INTEGRATION OF BRANDS IN GAMES

Although there are numerous definitions of games, we adhere to game theorist Jesper Juul's definition of a game as a rule-based system with a variable and quantifiable outcome, where different outcomes are assigned different values, the player exerts effort in order to influence the outcome, the player feels emotionally attached to the outcome, and the consequences of the activity are optional and negotiable (Juul, 2003). This definition highlights the variable nature of the entertainment, as well as the effort by the player and emotional engagement. In this chapter, we focus on digital games, which include arcade, video game console, PC, mobile, social networking, etc. Because we are examining multiple forms of brand content, it is important to note that branded entertainment consists of "… ideas that bring entertainment value to brands, and ideas that integrate brands into entertainment" (Aitchison, 2004 cf.; Hudson & Hudson, 2006).

Branded content appears in digital games in various ways. Although the terms *advergame* and *advergaming* are frequently used in academic and practitioner publications, there is no consensus on what exactly these terms mean (Svahn, 2005). Some authors used the term *advergame* in a broad sense for all forms of advertising or product and brand placement in video and computer games and even in virtual worlds such as *Second*

Life (e.g., Winkler & Buckner, 2006). However, it is important to differentiate between various forms of advertising and product placement in games (Nelson, 2002; Svahn, 2005) as different types of brand and product placement in games are possible and the psychological processes may not be uniform. The two most common methods of brand appearances are advergames and in-game advertising (or product placement in games).

Advergames

Advergames are games specially designed to promote one company's brand or products; in this way, they most closely resemble a traditional advertisement. They can be found on almost every game platform and device and can vary from "reskinned games" that simply insert a brand's artwork into an existing game (e.g., *Fandango's Popcorn Blaster*) to custom games created for the brand (e.g., *National Geographic's* fishing game, *Hooked*) to an entire Web game arena on the brand's web site (e.g., *Seventeen* magazine's "fun games"). In all cases, advergames seek to combine two key elements: the brand and entertainment (Kretchmer, 2004). The focus on a sole brand and the primary goal of persuasion are distinct from other forms of branded content in games. Therefore, advergames may be described as ideas that bring entertainment value to brands.

Although the term *advergame* is fairly new (Brent, 2000), the practice is not. The earliest forms of advergames, in the 1980s, were sent directly to consumers. These include *Tooth Protector*, a game where the player must protect teeth from cubes being thrown by the Snack Attackers, using Johnson & Johnson's products (toothbrush, floss, dental rinse), *Chase the Chuck Wagon* (showing a wagon rolling away from Ralston Purina dog food), and *Kool-Aid Man* (Vedrashko, 2006). These early brand-entertainment games were often tied to the brand's television commercials and were regarded as an ancillary promotional technique. Advergames later developed from small casual games into full-length games for PCs and consoles, such as Volvo's *Drive for Life* and *Mercedes-Benz World Racing*. In 2006, Burger King and Microsoft created *Sneak King,* which was available for the Xbox 360 at Burger King restaurants for only $3.99. The game featured the brand's mascot King, whose job is to deliver food to hungry people before they see the King and lose their appetite. Other full-length advergames include Doritos' *Dash of Destruction, Harm's Way,* and *Crash Course* (all available for free from the Xbox website) and a game targeted to tween girls called *Busy Scissors* (by Redken for the Nintendo Wii console, 2010). Despite the focus on the brand and the control over creative content and game play, advertisers generally do not create console advergames due to the expense in producing them and long lead times for development (Treffiletti, 2011).

Instead, most advergames today are easy to learn and simple to play. They offer quick rewards with forgiving gameplay, which makes a fun experience (Kuittinen, Kultima, Niemelä, & Paavilainen, 2007). They are usually downloadable for free (or a small fee) from the company's website (Buckner, Fang, & Qiao, 2002; Moore, 2006) as a way to promote the brand and achieve higher traffic and greater engagement on brand websites (Santos, Gonzalo, & Gisbert, 2007). One of the earliest examples of this kind of advergame was created in the mid-1990s as two game developers explored ad-supported Internet games as a viable business model (Radd, 2007); they created a game for LifeSavers candy, which eventually became a portal of similar fun games called candystand.com, which was bought out by Kraft and then Wrigley.

Branded applications (apps) in the form of advergames on smartphones are predicted to be the next growth market; analysts suggest that mobile game ad spending may reach $894 million in 2015, up from an estimated $87 million in 2010 (Orland, 2011). For example, Barclay's bank launched *Waterslide Extreme,* a free iPhone application that surpassed the 10 millionth download mark, which was part of a larger integrated marketing communication campaign (Dredge, 2010). In sum, advergames are regarded as games that are created for the primary purpose of advertising a particular brand or product. Although they are also designed to be entertaining, they do not typically feature other brands.

In-Game Advertising

In-game advertising, or product placement in games, is the inclusion of a product or brand within an existing digital game that also features other brands and products. The primary purpose of the game is entertainment and not promotion of a singular brand within it. In this way, the game provides ideas that integrate brands into entertainment. In fact, the earliest forms of brand appearances in games were not intended as a persuasion device. Instead, the brands were included to help increase the game's realism and came about as a result of licensing deals. These early placements were found, for example, in racing games, such as Ferrari, Renault, and Lotus in *Formula One* (1983; Vedrashko, 2006), and in later versions of the game, the brands became paid placements.

There are several forms for these placements today. Brands can appear in the background on static billboards or as part of the scenery or they can appear more prominently as they are incorporated into gameplay as props, clothing, game tools, etc. In most cases, the brands act as they would in a movie, essentially as visual or verbal mentions that can vary in prominence and integration into the story (see Chapter 2 in this volume). Typically, the brands do not interrupt the game experience and are thought to work best when seamlessly incorporated into gameplay (Nelson, Keum, & Yaros, 2004). However, in games, players can also interact directly with the brands (Nelson, 2005) and can even customize the branded content (Kwak, Clavio, Eagleman, & Kim, 2010). In addition, games offer the opportunity for hidden branded content (not subliminal) but in the form of cheat codes or Easter eggs (essentially, tiny bits of computer code written into the game to be "found" and then entered into the game in order to unlock additional content). Cheat codes help players advance through a level or reach a particular goal; they can be discovered by exploring sections of the game or from game forums online or even through YouTube tutorials posted by other game players. Easter eggs, on the other hand, usually offer a creative diversion (e.g., a different small game within the game, a change of music, etc.) but are not related to advancing gameplay. These codes are usually in the form of text-based commands that the player types into the game. Although they are not common, some of these cheat codes and Easter eggs also feature branded content (Vedrashko, 2006). For example, the game *NASCAR 2005: Chase for the Cup* includes the following branded cheat codes: "oldspice," "race dodge," "walmart nascar," and "dodge stadium." When players typed those brands into the game commands, they were rewarded with Old Spice racing tracks, virtual money, and vanity plates. In this case, the branded codes may offer a novel and subversive way to gain brand recognition.

To circumvent advertising wear-out, to offer flexibility for brands and brand placement options, and to better mirror existing media planning models for other media, dynamic in-game advertising was launched in 2005. Dynamic advertising allows for brands to buy space in an existing console game for a certain period of time (just as they do for outdoor billboard ads or magazine ads). For example, advertising posters and billboards were sold in virtual life (*Sims 3*) for movies such as Indiana

Jones and Ironman much in the same way that they are sold in real life (Marketing-Vox, 2008).

Beyond game consoles, product placements are also found in online games, especially social network games such as *FarmVille* and *CarTown*. These virtual spaces allow an opportunity for brands to be integrated into gameplay for short or long periods of time. For example, the movie *MegaMind* was featured in a 24-hour campaign within *FarmVille* (Marshall, 2010), which featured a MegaMind Farm. Game players could visit the farm to unlock the blue alien's contraption and watch a movie promo in exchange for receiving some special crop enhancer/protector called MegaGrow and decorative features called MegaDecoration. Apparently, 9 million users interacted with the MegaMind content during the 24-hour campaign.

Thus, branded content can appear in more or less overt ways in digital games and can appear alone or with other brands. What is shared across these brand appearances is the focus on entertainment, in essence: branded entertainment. The relationship between brand and entertainment in the context of games and the resultant psychological processing for understanding advertising effectiveness is reviewed next.

PSYCHOLOGICAL PROCESSING OF BRANDED ENTERTAINMENT IN GAMES

To illustrate the media context of branded entertainment and games, the following scenario, from the first author's life, is provided:

Mom: John, please turn off the game, it's time to eat.

John: [intensely playing the game; silence, sounds of car tires screeching around corners]

Mom: [walking into the room where game is played] John, I said it's time to eat, didn't you hear me?

John is not aware of the world around him. He is fully immersed in the seat of his car in the Formula 1 game (2009) heading into the final lap. All sense of time and space and other externalities of the real world (including his mother's voice) are oblivious to him. When he "comes to" after his mom turned off the game, John is flushed from the excitement of the game and a little angry that the game had finished. He was having fun despite the difficulty of keeping the car on the track. He had almost beaten his highest score and can't wait to finish dinner and try again.

Mom: How did you do?

John: Not bad, I *almost* won.

Mom: Interesting. I wonder why DHL was in there.

John: Where?

Mom: On the billboard as you drove by.

John: What?

This is an example of the media context of games. Media context has been shown to influence individuals' cognitive and emotional states and can influence subsequent processing of embedded brand messages (Moorman, Neijens, & Smit, 2002). In this case, John was so engrossed in the game that he did not remember seeing the DHL brand. Games are described as "lean-forward media" in contrast with lean-back media such as radio or outdoor (Katz, 2010). As such, games are similar to other active (lean forward) experiences such as participating in sports matches, creating art, or creative writing, etc., and different from more passive (lean back) experiences such as watching sports or gambling (Nakatsu, Rauterberg, & Vorderer, 2005). This distinction relates to differences in immersion and cognitive processing between the game context and other entertainment media.

Game players such as John can become so physically, cognitively, and emotionally engaged in the game that they lose all sense of time and space and feel transported into the game, i.e., telepresence: a state of mind where a subject experiences being "there" in a virtual or fictional world (Minsky, 1980). As such, players may completely forget about the external context or externalities (such as background brands) in the game itself. In addition, while playing the game, the audience may be entertained and feel joy, but also may feel other emotions such as frustration, pride, or even boredom. How that media context and emotional state influence the psychological processing of the brands within the games and subsequent brand effectiveness is discussed in the following section. First, we describe the meaning of entertainment in games and how it is manifested and related to psychological processes. Based on this understanding, we then discuss the effectiveness of brands in games, which is usually gauged by memory (e.g., recall or recognition; Nelson, Yaros, & Keum, 2006) or by persuasion (e.g., attitude toward the ad/brand, brand choice or preference, sales). Table 5.1 provides a review of some of the relevant research articles on

TABLE 5.1

Summary Review of the Published Advergaming and In-Game Advertising Literature

Author(s), Year	In-Game Advertising (IGA) or Advergaming (Exposure to Game in the Study?), Research Design	Independent Variables	Dependent Variables	Game-Genre and Sample (Country)	Major Findings
Nelson, 2002, 2005	IGA (yes), survey	Brand placements in the game	Recall (unaided/aided) attitude toward IGA in games	*Gran Turismo*, online Racing game; adults 18–25, $n = 20$ (U.S.)	30% recall of integrated brands immediately after gameplay; only 10% after 5 months. The interaction with the car improves recognition. PPL is seen as adding realism to games.
Chaney et al., 2004	IGA (yes), experimental	Billboards in the game, level of game experience	Recall, buying intention	Multiplayer First Person Shooter Game, Adult Male Gamers, $n = 42$ (U.K.)	Users primarily remember the product categories (43% recalled the soda can, 38% the pizza, 29% the camera) over brand names (21%, 14%, 5%, respectively). No significant influence of experience on recall; no influence on buying intentions.

Griorivici & Constantin, 2004	IGA (yes), experimental	Arousal (Task Performance Time), placement (billboard versus on-set), product type.	Recall, recognition of object and brand, brand preference. Also measured cognitive load, presence.	Interactive virtual environment, university students, N = 141 (U.S.)	Objects on billboards recalled more than in product placements (no effect on recognition, preference). Arousal led to lower recall of objects, but higher brand preference for cell phone. Faster reaction times showed higher brand recall/recognition; slower reaction times related to brand preference for Nokia. Lower engagement led to increased brand recall and preference.
Nelson et al., 2004	IGA (yes), netnography, survey		Attitude toward product placement (APPL), attitude toward advertising (Aadv), buying intentions (perceived)	Study 1: Comments on Slashdot, Study 2: *Gran Turismo*, Racing Game, Adults 18–30, n = 62 (U.S.)	Persuasion knowledge is developed through discussion (Study 1); Aadv is positively directly and mediated (via APPL) related to buying intentions. (Study 2)

(Continued)

TABLE 5.1 (CONTINUED)

Summary Review of the Published Advergaming and In-Game Advertising Literature

Author(s), Year	In-Game Advertising (IGA) or Advergaming (Exposure to Game in the Study?), Research Design	Independent Variables	Dependent Variables	Game-Genre and Sample (Country)	Major Findings
Hernandez et al., 2004	Advergames (yes), survey	Entertainment, extended exposure, congruence, intrusiveness and irritation	Negative attitude toward the advergame	*Arctic 3D Racer, Mini Minigolf (Nabisco* Advergames with 3 subbrands), $N = 315$, university students (U.S., Mexico, Peru)	Only entertainment has a significant negative influence on negative attitude toward the advergame.
Hernandez et al., 2005	Advergames (yes), quasi-experimental	Expertise, difficulty level, country	Brand recall	*Arctic 3D racer (racing game), Mini-Golf,* students $n = 260$ (U.S., Mexico, Korea, Chile)	Advergames lead to superior brand recall over banner ads. No cross-country differences were found.
Schneider & Cornwell, 2005	IGA (yes), experimental	Placement proximity, gaming experience, flow	Recall and recognition	*Rallisport Challenge,* racing, male students, $n = 46$ (Australia)	Proximity and gaming experience have a positive impact on recall and recognition. No significant effect of flow on memory.

Nicovich, 2005	IGA (yes), experimental	Involvement with the event, presence	Communication judgment: degree of ad believability (logos) and ad emotionality (pathos)	*Morrowind* (multiplayer role game), students, n = 152 (U.S.)	Involvement and presence significant positive effect on communication judgments. Presence mediates the involvement–judgment link.
Nelson et al., 2006	IGA (yes), experimental	Playing versus watching game, real and fictitious brands, presence	Recall, perceived persuasion, presence, liking the game	Playing versus watching PC racing game; adults, n = 62 (U.S.)	Recall of brands is related to watching or playing the game. When playing, the user is more likely to be distracted from brand information. Real brands received a greater recall than fictitious brands. Game liking and telepresence were positively related to perceived persuasion for the real brand setting.
Winkler & Buckner, 2006	Advergame (yes), quasi-experimental survey	Game exposure, attitude toward advertising	Recall, attitude toward IGA	*M&M Advergame, BMW X3 Advergame, Minigolf* by Nabisco, adults n = 42 (mainly German)	BMW received the highest recall value as it was the best brand–game fit. Positive attitude toward advertising does not automatically lead to positive attitude tow. PPL in games.

(Continued)

TABLE 5.1 (CONTINUED)

Summary Review of the Published Advergaming and In-Game Advertising Literature

Author(s), Year	In-Game Advertising (IGA) or Advergaming (Exposure to Game in the Study?), Research Design	Independent Variables	Dependent Variables	Game-Genre and Sample (Country)	Major Findings
Yang, Roskos-Ewoldsen, Dinu, & Arpan, 2006	IGA (yes), experimental	Game condition (sports, racing versus control)	Implicit (word fragment), explicit memory (recognition)	Formula 1 (2001), FIFA 2002, students, n = 153 (U.S.)	Players exposed to brands showed greater implicit memory for brands (as compared to controls, those not exposed to brands). Players showed above-chance recognition for brands they were exposed to in the games.
Glass, 2007	IGA (yes), experimental	Game exposure	Implicit association test (brand attitudes—good-bad)	Branded fighting game, students, n = 28 (U.S.)	Placed brands were more likely to be rated "faster" and as "good" than were nonplaced brands.
Lee & Faber, 2007	IGA (yes), experimental	Placement Proximity (focal, peripheral), game involvement (high, moderate),	Recall, recognition	Online racing game, students, n = 115 (U.S.)	Low levels of brand memory overall. Focal brands were better recalled and recognized than peripherally placed brands. Gaming experience,

Study	Design	Independent variable	Context/sample	Dependent measures	Findings
		gaming experience, game–product congruency			congruency, and involvement significantly interact with recall and/or recognition. Incongruent brands better recalled.
Mallinckrodt & Mizerski, 2007	Advergame (yes), experimental	Playing the game versus control	*Froot Loops Advergame*, children, 5–8 years, *n* = 294 (Australia)	Recall, preference, identification of the supplier of the game, brand beliefs that Froot Loops are healthy	Older children were more likely to understand the commercial character of the advergame. Playing the advergame had a positive influence on preference for the brand.
Yang & Wang, 2008	Advergame (yes), experimental	Form of the placement (branded or nonbranded), product type (symbolic, enhancement, tool)	Shooting/puzzle games *n* = 153 (Taiwanese students)	Recall, attention, interest, desire, action (AIDA); free/aided recall at a two-week delay	Product type and placement type are significantly related to the attention. After a two-week delay, 87% of respondents could recall the products and with aided recall 97% could recall.
Gurău, 2008	Advergame (yes), quasi-experimental survey	Game, previous knowledge of the game	*Coca-Cola and Pepsi-Cola Advergame*, students, *n* = 200, (France)	Entertainment (boring/absorbing), consumption of the placed brands	Knowledge of the game yielded a higher percentage of bored students. Playing the game had a slightly positive effect on consumption habits of both drinks compared to previous consumption.

(Continued)

TABLE 5.1 (CONTINUED)

Summary Review of the Published Advergaming and In-Game Advertising Literature

Author(s), Year	In-Game Advertising (IGA) or Advergaming (Exposure to Game in the Study?), Research Design	Independent Variables	Dependent Variables	Game-Genre and Sample (Country)	Major Findings
Mau et al., 2008	IGA (yes), experimental survey	Brand familiarity, brand placement in game (versus none-control), flow	Attitude toward the game, attitude toward the brand	*Counter-Strike*, First person shooter gaming community members (mainly, N = 521 Germany)	For attitude toward the game as well as for attitude toward the brand with the familiar brand (Coca-Cola), a negative influence after playing the game was observed. For the unfamiliar brand (Jolt), attitude toward brand increases after game play. No direct influence of flow on brand attitudes.
Walsh et al., 2008	IGA (yes), experimental	Video of NASCAR-car race versus game of NASCAR race	Brand recall, brand recognition	*NASCAR racing game versus NASCAR race (TV)*, students n = 72 (U.S.)	Recognition and brand recall were higher in the video setting (TV race) than in the game setting.

Wise et al., 2008	Advergame (yes), experimental	Thematic relevance of the game	Attitude toward the game, attitude toward the brand	Four different advergames of *Orbitz* (2 related to traveling, 2 not related to traveling), adults, n = 40 (U.S.)	Attitude toward the game predicts the attitude toward the brand. The relationship was significantly higher in the high thematic relevance group.
Bailey et al., 2009	Advergames (yes), experimental	Avatar type (assigned, chosen, customized), customization of the avatar in three different advergames	Arousal (skin conductance), reported presence	*Fruit by the Foot: Skate boarding game; Wonka-biking game; Go-Tarts fashion game*, children 8–12, n = 30 (U.S.)	Customization of avatar related to increased presence and arousal.
MacKay et al., 2009	IGA (yes), quasi-experimental survey	Predisposition toward a brand (pre-posttest versus control group), placed car brand in the game	Attitude toward the brand, recall	Racing game (*Gran Turismo 5*), students + non-students, n = 154 (Australia)	Positive predisposition toward brand positively influences recall. After game play those with more negative brand attitude initially showed more favorable brand attitudes. No results of game play were found on those who held preexisting favorable brand attitudes.

(Continued)

TABLE 5.1 (CONTINUED)

Summary Review of the Published Advergaming and In-Game Advertising Literature

Author(s), Year	In-Game Advertising (IGA) or Advergaming (Exposure to Game in the Study?), Research Design	Independent Variables	Dependent Variables	Game-Genre and Sample (Country)	Major Findings
Cauberghe & De Pelsmacker, 2010	Advergame (yes), experimental	Prominence of the placement, product involvement, repetition of the game	Recall, attitude toward the brand	Advergame "*Snag*" (Snake), mixed adults and students, $n = 480$ (Belgium)	Repetition led to negative effects on brand evaluation but not effects on recall. Prominent placement brand was better recalled.
Chang et al., 2010	IGA (yes), survey	Perceived congruity, prominence, integration	Interest in in-game advertising, purchase intention of featured brand	Five games with one inserted brand: *Free Fantasy* (Wahaha Nutri-express), *World of Warcraft* (Coca-Cola), QQ X5 (KFC), *Fantasy Westward Journey* (Li-ning), and QQ R2 (KFC), mostly students, $n = 443$ (China)	Perceived congruity, prominence, and integration all positively related to interest in IGA and purchase intention, with "integration" showing strongest results.

Gross, 2010	IGA (yes), experimental	Product–game congruency, prior gaming experience	Implicit and explicit memory (7-day delay), attitude toward the game	*Oreo Marble shooter* (trivia game, low congruent), *Oreo race for the stuff* (sports game, high congruent), students, *n* = 47 (U.S.)	High congruent games lead to higher implicit and explicit memory effects. Attitude toward the game was higher for the incongruent setting. Gaming experience had no significant influence.
Kwak et al., 2010	IGA (no), survey	Past experience with the game, perceived gaming skills	Personalize Intention ("Career Mode"), enjoyment, repurchase intention of game, playing time of game	*Sport video game—FIFA 06 Live*; FIFA game players *n* = 459 (Korea)	Past experience and perceived skill positively related to game personalization. Those who personalized the game were more likely to enjoy the game, repurchase it, and play it for longer periods of time.
Lewis & Porter, 2010	IGA (yes) quasi-experimental	Congruency	Acceptance of IGA	*Anarchy online* (Multiplayer role game), students, *n* = 100 (U.S.)	Congruency led to a better acceptance of ads in the game. Males were more favorable to fictional brands than to real brands in games, and they also find ads in games more annoying. Also, heavy game players are more likely to be annoyed by IGA. *(Continued)*

TABLE 5.1 (CONTINUED)

Summary Review of the Published Advergaming and In-Game Advertising Literature

Author(s), Year	In-Game Advertising (IGA) or Advergaming (Exposure to Game in the Study?), Research Design	Independent Variables	Dependent Variables	Game-Genre and Sample (Country)	Major Findings
Nicovich, 2010	IGA (yes), quasi-experimental survey	Presence, involvement with the "event," visual placement of brands within environment versus word-of-mouth interactions with avatars	Communication Judgment, "Ethos" (Source)	*Morrowind* (Multiplayer role game), students, $n = 302$ (U.S.)	Presence and involvement positively influence the communication judgment. The involvement–persuasion link is also partly mediated by presence.
van Reijmersdal et al., 2010	IGA (yes), experimental survey	Interactive brand placement (yes/no) moderators: age, prior brand usage,	Attitude toward the game, top of mind awareness of the brand, brand image, behavioral intentions toward the brand	*GoSupermodel!* (simulation/interaction game, massive multiplayer online game), 11- to 17-year-old female children/adolescents	Attitude toward the game increases when brands are integrated. Placement of the brand positively affects the top of mind awareness, brand image and behavioral intentions. Prior brand usage positively influences the effect of the advergame and is moderated by the age of the children,

					where younger girls with no prior product usage showed a slightly higher preference.
Waiguny & Terlutter, 2011	Advergame (yes), experimental	Game versus TV commercial; identification of the commercial character, time	Brand attitude, liking the advergame, recommendation intention of the game, replay intention, brand choice, pester intention	*Nesquik Duo* advergame, children 8–10, n = 51 (Austria)	Children exposed to the TV commercial were less entertained and subsequently less favorable toward all dependent variables except preference. Identifying the advergame as a form of commercial does not have negative effects, while in the TV setting all dependent variable values decrease. The longer children were exposed to the advergame, the more likely they could recall elements of the game and of the brand-related content.
Hang & Auty, 2011	IGA (yes), experimental	Exposure to product placement, interactivity with product placement	Brand choice, brand recall	FIFA game, children ages 9–10, n = 207 (China)	Brand recall less than chance; interactivity with product placement can lead to conceptual fluency—enhances recall and choice.
An & Stern, 2011	Advergame (yes), experimental	Ad Break (disclosure): verbal, auditory	Persuasion knowledge, brand recall, preference	Popstopia.com. "Be a Popstar"; Kraft Foods, children 8–11, n = 112 (U.S.)	No effect of ad break on persuasion or agent knowledge; ad breaks diminished brand recall and preference.

in-game advertising and advergaming published in peer-reviewed journals. Although the two forms of branded content in games are different in some respects noted earlier, we discuss each of the processes and ramifications for cognition and persuasion.

Understanding Entertainment in Games

Games arouse players strongly (Grodal, 2000). Arousal has been defined as an affective state: a feeling state of activation that varies from drowsiness to frantic excitement (Mehrabian & Russell, 1974). That excitement is part of the entertainment value. However, one common misunderstanding of the term *entertainment* is that it is always positively loaded, as implied by early definitions in which media enjoyment is understood as the experiencing of pleasure from the mass media of communication (Mendelsohn, 1966). There are several broader theories about what entertainment constitutes, what entertainment is, and how it is manifested (for an overview, see Bryant, Roskos-Ewoldsen, & Cantor, 2003; Bryant & Vorderer, 2006; Shrum, 2004, and Chapter 1, this volume). Selected relevant theories for processing games are reviewed next.

Emotional Engagement

Anyone who has ever played a computer game for the first time understands that playing a game is usually "... challenging and rewarding but may also be frustrating" (Vorderer, Klimmt, & Ritterfeld, 2004, p. 391). Thus, beyond joy or pleasure, several emotions constitute the entertainment experience. Entertainment itself may elicit a complex meta-emotion, that is appraised in a secondary process by the evaluation of primary emotions during the media consumption context (Bartsch, Vorderer, Mangold, & Viehoff, 2008). For example, if someone is reading a horror book or playing *Doom*, he or she *expects* to feel fear, which is not a positively loaded emotion. However, because the person expects the emotions, and when he or she feels it, he or she experiences a positive meta-emotion in the form of a pleasurable consumption experience. Based on this theory, the processing of entertaining media is related to a huge variety of different emotions, which affect the information processing as well as the evaluation of the media. For example, joy and excitement (as well as boredom) may transfer directly to the brand inside the game (Gurău, 2008; Wise, Bolls, Kim, Venkataraman, & Meyer, 2008).

Cognitive Immersion

Games offer a highly complex media environment, one that requires skills for processing complex mental representations and inferences (Azai & Patel, 1992) while simultaneously and selectively attending to different images in the game (Sweller & Chandler, 1994), often under time constraints. Games, unlike other media, (1) require gamers to concentrate on the gaming situation to control it, (2) demand a lot of mental resources to understand causalities in the gameplay and draw cognitive maps to solve the game, and (3) must be directed physically with control devices (Grodal, 2000). As a result of this context, the gaming situation arouses the gamer physically as well as mentally (Nakatsu et al., 2005). In essence, focusing on the controls and content necessitates full-bandwidth where multiple senses are employed simultaneously, which requires constant attention and active control of the setting, props, avatar, etc. (Vedrashko, 2006). The rich, multisensory media environment and full cognitive immersion often result in a sense of flow experienced by the game player.

Flow (a state or sensation of total involvement during an event, object, or activity; Csikszentmihalyi, 1990) is a psychological dimension that has been found to be a pleasurable experience—one where the person loses all track of space and time—and a positive feeling that encourages repetition (Trevino & Webster, 1992). Although Csikszentmihalyi (1990) observed the concept of flow for everyday life and work, flow has been used to describe feelings experienced from the entertainment of leisure activities and computer gaming (Ozok & Zaphiris, 2009; Sherry, 2004). For example, many video game players report the sensation of flow or being "in the zone" (i.e., totally engrossed, losing sense of time; Bryce & Rutter, 2001). Using in-depth interviews, Moore, Mazvancheryl, & Rego (1996) found that online game players referred to the fun of game playing but also to factors of intense involvement and distorted notions of time and space. Many players also mentioned the pleasure and adrenaline rush (also a part of the flow experience) they received from playing games, similar to playing real-life sports. The flow state may lead to focused attention on the flow-eliciting action, which leads to a loss of time, a loss of self-consciousness, a feeling that performing the action is rewarding, and a feeling related to the pleasure of control (Nakamura & Csikszentmihalyi, 2002; Sherry, 2004).

Generally speaking, flow is a holistic, optimal situation for a person, which is achieved if the challenge meets the individual's skills (Csikszentmihalyi, 1988). However, flow does not automatically occur; rather, it is experienced through a balance between skills and challenge (Moneta & Csikszentmihalyi, 1996). Suboptimal solutions are either a too-challenging situation in which the person is overloaded, which leads to anxiety and anger, or a less challenging situation, which leads to boredom (Nakamura & Csikszentmihalyi, 2002). This optimal level of challenge is also what game designers take into account, that the challenge of the game meets the skills of the game player (Chen, 2007; Lazzaro, 2008). Several game elements such as levels, tasks, and the reality and the fit of the gameworld can be used to generate a flow experience (Cowley, Charles, Black, & Hickey, 2008). Thus, flow can be used to explain the underlying processes of perception and persuasion related to in-game advertising as it is related to cognitive as well as affective processes.

One construct of flow is telepresence (Hoffman & Novak, 1997; Novak, Hoffman, & Yung, 2000). Telepresence (presence) has been conceptualized in numerous ways (for a review, see Lombard & Ditton, 1997). In the media and marketing literature, it is typically defined as a sense of being there—virtually feeling as though one were transported inside the mediated environment (e.g., Coyle & Thorson, 2001; Li, Daugherty, & Biocca, 2002; Steuer, 1995). Antecedents to telepresence include the multisensory nature of the media, image size/quality, viewing distance, dimensionality of visual field, camera techniques, aural realism, and interactivity; they can also include content characteristics of the medium and individual characteristics (Lombard & Ditton, 1997). Although all media can evoke feelings of telepresence (Shih, 1998), factors that lead to increased telepresence in web environments are greater interactivity, increased vividness, and three-dimensional visuals (Coyle & Thorson, 2001; Li et al., 2002).

Consequences of telepresence include physiological effects such as increased arousal levels (as evidenced by skin resistance measures, heart rate, and respiration rates (Riva, Waterworth, & Waterworth, 2004), motion sickness (e.g., Biocca, 1992), and automatic physical responses such as ducking or flinching (Lombard & Ditton, 1997)). Psychological effects are increased enjoyment, involvement, persuasion, and memory (Lombard & Snyder-Duch, 2001) and, for advertisers, telepresence can lead to enhanced product knowledge, brand attitudes, and purchase intentions (Kim & Biocca, 1997; Li et al., 2002).

In summary, digital games combine cognitive, emotional, and physical activities. In the optimal game-player context, the game player experiences feelings of flow and telepresence, which include a loss of time, a focus on the action, and strong emotions. When such emotions are expected, a pleasurable experience for the recipient occurs. How those experiences relate to psychological processing, memory, and persuasion of embedded brands is discussed next.

The Relationship Between Entertainment and Brand Memory

Memory-based measures (recognition, implicit and explicit recall) of the brands in the game are often used as a gauge of cognition and advertising effectiveness (Nelson, 2005). Much of the published research to date does not employ a theoretical framework to explain results of psychological processing on memory. A review of the literature shows that one theoretical framework used to explain psychological processing and cognition in games (e.g., Lee & Faber, 2007) and other media is the limited capacity model for mediated message processing (Lang, 2000, 2009). This model explains how the encoding, storage, and retrieval of messages in mediated media settings work. Central to the model is the basic assumption that mental resources for processing stimuli are limited and allocated to primary and secondary tasks (e.g., Eysenck & Keane, 2000). Although the model was originally developed for analyzing television watching, it has been adapted to other media by considering (1) the structure of the situation or medium; (2) aspects of the content, which engage the automatic resource allocation; (3) the demands the medium places on the cognitive load; and (4) the aspects of the situation or medium that influence the automatic allocation processes (Lang, 2000, 2009).

Given these aspects, digital games appear well suited for this theory: Games are a very rich medium as they combine narrative, rhetorical, verbal, acoustic, and visual stimuli (Bogost, 2007) as well as physical action by controlling the situation (Nakatsu, et al., 2005). The multisensory environment is characterized by a very strong activation of the game player. Further, compared to television, where the structure and the storyline of the content is fixed, the plot of games is related to the playing behavior (Grodal, 2000) Thus, the player has to understand and learn the content and the gameplay, and this is seen as the primary task in a gaming situation. The nature of the medium (lean forward, active engagement) requires full cognitive efforts. Researchers have suggested that the player will allocate most of his or her cognitive resources to the gameplay (e.g., Lee & Faber, 2007). As a result, peripheral elements, such as background ads displayed in a complex multisensory media environment such as a game, will suffer in terms of processing because players will focus on central elements.

The distinction between advergame and in-game advertising is important here. Typically, brands are more centrally featured in advergames (games are often written about or for the brand), whereas in in-game advertising the centrality or peripheral nature of the brand can vary. In addition, brand clutter is reduced in an advergame because there is only one brand present, whereas in in-game advertising situations there are usually multiple brands, all competing for the players' attention. Because of the difference in brand prominence and clutter, the results for memory vary a great deal between these two gaming contexts.

Memory-based measures for brands featured in advergames often garner fairly high results. For example, in one study, respondents played one of three different advergames, each featuring a single brand (Winkler & Buckner, 2006). Directly after gameplay, 86% of respondents remembered seeing the brand logo and 97% of those could recall at least one specific position of the logo within the game. Such high scores are even found after a delay. Gross (2010) reported that 100% of the players of a congruent brand-game advergame (*Oreo's Race for the Stuff*) recalled that the game was about cookies and could identify Oreo when asked 1 week after gameplay. The game asked participants to race against a clock to "twist, lick, and dunk" the Oreo icons. Even those in the incongruent game condition (*Oreo's Marble Shooter*) displayed a relatively high level of recall (95% recalled the game was about cookies, and 80% identified Oreo as the featured brand). In this game, the players were using a slingshot to knock marbles off the board; Oreos were not prominently featured. Finally, players of shooting and puzzle games that featured a single brand showed similarly high levels of recall after a 2-week delay (Yang & Wang, 2008). Results showed that 87% of respondents could recall the products with free recall measures, and with aided recall measures 97% could recall the product. All of the aforementioned studies featured online games where only one brand was featured in the game play. Thus, it is not surprising that the players recalled the only brand in the game.

Conversely, studies from in-game advertising report more mixed results with respect to player memory for the featured brands. For example, when Mau et al. (2008) placed only one very well-known brand, Coca-Cola, in a prominent position (billboard) in the game *Counter-Strike*, 71% of the players recalled the brand correctly. However, that high recall rate is unusual for in-game advertising studies. Numerous other studies have shown very low levels of recognition or recall, some at or just above the just-chance level (Hang & Auty, 2011; Lee & Faber, 2007; Yang, Roskos-Ewoldsen, Dinu, & Arpan, 2006).

Some research has provided insight into how memory may operate within limited capacity in-game advertising situations. For example, Yang et al. (2006) reported results of both explicit memory (recognition) and implicit memory for players of sport and racing games. They showed that those respondents exposed to the brands in a game showed significantly higher implicit memory (according to a word fragment test) than those not exposed to the brands in the game (i.e., control condition, other game condition). Implicit memory results were much stronger than explicit memory results.

Also, across advertising game context (advergames, in-game advertising), brands that are placed more prominently are more likely to be recalled than less prominently placed brands (e.g., Lee & Faber, 2007; Nelson, 2002; Schneider & Cornwell, 2005). For instance, Lee and Faber (2007) showed that in-game brand advertising placed in focal positions (e.g., the gates that car drivers had to pass through) were more likely to be recognized and recalled than in-game brands placed along the periphery (billboards on the far left of the track). Also in a racing game context, Nelson (2002, 2005) found a relatively high brand recall of about 30% directly after game-play, but after 5 months, the recall decreased to about 10%. The majority of players remembered the brand of racing car they selected, but were significantly less likely to remember brands along the periphery. Further, a few players were more likely to recall product category (e.g., soda) over a particular brand at a delay. Similarly, Chaney et al. (2004) tested unaided recall of brands placed on billboards within a multiplayer first-person shooter game. They reported superior recall results for the product category over the brand itself. The authors suggest that "the gamer could remember pictures (product) much easier than the actual words (brand)." Thus, players are more likely to recall brands that are central to gameplay (e.g., the car brand they are driving) and to perform better on implicit memory and recognition tests than explicit tests (free recall).

A small body of research has tested the relationship between the entertainment of games and memory-based measures of brand effectiveness. Some of these studies have found that a flow or flowlike situation such as (tele)presence reduces brand recall, in particular for brands that are not central to gameplay (Gangadharbatla, 2008; Schneider & Cornwell, 2005). Anecdotal evidence from an Internet Relay Chat (real-time Internet text messaging) of game players after an advertising experiment included the following reasons for not remembering the billboards: "too busy killing," "too focused," and "in the zone" (Chaney et al., 2004). Another set of studies has found no significant relationship between flow (Schneider & Cornwell, 2005), entertainment (Chaney et al., 2004), or the difficulty of the game (Hernandez, Minor, Suh, Chapa, & Salas, 2005) and in-game brand recall or recognition. Due to different game genres, in-game advertising placements, and measurements of entertainment, flow, and telepresence across these studies, it is difficult to form conclusions in this area.

Finally, studies comparing brand memory effects for game playing with a spectator situation have revealed that recall is lower in the more active gaming environment than in the less active, spectator situations. These results are also in line with predictions from the limited capacity model of media effects. For example, Walsh et al. (2008) discovered that embedded brands in a NASCAR racing game were less likely to be recalled than were sponsored brands in a NASCAR race on television. A three-times higher recall for real brands and a nine-times higher recall for fictitious brands were found for subjects who only watched a game compared with subjects who played the computer racing game (Nelson et al., 2006). Similar results were noted when researchers contrasted recall for an advergame versus a television commercial. Waiguny and Terlutter (2010) compared a content-equal advergame to a television commercial with children aged 8 to 10. Recall for the brand in the television commercial was about 82%, whereas it was only 45% in the advergame. All of these studies suggest that explicit brand recall suffers when the brand message is delivered by the game, irrespective of game format. Thus, if cognitive effects such as recall are the goal of the advertising campaign via advergames or in-game advertising, the brand should be placed in the game in a prominent and central position (Chen & Ringel, 2001). Otherwise, due to the focused attention on the gameplay and its central elements and due to limited cognitive capacity of the player, the brands or messages ancillary to the gameplay are not actively recalled or remembered at a very high level.

However, there is still debate over whether explicit (conscious) or implicit (unconscious) memory is the best goal and measure of effectiveness (Law & Braun-LaTour, 2004). It may be too difficult for participants to consciously retrieve brands using recognition or recall tests, even though the brands may later influence respondents (see also Chapter 4 in this volume).

The Relationship Between Entertainment and Persuasion

The persuasive power of a brand message in a game is related to (1) the design of the game and the gameplay and the way the brand message is included in the game, and (2) the level of entertainment. Each of these will be discussed in the following sections. The first set of psychological processes relates to the affective experience during and after the gameplay; the second set of processes relates to implicit learning effects.

How Entertainment and Affect Relate to Persuasion: The Transfer of "Positive" and "Negative" Experience

Persuasion via advergames or in-game advertising occurs passively (Smith & Just, 2009). Most common advergames do not include explicit information about products. Rather, any relevant information is integrated into the gameplay: Mascots are the avatars in the game or to collect ingredients or brand symbols is a goal of the game. Often, also, in the case of advergames, the entire gameplay is thematically built around the intended message (Wise et al., 2008). For example, in the advergame *Dino-Race* from Haribo (in the style of *Super Mario Kart*), children must collect jelly sweets in the form of a cola bottle (indicating fuel) and pacifier-shaped jelly sweets for a turbo boost. But they should avoid driving into timber and banana peels. Hence, this game action indicates that collecting the product has a positive impact on performance.

From this perspective, the persuasion effects of embedded brands are mainly based on two different processes. First, on conditioning, where the positive experience of the game is frequently combined with the brand. So evaluative (emotional) conditioning is happening (De Houwer, 2007; De Houwer, Baeyens, & Field, 2005; De Houwer, Thomas, & Baeyens, 2001; Kroeber-Riel, 1984), where an emotional stimuli (the enjoyable gaming situation) is combined with a neutral stimuli (brand). When conditioned, every time the brand is seen, the emotional experience will also be remembered and a positive feeling toward the brand increases. A separate but related process may occur when persons in a good mood or feeling positive tend to evaluate subjects and objects more positively (Bagozzi, Gopinath, & Nyer, 1999). As the gaming situation usually is pleasing, game players will evaluate not only the game more positively, but they may also evaluate the embedded brand more positively. This classic affect transfer is also well known in traditional advertising research (e.g., Bagozzi et al., 1999; Batra & Stayman, 1990; Brown & Stayman, 1992; Lutz, MacKenzie, & Belch, 1983; MacKenzie, Lutz, & Belch, 1986). It could be assumed as rather strong in the case of advergames or in-game advertising as the potential to produce positive emotions of an entertaining format is higher than in traditional advertising formats (Waiguny & Terlutter, 2011).

In order for evaluative conditioning to happen, at first a positive evaluation of the stimulus (game) is needed. For a game to be liked, it should be fun. Hence, delivering fun is the most important attribute for the evaluation of games (Gao, 2004; Lazzaro, 2008). In fact, Youn and Lee (2005) found that fun is the strongest motivation to play advergames. However, fun may depend on several factors, including interaction with other players or characters (Lazzaro, 2008) or the ability to customize avatars or game content (Bailey, Wise, & Bolls, 2009; Kwak et al., 2010). Hernandez also found that entertainment is the strongest antecedent of attitude toward an advergame (Hernandez, 2008). Games are evaluated positively if they can get the user into a flow state or sense of telepresence (i.e., "being there"; Nelson et al., 2006), which causes strong emotions, namely, fun. These positive feelings from and about the game may then transfer to the embedded brand stimuli through a halo effect, or through affect transfer in positive context effects (e.g., Goldberg & Gorn, 1987).

Indeed, across advergame and in-game advertising contexts, studies have reported a positive relationship between attitude toward the game (or game liking) and attitude toward the embedded brand (Bambauer-Sachse, 2007; Mau et al., 2008; Redondo, 2009; Waiguny, Terlutter, Wiegele, & Nelson, 2010; Wise et al., 2008). Further, some studies have found that a sense of flow or (tele)presence has direct and indirect effects on persuasion. For example, Nicovich (2010) reported that the level of presence in an online role-playing game had a positive effect on commmunication judgment for in-game brand placement ads as well as for word-of-mouth auditory brand conversations from avatars in the game environment. In addition, the sense of presence mediated the relationship between players' involvement in the situation and the communication judgment. In another in-game advertising study, Nelson et al. (2006) demonstrated that the sense of (tele)presence positively related to perceived persuasion for real and fictious brands; further, telepresence mediated the effect of game liking on persuasion. Therefore, it seems that some sense of telepresence (feeling in the game) or flow enhances the game experience and also the embedded brand.

However, as described earlier, a sense of flow may not always occur in a game situation, depending on the level of challenge of the game and the skills and motivations of the game player. On the one hand, feelings of flow and fun can arise if a game is challenging and delivers the pleasure of handling the challenge. On the other hand, easy games can also deliver fun as they offer a quick possibility to get entertained; however, after a time, easy games may cause boredom. Therefore, an optimal balance between challenge and skills is needed. One study showed how challenge relates to persuasion. Waiguny, Nelson, and Terlutter (2011) found that children (ages 7–10) who were optimally challenged reported the highest brand attitudes for the featured brand in the advergame, whereas those who were underchallenged (bored) showed the lowest overall brand attitudes. However, not much research to date has explored the relationships between game challenge, flow, and persuasion.

In sum, if a game entertains as expected, the positive emotions garnered from the experience can lead to a positive evaluation of the game, which could be transferred to the brand, especially if the brand (or brand elements) is placed centrally (Glass, 2007; Redondo, 2009). In addition, emotions as a result of gameplay do not only lead to affect transfer; emotions can also influence the willingness and ability to process the conveyed messages. These processing effects will be discussed next.

Entertainment and Implicit Learning Effects

In addition to positive affect transfer from game to brand, a second body of literature explains embedded brand persuasion according to implicit learning effects (e.g., Hang & Auty, 2011). Such processes are especially important for branded entertainment formats since past research has shown that although brand recall rates are rather low, positive effects on brand attitudes, preferences, and beliefs are often significant (Van Reijmersdal, 2009). These effects are based on the fact that the learning effects of games are often implicit and incidental (Ritterfeld & Weber, 2006) and, similar to product placement in movies, they are also more likely to address the procedural/implicit memory than the explicit memory (Auty & Lewis, 2004a, 2004b).

Different from traditional television advertising, entertainment formats such as advergames or other digital games typically give the brands embedded into them a much longer exposure time. Games are often played longer than 30 seconds and brand exposures may occur frequently in the game. Such repeated exposures are thought to influence audiences' perceptions of the brand through incidental and implicit learning, and predicted fluency effects may occur. First, a perceptual fluency effect (or subjective ease of processing presemantic or visual features of stimuli; Tulving & Schacter, 1990) is caused by longer exposure times to the embedded brand and frequent repetition. As a result, the more familiar a stimuli (embedded brand) is to the game player, the more likely it will be processed quicker; this familiarity generally leads to a more favorable evaluation (e.g., Albarracín & Vargas, 2010; Conroy, Hopkins, & Squire, 2005). Indeed, implicitly processed stimuli are typically evaluated as better, more beautiful, and pleasing (Reber & Schwarz, 1999; Reber, Schwarz, & Winkielman, 2004; Reber, Winkielman, & Schwarz, 1998; Winkielman, Schwarz, Fazendeiro, & Reber, 2003). Thus, exposure time has a major impact on implicit and incidental learning effects. Subsequently, respondents (especially those who do not actively recall the brand/stimulus) may then misattribute the positive feelings (as a result of fluency) to brand preference or choice (e.g., Schwarz, 2004).

A handful of studies have investigated fluency effects in a game context. For example, after asking respondents to play a fighting game, Glass (2007) used the Implicit Association Test (IAT) to compare the response times for the words *good* and *bad* for brands placed in a fighting game (e.g., Burger King) versus equivalent brands that were not in the game (e.g., McDonald's). Results show that respondents replied faster (reaction time) and were more likely to pick "good" for brands viewed in the game. Although the researcher did not set out to test for fluency effects (nor did he check for recall), the results are generally in line with this theoretical framework. Brands that were viewed in the game were likely processed more fluently (faster response times) and were evaluated more positively than those not in game.

In a more recent study, Hang and Auty (2011) asked children ages 9–10 to play a sports game (FIFA) where they manipulated exposure to in-game advertising and opportunity to interact with the brand. They then assessed children's perceptual fluency by asking them their brand choice on a stimulus-based task (where the visual logo was provided), but only for those children who did not recall the brand. Results show that those children who interacted with the brand (i.e., children were allowed to indicate their favorite branded T-shirt) demonstrated the highest perceptual fluency across experimental conditions; that is, 95% of children who were allowed to interact with the game and then were exposed to the brand in the game selected that brand in a choice task, versus 43.5% who were exposed to the brand but did not interact with it, 39% of children who interacted with the brand but did not play the game, and 9.1% in a control group (no interaction, no game play). The authors conclude that the synergistic effects of exposure and interactivity led to superior brand evaluations.

In addition to perceptual processing fluency, games also provide the possibility to convey messages rhetorically or procedurally (Bogost, 2007; Smith & Just, 2009), which allows learning effects through conceptual fluency (ease of processing language or conceptual information; Whittlesea, 1993) or associative learning (Auty & Lewis, 2004a; Ritterfeld & Weber, 2006; Shapiro, 1999). In this case, the associative (semantic) networks in the brain are more and more activated, created, and confirmed. So an existing association could be strengthened via this effect and could then influence cognitive and affective judgments (Grimes & Kitchen, 2007).

A good example of instigating implicit learning effects is through the antiadvergame, sponsored by PETA, against Kentucky Fried Chicken (KFC) in the style of Super Mario. In the game, the enemies are the mascot of KFC, and the hero is a small chicken. Jumping on the enemies kills them, but getting in contact with them harms the chicken. Often repeated, this game action likely fosters the association that KFC is bad to chickens, so an implicit learning effect via conceptual fluency occurs as the associative network is consequently influenced and enhanced.

Studies confirming the learning effects in this area are in an initial phase. For example, Ahn (2008) demonstrated that playing an antiadvergame against McDonald's affects the negative brand personality dimensions of the brand (in line with the intent of the game). Another study showed that children's gameplay influenced their health-related beliefs about the featured brand (e.g.; Waiguny, 2011; Waiguny, Nelson, & Terlutter, 2010).

Specifically, after children aged 7–10 played the Nesquik advergame *Garden Quest*, where one of their tasks was to collect whole grain symbols and the brand mascot was a strong and quick animal, they were more likely to believe that Nesquik cereal is a "healthy product."

Finally, in the Hang and Auty (2011) study described earlier, conceptual fluency was assessed according to children's propensity to write down the featured in-game brand name in a memory-based choice task. Results showed that conceptual fluency effects were only realized for those children who could not recall the brand but had the opportunity to interact with it (39% vs. 12.5% in a control group). Mere exposure to the brand in the game (without interaction) did not elicit conceptual fluency effects. Further, the authors suggest their study provides new evidence that "interactivity can integrate conceptual fluency with perceptual fluency to achieve a greater effect on choice" (p. 70). Future research should assess the conditions for which perceptual and conceptual fluency may operate in game situations.

Factors That Influence Brand Memory and Persuasiveness in Advergames and In-Game Advertising

In addition to the main psychological processes described earlier, there are several factors that may influence memory and persuasion. Although some of them have been mentioned briefly, each of these will be discussed in more detail next.

Brand–Game Congruency

In a review of the literature, McCarty (2004) writes, "... a good product placement may be one that fits with the story in such a way as to make us forget that it is there to persuade us. This idea of fit of product placement is critical and relates to the notion of seamlessness" (p. 50–51). Perceived fit may relate to product, medium, communicator, and message dimensions (Bhatnagar, Aksoy, & Malkoc, 2004). In a game context, advertisers want to know whether it is appropriate to place their brand in a particular game or game genre and whether it will be effective.

Theories related to the effects of congruency on cognition present opposing views. On the one hand, congruence between media theme and the ad might enhance memory for an ad, according to the effects of cognitive priming (e.g., Yi, 1990). The explanation is that congruent ads attract atten-tion unconsciously and automatically and are, therefore, easier to retrieve. This process is facilitated by the fact that the subject of the ad has been primed in the media context and that "the ad can be stored at 'the inter-section' of a greater number of classificatory features, making information easier to locate in memory" (Lambert, 1980, p. 38). This theory lends sup-port to other research in the product placement literature that suggests a good fit of the context with the placed products should *enhance* attention to and memory for the products (Bhatnagar, et al., 2004). With respect to advergames or in-game advertising featuring one brand where the brand is central to gameplay, two studies have found such effects: Congruence between brand and game increases implicit and explicit brand recall (Peters, Leshner, Bolls, & Wise, 2009; Winkler & Buckner, 2006).

However, an opposing theoretical view proposes that novel or unex-pected information can be more memorable than expected information (Von Restorff, 1933). New (1991, p. 100) suggested that the "route to visibil-ity" provided by incongruent ads might increase prominence. These views are supported by schema theory (Cornwell & Maignan, 1998), in which the association of knowledge develops through experiences over time and affects one's information processing (Taylor & Crocker, 1981). Presumably, incongruence, yielding a greater number of inferences than congruence, enhances recall by producing stronger and more elaborate schema (Hastie, 1984). In fact, in a review of the literature on product placement (not just in games), Balasubramanian et al. (2006) suggest: In general, incongru-ent placements produce higher cognitive outcomes than congruent place-ments. Within the game literature, studies of in-game advertising, where numerous brands are featured in both central and peripheral positions, have shown such results. For example, in a racing game, Nelson, Yang, and Yaros (2008) reported that perceived fit between brand and game was negatively related to recall when brands were placed along the side of the racing track. Also in a racing game context, Lee and Faber (2007) found that highly incongruent brands (e.g., pet food brands in a car racing game) were significantly more likely to be recalled than moderately incongruent brands (e.g., deodorant) or congruent brands (gasoline). These results were primarily attributed to the high recall ratings among inexperienced game players who were highly involved in the game. In sum, the superiority of incongruent or congruent brands appears to relate to the game context (advergame, in-game advertising) and where the featured brand is placed (central, periphery). Congruent brands fare better in advergame situations when the brand is central to gameplay without interference from other brands; incongruent brands fare better in in-game advertising situations.

Congruency and Persuasion

Advertisers often select media content that fit their brands with the goal of thematic congruence between context and ad. When the content and the ad are perceived to fit or be congruent, consumers can more easily and confidently evaluate the ad and the brand compared with incongruence (Campbell & Goodstein, 2001; Goodstein, 1993). This ease and confidence for the consumer can lead to more favorable evaluations (Maoz & Tybout, 2002; Sengupta, Goodstein, & Boninger, 1997). Other possible explanations for effects related to negative or positive affect may be due to out-of-context placements. Bhatnagar et al. (2004) suggest that placed brands that do not fit are likely to be noticed "as well as raise suspicions of superfluity and of media motives other than artistic expression" (p. 107). In this view, out-of-context genre-brand placements might arouse negativity and lower levels of brand trust. Similarly, Balasubramanian, Karrh, and Patwardhan (2006) suggest that congruence may follow the peripheral route to persuasion (Petty & Cacioppo, 1986). If the placements are considered seamless, the placements might avoid counterarguments such as those discussed earlier. Thus, Theoretical Proposition 9b in Balasubramanian et al. (2006), p. 128, predicts that: In general, congruent placements yield higher affective outcomes (brand attitudes) than incongruent placements.

A handful of studies in the game literature have investigated the influence of congruence on persuasion. Across genre and research method, results suggest that congruity between brand and game leads to better acceptance of ads. For example, game players who played *Anarchy online* (a multiplayer game) featuring fictitious (Dreadloch Arms & Gear, a weapons manufacturer) and congruent brands were more likely to report that they accept in-game advertising as "an unobtrusive addition to the game" than those players exposed to incongruent brands (e.g., Garnier Fructis hair styling products). Similarly, across a range of game genres or advergames (e.g., *Free Fantasy: Wahaha Nutri-express, World of Warcraft: Coca-Cola, QQ X5: KFC, Fantasy Westward Journey: Li-ning*, and *QQ R2: KFC*), players indicated that perceived congruity, prominence, and integration all positively related to their interest in in-game advertising and purchase intention, with integration showing strongest results (Chang et al., 2010).

These results are in line with discussions among game players in a netnography (Nelson et al., 2004), where real brands—when placed seamlessly—were thought to add to a game's verisimilitude. In an experimental setting of in-game advertising, Nelson, Yang, and Yaros (2008) reported that perceived fit between brand and game genre was positively related to brand attitudes and purchase intentions for Coca-Cola. Finally, in an advergame, respondents played either product-relevant or product-irrelevant advergames for Orbitz travel (Wise et al., 2008). Results of their study showed that attitude toward the game predicts the attitude toward the brand, and that this relationship was significantly higher in the product-relevant (i.e., high thematic relevance) group.

As a whole, it appears that the degree to which the brand and game genre are relevant or match offers important consequences for cognitive and affective processes. For cognitive processes, incongruency is sometimes better (in-game advertising), but for affect and persuasion, it appears that congruency between brand and genre is better liked, which can translate into superior brand effects.

Placement Strength: Prominence and Repetition

Placement strength has been defined as "the number of brand mentions, visual or verbal inclusions or both, appearance in the foreground or background, actual usage and integration with the contents" (Bhatnagar et al., 2004, p. 108). More recently, Cauberghe and De Pelsmacker (2010) used brand prominence and repetition as two separate aspects of placement strength. Each of these aspects will be reviewed next.

Prominent placements are those in which the product (or other brand identifier) is made highly visible by virtue of size or position on the screen or its centrality to the action in the scene. Subtle placements are when the brand is not shown prominently because it is small or appears in the background along with other objects for a low exposure time (Gupta & Lord, 1998). Similar to effects reported in a movie-viewing context (e.g., Gupta & Lord, 1998), most research studies within an advergame (Cauberghe & De Pelsmacker, 2010) or in-game advertising context (e.g., Lee & Faber, 2007; Schneider & Cornwell, 2005) have found that the more prominently brands are placed in the game, the higher the recall compared to brands placed along the periphery. These findings are often true despite the level of product involvement (Cauberghe & De Pelsmacker, 2010).

The effects of multiple advertising exposures on brand attitudes are important for understanding advertising effects (for example, see the perceptual fluency section discussed earlier). However, in most of the reviewed studies, participants were exposed at only one session to the featured brand. Yet, a single exposure to a game is not usual. Gamers (especially those aged 15–19 years of age) typically spend several hours a week playing games, according to results of the 2009 American Time Use Survey (Bureau of Labor Statistics, 2009).

Thus, it is likely that by repeated exposure to brands in the game, the learning and affective processes cited previously may be strengthened but also diminished by frequent repetition of a game. These differing effects are based on wear-in and wear-out effects (Berlyne, 1970) of communication. The idea is that an optimal level of exposure will lead to increased recall or persuasion, but after a certain level of exposures, ceiling effects for recall will be realized and persuasion may suffer. Only a handful of studies in the gaming literature to date have explored the effects of repetition on recall or persuasion. For example, in a study of 480 players of *Snag* (a mobile game), the level of repetition (i.e., playing the game two or four times) had no effect on brand recall for low- or high-involvement fictitious brands (Cauberghe & De Pelsmacker, 2010). However, a high level of repetition (four times) led to significantly less favorable brand attitudes for the fictitious brands. This was especially true for the high-involvement product (car). Interestingly, such "wear-out" effects occurred regardless of game liking. In another study, Waiguny (2011) found that children who played a Nesquik advergame during a 2-week period demonstrated a significant increase in the beliefs that the brand is healthy as compared with children who only played the game once. Such preliminary results, therefore, suggest that repetition can help build positive brand beliefs or affect, but too much exposure will cause the brand attitudes to suffer. Future research should explore varying levels of repetition to discern optimal levels of fluency and effects.

Dispositional Factors of the Gamer

Besides the factors directly delivered by the game, several other factors influence the relationship between entertainment and persuasion. We point out three of them: the familiarity with or prior use of the featured brands, the gaming experience of the player, and the level of persuasion knowledge of the game player. All three factors regulate the level of entertainment of the game as well as the likelihood of persuasion with games.

Brand Familiarity and Use

Research in other advertising domains has found that the familiarity or prior use of brands relates to differing effects for memory and persuasion. For example, familiar brands are processed quicker and evaluated better; however, given that such brands typically engender stable attitudes, attitude shifts and persuasive effects are rather weak for familiar brands (Machleit & Wilson, 1988). In the product placement literature, studies have shown that familiar brands are recognized (Brennan & Babin, 2004) and in games, are also recalled more often than unfamiliar brands (Nelson, 2002; Nelson et al., 2006). It also appears that game players may be somewhat conscious of this influence on their memory. An open-ended question that asked game players why they recalled certain brands yielded the common response of brand familiarity (Schneider & Cornwell, 2005). Interestingly, the players attributed brand familiarity (of Castrol) from actual racing events, brand promotions, or other computer games of a similar genre.

Despite these results, Balasubramanian et al. (2006) suggest that unfamiliarity is likely to increase cognitive outcomes (such as recall) (proposition 8a) in product placement settings. Perhaps the interactive game environment, where cognitive capacity is constrained (as compared with film settings), limits the generalizability of that prediction. Although familiarity and brand attitudes are not the same construct, it is likely that prior brand attitudes presuppose a level of familiarity with the brand. In line with results discussed earlier, MacKay, Ewing, Newton, and Windisch (2009) showed that a positive predisposition toward a brand placed in a racing game positively influences recall.

The relationship between brand familiarity and persuasion is mixed. On the one hand, game players like the enhanced realism with the inclusion of real (familiar) brands in game settings; however, they also enjoy the creativity and humor offered when unfamiliar (fictitious) brands are included (Nelson et al., 2004). In an quasi-experimental study using advergames, Waiguny (2011) reported that brand familiarity positively influenced liking the advergame, but did not affect the attitude toward the brand or beliefs about the brand (Waiguny, 2011). On the other hand, brand familiarity can also impair brand attitudes. Mau et al. (2008) found that brand attitudes suffered for the familiar brand of Coca-Cola as a result of integration into a game (CounterStrike); that is, brand attitudes were significantly lower among players after gameplay than they were before. Conversely, brand attitudes for the unfamiliar brand (Jolt Cola in the German market) were significantly higher after gameplay than before (Mau et al., 2008). In terms of prior brand use, MacKay et al. (2009) showed that after playing a racing game, those players with initially *negative* brand attitudes showed more favorable brand attitudes after game play; however, no results of gameplay were found for those who held preexisting favorable brand attitudes.

Finally, a study with 2,746 10- to 17-year-old girls demonstrated that nonbrand users were more likely to be influenced by interactive brand placement in the game GoSupermodel! than brand users (Van Reijmersdal, Jansz, Peters, & Van Noort, 2010). As a whole, prior familiarity or brand use tends to be positively related to memory for those brands (as compared with unfamiliar or nonused brands). For persuasion, it appears that those brands with which participants are not highly familiar and do not already feel positively toward will gain the most from appearing in games. In other words, persuasion may be best for new brands or for those toward which players feel negatively predisposed.

Game Experience

Research on how different people experience games is a largely neglected topic so far. But it is obvious that not everyone is entertained in the same way by a digital game, so simple usage models need to be extended (Cowley et al., 2008). Some studies have considered the role that game experience may play in psychological processing of embedded brands (Gross, 2010; Schneider & Cornwell, 2005). However, the way that game experience is conceptualized and measured varies considerably within and between studies, which makes it difficult to understand how the research findings fit together. For example, to understand the influence of prior gaming experience, researchers must distinguish between experience with a game in particular and general experience in gaming.

If a player already has substantial experience with a specific game, the novelty and complexity of the game decrease (Rauterberg, 1995; van Lankveld, Spronck, van den Herik, & Rauterberg, 2010), resulting in high levels of repetition and wear-out effects. As a result, it is more likely that the game may be perceived as boring (Cowley et al., 2008) and, thus, attitudes toward the game and embedded brands may suffer; this may be especially true of casual advergames. For example, Gurău (2008) found that significantly more students rated the Coke or Pepsi advergame as boring if they had played the game before.

The experience with gaming in general influences the skills of gamers. Expert gamers have better capabilities in understanding a game, decoding the gameplay more quickly and perceiving visual stimuli. Furthermore, experts have better eye-hand coordination in controlling the game than do novice players (Greenfield, DeWinstanley, Kilpatrick, & Kaye, 1994). Thus, experts may have an easier time of attending to items in the periphery than novices do or may not need to allocate as many resources to gameplay as less experienced players. As a result, experienced game players have been found to recall and recognize a greater number of brands than do novices in an in-game advertising context (Schneider & Cornwell, 2005). Further, Lee and Faber (2007) reported interactions between player involvement, experience, and placement proximity. Namely, the authors suggest that those players who were less experienced (and irrespective of involvement) required more resources to play the game (as compared to more experienced players) and did not know where to focus; thus, the results for peripheral brands (but not focal brands) suffered considerably as compared with experienced players. However, despite the superior findings for game experience and recall, a few studies have found no effects for the relationship between game experience in general and with a particular game and recall in in-game advertising (e.g., Chaney et al., 2004; Gross, 2010).

For in-game advertising acceptance and persuasion, results of one study suggest that experienced game players may be less accepting of advertising in general and in games than nongame players (Lewis & Porter, 2010). Further, as players gain expertise and skills, the optimal balance between skills and challenge is shifted, and more experienced players need an increased challenge to enter a flow state (Chen, 2007). One way to increase challenge or at least interest in the game relates to the likelihood of investigating additional features of the game. For example, one study found that more experienced game players and those who are perceived to have a greater gaming skill were also more likely to customize content within the game (e.g., enter Career Mode of *FIFA 06 Live*) than those who were less experienced and skilled. Further, the more likely players were to indicate they would personalize the game, the more likely they were to enjoy the game. For experienced game players, customization offers one way to alleviate boredom once they have mastered the game action and controls (Kwak et al., 2010).

Thus, expert gamers are less likely to be entertained unless they are offered specific challenges or opportunities. For example, Rau et al. (2006) found that experts were less excited by playing an online game than were novices. Hence, as a result of less entertainment and the lower cognitive load, experienced players are less likely to evaluate the game positively, and subsequently a negative affect transfer to the embedded brand could occur. This effect was demonstrated in a study by Waiguny (2011). In this study, 101 children were instructed to play an advergame, then were questioned about it directly after gameplay and after a two-week delay. Although no significant differences in game experience and game or brand attitudes were found directly after gameplay, after 2 weeks, expert gamers (children who play games daily or at least 3–4 times a week) showed lower values in the judgment of the game and for brand attitude of the embedded brand as compared to novice game players (Waiguny, 2011). Future research should investigate more carefully how different measurements of game expertise (in general, for a particular game) might impact cognitive resources, fluency, and processing of embedded brands.

Persuasion Knowledge

How individuals learn to identify, understand, and cope with messages relates to their knowledge about the persuasion context itself. Friestad and Wright's (1994) persuasion knowledge model examines the general set of beliefs people hold about how persuasion agents (e.g., marketers, advertisers) operate, including perceptions of agents' goals and tactics, evaluation of the effectiveness or appropriateness of persuasion attempts, and self-reflections of the targets' own ability to cope with these attempts (Friestad & Wright, 1994). People learn about persuasion tactics from many sources, including discussions with family and friends, media literacy efforts, direct experiences with persuasion agents and tactics, and commentary in the media (Friestad & Wright, 1994). Thus, persuasion knowledge, as a form of advertising literacy, is developmental and increases over time. It may also vary from individual to individual and from advertising tactic to tactic.

In addition to long-term development, persuasion knowledge may be heightened in a particular persuasion attempt and may influence subsequent persuasion outcomes. For example, the persuasion knowledge model implies that consumers will process a message in a perceived nonpersuasion setting quite differently from a setting in which they believe a persuasion attempt is being made (Wei, Fischer, & Main, 2008). Acquisition of persuasion knowledge may therefore heighten suspicion or skepticism and negatively influence the source of the persuasion, attitude toward the tactic itself, or the featured brand. In the case of advergames or in-game advertising, the knowledge that the entertainment context presents a persuasion setting may not be pervasive among players, especially children (Mallinckrodt & Mizerski, 2007). Unlike traditional broadcast advertising, where most people of cognitive ability understand its persuasive intent, in-game advertising or advergames typically present a noncommercial face with the focus on entertainment (Thomson, 2010).

A few studies have explored how persuasion knowledge of advergames may influence persuasion outcomes among children (see also Chapter 4, this volume). In an Australian context, Mallinckrodt and Mizerski (2007) showed that the older children (ages 7–8) who played an advergame featuring Froot Loops cereal were more likely than controls to select Froot Loops cereal. The researchers assessed the children's persuasive knowledge (knowledge of the commercial nature of the game, its persuasive intent; Friestad & Wright, 1994) and expected that higher persuasion knowledge may lead to skepticism and result in decreased brand attitudes and selection. However, the researchers found no significant *negative* effects of persuasion knowledge on brand preferences or intention to request the cereal from parents. In fact, the older children with persuasion knowledge in the sample were even more likely to select Froot Loops; rather, the more they identified the game's intent, the more they preferred the brand. A second study conducted with children in Austria showed that persuasion knowledge (understanding the advergame's commercial intent) only negatively influence brand attitudes for the featured brand when the children were underchallenged by the game (Waiguny et al., 2011). For those children who were optimally challenged (and in the flow state), the critical evaluation of the brand did not occur. The authors suggest that the ability to critically perceive and process information is strongly influenced by the entertainment of games. In essence, people like to remain in a positive mood; they like situations of positive affect. As a result, cognitive resources are allocated to maintain in the entertaining situation rather than to critical processing (Mackie & Worth, 1989, p. 27).

Finally, An and Stern (2011) tested whether persuasion knowledge would be activated when children (ages 8–11) saw or heard an "ad break" (disclosure) while playing an advergame. Their results showed that even though the ad breaks did not increase children's persuasion knowledge, the breaks did reduce the children's recall of and preference for the embedded brand. Future research should investigate the process by which children activate persuasion knowledge and discern how best to measure the construct.

EFFECTS AND ETHICS

The chapter thus far has discussed the effectiveness of brands in games based on psychological processing and persuasion. Given the potential for persuasion, especially along the lines of implicit learning, the effects of brands in games on audiences and society must also be considered. Two interrelated issues are raised and policy issues discussed. The first issue relates to the persuasion knowledge or advertising literacy about advergames and in-game advertising placements. If such persuasion techniques are largely unknown to audiences (Evans & Hoy, 2011; Nelson, 2008), especially among children, whom most of the games target (An & Park, 2011; Thomson, 2010), then advertising literacy in the form of education and disclosure should be enacted. On the first point, the Federal Trade Commission in the United States developed a game entitled *Admongo* to help children aged 8–12 gain advertising literacy in general and to answer the following questions with respect to a variety of advertising formats: *Who is responsible for the ad? What is the ad actually saying? And what does the ad want me to do?* Such literacy efforts may help children identify commercial intent, but further disclosure means are necessary. In line with the International Chamber of Commerce (ICC) Consolidated Code of Advertising and Marketing Communication Practice, we advocate that all electronic communications with a clearly commercial purpose should be identified. As Thomson (2010) notes, some advergame websites are already doing so, albeit in more or less obvious ways. On the subtle end of the spectrum, Luckycharms.com includes an "Ad Spot" logo on the bottom of the page but does not explain or identify the commercial content. Conversely, the disclosure "This pages contains advertisements" is explicitly stated on the Millsberry.com website, and the Frootloops.com website states at the bottom of the page in small letters: "KIDS: this page may contain a product or promotion advertisement." Perhaps a standard explicit disclosure could be enacted for advergames or in-game advertising along the lines of the new rules on broadcast television in the United Kingdom, where a P logo (for product placement) is inserted during UK-produced programs containing product placement (Farey-Jones, 2011). This might be a more powerful hint for children, as just a short break to inform them that the game is some form of advertising is maybe not effective (An & Park, 2011; Wollslager, 2009). Future research might examine the level of advertising literacy or persuasion knowledge about advergames or in-game advertising among children, parents, educators, and policymakers.

CONCLUSION

Increasingly, branded content is found across media, including in digital games. Whereas brands may increase the verisimilitude of the gaming experience, they are also consciously placed or turned into a game as a persuasion device. In this way, the fun of digital games is combined with the brand for new forms of branded entertainment. How that fun relates to psychological processing and persuasion is only beginning to be understood. Future programmatic research that clarifies terms and employs theoretical frameworks to better explain the explicit and implicit effects of embedded brands in digital games is needed. Although the formats and metrics of digital games will undoubtedly evolve, the psychological effects related to the emotions, affect, and cognitive processing may not. As advocated by Mediapost blogger Cory Treffiletti (2011), if researchers can make known the efficacy of game placements, there is "… nowhere to go but up for in-game marketing!" (March 4, 2011).

REFERENCES

Ahn, D. (2008). *The interpretation of the messages in an advergame: The effects on brand personality perception*. Paper presented at the annual meeting of the Association for Education in Journalism and Mass Communication. Retrieved from http://www.allacademic.com/meta/p272095_index.htm

Aitchison, J. (2004). Making the move from commercials to content. *Media Asia, 18*(June), 23–24.

Albarracín, D., & Vargas, P. (2010). Attitudes and persuasion. In S. T. Fiske, D. T. Gilbert, & G. Lindzey (Eds.), *Handbook of social psychology* (pp. 394–427). Hoboken, NJ: Wiley.

An, S., & Park, E. H. (2011). *Do kids understand that advergames are advertising?* Paper presented at the annual conference of the American Academy of Advertising.

An, S., & Stern, S. (2011). Mitigating the effects of advergames on children. *Journal of Advertising, 40*(1), 43–56.

Auty, S., & Lewis, C. (2004a). The "delicious paradox": Preconscious processing of product placements by children. In L. J. Shrum (Ed.), *The psychology of entertainment media: Blurring the lines between entertainment and persuasion* (pp. 117–133). Mahwah, NJ: Lawrence Erlbaum.

Auty, S., & Lewis, C. (2004b). Exploring children's choice: The reminder effect of product placement. *Psychology and Marketing, 21*(9), 697–713.

Bagozzi, R., Gopinath, M., & Nyer, P. (1999). The role of emotions in marketing. *Journal of the Academy of Marketing Science, 27*(2), 184–206.

Bailey, R., Wise, K., & Bolls, P. (2009). How avatar customizability affects children's arousal and subjective presence during junk food–sponsored online video games. *CyberPsychology & Behavior, 12*, 277–283.

Balasubramanian, S. K., Karrh, J. A., & Patwardhan, H. (2006). Audience response to product placements: An integrative framework and future research agenda. *Journal of Advertising, 35*(3), 115–141.

Bambauer-Sachse, S. (2007). Welche Effekte hat brand placement in PC-/Videospielen. *der markt, 46*(183), 139–147.

Bartsch, A., Vorderer, P., Mangold, R., & Viehoff, R. (2008). Appraisal of emotions in media use: Toward a process model of meta-emotion and emotion regulation. *Media Psychology, 11*(1), 7–27.

Batra, R., & Stayman, D. M. (1990). The role of mood in advertising effectiveness. *Journal of Consumer Research, 17*(2), 203–214.

Berlyne, D. E. (1970). Novelty, complexity, and hedonic value. *Perception & Psychophysics, 8*, 279–289.

Bhatnagar, N., Aksoy, L., & Malkoc, S. (2004). Embedding brands within media content: The impact of message, media, and consumer characteristics on placement efficacy. In L. J. Shrum (Ed.), *The psychology of entertainment media: Blurring the lines between entertainment and persuasion* (pp. 99–116). Mahwah, NJ: Lawrence Erlbaum.

Biocca, F. (1992). Will simulation sickness slow down the diffusion of virtual environment technology? *Presence: Teleoperators and Virtual Environments, 1*(3), 334–343.

Bogost, I. (2007). *Persuasive games: The expressive power of video games.* Cambridge, MA: MIT Press.

Brennan, I., & Babin, L. A. (2004). Brand placement recognition: The influence of presentation mode and brand familiarity. *Journal of Promotion Management, 10*(1/2), 185–202.

Brown, S. P., & Stayman, D. M. (1992). Antecedents and consequences of attitude toward the ad: A meta-analysis. *Journal of Consumer Research, 19*, 34–51.

Bryant, J., Roskos-Ewoldsen, D. R., & Cantor, J. (Eds.). (2003). *Communication and emotion: Essays in honor of Dolf Zillmann.* Mahwah, NJ: Lawrence Erlbaum.

Bryant, J., & Vorderer, P. (Eds.). (2006). *Psychology of entertainment.* Mahwah, NJ: Lawrence Erlbaum.

Bryce, J., & Rutter, J. (2001). *In the game—in the flow: Presence in public computer gaming.* Paper presented at the computer games and digital textualities. Retrieved from http://www.digiplay.org.uk

Buckner, K., Fang, H., & Qiao, S. (2002). Advergaming: A new genre in Internet advertising. *SoChytes Journal, 2*(1).

Bureau of Labor Statistics. (2009). Retrieved from http://www.bls.gov/news.release/atus.t11.htm

Campbell, M. C., & Goodstein, R. C. (2001). The moderating effect of perceived risk on consumers' evaluations of product incongruity: Preference for the norm. *Journal of Consumer Research, 28*(3), 439–449.

Cauberghe, V., & De Pelsmacker, P. (2010). Advergames: The impact of brand prominence and game repetition on brand responses. *Journal of Advertising, 39*(1), 5–18.

Chaney, I. M., Lin, K.-H., & Chaney, J. (2004). The effect of billboards within the gaming environment. *Journal of Interactive Advertising, 5*(1), 37–45.

Chang, Y., Yan, J., Zhang, J., & Luo, J. (2010). Online in-game advertising effect: Examining the influence of a match between games and advertising. *Journal of Interactive Advertising, 11*(1), 63–73.

Chen, J. (2007). Flow in games (and everything else). *Commnications of the ACM, 50*(4), 31–34.

Chen, J., & Ringel, M. (2001). Can advergaming be the future of interactive advertising? *kpe*, 1–7.

Conroy, M. A., Hopkins, R. O., & Squire, L. R. (2005). On the contribution of perceptual fluency and priming to recognition memory. *Cognitive, Affective, & Behavioral Neuroscience, 5*(1), 14–20.

Cornwell, T. B., & Maignan, I. (1998). An international review of sponsorship research. *Journal of Advertising, 27*(1), 1–21.

Cowley, B., Charles, D., Black, M., & Hickey, R. (2008). Toward an understanding of flow in video games. *Computers in Entertainment, 6*(2), 1–27.

Coyle, J. R., & Thorson, E. (2001). The effects of progressive levels of interactivity and vividness in web marketing sites. *Journal of Advertising, 30*(3), 65–77.

Csikszentmihalyi, M. (1988). The flow experience and its significance for human psychology. In M. Csikszentmihalyi & I. S. Csikszentmihalyi (Eds.), *Optimal experience: Psychological studies of flow in consciousness* (pp. 15–35). New York: Cambridge University Press.

Csikszentmihalyi, M. (1990). *Flow: The psychology of optimal experience.* New York: Harper Collins.

De Houwer, J. (2007). A conceptual and theoretical analysis of evaluative conditioning. *Spanish Journal of Psychology, 10*(2), 230–241.

De Houwer, J., Baeyens, F., & Field, A. P. (2005). Associative learning of likes and dislikes: Some current controversies and possible ways forward. *Cognition and Emotion, 19*(2), 161–174.

De Houwer, J., Thomas, S., & Baeyens, F. (2001). Associative learning of likes and dislikes: A review of 25 years of research on human evaluative conditioning. *Psychological Bulletin, 127*(6), 853–869.

Dredge, S. (2010, June 24). *Barclaycard launches rollercoaster extreme iPhone advergame.* http://www.mobile-ent.biz/news/read/barclaycard-launches-rollercoaster-extreme-iphone-advergame

138 • *Michelle R. Nelson and Martin K. J. Waiguny*

Evans, N., & Hoy, M. (2011). *Got game? An investigation of parents' understanding of and attitudes toward advertising.* Paper presented at the annual conference of the American Academy of Advertising.

Eysenck, M. W., & Keane, M. T. (2000). *Cognitive psychology: A student's handbook.* Hove, UK: Psychology Press.

Farey-Jones, D. (2011, March 18). *First TV product placement returns 5:1 media value.* http://www.brandrepublic.com/news/1060352/First-TV-product-placement-returns-51-media- value/?DCMP=ILC-SEARCH

Friestad, M., & Wright, P. (1994). The Persuasion Knowledge Model: How people cope with persuasion attempts. *The Journal of Consumer Research, 21*(1), 1–31.

Gangadharbatla, H. (2008). Gender, arousal, and presence as predictors of recall of brands placed in video games. In S. Rodgers (Ed.), *Proceedings of the 2008 Conference of the American Academy of Advertising* (pp. 72–82). Columbia, MO: AAA.

Gao, Y. (2004). Appeal of online computer games: A user perspective. *The Electronic Library, 22*(1), 74–78.

Gartenberg, M., & Horwitz, J. (2004). *Game software publishing: Understanding motivations to combat publishing uncertainties* (pp. 22). New York: JupiterResearch.

Glass, Z. (2007). The effectiveness of product placement in video games. *Journal of Interactive Advertising, 8*(1), 1–27.

Goldberg, M. E., & Gorn, G. J. (1987). Happy and sad TV programs: How they affect reactions to commercials. *Journal of Consumer Research, 14*, 387–402.

Goodstein, R. C. (1993). Category-based applications and extensions in advertising: Motivating more extensive ad processing. *Journal of Consumer Research, 20*(1), 87–99.

Greenfield, P. M., DeWinstanley, P., Kilpatrick, H., & Kaye, D. (1994). Action video games and informal education: Effects on strategies for dividing visual attention. *Journal of Applied Developmental Psychology, 15*(1), 105–123.

Grimes, A., & Kitchen, P. J. (2007). Researching mere exposure effects to advertising. *International Journal of Market Research, 49*(2), 191–219.

Grodal, T. (2000). Video games and the pleasures of control. In D. Zillmann & P. Vorderer (Eds.), *Media entertainment: The psychology of its appeal* (pp. 197–213). Mahwah, NJ: Lawrence Erlbaum.

Gross, M. L. (2010). Advergames and the effects of game-product congruity. *Computers in Human Behavior, 26*(6), 1259–1265.

Gupta, P. B., & Lord, K. L. (1998). Product placement in movies: The effect of prominence and mode on audience recall. *Journal of Current Issues and Research in Advertising, 20*(1), 47–59.

Gurău, C. (2008). The influence of advergames on players' behaviour: An experimental study. *Electronic Markets, 18*(2), 106–116.

Hang, H., & Auty, S. (2011). Children playing branded video games: The impact of interactivity on product placement effectiveness. *Journal of Consumer Psychology, 21*(1), 65–72.

Hastie, R. (1984). Causes and effects of causal attribution. *Journal of Personality and Social Psychology, 46*(1), 44–56.

Hernandez, M. D. (2008). Determinants of children's attitudes towards "advergames": The case of Mexico. *Young Consumers, 9*(2), 112–120.

Hernandez, M. D., Minor, M. S., Suh, J., Chapa, S., & Salas, J. A. (2005). Brand recall in the advergaming environment. In M. R. Stafford & R. J. Faber (Eds.), *Advertising, promotion and new media* (pp. 298–319). Armonk, NY: M.E. Sharpe.

Hoffman, D. L., & Novak, T. P. (1997). A new marketing paradigm for electronic commerce. *The Information Society, 13*(Jan–Mar), 43–54.

Hudson, S., & Hudson, D. (2006). Branded entertainment: A new advertising technique or product placement in disguise? *Journal of Marketing Management, 22*(5/6), 489–504.

Juul, J. (2003). *The game, the player, the world: Looking for a heart of gameness.* Paper presented at the Level Up: Digital Games Research Conference.

Katz, H. (2010). *The media handbook, 4th ed.* New York: Routledge.

Kim, T., & Biocca, F. (1997). Telepresence via television: Two dimensions of telepresence may have different connections to memory and persuasion. *Journal of Computer-Mediated Communication, 3*(2).

Kretchmer, S. B. (2004). Advertainment: The evolution of product placement as a mass media marketing strategy. *Journal of Promotion Management, 10*(1/2), 37–54.

Kroeber-Riel, W. (1984). Emotional product differentiation by classical conditioning (with consequences for the "low-involvement hierarchy"). *Advances in Consumer Research, 11*, 538–453.

Kuittinen, J., Kultima, A., Niemelä, J., & Paavilainen, J. (2007). *Casual games discussion.* Paper presented at the 2007 conference on Future Play Toronto.

Kwak, D. H., Clavio, G. E., Eagleman, A. N., & Kim, K. T. (2010). Exploring the antecedents and consequences of personalizing sport video game experiences. *Sport Marketing Quarterly, 19*, 217–225.

Lambert, D. R. (1980). Transactional analysis as a congruity paradigm for advertising recall. *Journal of Advertising, 9*(2), 37–41.

Lang, A. (2000). The limited capacity model of mediated message processing. *Journal of Communication, 50*(1), 46–70.

Lang, A. (2009). The limited capacity model of motivated mediated message processing. In R. L. Nabi & M. B. Oliver (Eds.), *The SAGE handbook of media processes and effects* (pp. 193–204). Los Angeles: SAGE.

Law, S., & Braun-LaTour, K. A. (2004). Product placements: How to measure their impact. In L. J. Shrum (Ed.), *The psychology of entertainment media* (pp. 63–78). Mahwah, NJ: Lawrence Erlbaum.

Lazzaro, N. (2008). Why we play: Affect and the fun of games: Designing emotions for games, entertainment interfaces and interactive products. In A. Sears & J. A. Jacko (Eds.), *The human-computer interaction handbook: Fundamentals, evolving technologies, and emerging applications* (pp. 679–700). New York: Lawrence Erlbaum.

Lee, M., & Faber, R. J. (2007). Effects of product placement in on-line games on brand memory. *Journal of Advertising, 36*(4), 75–90.

Lewis, B., & Porter, L. (2010). In-game advertising effects: Examining player perceptions of advertising schema congruity in a massively multiplayer online role-playing game. *Journal of Interactive Advertising, 10*(2), 46–60.

Li, H., Daugherty, T., & Biocca, F. (2002). Impact of 3-D advertising on product knowledge, brand attitude, and purchase intention: The mediating role of presence. *Journal of Advertising, 31*(3), 43–57.

Lombard, M., & Ditton, T. (1997). At the heart of it all: The concept of presence. *Journal of Computer-Mediated Communication, 3*(2).

Lombard, M., & Snyder-Duch, J. (2001). Interactive advertising and presence: A framework. *Journal of Interactive Adertising, 1*(2), 56–65.

Lutz, R. J., MacKenzie, S. B., & Belch, G. E. (1983). Attitude toward the ad as a mediator of advertising effectiveness: Determinants and consequences. *Advances in Consumer Research, 10*, 532–539.

Machleit, K. A., & Wilson, R. D. (1988). Emotional feelings and attitude toward the advertisement: The roles of brand familiarity and repetition. *Journal of Advertising, 17*(3), 27–35.

MacKay, T., Ewing, M., Newton, F., & Windisch, L. (2009). The effect of product placement in computer games on brand attitude and recall. *International Journal of Advertising, 28*(3), 423–438.

MacKenzie, S. B., Lutz, R. J., & Belch, G. E. (1986). The role of attitude toward the ad as a mediator of advertising effectiveness: A test of competing explanations. *Journal of Marketing Research, 23*(2), 130–143.

Mackie, D. M., & Worth, L. T. (1989). Processing deficits and the mediation of positive affect in persuasion. *Journal of Personality and Social Psychology, 57*(1), 27–40.

Mallinckrodt, V., & Mizerski, D. (2007). The effects of playing an advergame on young children's perceptions, preferences, and requests. *Journal of Advertising, 36*(2), 87–100.

Maoz, E., & Tybout, A. M. (2002). The moderating role of involvement and differentiation in the evaluation of brand extensions. *Journal of Consumer Psychology, 12*(2), 119–131.

Marketing-Vox. (2008). Retrieved from http://www.marketingvox.com/dynamic-in-game-ads -invade-sims-3-041347

Marshall, J. (2010, November 16). *Zynga ramps up in-game ads, extends beyond FarmVille.* Retrieved from http://www.clickz.com/clickz/news/1898138 zynga-ramps-game-ads-extends-farmville

Mau, G., Silberer, G., & Constien, C. (2008). Communicating brands playfully. *International Journal of Advertising, 27*, 827–851.

McCarty, J. A. (2004). Product placement: The nature of the practice and potential avenues of inquiry. In L. J. Shrum (Ed.), *The psychology of entertainment media: Blurring the lines between entertainment and persuasion* (pp. 45–61). Mahwah, NJ: Lawrence Erlbaum.

Mehrabian, A., & Russell, J. A. (1974). *An approach to environmental psychology.* Cambridge, MA: The MIT Press.

Mendelsohn, H. (1966). *Mass entertainment.* New Haven, CT: College & University Press.

Minsky, M. (1980). Telepresence. *Omni, 2*(June), 45–51.

Moneta, G. B., & Csikszentmihalyi, M. (1996). The effect of perceived challenges and skills on the quality of subjective experience. *Journal of Personality, 64*(2), 275–310.

Moore, E. G., Mazvancheryl, S. K., & Rego, L. L. (1996). The Bolo game: Exploration of a high-tech virtual community. *Advances in Consumer Research, 23*(1), 167–171.

Moore, E. S. (2006). *It's a child's play: Advergaming and the online marketing of food to children.* Kaiser Family Foundation: University of Notre Dame.

Moorman, M., Neijens, P. C., & Smit, E. G. (2002). The effects of magazine-induced psychological responses and thematic congruence on memory and attitude toward the ad in a real-life setting. *Journal of Advertising, 31*(4), 27–40.

Nakamura, J., & Csikszentmihalyi, M. (2002). The concept of flow. In S. J. Lopez & C. R. Snyder (Eds.), *Handbook of positive psychology* (pp. 89–105). London: Oxford University Press.

Nakatsu, R., Rauterberg, M., & Vorderer, P. (2005). A new framework for entertainment computing: From passive to active experience. *Entertainment Computing—ICEC 2005*, 1–12.

Nelson, M. R. (2002). Recall of brand placements in computer/video games. *Journal of Advertising Research, 42*(2), 80–92.

Nelson, M. R. (2005). Exploring consumer response to "advergaming." In C. P. Haugtvedt, K. A. Machleit, & R. Yalch (Eds.), *Online consumer psychology: Understanding and influencing consumer behaviour in the virtual world* (pp. 167–194): Mahwah, NJ: Lawrence Erlbaum.

Nelson, M. R. (2008). The hidden persuaders. *Journal of Advertising, 37*(1), 113–126.

Nelson, M. R., Keum, H., & Yaros, R. A. (2004). Advertainment or adcreep? Game players' attitudes toward advertising and product placements in computer games. *Journal of Interactive Advertising, 5*(1), 3–21.

Nelson, M. R., Yang, J. J., & Yaros, R. (2008). *Fit and effectiveness: Investigating game genre-brand congruence for brand placements.* In S. Rodgers (Ed.), Annual Conference Proceedings of the American Academy of Advertising (p. 197). Columbia, MO: University of Missouri.

Nelson, M. R., Yaros, R. A., & Keum, H. (2006). Examining the influence of telepresence on spectator and player processing of real and fictitious brands in a computer game. *Journal of Advertising, 35*(4), 87–99.

New, K. (1991). Media planning to build brands. In Don Cowley (Ed.), *Understanding brands: By 10 people who do* (pp. 85–116). London: Kogan.

Nicovich, S. G. (2010). The effect of involvement on ad judgement in a computer-mediated environment: The mediating role of presence. *International Journal of Advertising, 29*(4), 597–620.

Novak, T. P., Hoffman, D. L., & Yung, Y. F. (2000). Measuring the customer experience in online environments: A structural modeling approach. *Marketing Science, 19*(1), 22–42.

Orland, K. (2011, January 6). *Analyst: Mobile game ad spending to increase tenfold by 2015.* http://www.gamasutra.com/view/news/32312/Analyst_Mobile_Game_Ad_ Spending_To_Increase_Tenfold_By_2015.php

Ozok, A. A., & Zaphiris, P. (2009). Online communities. *LNCS*(5621), 574–583.

Peters, S., Leshner, G., Bolls, P., & Wise, K. (2009). *The effects of advergames on game players' processing of embedded brands.* Paper presented at the annual meeting of the International Communication Association. Retrieved from http://www.allacademic. com/meta/p301128_index.html

Petty, R. E., & Cacioppo, C. (1986). The elaboration likelihood model of persuasion. *Advances in Experimental Social Psychology, 19*, 123–195.

Radd, D. (2007). The secrets of advergaming. *Businessweek.* Retrieved from http://www. businessweek.com/innovatecontent/may2007/d20070523_844955.htm

Rau, P. L. P., Peng, S. Y., & Yang, C. C. (2006). Time distortion for expert and novice online game players. *Cyberpsychology and Behavior, 9*(4), 396–403.

Rauterberg, M. (1995). About a framework for information and information processing of learning systems. In E. Falkenberg, W. Hesse, & A. Olive (Eds.), *Information system concepts—Towards a consolidation of views* (pp. 54–69). London: Chapman & Hall.

Reber, R., & Schwarz, N. (1999). Effects of perceptual fluency on judgments of truth. *Consciousness and Cognition, 8*(3), 338–342.

Reber, R., Schwarz, N., & Winkielman, P. (2004). Processing fluency and aesthetic pleasure: Is beauty in the perceiver's processing experience? *Personality and Social Psychology Review, 8*(4), 364–382.

Reber, R., Winkielman, P., & Schwarz, N. (1998). Effects of perceptual fluency on affective judgments. *Psychological Science, 9*(1), 45–48.

Redondo, I. (2009). *Measuring the influence of advergames on adolescents: The role of placement conspicuousness and play time on brand.* Paper presented at the EMAC 2009.

Ritterfeld, U., & Weber, R. (2006). Video games for entertainment and education. In P. Vorderer & J. Bryant (Eds.), *Playing video games: Motives, responses and consequences* (pp. 399–412). Mahwah, NJ: Lawrence Erlbaum.

Riva, G., Waterworth, J. A., & Waterworth, E. L. (2004). The layers of presence: A bio-cultural approach to understanding presence in natural and mediated environments. *Cyberpsychology and Behavior, 7*(4), 402–416.

Santos, E., Gonzalo, R., & Gisbert, F. (2007). Advergames: Overview. *International Journal Information Technologies and Knowledge, 1*, 203–208.

Schneider, L.-P., & Cornwell, T. B. (2005). Cashing in on crashes via brand placement in computer games. *International Journal of Advertising, 24*(3), 321–343.

Schwarz, N. (2004). Metacognitive experiences in consumer judgment and decision making. *Journal of Consumer Psychology, 14*(4), 332–348.

Sengupta, J., Goodstein, R. C., & Boninger, D. S. (1997). All cues are not created equal: Obtaining attitude persistence under low-involvement conditions. *Journal of Consumer Research, 23*(4), 351–361.

Severin, W. J., & Tankard, J. W., Jr. (1997). *Communication theories: Origins, methods, and uses in the mass media* New York: Longman.

Shapiro, S. (1999). When an ad's influence is beyond our conscious control: Perceptual and conceptual fluency effects caused by incidental ad exposure. *Journal of Consumer Research, 26*(1), 16–36.

Sherry, J. L. (2004). Flow and media enjoyment. *Communication Theory, 14*(4), 328–347.

Shih, C.-F. (1998). Conceptualizing consumer experiences in cyberspace. *European Journal of Marketing, 32*(7/8), 655–663.

Shrum, L. J. (Ed.). (2004). *The psychology of entertainment media: Blurring the lines between entertainment and persuasion.* Mahwah, NJ: Lawrence Erlbaum.

Smith, J. H., & Just, S. N. (2009). Playful persuasion: The rhetorical potential of advergames. *Nordicom Review, 30*(2), 53–68.

Steuer, J. (1995). Defining virtual reality: Dimensions determining telepresence. In F. Biocca & M. R. Levy (Eds.), *Communication in the age of virtual reality* (pp. 33–56). Hillsdale, NJ: Lawrence Erlbaum.

Svahn, M. (2005). Future-proofing advergaming: A systematisation for the media buyer. *Proceedings of the second Australasian conference on interactive entertainment* (Vol. 123, pp. 187–191). Sydney, Australia: Creativity & Cognition Audios Press.

Sweller, J., & Chandler, P. (1994). Why some material is difficult to learn. *Cognition and Instruction, 12*(3), 185–233.

Taylor, S. E., & Crocker, J. (1981). Schematic bases of social information processing. In E. T. Higgins, C. P. Herman, & M. P. Zanna (Eds.), *Social cognition: The Ontario symposium* (pp. 89–134). Hillsdale, NJ: Lawrence Erlbaum.

Thomson, D. M. (2010). Marshmallow power and frooty treasures: Disciplining the child consumer through online cereal advergaming. *Critical Studies in Media Communication, 27*(5), 438–454.

Treffiletti, C. (2011, March 4). *Dear marketers: Start playing (in) games.* http://www.treffiletti. com/blog/2011/03/dear-marketers-start-playing-in-games-mediapost-3211.html

Trevino, L. K., & Webster, J. (1992). Flow in computer-mediated communication: Electronic mail and voice mail evaluation and impacts. *Communication Research, 19*(5), 539–573.

Tulving, E., & Schacter, D. L. (1990). Priming and human memory systems. *Science, 247,* 301–306.

van Lankveld, G., Spronck, P., van den Herik, H., & Rauterberg, M. (2010). Incongruity-based adaptive game balancing. In H. van den Herik & P. Spronck (Eds.), *Advances in computer games* (Vol. 6048, pp. 208–220). Berlin/Heidelberg: Springer.

van Reijmersdal, E. A. (2009). Brand placement prominence: Good for memory! Bad for attitudes? *Journal of Advertising Research, 49*(2), 151–153.

van Reijmersdal, E. A., Jansz, J., Peters, O., & Van Noort, G. (2010). The effects of interactive brand placements in online games on children's cognitive, affective, and conative brand responses. *Computers in Human Behavior, 26*(6), 1787–1794.

Vedrashko, I. (2006). *Advertising in computer games.* Cambridge, MA: Massachusetts Institute of Technology.

Von Restorff, H. (1933). Über die Wirkung von Bereichsbildungen im Spurenfeld. *Psychological Research, 18*(1), 299–342.

Vorderer, P., Klimmt, C., & Ritterfeld, U. (2004). Enjoyment: At the heart of media entertainment. *Communication Theory, 14*(4), 388–408.

Waiguny, M. K. J. (2011). *Entertaining Persuasion: Die Wirkungen von Advergames auf Kinder.* Wiesbaden, Germany: Gabler.

Waiguny, M. K. J., Nelson, M. R., & Terlutter, R. (2010). Persuading playfully? The effects of persuasion knowledge and positive affect on children's attitudes, brand beliefs and behaviors. In W.-N. Lee (Ed.), *Proceedings of the 2010 conference of the American Academy of Advertising* (pp. 67–70). Minneapolis, MN.

Waiguny, M. K. J., Nelson, M. R., & Terlutter, R. (2011). *Go with the flow: How persuasion knowledge and game challenge and flow state impact children's brand attitude.* Paper presented at the annual conference of the American Academy of Advertising.

Waiguny, M. K. J., & Terlutter, R. (2010). Commercial or not? Differences in the perception of TV-advertisments and advergames by children. In S. Okazaki (Ed.), *Proceedings of the 9th international conference on research in advertising.* Madrid: ESIC.

Waiguny, M. K. J., & Terlutter, R. (2011). Differences in children's processing of advergames and TV commercials. In S. Okazaki (Ed.), *Advances in advertising research* (Vol. 2, pp. 35–51). Wiesbaden, Germany: Gabler.

Waiguny, M. K. J., Terlutter, R., Wiegele, M., & Nelson, M. R. (2010). *In-game advertising drives brand recall and liking for motorsport game among heavy users.* Paper presented at the EMAC 2010.

Walsh, P., Kim, Y., & Ross, S. D. (2008). Brand recall and recognition: A comparison of television and sport video games as presentation modes. *Sport Marketing Quarterly, 17,* 201–208.

Wei, M. L., Fischer, E., & Main, K. J. (2008). An examination of the effects of activating persuasion knowledge on consumer response to brands engaging in covert marketing. *Journal of Public Policy and Marketing, 27*(1), 34–44.

Whittlesea, B. W. A. (1993). Illusions of familiarity. *Journal of Experimental Psychology: Learning, Memory & Cognition, 19*(6), 1235–1253.

Winkielman, P., Schwarz, N., Fazendeiro, T., & Reber, R. (2003). The hedonic marking of processing fluency: Implications for evaluative judgment. In J. Musch & K. C. Klauer (Eds.), *The psychology of evaluation: Affective processes in cognition and emotion* (pp. 189–217). Mahwah, NJ: Erlbaum.

Winkler, T., & Buckner, K. (2006). Receptiveness of gamers to embedded brand messages in advergames: Attitudes towards product placement. *Journal of Interactive Advertising, 7*(1), 37–46.

Wise, K., Bolls, P. D., Kim, H., Venkataraman, A., & Meyer, R. (2008). Enjoyment of advergame and brand attitudes: The impact of thematic relevance. *Journal of Interactive Advertising, 9*(1), 1–11.

Wollslager, M. E. (2009). Children's awareness of online advertising on Neopets: The effect of media literacy training on recall. *SIMILE, 9*(2), 31–53.

Yang, H. L., & Wang, C. S. (2008). Product placement of computer games in cyberspace. *Cyberpsychology and Behavior, 11*(4), 399–404.

Yang, M., Roskos-Ewoldsen, D. R., Dinu, L., & Arpan, L. M. (2006). The effectiveness of "in-game" advertising: Comparing college students' explicit and implicit memory for brand names. *Journal of Advertising, 35*(4), 143–152.

Yi, Y. (1990). Cognitive and affective priming effects of the context for print advertisements. *Journal of Advertising, 19*(2), 40–48.

Youn, S., & Lee, M. (2005). Advergame playing motivations and effectiveness. In M. R. Stafford & R. J. Faber (Eds.), *Advertising, promotion and new media* (pp. 320–347). Armonk, NY: M.E. Sharpe.

Section II

The Programs Between the Ads: The Persuasive Power of Entertainment Media

6

The Stories TV Tells: How Fictional TV Narratives Shape Normative Perceptions and Personal Values

L. J. Shrum
University of Texas at San Antonio
San Antonio, Texas

Jaehoon Lee
University of Houston–Clear Lake
Houston, Texas

Narrative entertainment television is all about the stories. These stories can be gripping, arousing, heartrending, amusing—they run the entire gamut of emotions. We often become spellbound by the stories, even transported into them (Carpenter & Green, this volume). But they are just stories. They are quite often fictional, sometimes fantastical, and thus surely have little effect on us past the momentary thoughts and emotions that are elicited while we view. Or at least that's what most people seem to think (Shrum, Burroughs, & Rindfleisch, 2005; see Comstock & Powers, this volume). However, there is actually considerable evidence to the contrary (Morgan, Shanahan, & Signorielli, 2012). In this chapter, we put forth the argument that the programs we watch on television, even the fictional ones, do have enduring effects on us. Every piece of information we process gets stored in memory for potential use later. Moreover, whether and how that information is used in the judgment process depends on a variety of factors, including the type of judgment that is required, television viewing frequency, and characteristics of the viewing experience.

In the following sections, we review a program of research spanning the last 20 years that has focused on not only documenting the particular effects of television viewing, but also specifying the cognitive processes that account for how the effect occurs in the head. We discuss two separate but complementary models that reflect two different types of underlying psychological processes. The separate models reflect the fact that the way in which television influences judgments depends on the type of judgment (Shrum, 2004). Thus, we specify a model for how television influences normative perceptions (e.g., what others have and do) and a model for how television influences attitudes, values, and beliefs. As we demonstrate, not only are these distinct models, but the manner in which television influences the two types of judgments is in many ways opposite of each other.

CULTIVATION THEORY

Our research on the psychological processes underlying television viewing effects takes its starting point from cultivation theory. Cultivation theory is a broad theory that relates media content with particular outcomes. The theory has two components. The first is that the content of television programs—whether they be "fiction" such as soap operas or "fact" such as news—present a systematic distortion of reality.[1] That is, the world as it is portrayed on television differs in important and sometimes dramatic ways from how the real world is constituted. For example, the world of television tends to be more affluent (O'Guinn & Shrum, 1997), more violent (Gerbner, Gross, Morgan, & Signorielli, 1980), more maritally unfaithful (Lichter, Lichter, & Rothman, 1994), and more populated with doctors, lawyers, and police officers (DeFleur, 1964; Head, 1954; Lichter et al., 1994; Smythe, 1954) than the real world.

The second component is that frequent exposure to these distorted images results in their internalization: The more people watch television, the more they develop values, attitudes, beliefs, and perceptions that are consistent with the world as it is portrayed on television. The internalization of the television message may result in the learning of television "facts": TV viewing has been shown to be positively correlated with estimates of the number of doctors, lawyers, and police officers in the real world (Shrum, 1996, 2001), the prevalence of violence (Gerbner et al., 1980; Shrum, Wyer, & O'Guinn, 1998), and the prevalence of ownership of expensive products (O'Guinn & Shrum, 1997; Shrum, 2001). In addition, internalization can take the form of learning the lessons of television: Heavy television viewing has been shown to be associated with greater anxiety and fearfulness (Bryant, Carveth, & Brown, 1981), greater faith in doctors (Volgy & Schwarz, 1980), greater pessimism about marriage (Shrum, 1999), and greater interpersonal mistrust (Gerbner et al., 1980; Shrum, 1999).

Research on aspects of the cultivation effect has been a contentious area. Although studies supporting cultivation theory are not in short supply, there have been a number of critiques of cultivation, including critiques of theory, method, analysis, and interpretation (cf. Hirsch, 1980; Hughes, 1980; Newcomb, 1978). These critiques, while having some validity, have been dealt with at length elsewhere (Gerbner, Gross, Morgan, & Signorielli, 1994; Morgan & Shanahan, 1997; Shanahan & Morgan, 1999). Suffice it to say that the critiques revolve around trade-offs in the measurement of the independent variable, television viewing, and consequent issues of causal direction. Gerbner and colleagues take the position that measurement of television viewing best captures their concept of cultivation (Gerbner et al., 2002). More specifically, it better approximates a pattern of viewing over years, because television, in their view, tends to be a habitual process, and thus measurement of viewing provides more validity than does a brief exposure to a particular stimulus (e.g., a program segment, an entire program, or even a series of programs) under experimental conditions. Others point out that the resulting correlational data leave causality ambiguous. Indeed, most of the critiques of cultivation revolve around third variable or reverse causality explanations (Hirsch, 1980; Hughes, 1980; Zillmann, 1980). Experiments have been used to address these causal issues (for a review, see Ogles, 1987). However, experiments can be criticized because they may provide only a short exposure to particular television or film content, which may not fully capture the long-term nature of cultivation. Nevertheless, as we discuss presently, experiments can be useful in testing some of the processes underlying cultivation effects.

Three important (and somewhat interrelated) reasons for the contentious debate regarding the reliability and validity of the cultivation effect are that the effects are for the most part small ones (Morgan & Shanahan, 1997), the effects are not always consistently obtained (Hawkins & Pingree, 1982), and when they are obtained, implementation of certain statistical controls (e.g., demographics, activities outside the home, population size) has been shown to reduce the cultivation effect to nonsignificance (cf. Hirsch, 1980; Hughes, 1980). Indeed, meta-analyses of studies investigating the cultivation effect find an overall correlation coefficient of about .09, and this relation tends to vary slightly, but not significantly, across various demographic and situational variables (Morgan & Shanahan, 1997). The issues of small effect size and lack of reliability make cultivation effects particularly vulnerable to claims that the noted effects are spurious. That is, some other unmeasured variable may easily account for the entire relation between television viewing and judgments when the effect's size is small.

The issue of small effect sizes has been addressed through a variety of arguments. First, small effect sizes, if real, are not trivial. As Gerbner et al. (2002) note, there are many instances in which a very small shift on some variable (e.g., global warming, voting behavior) has important consequences. Variables such as violence and aggression likely fall into this category as well (Bushman & Anderson, 2001). Second, and more pertinent to the focus of this chapter, small main effects may simply be masking larger effects within certain groups. This notion formed the basis of Gerbner et al.'s (1980) refinements to cultivation theory that introduced the concepts of mainstreaming and resonance, which postulated that direct experience variables may moderate the cultivation effect (see also Shrum & Bischak, 2001). The notion also forms the basis of our focus on psychological processes: Variables that affect the judgment process may also moderate the cultivation effect.

First-Order and Second-Order Cultivation Effects

Early cultivation research used a number of ways to measure possible effects of television viewing. One general type measured people's perceptions of the frequency with which certain things occur in the real world (e.g., percentage of people who have been victims of violence, percentage of the work force made up of lawyers or doctors) or the risk of something occurring (e.g., probability of being involved in a crime). A second general type assessed people's personal beliefs and values, such as their level of trust of the average person or their own level of anomie (for reviews, see Shanahan & Morgan, 1999). Although Gerbner and colleagues treated these measures as indicators of a common underlying concept, Hawkins and Pingree (1982) noted that the two types of measures seemed to represent different psychological concepts. The frequency and probability measures, which they termed first-order measures, represented estimates that often had actual answers, and thus these estimates could be objectively determined for actual occurrence in both society and the world of television (e.g., frequency of violent crime). In contrast, the belief measures, which they termed second-order measures, were subjective judgments that assessed personal attitudes, values, and beliefs, and thus had no direct counterpart in the television world, but could only be inferred.

Hawkins and Pingree (1982; see also Hawkins & Pingree, 1990) went on to make two other observations about these two measures. The first was that cultivation effects based on the two measures seemed to differ in both size and reliability: First-order measures tended to be larger and more reliable than second-order ones. The second observation was that the two measures were relatively uncorrelated. Based on these two observed patterns, Hawkins and Pingree thus speculated that the processes underlying the two types of cultivation effects might be different.

As it turns out, they were right, and this distinction in underlying processes for first- and second-order measures is embodied in the two models we present next. The distinction between the two types of measures is captured by the concept of online versus memory-based processes (Hastie & Park, 1986). First-order judgments are generally memory-based; they are formed by recalling information currently stored in memory. Second-order judgments are generally constructed through an online process; information that is being processed in real time (reading the newspaper, watching a TV program) is used to update current judgments or construct new ones. Given this, it follows that the ways in which online and memory-based judgments differ should mirror differences in processing between first- and second-order cultivation measures. This has two important implications: Television may influence each of the two types of judgments in different ways, and different factors may mediate or moderate the relation between television viewing and the two types of judgments. In the following sections, we build on this reasoning by describing independent models for first-order (memory-based) and second-order (online) cultivation judgments.

THE ACCESSIBILITY MODEL FOR FIRST-ORDER CULTIVATION EFFECTS

Model Assumptions

The accessibility model begins with two general propositions. The first is that viewing increases the accessibility of information in memory that pertains to typical cultivation judgments (e.g., violence, occupations, affluence). Accessibility refers to the ease of recalling information from memory; the more accessible information is in memory, the easier it is to recall. The second general proposition is that first-order, memory-based judgments are constructed through heuristic processing. When people process heuristically, they do not carefully consider all information in memory before constructing their judgments; instead, they take a cognitive shortcut and consider only a small subset of available information. More specifically, the model assumes that people apply the availability heuristic (Tversky & Kahneman, 1973), and base their judgments on the ease with which relevant information can be recalled, or apply the simulation heuristic (Kahneman & Tversky, 1982), and base their judgments on the ease with which a particular thing or event can be imagined.

In using the availability heuristic, people base their judgments of things such as frequency or probability on how easily a relevant example comes to mind: The easier it is to recall, the higher the estimate. Thus, people tend to estimate that words in the English language that start with the letter *K* occur more often than words that have *K* as the third letter (Tversky & Kahneman, 1973, study 3), even though the opposite is in fact the case. This result is presumably because words tend to be organized in memory according to their first letter, and thus words that start with *K* are more easily recalled. Similarly, 80% of people tend to estimate that accidents account for more deaths than strokes, even though strokes account for about 85% more deaths than accidents (Lichtenstein, Slovic, Fischhoff, Layman, & Combs, 1978). Again, this is presumably because accidents are easier to recall or imagine than strokes.

When judging frequency or probability, a relevant example may not be available in memory (i.e., present in memory) or if available, not particularly accessible (i.e., not easily retrieved). Thus, the availability heuristic cannot be applied. In these instances, people may resort to basing their estimates on the ease with which a relevant exemplar can be imagined. This is an example of the simulation heuristic. Supporting this notion, research has shown that when people are induced to imagine a particular event such as winning a contest (Gregory, Cialdini, & Carpenter, 1982) or contracting a disease (Sherman, Cialdini, Schwartzman, & Reynolds, 1985), they provide higher estimates of the probability that they will experience these events compared to people who are not induced to imagine such events. These relations are mediated by ease of imagining (Sherman et al., 1985).

Relation to media consumption. The studies just noted, along with numerous others, clearly document that accessibility of relevant examples or ease of construction of a scenario influences estimates of frequency and probability. Those with more accessible examples or greater ease of construction provide higher estimates. This is shown to occur in both experimental studies and field studies—but what influences this accessibility? Clearly, in the experimental studies, accessibility is manipulated. And what of the field studies of Lichtenstein et al. (1978)? Why did people tend to greatly overestimate the number of deaths caused by accidents, but greatly underestimate deaths caused by strokes? Lichtenstein et al. speculate that accessibility is influenced by media coverage, suggesting that media publicity of such dramatic events as accidents and homicides increase accessibility of these examples relative to less dramatic and publicized causes of death such as strokes. This speculation was supported by a content analysis of newspaper articles showing just such differences in coverage (Combs & Slovic, 1979).

These studies suggest that media consumption may influence the accessibility of constructs that are commonly portrayed in television programs. It follows, then, that differences in media consumption (all other things being equal) may influence levels of accessibility of relevant constructs. If so, then for memory-based judgments, if the availability or simulation heuristic is used, then heavier media consumers should provide higher estimates of frequency or probability than lighter media consumers should. In fact, this is exactly what cultivation theory predicts.

Model Propositions

Based on the general propositions related to accessibility and heuristic processing, five specific propositions can be formulated that comprise the accessibility model: (1) television viewing influences accessibility, (2) accessibility mediates the cultivation effect, (3) television exemplars are not source-discounted, (4) motivation to process information moderates the cultivation effect, and (5) ability to process information moderates the cultivation effect.

Proposition 1: Viewing increases accessibility. Proposition 1 posits that television viewing increases the accessibility of constructs that are frequently portrayed in television programs. Examples include crime, violence, affluence, marital strife, and occupations such as doctors, lawyers, and police officers. All are very common television fare. Proposition 1 was first tested in a study that operationalized accessibility as the speed with which judgments could be generated (Shrum & O'Guinn, 1993; Shrum, O'Guinn, Semenik, & Faber, 1991). In the first part of the study, participants were asked to generate a number of different estimates, such as the percentage of Americans who are victims of a crime in an average year or percentage of Americans who have maids or servants. Later, we measured participants' frequency of television viewing. The results showed that heavy viewers not only gave higher estimates than light viewers (cultivation effect), they also made the judgments faster (accessibility effect). Other studies replicated those findings using multiple operationalizations of viewing frequency, accessibility, dependent measures, and control variables (Busselle & Shrum, 2003; O'Guinn & Shrum, 1997; Shrum, 1996).

Proposition 2: Accessibility mediates the cultivation effect. Proposition 2 is based on the assumption regarding the application of the availability heuristic, and combines the effects of television viewing frequency on magnitude of estimates and degree of accessibility into one test:

Proposition 2 received a partial test by Shrum & O'Guinn (1993). In that

study, when speed of response was used as a statistical control variable, the cultivation effect was eliminated, which provides limited support for mediation. In a later study, Shrum (1996) provided more direct evidence of mediation, showing that viewing frequency was related to both speed of response and magnitude of estimates, that speed of response was related to the magnitude of the estimates, and that controlling for speed of response significantly reduced the cultivation effect (see Figure 6.1). This pattern of results is consistent with partial mediation (Baron & Kenny, 1986).

Proposition 2 also received support in a study by Busselle (2001). That study directly manipulated accessibility. This was accomplished by having some participants provide their cultivation judgments in the usual manner (provide judgments, followed by television viewing frequency), but had others first recall an example of the construct being estimated (e.g., percentage of people who cheat on their spouses). The latter procedure eliminated the cultivation effect. Presumably, having both heavy and light viewers recall an example made those examples equally accessible in memory,

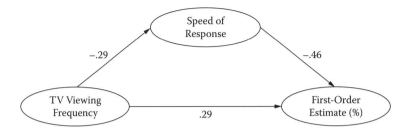

FIGURE 6.1
Path model showing mediating role of accessibility in the cultivation effect. Coefficients represent average of results across dependent variables (see Shrum, L. J., *Human Communication Research, 22,* 482–509, 1996).

thus eliminating the accessibility advantage of heavier viewers, and in turn eliminating the accessibility bias in judgments of heavier viewers.

Proposition 3: Television exemplars are not source-discounted. The third proposition is that the television-related exemplars that are recalled from memory in the process of constructing a judgment are not source-discounted. For example, propositions 1 and 2 state that when forming a first-order cultivation judgment (e.g., what percentage of Americans are millionaires), people will attempt to recall an example of one, and base their frequency judgment on how easy it is to generate an example (or imagine one). Television viewing increases the accessibility of these exemplars, and thus heavy viewers find them easier to recall, and thus make higher estimates. However, most people would not knowingly base real-world estimates on the recall of fictional television information. Thus, in order for the television exemplars to still have an effect, people must not generally attend to source information when constructing the judgment, and thus do not source-discount. This process is consistent with one that is relatively automatic and made without much effort or scrutiny.

We tested proposition 3 in two experiments (Shrum et al., 1998). To do so, we created conditions in which we induced people to source-discount prior to their judgments. If source-discounting occurs spontaneously (i.e., people normally source-discount), the source-discounting conditions should have no effect on judgments. However, if people normally do not source-discount, then inducing them to do so should eliminate the cultivation effect. This was what we found. When we induced participants to source-discount by reminding them of their television viewing habits prior to their judgments (source priming) or reminding them of their viewing habits as well as their possible relation to the judgments (relation priming), the cultivation effect was eliminated. However, under normal (no-prime) conditions in which participants were not primed with source information, the usual robust cultivation effect was observed. These findings were observed for estimates of both crime and occupational prevalence.

The general pattern of results can be seen in Figure 6.2. One additional point regarding the pattern of results is worth noting. As hypothesized, the slope of the line was significant (indicating a cultivation effect) only in the no-prime (control) condition. Moreover, as the figure shows, this effect occurred because only heavier viewers were affected by the source- and relation-priming conditions. This pattern is also consistent with our general model. Because light viewers should have relatively little television information stored in memory, inducing them to source-discount television should have little effect. And that too is what we found.

Tests of propositions 1–3 have focused on showing aspects of heuristic processing and demonstrating its influence on the cultivation effect. Propositions 4 and 5 focus on manipulating heuristic processing. Because heuristics are judgment simplification processes, they are usually made

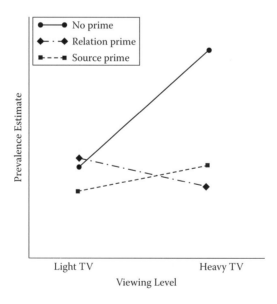

FIGURE 6.2

Prevalence estimates as a function of priming condition and level of TV viewing. Represents pattern of results across dependent variables (see Shrum, L. J., Wyer, R. S., & O'Guinn, T. C., *Journal of Consumer Research,* 24, 447–458, 1998).

automatically, without conscious awareness (Kahneman & Frederick, 2002). Moreover, simplifying judgments is generally desirable when either the motivation or ability to process information is low (Petty & Cacioppo, 1986). Propositions 4 and 5 pertain to these types of situations.

Proposition 4: Motivation to process information moderates the cultivation effect. Heuristic processing tends to be accentuated when motivation to process information is low, and conversely, reduced when motivation to process information is high (Sherman & Corty, 1984). If so, and the cultivation effect occurs because people process heuristically, then inducing them to reduce their reliance on heuristics should reduce or eliminate the cultivation effect. This position was tested by manipulating motivation to process, and specifically, by inducing some participants to be motivated to provide accurate judgments (Shrum, 2001). We expected this manipulation to reduce heuristic processing, and thus reduce the cultivation effect. In contrast, we also gave some participants instructions to process heuristically (answer with the first impression that comes to mind), and a third (control) group was given no instructions other than to simply provide the estimates.

We expected that the heuristic group and the control group would exhibit cultivation effects, and of roughly the same magnitude. In other words, if people generally process heuristically when forming their judgments, as we have proposed, then giving them instructions to do what they would otherwise do anyway should have no effect. In contrast, motivating them to be accurate in their judgments should cause them to consider information other than that which is most accessible, and thus decrease reliance on television information. Moreover, this decrease in reliance should occur only for heavy viewers, because they were the only ones using television information in the first place. The results supported our hypotheses, and the general pattern can be seen in Figure 6.3. Across three different dependent variables (estimates of crime, occupation, and affluence), cultivation effects were observed in the heuristic and control condition, but were eliminated in the systematic condition. Moreover, just as with the source-discounting results described earlier, the motivation manipulation only affected heavy viewers.

Proposition 5: Ability to process information moderates the cultivation effect. The final proposition tests the second condition under which heuristic processing tends to be accentuated versus attenuated. Along with motivation to process information, the ability to process also affects heuristic processing. When ability to process information is low, such as when someone is

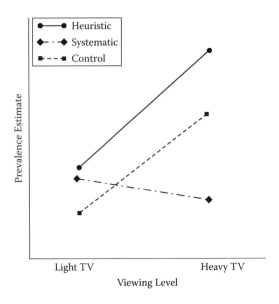

FIGURE 6.3
Prevalence estimates as a function of processing condition and level of TV viewing. Represents pattern of results across dependent variables (see Shrum, L. J., *Human Communication Research*, 27, 94–120, 2001).

distracted, under time pressure, or the material is difficult to read or understand, people again turn to cognitive shortcuts to simplify the judgment process.

To test this proposition, we constructed a field experiment that manipulated these variables naturally (Shrum, 2007). We did this by manipulating whether respondents completed our study through a mail survey or a telephone survey. Because people tend to feel under more time pressure in telephone surveys than mail surveys (but express the same level of involvement), we expected the telephone survey participants to engage in more heuristic processing than those in the mail survey, and thus exhibit larger cultivation effects. The results were consistent with our theoretical reasoning. Across five different dependent variables, the cultivation effect was substantially stronger in telephone survey conditions (average β = .26) than in mail survey conditions (average β = .10).

Model Integration

Taken together, the five propositions can be integrated to provide a model that describes when and how cultivation effects occur for first-order cultivation judgments. This model integration can be seen in Figure 6.4. Starting from when a cultivation-related judgment is required (top of diagram), the flow diagram traces the steps (and conditions) that dictate whether a cultivation effect is obtained. Note that there are in fact a number of barriers that can inhibit cultivation effects (ability to process,

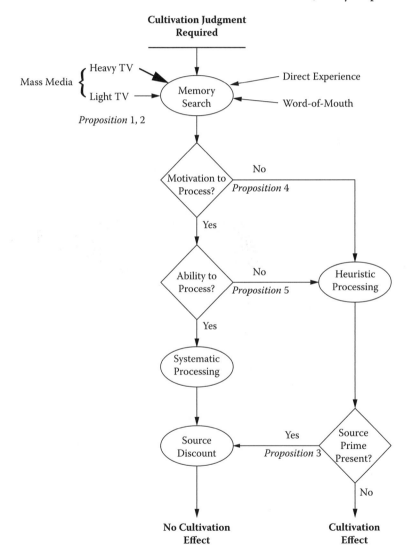

FIGURE 6.4

Flow diagram of the heuristic processing model of television effects. Circles represent mental processes. The thicker arrow from Heavy TV to Memory Search indicates a greater contribution to the search process.

motivation to process, source discounting), which may explain why cultivation effects that are often observed in research tend to be small. However, when conditions that accentuate the propensity to process heuristically are present, cultivation effects tend to be very robust.

As noted earlier, the accessibility model pertains only to first-order cultivation effects. Next, we turn to understanding second-order cultivation effects. Because first-order and second-order judgments are made through fundamentally different processes, as we argue and demonstrate next, the models that explain first- and second-order cultivation processes are also fundamentally different.

THE ONLINE PROCESS MODEL FOR SECOND-ORDER CULTIVATION EFFECTS

The accessibility model just reviewed pertains to judgments that are memory-based. However, these judgments are actually made relatively infrequently (Hastie & Park, 1986). In contrast, online judgments are made all the time. They occur spontaneously and with little effort. Examples include forming an impression of someone as he or she passes by, forming or updating an attitude about a person or situation while watching a television program or reading an advertisement, or deciding whom to vote for based on watching a debate. All (or at least much of) the information used to make the judgments comes from information that is received and processed in real time, rather than through the recall of information from memory.

For the online process model we have proposed for second-order cultivation judgments, we have adopted a persuasion model. In this model, television portrayals operate like a persuasive communication. The consistent messages that are woven throughout television portrayals (e.g., freedom, self-reliance, just world, dangerous world, money indicates success) have an influence on viewers' attitudes, values, and beliefs, and the influence is proportionate to the amount of viewing. Hence, the more people watch television, the more their attitudes, values, and beliefs resemble those that are espoused in television narratives.

If the persuasion model analogy is valid, there are a number of implications that flow from it for the processes that underlie second-order cultivation effects. First, frequent viewing of the same messages should result in attitude shifts toward the dominant messages of television narratives. This is precisely what cultivation posits (Gerbner & Gross, 1976). The persuasion model also has implications for how different processing factors may influence the cultivation effect. For example, the Elaboration Likelihood Model (Petty & Cacioppo, 1986) posits that motivation to process information increases persuasion (at least when the message arguments are strong ones). Under high motivation conditions, people follow the central route to persuasion. They consider arguments more carefully and engage in greater depth of processing. Thus, in applying these concepts to the cultivation effect, higher motivation to process information should increase cultivation effects. Similarly, ability to process information also increases persuasion. That is, when conditions allow people to pay close attention to a message, persuasion increases. Applied to the cultivation effect, a higher ability to process information should result in a larger cultivation effect. Note that these two predictions are actually the opposite of the effects of motivation and ability described in the accessibility model for first-order cultivation effects (cf. Shrum, 2001, 2007).

Tests of the Model

Motivation and ability. Although testing of the online processing model has not been as extensive as testing of the accessibility model, two sets of studies have tested different aspects of the online processing model. The first tested the proposition that both motivation and ability to process information during the television viewing process moderate second-order cultivation effects (Shrum, Burroughs, & Rindfleisch, 2005). To do so, the studies examined the cultivation of materialism. Whereas research on the relation between television viewing and perceptions of societal affluence (first-order judgment) have been frequent, cultivation research on materialism has been relatively scarce. However, television portrays very clear and consistent messages that possessions increase happiness and signal success (O'Guinn & Shrum, 1997). Thus, we expected that frequency of viewing frequency should be positively correlated with levels of materialism.

However, the persuasion model (specifically, the Elaboration Likelihood Model) suggests that motivation and ability will moderate this effect. Greater motivation and ability should each be associated with stronger cultivation effects. To test these propositions, we used need for cognition as a surrogate measure of motivation to process information (Cacioppo & Petty, 1982). Need for cognition refers to the extent to which people enjoy processing information and being cognitively engaged. For ability to process, we used a measure of chronic attention to programming during viewing (Rubin, Perse, & Taylor, 1988). The results supported our predictions. As can be seen in Figure 6.5, cultivation effects were stronger for those higher in need for cognition and for those who generally pay more attention during viewing (although cultivation effects were obtained for everyone). A follow-up experiment provided additional support, showing that viewers who are high in need for cognition tend to elaborate more during viewing, have more positive cognitions, and tend to become more transported into the narrative than low-need-for-cognition viewers.

Narrative transportation. Although the research just described is consistent with the online processing model, there were several study limitations. First, the studies were primarily correlational, and thus limit claims of causality. Second, the retrospective nature of survey methods hampered the understanding of what is actually going on during the viewing process. To address these limitations, we conducted an experiment that manipulated exposure to narratives related to materialism (Shrum, Lee,

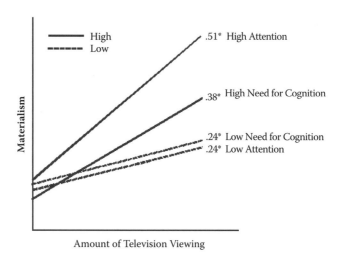

* *p* < .001

FIGURE 6.5
Materialism as a function of need for cognition and television viewing and as a function of the attention and television viewing. (see Shrum, L. J., Burroughs, J. E., & Rindfleisch, A., *Journal of Consumer Research*, 32, 473–479, 2005).

Burroughs, and Rindfleisch, 2011). Under the guise of investigating the relations between ads and television content, we had some participants view a 20-min clip from the movie *Wall Street* (high materialism condition) and other participants view a 20-min excerpt from the movie *Gorillas in the Mist* (low materialism condition). We also had participants indicate the extent to which they were transported into the narrative while they viewed the clips (Busselle & Bilandzic, 2008; Green & Brock, 2000). Narrative transportation is an individual difference variable that measures the extent to which audience members (readers, listeners, viewers) are absorbed into the world of the narrative. Transported viewers become engrossed in the story, are highly involved and cognitively engaged, think vivid thoughts, and react emotionally to the narrative (Green & Brock, 2000; see Carpenter and Green, this volume). When viewers are highly transported into the narrative, they may suspend disbelief, actively avoid counterarguing, and ignore facts that may contradict the narrative's message (Green, Garst, & Brock, 2004).

Based on these findings, we expected that those viewing the high materialistic narrative (*Wall Street*) would indicate more support for material values (Richins & Dawson, 1992) than those viewing the low materialistic narrative. However, we also expected that narrative transportation would moderate this effect, such that viewers who reported being more transported into the narrative would be the most persuaded. The results confirmed these hypotheses (see Figure 6.6). In fact, only those who were highly transported into the narrative showed a cultivation effect.

Taken together, the two sets of studies test aspects of the online processing model, and these tests provide considerable support for the theoretical framework. For second-order (online) cultivation judgments such as attitudes, values, and beliefs, television information influences judgments during viewing, as information is processed. These judgments are spontaneous, internally generated, and affected by viewer involvement, attention, and transportation into the narrative. In contrast, for first-order (memory-based) cultivation judgments, which are externally generated through some elicitation, television information influences judgments at the time the judgment is elicited, and does so through the recall of relevant information from memory. Moreover, the judgments are influenced by the people's motivation and ability to search memory for relevant information. Thus, the processes by which television viewing influences first- and second-order cultivation judgments are very different.

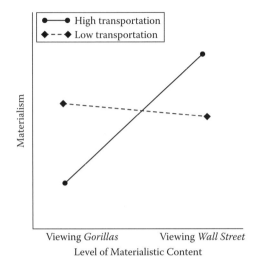

FIGURE 6.6

Materialism as a function of narrative transportation and television viewing. Represents the general pattern of effects (see Shrum, L. J., Lee, J., Burroughs, J. E., & Rindfleisch, A., *Human Communication Research*, 37, 34–57, 2011).

CONCLUSION

In this review of research on the processes underlying the effects of television viewing, we have described two different models for how television influences viewers. The premise of the two models is that the ways in which television information exerts its effects depend on the types of judgments that are addressed. As we have detailed, certain types of processes (e.g., motivation and ability to process) may actually have very different, and even opposite, effects on first- versus second-order cultivation judgments. Understanding this helps to explain why cultivation research that has investigated these processes (motivation, ability) seems to produce very inconsistent results. In some instances, if first- and second-order judgments are conflated, it may cancel out the effects of motivation and ability. In other instances, motivation and ability may influence some cultivation effects but not others. Although seemingly inconsistent, as we have detailed, not only are such patterns expected, they can be predicted. Thus, providing these more complex theoretical explanations provides more confidence in the validity of the cultivation effect.

REFERENCES

Bryant, J., Carveth, R. A., & Brown, D. (1981). Television viewing and anxiety: An experimental examination. *Journal of Communication, 31*(1), 106–119.

Bushman, B.J., & Anderson, C.A. (2001). Media violence and the American public: Scientific facts versus media misinformation. *American Psychologist, 56*(6–7), 477–489.

Busselle, R. W. (2001). The role of exemplar accessibility in social reality judgments. *Media Psychology, 3*, 43–67.

Busselle, R., & Bilandzic, H. (2008). Fictionality and perceived realism in experiencing stories: A model of narrative comprehension and engagement. *Communication Theory, 18*, 255–280.

Busselle, R. W. &, Shrum, L. J. (2003). Media exposure and the accessibility of social information. *Media Psychology, 5*, 255–282.

Cacioppo, J. T., & Petty, R. E. (1982). The need for cognition. *Journal of Personality and Social Psychology, 42*, 116–131.

Combs, B., & Slovic, P. (1979). Newspaper coverage of causes of death. *Journalism Quarterly, 56*, 837–849.

DeFleur, M. L. (1964). Occupational roles as portrayed on television. *Public Opinion Quarterly, 28*, 54–74.

Dixon, T., & Linz, D. (2000). Overrepresentation and underrepresentation of African Americans and Latinos as lawbreakers on television news. *Journal of Communication*, 50, 131–154.

Gerbner, G., & Gross, L. (1976). Living with television: The violence profile. *Journal of Communication, 26*(2), 172–194.

Gerbner, G., Gross, L., Morgan, M., & Signorielli, N. (1980). The "mainstreaming" of America: Violence profile no. 11. *Journal of Communication, 30*(Summer), 10–29.

Gerbner, G., Gross, L., Morgan, M., & Signorielli, N. (1994). Growing up with television: The cultivation perspective. In J. Bryant & D. Zillmann (Eds.), *Media effects: Advances in theory and research* (pp. 17–41). Hillsdale, NJ: Erlbaum.

Gerbner, G., Gross, L., Morgan, M., Signorielli, N., & Shanahan, J. (2002). Growing up with television: Cultivation processes. In J. Bryant & D. Zillmann (Eds.), *Media effects: Advances in theory and research* (2nd ed., pp. 43–67). Mahwah, NJ: Erlbaum.

Green, M. C., & Brock, T. C. (2000). The role of transportation in the persuasiveness of public narratives. *Journal of Personality and Social Psychology, 79*, 701–721.

Green, M. C., Garst, J., & Brock, T. C. (2004). The power of fiction: Determinants and boundaries. In L. J. Shrum (Ed.), *The psychology of entertainment media: Blurring the lines between entertainment and persuasion* (pp. 161–176). Mahwah, NJ: Erlbaum.

Gregory, W. L., Cialdini, R. B., & Carpenter, K. M. (1982). Self-relevant scenarios as mediators of likelihood estimates and compliance: Does imagining make it so? *Journal of Personality and Social Psychology, 43*, 89–99.

Hastie, R., & Park, B. (1986). The relationship between memory and judgment depends on whether the judgment task is memory-based or online. *Psychological Review, 93*, 258–268.

Hawkins, R. P., & Pingree, S. (1982). Television's influence on constructions of social reality. In D. Pearl, L. Bouthilet, & J. Lazar (Eds.), *Television and behavior: Ten years of scientific progress and implications for the eighties* (Vol. 2, pp. 224–247). Washington, DC: Government Printing Office.

Hawkins, R. P., & Pingree, S. (1990). Divergent psychological processes in constructing social reality from mass media content. In N. Signorielli & M. Morgan (Eds.), *Cultivation analysis: New directions in media effects research* (pp. 33–50). Newbury Park, CA: Sage.

Head, S. W. (1954). Content analysis of television drama programs. *Quarterly of Film, Radio, and Television, 9,* 175–194.

Hirsch, P. (1980). The scary world of the nonviewer and other anomalies: A reanalysis of Gerbner et al.'s findings on cultivation analysis. *Communication Research, 7,* 403–456.

Hughes, M. (1980). The fruits of cultivation analysis: A reexamination of some effects of television watching. *Public Opinion Quarterly, 44,* 287–302.

Kahneman, D. & Frederick, S. (2002). Representativeness revisited: Attribute substitution in intuitive judgment. In T. Gilovich, D. Griffin, & D. Kahneman (Eds.), *Heuristics and biases: The psychology of intuitive judgment* (pp. 49–81). Cambridge, England: Cambridge University Press.

Kahneman, D., & Tversky, A. (1982). The simulation heuristic. In D. Kahneman, P. Slovic, & A. Tversky (Eds.), *Judgment under uncertainty: Heuristics and biases* (pp. 201–208). New York: Cambridge University Press.

Lichtenstein, S., Slovic, P., Fischhoff, B., Layman, M., & Combs, B. (1978). Judged frequency of lethal events. *Journal of Experimental Psychology: Human Learning and Memory, 4,* 551–578.

Lichter, S. R., Lichter, L. S., & Rothman, S. (1994). *Prime time: How TV portrays American culture.* Washington, DC: Regnery Publishing.

Morgan, M., & Shanahan, J. (1997). Two decades of cultivation research: An appraisal and meta-analysis. In B. R. Burleson (Ed.), *Communication yearbook 20* (pp. 1–45). Newbury Park, CA: Sage.

Morgan, M., Shanahan, J., & Signorielli, N. (Eds.). (2012). *The cultivation differential: State of the art research in cultivation theory.* New York: Peter Lang Publishers.

Newcomb, H. (1978). Assessing the violence profile studies of Gerbner and Gross: A humanistic critique and suggestion. *Communication Research, 5,* 264–282.

Ogles, R. M. (1987). Cultivation analysis: Theory, methodology and current research on television-influenced constructions of social reality. *Mass Communication Review 14*(1 and 2), 43–53.

O'Guinn, T. C., & Shrum, L. J. (1997). The role of television in the construction of consumer reality. *Journal of Consumer Research, 23,* 278–294.

Oliver, M. B. (1994). Portrayals of crime, race, and aggression in "reality based" police shows: A content analysis. *Journal of Broadcasting & Electronic Media, 38,* 179–192.

Petty, R. E., & Cacioppo, J. T. (1986). *Communication and persuasion: Central and peripheral routes to attitude change.* New York: Springer-Verlag.

Richins, M. L., & Dawson, S. (1992). A consumer values orientation for materialism and its measurement: Scale development and validation. *Journal of Consumer Research, 19,* 303–316.

Rubin, A. M., Perse, E. M., & Taylor, D. S. (1988). A methodological examination of cultivation. *Communication Research, 15,* 107–134.

Shanahan, J., & Morgan, M. (1999). *Television and its viewers: Cultivation theory and research.* New York: Cambridge University Press.

Sherman, S. J., Cialdini, R. B., Schwartzman, D. F., & Reynolds, K. D. (1985). Imagining can heighten or lower the perceived likelihood of contracting a disease: The mediating effect of ease of imagery. *Personality and Social Psychology Bulletin, 11,* 118–127.

Sherman, S. J., & Corty, E. (1984). Cognitive heuristics. In R. S. Wyer & T. K. Srull (Eds.), *Handbook of social cognition* (Vol. 1, pp. 189–286). Hillsdale, NJ: Erlbaum.

Shrum, L. J. (1996). Psychological processes underlying cultivation effects: Further tests of construct accessibility. *Human Communication Research, 22,* 482–509.

Shrum, L. J. (1999). The relationship of television viewing with attitude strength and extremity: Implications for the cultivation effect. *Media Psychology, 1,* 3–25.

Shrum, L. J. (2001). Processing strategy moderates the cultivation effect. *Human Communication Research, 27,* 94–120.

Shrum, L. J. (2004). The cognitive processes underlying cultivation effects are a function of whether the judgments are on-line or memory-based. *Communications, 29,* 327–344.

Shrum, L. J. (2007). The implications of survey method for measuring cultivation effects. *Human Communication Research, 33,* 64–80.

Shrum, L. J., & Bischak, V. D. (2001). Mainstreaming, resonance, and impersonal impact: Testing moderators of the cultivation effect for estimates of crime risk. *Human Communication Research, 27*(2), 187–215.

Shrum, L. J., Burroughs, J. E., & Rindfleisch, A. (2005). Television's cultivation of material values. *Journal of Consumer Research, 32,* 473–479.

Shrum, L. J., Lee, J., Burroughs, J. E., & Rindfleisch, A. (2011). An online process model of second-order cultivation effects: How television cultivates materialism and its consequences for life satisfaction. *Human Communication Research, 37,* 34–57.

Shrum, L. J., & O'Guinn, T. C. (1993). Processes and effects in the construction of social reality: Construct accessibility as an explanatory variable. *Communication Research, 20,* 436–471.

Shrum, L. J., O'Guinn, T. C., Semenik, R. J., & Faber, R. J. (1991). Processes and effects in the construction of normative consumer beliefs: The role of television. In R. H. Holman & M. R. Solomon (Eds.), *Advances in consumer research* (Vol. 18, pp. 755–763). Provo, UT: Association for Consumer Research.

Shrum, L. J., Wyer, R. S., & O'Guinn, T. C. (1998). The effects of television consumption on social perceptions: The use of priming procedures to investigate psychological processes. *Journal of Consumer Research, 24,* 447–458.

Smythe, D. W. (1954). Reality as presented by television. *Public Opinion Quarterly, 18,* 143–156.

Tversky, A., & Kahneman, D. (1973). Availability: A heuristic for judging frequency and probability. *Cognitive Psychology, 5,* 207–232.

Volgy, T., & Schwarz, J. (1980). Television entertainment programming and sociopolitical attitudes. *Journalism Quarterly, 57,* 150–155.

Zillmann, D. (1980). Anatomy of suspense. In P. H. Tannenbaum (Ed.), *The entertainment functions of television* (pp. 133–163). Hillsdale, NJ: Erlbaum.

ENDNOTE

1. We put *fact* and *fiction* in quotes to signify that, like the topic of the book, the lines between what is fact and fiction are quite blurry. On the one hand, soap operas are clearly fictional in the technical sense, but they also hold a grain of truth, or at least "ring true" to some degree. On the other hand, news programs presumably present factual information, and yet content analyses consistently show that news presentations can be significantly distorted, for example, emphasizing dramatic crimes such as murder and other violence and tending to show African-Americans and Latinos as criminals more often than base-rates would suggest is representative (Dixon & Linz, 2000). In the middle is "reality TV," which shows heavily edited but nevertheless actual footage of such events as crime and police response. But just as with the editing process for news, selective editing tends to portray certain classes of people (e.g., black and Hispanic characters) as perpetrators more often but as police officers less often than white characters (Oliver, 1994).

7

Flying With Icarus: Narrative Transportation and the Persuasiveness of Entertainment

Jordan M. Carpenter and Melanie C. Green
University of North Carolina at Chapel Hill
Chapel Hill, North Carolina

INTRODUCTION

Think of the story of Icarus. Imagine the brash young man first stumbling terrified through the maze of the Minotaur. Suddenly, he escapes and finds himself free not only from the threat of the monster and from darkness but also, incredibly, from the earth itself. He can *fly*. Ignoring his father's warnings, he swoops and twirls through the air, climbing higher and higher with joy. But his exuberance brings him too near the sun, the wax holding his wings together melts, and he plummets into the sea.

We mention this example to illustrate two phenomena. First, narratives are universal and pervasive. Stories predate the invention of any sort of media, living as storytelling, and once technology allowed people to record their stories, they began doing so. Communicating narratives has become a major part of most entertainment media, from the written word to video games. Individuals seeking entertainment frequently look for narratives, in forms ranging from sitcoms to novels.

Second, we wish to demonstrate the effect narratives can have on readers. Despite being written hundreds of years ago, this fictional world and its characters have the power to grab readers of today and place them back into that scene, swooping through the air with Icarus. Entertainment narratives can not only provide enjoyment and emotional experiences, but can also affect individuals' real-world attitudes and beliefs. Narratives can convey lessons; a listener may come away from the story of Icarus with a stronger belief in the importance of caution or of listening to one's parents.

Narratives are a major way we communicate and think. Developmental psychologists have found that in most cultures, children as young as 3 years old have internalized basic narrative structure or grammar (Mancuso, 1986). The universality and automaticity of viewing or reading narratives makes them potent media experiences, embedding the reader in the author's world, following along rather than focusing on his or her own life or surroundings.

The theory of narrative transportation (transportation into a narrative world; Green & Brock, 2000, 2002; see also Gerrig, 1993) attempts to quantify and examine the consequences of this phenomenon. Transported readers have imaginatively left their immediate surroundings behind and entered the narrative world. Importantly, being transported into a story has strong cognitive and emotional consequences and leaves a reader especially susceptible to attitude change from the themes of a story they are experiencing (Green & Brock, 2000).

This chapter will examine the features and mechanisms of narrative transportation, compare it to similar concepts such as identification and presence, discuss examples of real-world applications of transportation, and finally describe individual differences that may facilitate transportation in media users.

TRANSPORTATION INTO A NARRATIVE WORLD

Transportation is a unique subjective state characterized by deep focus on a narrative. Transported readers are completely immersed in the world of the story. However, it is not simply the process of paying attention to words or media. Green & Brock (2000) found that they could reduce transportation by instructing readers to focus on a written story in an analytical, unemotional way, while other readers were transported into that same story by focusing on its narrative aspects. Thus, transportation not only involves attention, but also imaginative imagery and emotional involvement.

Transportation also involves a lack of focus on the outside world, and an unwillingness to doubt the "reality" of a transporting story. This acceptance of a story's reality is implied by the fact that readers have been found to be curiously unaffected by the knowledge that a story was made up or real; individuals are equally transported into stories when they are described as factual or fictional (and, as discussed later, typically show similar levels of attitude change in response to factual and fictional stories).

Transportation can be measured with a self-report scale (Green & Brock, 2000). The scale has eleven general items measuring cognitive and emotional engagement, and additional items measuring mental imagery related to characters and settings. An example items is, "The narrative affected me emotionally" (1 = not at all to 7 = very much). Although early work on transportation focused on written narratives, individuals can become transported into stories in any medium: written, spoken, video, or multimedia.

TRANSPORTATION-IMAGERY MODEL

The Transportation-Imagery Model (Green & Brock, 2002) contains five postulates for theory-driven research into this area. Though all of the postulates are useful to any researcher interested in pursuing transportation, it is especially important to note that levels of transportation into a given story are affected by variables within the story itself, within the situation, and within the audience member. All three elements must be studied to truly understand the process of transportation and narrative persuasion. We discuss the first two factors next, and individual differences in a later section.

Story Factors

Story characteristics are important in creating the experience of transportation. As the Transportation-Imagery Model states, "Propensity for transportation by exposure to a given narrative account is affected by attributes of the text. Among these moderating attributes are the level of artistic craftsmanship and the extent of adherence to narrative format" (Green & Brock, 2002, p. 327). Although initial research suggested that narrative quality is indeed associated with transportation (an adapted excerpt from a bestseller induced higher average transportation than a story created by psychology experimenters; Green & Brock, 2000), there are many factors that can contribute to narrative quality. Kreuter and colleagues (2007) outlined a number of these elements, including plot coherence, character development, emotional intensity, and production values (see also Kreuter et al., 2008).

Research has confirmed that the narrative structure is a key element: Wang and Calder (2006) found that disrupting the logical sequence of events made a story less transporting. Certain elements of a written story's diction and style are important as well. Stylistic elements such as metaphor, alliteration, rhyme, and allusion defamiliarize readers from the outside world and may draw people in. Stories containing these elements have been found to be more striking and more able to capture readers' attention (Miall & Kuiken, 1994; van Peer, 1986). These factors could play out in other media, such as film, television, or video games. Theoretically, elements such as directorial choices, cinematography, and music could engage viewers in ways similar to stylistic elements in text (e.g., Bezdek & Gerrig, 2008).

Story Medium

One of the postulates of the Transportation-Imagery Model (Green & Brock, 2002) holds that the medium and context in which a narrative is delivered can affect that narrative's ability to transport, particularly since some media can limit imaginative participation. Entertainment media often takes the form of video or multimedia presentations. In these contexts, imagery is provided to viewers, rather than being self-generated (as with written texts). This may have either positive or negative consequences for transportation. On the one hand, films can provide rich imagery that goes beyond the imagination of some readers, and the pacing of film presentations may be especially likely to evoke participatory responses. On the other hand, video presentations can somewhat constrain the imaginative involvement of the viewers, because they do not encourage alternative visions of settings and characters. Because the viewer has not done as much mental work to create the narrative world in his or her mind, the story may have reduced impact. Nonetheless, transportation has been demonstrated across media (e.g., Green et al., 2008; Shrum, Lee, Burroughs, & Rindfleisch, 2011; Williams, Green, Kohler, Allison, & Houston, 2010). Once individuals have become transported, the same basic psychological and persuasive processes should occur. However, there may be individual differences in the extent to which different media are transporting for different individuals; individuals who wish to exert less cognitive effort appear to prefer video presentations over text, whereas this effect is reversed for individuals who enjoy thinking (Green et al., 2008). An exciting new area for transportation research is highly immersive virtual worlds; engagement in these media experiences has generally been explored under the rubric of "presence," which we discuss later.

TRANSPORTATION AS A MECHANISM OF NARRATIVE PERSUASION

Besides the unique aspects of its subjective experience, the most important empirical aspect of transportation is its ability to leave people with attitudes changed by the narrative that drew them in. In the first test of this phenomenon, Green and Brock (2000) asked participants to read an engaging story about a furloughed mental patient who commits murder. Transported readers were more likely to later endorse attitudes implied by the story, such as a sense that violence is common, a belief that the world is unjust, and a feeling that the mentally ill should be confined. Research in this area in the decade since Green and Brock's (2000) publication of a scale to measure transportation has demonstrated transportation effects in a variety of domains. There are several ways in which transportation evokes belief change, including affective, cognitive, and imagery processes.

Affective Responses

Transportation may evoke belief change in narratives by influencing affective responses (Heath, Bell, & Sternberg, 2001; Mazzocco, Green, Sasota, & Jones, 2010; Oatley, 1999, 2002). Narratives typically address emotion-evoking events (e.g., some type of conflict or obstacle faced by a character, with perhaps a successful resolution) and create emotional connections to characters (Green, 2007). Transportation leads to stronger emotional responses to narratives (Green, Chatham, & Sestir, 2011;

see also Escalas, Moore, & Britton, 2004). Narratives, as opposed to rhetoric, may be a particularly effective means of forming and changing affectively based attitudes, as well as attitudes based in both affect and cognition.

Cognitive Responses

Furthermore, transportation tends to reduce counterarguing or negative cognitive responding (Green & Brock, 2000; Slater & Rouner, 2002). Transportation is a pleasurable state (Green, Brock, & Kaufman, 2004), and transported individuals are typically not motivated to interrupt this experience to critique the story, argue against implications of the story, or question the real-world validity of the story. The strong focus on narrative events that is part of transportation also may tend to reduce counterarguing, because the majority of an individual's mental resources are devoted to imagining the story. Thus, the cognitive capacity needed to generate counterarguments may be reduced. Indeed, narratives may be especially effective under conditions in which individuals might otherwise resist persuasion (Kreuter et al., 2007; Slater & Rouner, 1996).

Perceived Reality of Narratives

To the extent that readers become transported into narratives, they tend to react to events in the narrative as if they were real, increasing the likelihood of an emotional response (Green, 2004). Conversely, aspects of the narrative that are strikingly unrealistic or inconsistent with the rules of the narrative world can disrupt the reader's or viewer's formation of a mental model, and thus reduce engagement with the narrative (Busselle & Bilandzic, 2008). Direct experience with an attitude object is a powerful predictor of attitudes and behavior (Fazio & Zanna, 1981); a transporting narrative may provide a simulation that approaches direct experience. Studies on memory suggest that text narratives have memory qualities similar to imagination (e.g., more emotional content), whereas media-based narratives are remembered in ways more similar to reality (e.g., vividness, contextual detail), although real memories are more intense than memories based on narratives (Gordon, Gerrig, & Franklin, 2009). Thus, films or television programs might be especially good at creating a sense of reality through concrete visual representations.

Perhaps because they believe narratives to be representative of reality, transported readers are also likely to generalize story events, (Strange & Leung, 1999).

Participatory Responses

Even though readers cannot actually participate in the action of a story, research has indeed indicated that readers often react *as if* they were part of story events. Gerrig (e.g., Polichak & Gerrig, 2002) refers to these reactions as participatory responses or "p-responses." These p-responses can range from relatively automatic and reflexive "as if" responses, in which individuals respond as they would to a real situation (e.g., wanting to yell, "Watch out!" when the villain is sneaking up behind the hero) to relatively more complex responses such as problem solving (attempting to gain information to predict outcomes) or replotting responses (mentally undoing earlier narrative events to try to change the outcome). The kinds of participatory responses that readers have to a narrative can affect their emotional responses, their memory for narrative events, and their real-world judgments.

Imagery

Transportation may also lead to belief change through the production of mental imagery, as described by the Transportation-Imagery Model (Green & Brock, 2002). According to this model (Green & Brock, 2002), narrative persuasion is limited to story texts that are in fact narratives, in which images are evoked, and in which readers' (viewers') beliefs are implicated. Mental imagery can affect attitudes and behaviors (Gregory, Cialdini, & Carpenter, 1982), and may also re-evoke story themes and messages when recalled (see Green & Brock, 2002). Furthermore, images may increase resistance to counterpersuasion because images—and the affect or emotions they evoke—may be resistant to verbal counterarguments. For example, the *Jaws* viewer who retains a vivid image of a shark attack may continue to fear swimming despite hearing arguments about the rarity of shark attacks (e.g., Harrison & Cantor, 1999). Likewise, images of terrorism, and the associated fear, may override statistics about the rarity of terrorist attacks.

Concreteness

Similarly, because narratives are concrete and specific, it may be harder to argue against their conclusions, especially when the narratives reflect another person's lived experience (as in personal anecdotes). A person may not feel that affirmative action is helpful, but when hearing a story about a person who would not have had educational opportunities without affirmative action, the listener cannot deny that person's experience. This characteristic of narratives may also underlie Strange and Leung's (1999) finding that narratives are equally influential whether they are described as presenting a typical case or an atypical case. Concrete information, such as that provided in narratives, also evokes causal processing, which contributes to persistence (e.g., Anderson, 1983).

NARRATIVE PERSUASION ACROSS DOMAINS

Evidence for transportation as a mechanism of narrative persuasion has been found in a variety of domains. None of the mechanisms of transportation would be worth study if they did not play out in people's everyday lives. Luckily, there is evidence that persuasive power of narratives can occur outside of the lab, sometimes in powerfully trenchant ways. For instance, repeated, real-world exposure to narratives can subtly affect people by gradually convincing them of the themes common to these narratives (the cultivation effect; e.g., Gerbner et al., 2002; Shrum, Burroughs, & Rindfleisch, 2005). These effects are particularly powerful if individuals are transported into the narratives (Shrum et al., 2011; see also Shrum & Lee, this volume).

Social Values

As one example, simple stories, such as those common on television, feature events that happen for a clear reason. Researchers have found that avid watchers of fictional television programs are more likely to believe in a just world: that good deeds are necessarily rewarded and that a person who suffers misfortune somehow deserved that fate (Appel, 2008). However, viewers of nonfiction television were less likely to have that belief system, and in fact were more likely to believe the world is random and unfair. Similarly, television viewing can increase materialism, which can lead to reduced life satisfaction (Shrum et al., 2011).

Health

Researchers have been interested in using transportation effects for more socially beneficial aims. One of the most-studied bailiwicks for harnessing the potential of transportation is public health: Can a good story convince people to behave safely or protect themselves from disease? Researchers are optimistic. In the realm of cancer research, Kreuter and his colleagues (2007; see also Green, 2006) assert that narratives can have a positive social influence on every stage at which cancer can be addressed, from prevention to survivorship. For instance, narratives sidestep automatic resistance regarding certain behaviors or messages, such as smoking is unhealthy, and they can provide cancer sufferers with comfort by providing surrogate social connections.

In practice, transportation has been shown to have positive benefits in health communication. Narratives are especially good at stimulating self-relevant emotions, which can in turn cause people to perceive themselves as more at risk of an injury or disease and therefore more likely to protect themselves from it (Dunlop, Wakefield, & Kashima, 2008). Similarly, when directly pitted against statistical data, narrative testimonials can be more persuasive at raising people's personal risk perception and inducing a desire to behave self-protectively (de Wit, Das, & Vet, 2008; see also Baesler & Burgoon, 1994).

Morgan, Movius, and Cody (2009) found that network television media dramas, such as *House* and *Grey's Anatomy*, were effective at influencing viewers' knowledge of and intentions toward personal organ donation, a highly emotional topic. These programs efficiently give viewers both accurate information and misinformation, however, and could be effective at convincing people in either direction: For example, one show's ludicrous storyline in which a doctor amorally manipulates the donation system left viewers less likely to want to become a donor, while another show's sober, obvious dialogue about the virtues of donation left viewers more likely to indicate an intention to become a donor. Importantly, the emotional involvement of the viewers in the program predicted both learning and motivation, as did their transportation into the narratives.

Advertising

The most obvious and ubiquitous form of persuasive appeal is the advertisement, but the brief length of most ads may at first make them appear to be irrelevant to transportation theory. It is plausible that a reader will be drawn into an epic tale of adventure, but it is less believable for people to be carried away by a woman's 15-second-long struggle with static cling. However, some research has found that transportation (or transportation-like effects) can occur in even the shortest persuasive appeals.

One way for advertisements to induce transportation is to invite readers to imagine a fictional world that the writers do not have time or space to convey. This is often done by directly asking people to imagine themselves using the product. This technique is an effective way of invoking transportation and sidestepping elaboration: Escalas (2004) found that when an ad directed readers to imagine themselves using the product, their liking of the product was not affected by the quality of argument in favor of the product. Instead, these readers were transported into their own imagined simulation, leading to a decrease in critical thoughts about the product and an increase in positive feelings about the product.

However, not every advertisement invokes transportation so explicitly. Some are able to imaginatively involve viewers simply on the basis of their evocative imagery. Phillips and McQuarrie (2010) label these types of images *grotesque* (directly opposed to simple, pleasant, mundane, or cheerful) and propose that part of their effectiveness lies in their transporting nature. This research is partly important because it suggests a direct answer to the question of why an advertisement can be effective even (perhaps especially) if it does not associate the product with positive or happy things.

While advertisements can be transporting, they may be more salient in most people's entertainment experience as potential interrupters of transportation. On the one hand, commercials intrude into television programs, particularly shameless movies can linger on certain shots to make their product placement more obvious, and print ads appear on the pages in the middle of magazine stories. On the other hand, sometimes an advertisement can coexist with a narrative more harmoniously, such as a relevant commercial playing before a YouTube video. There are consequences for ads' effectiveness depending on how they appear with a story. In one set of studies, when an advertisement interrupted a highly transporting narrative, people were left with more negative attitudes toward the product

(Wang & Calder, 2006). However, when an ad accompanied a transporting story without interrupting the experience, people liked the product more than when not transported. Furthermore, under some circumstances, the experience of transportation into a narrative can transfer to the advertisement, which can increase ad effectiveness (Wang & Calder, 2009).

Fact and Fiction

Surprisingly, fictional narratives can often be just as powerful as factual ones in changing beliefs (Green, Garst, Brock, & Chung, 2006). For example, Slater (1990) found that fiction was especially effective for changing attitudes about unfamiliar (versus familiar) social groups. Strange and Leung (1999) showed that a narrative about a teenage school dropout could change readers' beliefs about the causes of students dropping out of high school, regardless of whether those narratives were described as news articles or as fictional stories. Green and Brock (2000) showed changes in beliefs related to a story about an attack on a young child at a shopping mall even when the narrative was clearly labeled as fiction. In general, individuals appear to be more concerned with plausibility than with real-world truth; if a story "rings true," it can influence beliefs even if the events and characters described are completely made up by an author. Furthermore, research in cognitive psychology demonstrates that individuals also learn "false facts" from fiction (Marsh, Meade, & Roediger, 2003; Marsh & Fazio, 2006). That is, individuals use even misinformation that appears in stories when they answer general knowledge questions.

Of course, research on entertainment-education has shown effects of fictional communication on a wide variety of health and social beliefs and behaviors (see Singhal, Cody, Rogers, & Sabido, 2004, for a review), and has been frequently used in developing countries. Entertainment-education presents fictional programs with embedded messages about topics ranging from literacy to family planning. These programs may take the form of radio serials, telenovelas (soap operas), or even the insertion of a persuasive storyline into an existing program. While entertainment-education studies typically do not explicitly compare the influence of fictional versus nonfictional material, they clearly demonstrate that messages from purely fictional worlds can affect real attitudes and actions.

Persistence of Narrative-Based Attitude Change

Many studies of narrative-based attitude change have examined only immediate effects. Of course, the persistence of these effects is important from both a theoretical and practical perspective. Although research on delayed effects is still underrepresented, initial studies are promising in demonstrating both persistence effects (Williams et al., 2010) and sleeper effects (that is, when a message becomes more effective over time; Appel & Richter, 2007).

TRANSPORTATION AND RELATED CONSTRUCTS

Transportation and Elaboration

Traditional theories of persuasion, most specifically the Elaboration Likelihood Model (Petty & Cacioppo, 1986) and the Heuristic-Systematic Model (Chaiken, 1980), have focused on two routes to persuasion: one requiring attention and effort and involving careful consideration of a persuasive attempt (high elaboration), and the other occurring automatically through heuristics and the influence of peripheral details (low elaboration; Petty & Cacioppo, 1986). Despite the ubiquity and predictive power of these models, narrative transportation does not fit cleanly into them. Both the Transportation-Imagery Model (Green & Brock, 2002) and the Extended Elaboration Likelihood Model (Slater & Rouner, 2002) have highlighted the different processes involved in narrative persuasion versus traditional rhetorical or argument-based persuasion.

The first difference is theoretical: Transportation causes readers to be centrally focused on the story, but in a way that is experiential and fraught with emotion, not in the cerebral, thoughtful manner described by the ELM (Petty & Cacioppo, 1986; Green & Brock, 2002). Meanwhile, transported readers are less likely to be influenced by information not contained within the narrative, such as the story source. Indeed, the immersion into the story renders people peculiarly unmoved by outside information, even something as important as whether a story was fictional or true or whether it represents a typical or atypical experience (Green & Brock, 2000; Strange & Leung, 1999).

Second, elaboration and transportation occur under different situations. Two of the most reliable ways of predicting high elaboration are when a persuasive appeal involves issues that are highly relevant to the listener, and when a listener is high in an individual difference called need for cognition, which measures how much individuals enjoy engaging in effortful thought (Cacioppo & Petty, 1982; Cacioppo, Petty, & Kao, 1984). These predictors are less relevant for transportation.

Although transportation is increased when individuals have some connection with narrative themes or characters (Green, 2004), relevance is not necessary for immersion. Indeed, one possible outcome of transportation is to make story events feel more personally relevant because of connections with characters; the concerns of a liked or admired character may seem more important to a transported reader. Need for cognition typically shows a low positive correlation with transportation (likely due to the fact that both need for cognition and transportation involve attention), but it generally does not predict the outcome of narrative persuasion.

Transportation and Identification

As a truism, the notion that media characters can be engaging is almost so obvious as to be inane. Would the myths of ancient Greece be immortal without brash Hercules or scheming Medea? Would anyone really care about rescuing Princess Toadstool without the charming, loveable Mario? Characters can be a doorway into a media experience, and people can have many ways of reacting to them. One of the most poignant is *identification*, immersing oneself in the viewpoint of the character (Cohen, 2001).

More than just a positive attitude or good feeling toward a fictional character, identification is more specifically thought of as an orientation; the character serves as an orientation through which the reader experiences the story. Identification involves losing track of one's own identity and then subsequently adopting the character's goals and perspective as one's own (Oatley, 1994; Sestir & Green, 2010). This is distinct from similar concepts such as wishful identification, where the reader looks up to and respects the character (Lonial & Van Auken, 1986); parasocial interaction, in which the reader feels as if she has a relationship with the media character (Horton & Wohl, 1956); and connectedness, where a viewer develops long-term relationships with characters and expresses their affection for the characters through activities such as imitating characters' fashion choices or ways of speaking, collecting objects related to the program, and wishing to be part of the program (Russell, Norman, & Heckler, 2004; see also Russell & Russell, this volume).

Bandura's social cognitive theory provides a model through which fictional characters can influence others. Social cognitive theory posits a model of human behavior that centers on personal agency (e.g., Bandura, 2001). Research has shown that, consistent with this model, if a person identifies with a fictional character taking active steps to be healthy, that person will be more likely to take on similar healthy behaviors from a raised sense of his or her own self-efficacy (Smith, Downs, & Witte, 2007). Social cognitive theory has provided the theoretical basis for much of the work in entertainment-education, which has demonstrated effects on health and social issues around the world (see Singhal et al., 2004, for a review).

Transportation and identification are similar processes, and are likely strongly related. Similar to transportation, identification involves a deep focus on a narrative, a subjective sense of "losing oneself," and a lack of critical analysis about the narrative. Also, similar to transportation, identification is inherently affective, involving an empathetic, experiential adoption of the media character's emotions. Finally, identification is possible in both fictional and nonfictional narratives across a variety of technologies and media (Cohen, 2001). Perhaps most importantly, identification makes people less critical of messages they encounter within a story and therefore more likely to be persuaded (Slater & Rouner, 2002).

However, unlike transportation, which is absorption into the whole world of a narrative, identification is focused through the perspective of a single media character. Also, transportation tends to be uninterrupted once engaged, while according to some theorists, identification is intermittent and easily interrupted (Cohen, 2001). While both transportation and identification are persuasive, some theorists have proposed that they work under different processes: transportation by reducing counterarguing of narrative themes, and identification by opening audience members to points of view they would otherwise avoid (Moyer-Guse, 2008; Tal-Or & Cohen, 2010).

Transportation and Presence

As technology improves, media immersion has become more complex. Rather than audience members or readers simply using their imaginations to enter the world of a narrative, now developers have the ability to create simulated locations so apparently real that users may feel as if they are actually located within them, able to interact with it like a physical space. This concept is called *presence* (Minski, 1980; Klimmt & Vorderer, 2003), and it is generally defined as a loss of awareness of the mediated nature of an environment, and the role of technology in its presentation (e.g., Ijsselstein, de Ridder, Freeman, & Avons, 2000). Presence is typically studied in interactive forms of new media: For example, virtual reality simulations, video games, and Java-enabled web portals. These are domains in which narrative transportation is understudied, leading to a dearth of connection between the two ideas; new-media researchers have even referred to the absorbing nature of text-based narratives as "the book problem" (Schubert & Crusius, 2002).

Nonetheless, the two concepts are similar. Both involve a deep level of undifferentiated attention on the mediated information, a loss of awareness of the outside world, and a sense of being personally involved in a fictional world. Much like a reader of a narrative using the familiar structure of a story to "fill in the blanks" of information and then place themselves into the story through identifying, users construct spatial schemata for a mediated physical environment, and then place themselves into that environment (Wirth et al., 2007). Measures of presence do typically include a component asking about physical experiences, however (e.g., feelings of being able to easily control a virtual avatar), which is not considered an aspect of transportation.

The connections between presence and transportation have not been fully explored. While presence is captivating, it is also unclear if it has consequences for persuasion similar to those of transportation. The Transportation-Imagery Model (Green & Brock, 2002) postulates that it may be the mental images evoked by a narrative that, when linked with story themes, serve as powerful pieces of information. The importance of images in this theory implies that presence may also be similarly engaging and lead to similar persuasive effects (Bracken, 2002). However, many virtual worlds do not have a strong narrative structure, which would limit the possibility for transportation-based attitude change.

TRANSPORTATION AND INDIVIDUAL DIFFERENCES

As we said earlier, all stories are not created equal. Some contain superior writing style, intense drama or suspense, timeliness and relevance to universal feelings or issues, or a high entertainment factor, and these stories will be more engaging and transporting than others. However, we should consider as well that not all readers are created equal. Some may be more likely to seek out transporting experiences, may be more likely to be drawn into stories even if they are of lower quality, and may reach a deeper level of immersion while engaged in a story. Because of this, not only is it important to look at *transportation*, but also *transportability*, the likelihood that a reader will become deeply involved in a story when situational factors and narrative features are held constant (Dal Cin, Zanna, & Fong, 2004; Green, 1996).

Transportability

Much like the state of transportation, transportability as a trait predicts the extent to which an individual is persuaded by the themes in a specific narrative, but not the amount of persuasion from an analogous rhetorical communication (Mazzocco et al., 2010). As might be obvious, the mechanism that drove this phenomenon was the level of engagement. Highly transportable individuals were more likely to be transported into the narratives that persuaded them. Perhaps less obviously, the relationship was mediated by emotional rather than rational responses to the story. Transportable individuals felt empathy for the characters in the story, which in turn affected their attitudes.

That individual differences affect the power of persuasive attempts is not news. Probably the most famous example is need for cognition (e.g., Cacioppo et al., 1984), a trait which has repeatedly been demonstrated to influence the likelihood a person will engage with a rhetorical appeal in a reasoned, careful, analytical way. That model, however, is very different from the picture of a transportable individual found by Mazzocco and colleagues: responding with empathy instead of reason to a well-written narrative (Mazzocco and colleagues did find that need for cognition correlated with transportability, but it was insufficient to explain the relationship between transportability and attitude change). Transportability, therefore, can be thought of as somewhat analogous to need for cognition, but moderating the effects of narrative transportation rather than rhetorical arguments.

Need for Affect

Another relevant trait is the need for affect, which is theorized to be the extent to which an individual will approach or avoid emotion-inducing situations (Maio & Esses, 2001). As discussed earlier, stories often affect people emotionally, a feature that may be pleasant or aversive to different individuals. Individuals with a higher need for affect are more willing to expose themselves to heartstring-tugging narratives, and are more drawn in to real-life, emotional events, such as the death of Princess Diana. More directly relevant, people high in need for affect are more drawn into narratives, which leads to higher levels of endorsement for narrative-relevant attitudes (Appel & Richter, 2010). This effect was stronger for highly emotional stories, which indicates an important feature of narrative persuasion: For certain types of people, stories may be uniquely effective at changing even tightly held, strongly valenced beliefs, a situation in which rhetorical arguments often fail (Mazzocco et al., 2010).

Transportation and Theory of Mind

Another aspect of cognition that might be important to narrative persuasion is theory of mind (also known as mind reading), the ability to recognize that another person has her own thoughts, perspectives, knowledge, and feelings (Premack & Woodruff, 1978). Mind reading is central to adult social interaction, and most children learn it as part of normal development. However, though all healthy adults have the ability, this type of perspective taking is not universal across situations; it is effortful, meaning it requires both motivation and ability. When one or the other of these elements is missing, people are likely to fail at their theory of mind inferences (Epley, 2004).

Because motivation is so important to successful theory of mind, we have developed the mind-reading motivation scale (Carpenter, 2008; Carpenter & Green, 2010), which measures the extent to which a person will expend effort to seek out the perspectives of others. This general orientation toward people indicates a particular kind of motivation not explained by extroversion or need for cognition. An example scale item is "There is just something intriguing about the insight different people can offer about someone else's motivations and perspective" (1 = not at all to 7 = very much). The items fall into three clusters, measuring perspective curiosity (seeking out the views of others), perspective defensiveness (avoiding the views of others), and perspective engagement (interest in others in the immediate social environment).

Mind-reading motivation has been shown to affect the kinds of behaviors that individuals engage in on social networking sites such as Facebook. Specifically, individuals who show more perspective curiosity are more likely to use Facebook in ways that enhance and support their offline or "real life" social engagement, such as organizing events with friends. In contrast, those higher in perspective defensiveness tend to use Facebook in more nonsocial ways, such as interacting with people who they only know on Facebook (Carpenter, Green, & LaFlam, 2011).

Besides the potential social benefits to this trait, it is also relevant to the focus of this chapter: Mind reading is central to narratives, and so an individual more motivated or interested in other's perspectives may be more likely to be transported. As Zunshine (2006) points out, theory of mind is necessary to comprehend written narrative, and may even be the reason people find narratives enjoyable. In a narrative, information comes from a variety of sources that readers must navigate and monitor in order to make sense of the story. Fiction allows people to use their mind-reading abilities in a much wider variety of circumstances than would otherwise be available, and so keeping track of who thinks what can be a challenging and fulfilling theory-of-mind exercise, essentially a form of play. As predicted, there does seem to be a relationship between mind-reading motivation and transportation (Carpenter, 2008). Mind-reading motivation was positively correlated with both transportability and transportation into a specific story. It was also related to participants' self-reported enjoyment of reading fiction, though not their enjoyment of reading nonfiction.

Mind-reading motivation may also be able to help predict differences in which elements of a narrative will be persuasive for different readers. For example, individuals high in mind-reading motivation may be more persuaded by story information conveyed by character thoughts and relationships, whereas those low in mind-reading motivation might be more influenced by general aspects of the narrative world itself or by other elements of the plot. Similarly, although people high in mind-reading motivation appear to be more transportable in general, they may be particularly likely to be transported into narratives with complex interactions between characters (e.g., mysteries, delicate courtships, deceptions, things left unsaid, webs of relationships), where understanding perspectives is essential to fully understanding the story. Individuals who enjoy exercising their theory-of-mind abilities may find special pleasure in solving these interpersonal puzzles created by an author. These hypotheses remain to be tested empirically, but illustrate the ways in which understanding this concept can potentially advance knowledge about how narratives may affect different viewers differently.

Other reader individual differences do have an impact on transportation and on narrative-based persuasion, but the list of tested traits remains small. Nonetheless, it is becoming increasingly clear that not everyone is equally drawn in to stories, and therefore that the reader, along with the situation and the narrative itself, is an important variable in this area of persuasion research.

FUTURE DIRECTIONS

Indirect Effects Over Time

Beyond any immediate effects from a narrative presentation, entertainment media may also create strong attitudes by sparking interpersonal discussion and by influencing the processing of later stories. Individuals may be likely to talk about the stories with others, and this discussion can reinforce story conclusions. Furthermore, individuals who have a bank of related stories stored in memory are more likely to be persuaded by a new, related narrative (Mazzocco, Green, & Brock, 2007). These social and cognitive effects may mean that entertainment media can have enduring effects in nonobvious ways; these socially and cognitively mediated pathways are a rich avenue for future research.

Implicit Attitudes

Although little research has explored the effect of narratives on implicit attitudes, theoretically, narratives should affect these types of attitudes as well. Implicit attitudes are unconscious associations that individuals have with an attitude object. Individuals may not be aware of these attitudes and cannot control their activation (e.g., Greenwald & Banaji, 1995). However, such attitudes can affect behavior. Implicit attitudes and explicit attitudes toward the same attitude object are not necessarily strongly correlated with one another (see Nosek, 2005, for a review), nor are they necessarily affected by the same kinds of information and experiences (Rydell & McConnell, 2006). For example, a former smoker might have negative explicit attitudes toward cigarettes, but positive implicit attitudes. The subtle associations that may be created by narratives may be especially influential with respect to implicit attitude change. Initial evidence from a study of popular movies suggests that stories can indeed alter implicit attitudes (Dal Cin et al., 2007).

New Technologies

Even beyond the intersection of presence and transportation that we discussed earlier, rapidly changing technology is altering the way many people engage with narratives. For example, Amazon's Kindle device is a relatively new medium through which people store, browse, and actually read written stories; other e-readers and e-book applications for smartphones and tablet computers are becoming more widely used. Some stories even come with an option for narrative information from other channels, such as sound effects or simulated shadows across the text, and some even include mild forms of interactivity, such as letting a reader trace his finger over the screen to move a simulated source of light. It is not clear whether these effects allow readers to be more fully absorbed or whether they lower transportation by focusing readers on features separate from the story's plot and characters. Readers may also respond differently to an e-book than they do to a heavy, tangible book with actual pages and weight. As more and more people start to read using these new technologies, it becomes increasingly important to see the consequences, positive or negative, they have on transportation.

Another constantly changing technology is video gaming, which is often successfully persuasive, even for in-game advertisements for products (Nicovich, 2005). Ivory and Kalyanaraman (2007) found that as the graphical and technical quality of a game increased, a player's immersion and propensity to be persuaded by that game also increased. However, they did not consider another way that video games are developing. Games are increasingly able to place players within a complete, surprising story: even the barest puzzle or action game now often comes with at least a rudimentary plot and characters. It is important to examine the effect of narrative transportation for players in these games, especially considering the fact that unlike readers of a story, players must act to move the storyline forward.

Transportation Overdose?

The rise of smartphones, tablet computers, and other ever-more powerful personal entertainment devices means that individuals can now spend even more of their time immersed in narrative worlds. Individuals waiting in line or commuting on public transportation may now be simultaneously watching movies, playing narrative video games, or otherwise mentally removing themselves from the world around them. Although these activities reduce boredom, one possibility is that they may also create a contrast effect where the real world comes to seem pale by comparison to the exciting or vivid narratives available elsewhere. Whereas the cultivation effect may create altered views of the world through assimilation processes, a general immersion in transporting media may in some cases create an overall contrast that causes individuals to devalue their everyday experiences. Such a phenomenon may not be common, but may underlie cases of video game addiction.

CONCLUSION

Entertainment media is a powerful force in today's world, and its influence will likely keep increasing as people become able to access entertainment programs on ever-growing numbers of channels and devices. The extent to which entertainment programs are able to shift individuals' beliefs, worldviews, and behaviors depends in part on the extent to which they transport viewers into a narrative world. Transportation is commonly experienced and sought out as a pleasurable state, and it is influenced by story factors, situational factors, and individual differences. This chapter has described transportation theory, highlighted the ways in which transportation functions as a mechanism for narrative persuasion, and explored the variety of domains where transportation effects have been demonstrated. Although significant knowledge exists about the process of narrative persuasion, we have also noted just a few of the many exciting research directions that remain to be explored. We look forward to continuing to unlock the mysteries of this distinctive phenomenon that has been a part of human experience from the ancient storytellers all the way through to today's high-tech media, and which will surely continue into whatever comes next.

REFERENCES

Anderson, C. A. (1983). Abstract and concrete data in the perseverance of social theories: When weak data lead to unshakeable beliefs. *Journal of Experimental Social Psychology, 19*, 93–108.

Appel, M. (2008). Fictional narratives cultivate just-world beliefs. *Journal of Communication, 58*, 62–83.

Appel, M., & Richter, T. (2007). Persuasive effects of fictional narratives increase over time. *Media Psychology, 10*, 113–134.

Appel, M., & Richter, T. (2010). Transportation and need for affect in narrative persuasion: A mediated moderation model. *Media Psychology, 13*, 101–135.

Baesler, E. J., & Burgoon, J. K. (1994). The temporal effects of story and statistical evidence on belief change. *Communication Research, 21*, 582–602.

Bandura, A. (2001). Social cognitive theory: An agentic perspective. *Annual Review of Psychology, 52*, 1–26.

Bezdek, M. A., & Gerrig, R. J. (2008). Musical emotions in the context of narrative film. *Behavioral and Brain Sciences, 31*(5), 578.

Busselle, R., & Bilandzic, H. (2008). Fictionality and perceived realism in experiencing stories: A model of narrative comprehension and engagement. *Communication Theory, 18*, 255–280.

Cacioppo, J. T., & Petty, R. E. (1982). The need for cognition. *Journal of Personality and Social Psychology, 42*, 116–131.

Cacioppo, J. T., Petty, R. E., & Kao, C. F. (1984). The efficient assessment of need for cognition. *Journal of Personality Assessment, 48*, 306–307.

Carpenter, J. M. (2008). *Need for social cognition: Devising and testing a measurement scale.* Unpublished masters thesis, University of North Carolina at Chapel Hill.

Carpenter, J. M., & Green, M. C. (2010). *Mind-reading motivation.* Manuscript in preparation.

Carpenter, J. M., Green, M. C., & LaFlam, J. (2011). People or profiles: Individual differences in online social networking use. *Personality and Individual Differences, 50*, 538–541.

Chaiken, S. (1980). Heuristic versus systematic information processing and the use of source versus message cues in persuasion. *Journal of Personality and Social Psychology, 39*, 752–766.

Cohen, J. (2001). Defining identification: A theoretical look at the identification of audiences with media characters. *Mass Communication & Society, 4*, 245–264.

Dal Cin, S., Gibson, B., Zanna, M. P., Shumate, R., & Fong, G. T. (2007). Smoking in movies, implicit associations of smoking with the self, and intentions to smoke. *Psychological Science, 18*, 559–563.

Dal Cin, S., Zanna, M. P., & Fong, G. T. (2004). Narrative persuasion and overcoming resistance. In E. S. Knowles & J. Linn (Eds.), *Resistance and persuasion* (pp. 175–191). Mahwah, NJ: Erlbaum.

de Wit, J., Das, E., & Vet, R. (2008). What works best: Objective statistics or a personal testimonial? An assessment of the persuasive effects of different types of message evidence on risk perception. *Health Psychology, 27*, 110–115.

Dunlop, S., Wakefield, M., & Kashima, Y. (2008). Can you feel it? Negative emotion, risk, and narrative in health communication. *Media Psychology, 11*, 52–75.

Escalas, J. E. (2004). Imagine yourself in the product: Mental simulation, narrative transportation, and persuasion. *Journal of Advertising, 33*(2), 37–48.

Escalas, J. E., Moore, M. C., & Britton, J. E. (2004). Fishing for feelings? Hooking viewers helps! *Journal of Consumer Psychology, 14*, 105–114.

Epley, N., Keysar, B., Van Boven, L., & Gilovich, T. (2004). Perspective taking as egocentric anchoring and adjustment. *Journal of Personality and Social Psychology, 87*, 327–339.

Fazio, R. H., & Zanna, M. P. (1981). Direct experience and attitude behavior consistency. In L. Berkowitz (Ed.), *Advances in experimental social psychology* (Vol. 14, pp. 162–202). New York: Academic Press.

Gerbner, G., Gross, L., Morgan, M., & Signorielli, N. (2002). Growing up with television: The cultivation perspective. In J. Bryant & D. Zillmann (Eds.), *Media effects: Advances in theory and research* (pp. 43–68). Hillsdale, NJ: Erlbaum.

Gerrig, R. J. (1993). *Experiencing narrative worlds: On the psychological activities of reading.* New Haven, CT: Yale University Press.

Gordon, R., Gerrig, R. J., & Franklin, N. (2009). Qualitative characteristics of memories for real, imagined, and media-based events. *Discourse Processes, 46*(1), 70–91.

Green, M. C. (1996). *Mechanisms of narrative-based belief change.* Unpublished master's thesis, Ohio State University.

Green, M. C. (2004). Transportation into narrative worlds: The role of prior knowledge and perceived realism. *Discourse Processes, 38*(2), 247–266.

Green, M. C. (2007). Linking self and others through narrative. *Psychological Inquiry, 18*, 100–102.

Green, M. C., & Brock, T. C. (2000). The role of transportation in the persuasiveness of public narratives. *Journal of Personality and Social Psychology, 79*, 701–721.

Green, M. C., & Brock, T. C. (2002). In the mind's eye: Transportation-imagery model of narrative persuasion. In M. C. Green, J. J. Strange, & T. C. Brock (Eds.), *Narrative impact: Social and cognitive foundations* (pp. 315–341). Mahwah, NJ: Erlbaum.

Green, M. C., Brock, T. C., & Kaufman, G. F. (2004). Understanding media enjoyment: The role of transportation into narrative worlds. *Communication Theory, 14*, 311–327.

Green, M. C., Garst, J., Brock, T. C., & Chung, S. (2006). Fact versus fiction labeling: Persuasion parity despite heightened scrutiny of fact. *Media Psychology, 8*, 267–285.

Green, M. C., Chatham, C., & Sestir, M. A. (2011). *Emotion and transportation into fact and fiction.* Manuscript under review.

Green, M. C., Kass, S., Carrey, J., Feeney, R., Herzig, B., & Sabini, J. (2008). Transportation across media: Repeated exposure to print and film. *Media Psychology, 11*(4), 512–539.

Greenwald, A. G., & Banaji, M. R. (1995). Implicit social cognition: Attitudes, self-esteem, and stereotypes. *Psychological Review, 102*, 4–27.

Gregory, W. L., Cialdini, R. B, & Carpenter, K. M. (1982). Self-relevant scenarios as mediators of likelihood estimates and compliance: Does imagining make it so? *Journal of Personality & Social Psychology, 43*, 89–99.

Harrison, K., & Cantor, J. (1999). Tales from the screen: Enduring fright reactions to scary media. *Media Psychology, 1*, 97–116.

Heath, C., Bell, C., & Sternberg, E. (2001). Emotional selection in memes: The case of urban legends. *Journal of Personality and Social Psychology, 81*, 1028–1041.

Horton, D., & Wohl, R. (1956). Mass communication and para-social interaction: Observations on intimacy at a distance. *Psychiatry, 19*, 215–29.

Ijsselsteijn, W. A., de Ridder, H., Freeman, J., & Avons, S. E. (2000). Presence: Concept, determinants, and measurement. Proceedings of the SPIE, 3959: 520–529.

Ivory, J., & Kalyanaraman, S. (2007). The effects of technological advancement and violent content in video games on players' feelings of presence, involvement, physiological arousal, and aggression. *Journal of Communication, 57*, 532–555.

Klimmt, C., & Vorderer, P. (2003). Media psychology "is not yet there": Introducing theories on media entertainment to the presence debate. *Presence: Teleoperators and Virtual Environments, 12*(4), 346–359.

Kreuter, M. W., Green, M. C., Cappella, J. N., Slater, M. D., Wise, M. E., Storey, D., et al. (2007). Narrative communication in cancer prevention and control: A framework to guide research and application. *Annals of Behavioral Medicine, 33*, 221–235.

Lonial, S. C., & van Auken, S. (1986). Wishful identification with fictional characters: An assessment of the implications of gender in message dissemination to children. *Journal of Advertising, 15*, 4–11.

Maio, G. R., & Esses, V. M. (2001). The need for affect: Individual differences in the motivation to approach or avoid emotions. *Journal of Personality, 69*, 583–615.

Mancuso, J. C. (1986). The acquisition and use of narrative grammar structure. In T. R. Sarbin (Ed.), *Narrative psychology: The storied nature of human conduct* (pp. 91–110). New York: Praeger.

Marsh, E. J., & Fazio, L. K. (2006). Learning errors from fiction: Difficulties in reducing reliance on fictional stories. *Memory & Cognition*, 34, 1140–1149.

Marsh, E. J., Meade, M. L., & Roediger, H. L. (2003). Learning facts from fiction. *Journal of Memory and Language, 49*(4), 519–536.

Mazzocco, P. J., Green, M. C., Sasota, J. A., & Jones, N. W. (2010). This story is not for everyone: Transportability and narrative persuasion. *Social Psychological and Personality Science, 1*(4), 361–368.

Mazzocco, P. J., Green, M. C., & Brock, T. C. (2007). The effects of a prior story-bank on the processing of a related narrative. *Media Psychology, 10*, 64–90.

Minsky, M. (1980). Telepresence. *Omni, 2*, 44–52.

Morgan, S., Movius, L., & Cody, M. (2009). The power of narratives: The effect of entertainment television organ donation storylines on the attitudes, knowledge, and behaviors of donors and nondonors. *Journal of Communication, 59*, 135–151.

Moyer-Guse, E. (2008). Toward a theory of entertainment persuasion: Explaining the persuasive effects of entertainment-education messages. *Communication Theory, 18*, 407–425.

Nicovich, S. (2005). The effect of involvement on ad judgment in a video game environment: The mediating role of presence. *Journal of Interactive Advertising, 6*, 29–39.

Nosek, B. A. (2005). Moderators of the relationship between implicit and explicit evaluation. *Journal of Experimental Psychology: General, 134*, 565–584.

Oatley, K. (1994). A taxonomy of the emotions of literary response and a theory of identification in fictional narrative. *Poetics, 23*, 53–74.

Oatley, K. (1999). Why fiction may be twice as true as fact: Fiction as cognitive and emotional simulation. *Review of General Psychology, 3*, 101–117.

Oatley, K. (2002). Emotions and the story worlds of fiction. In M. C. Green, J. J. Strange, & T. C. Brock (Eds.), *Narrative impact: Social and cognitive foundations* (pp. 39–69). Mahwah, NJ: Erlbaum.

Petty, R. E., & Cacioppo, J. T. (1986). The elaboration likelihood model of persuasion. In L. Berkowitz (Ed.), *Advances in Experimental Social Psychology* (Vol. 19, pp. 123–205). New York: Academic Press.

Phillips, B., & McQuarrie, E. (2010). Narrative and persuasion in fashion advertising. *Journal of Consumer Research, 37*, 368–392.

Polichak, J. W., & Gerrig, R. J. (2002). "Get up and win!": Participatory responses to narrative. In M. C. Green, J. J. Strange, & T. C. Brock (Eds.), *Narrative impact: Social and cognitive foundations* (pp. 71–95). Mahwah, NJ: Erlbaum.

Premack, D., & Woodruff, G. (1978). Does the chimpanzee have a theory of mind? *Behavioral and Brain Sciences, 1*, 515–526.

Russell, C. A., Norman, A. T., & Heckler, S. E. (2004). The consumption of television programming: Development and validation of the connectedness scale. *Journal of Consumer Research, 31*(1), 150–161.

Rydell, R. J., & McConnell, A. R. (2006). Understanding implicit and explicit attitude change: A systems of reasoning analysis. *Journal of Personality and Social Psychology, 91*, 995–1008.

Sestir, M., & Green, M. C. (2010). You are who you watch: Identification and transportation effects on temporary self-concept. *Social Influence, 5*(4), 272–288.

Shrum, L. J., Burroughs, J. E., & Rindfleisch, A. (2005). Television's cultivation of material values. *Journal of Consumer Research, 32*, 473–479.

Shrum, L. J., Lee, J., Burroughs, J. E., & Rindfleisch, A. (2011). An online process of second-order cultivation effects: How television cultivates materialism and its consequences for life satisfaction. *Human Communication Research, 37*, 34–57.

Singhal, A., Cody, M. J., Rogers, E. M., & Sabido, M. (Eds.). (2004). *Entertainment-education and social change: History, research, and practice*. Mahwah, NJ: Erlbaum.

Schubert, T., & Crusious, J. (2002). Five theses on the book problem: Presence in books, film and VR. Paper Presented at PRESENCE — 5th Annual International Workshop. Porto, Portugal.

Slater, M. D. (1990). Processing social information in messages: Social group familiarity, fiction versus nonfiction, and subsequent beliefs. *Communication Research, 17*, 327–343.

Slater, M. D., & Rouner, D. (1996). Value-affirmative and value-protective processing of alcohol education messages that include statistical evidence or anecdotes. *Communication Research, 23*, 210–235.

Slater, M. D., & Rouner, D. (2002). Entertainment-education and elaboration likelihood: Understanding the processing of narrative persuasion. *Communication Theory, 12*(2), 173–191.

Smith, R., Downs, E., & Witte, K. (2007). Drama theory and entertainment education: Exploring the effects of a radio drama on behavioral intentions to limit HIV transmission in Ethiopia. *Communication Monographs, 74*(2), 133–153.

Strange, J. J., & Leung, C. C. (1999). How anecdotal accounts in news and in fiction can influence judgments of a social problem's urgency, causes, and cures. *Personality and Social Psychology Bulletin, 25,* 436–449.

Tal-Or, N., & Cohen, J. (2010). Understanding audience involvement: Conceptualizing and manipulating identification and transportation. *Poetics, 38,* 402–418.

Van Peer, W. (1986). *Stylistics and psychology: Investigations of foregrounding.* London: Croom Helm.

Wang, J., & Calder, B. (2006). Media transportation and advertising. *Journal of Consumer Research, 33,* 151–162.

Wang, J., & Calder, B. J. (2009). Media engagement and advertising: Transportation, matching, transference and intrusion. *Journal of Consumer Psychology, 19*(3), 546–555.

Williams, J. H., Green, M. C., Kohler, C., Allison, J. J., & Houston, T. K. (2010). Stories to communicate risks about tobacco: Development of a brief scale to measure transportation into a video story. *Health Education Journal, 70,* 184–191.

Wirth, W., Hartmann, T., Bocking, S., Vorderer, P., Klimmt, C., Schramm, H. et al. (2007). A process model of the formation of spatial presence experiences. *Media Psychology, 9,* 493–525.

Zunshine, L. (2006). *Why we read fiction: Theory of mind and the novel.* Columbus: The Ohio State University Press.

8

Seeing Is Believing: Toward a Theory of Media Imagery and Social Learning

Karen E. Dill
Fielding Graduate University
Santa Barbara, California

Melinda C. R. Burgess
Southwest Oklahoma State University
Weatherford, Oklahoma

> The image is more than an idea. It is a vortex or cluster of fused ideas and is endowed with energy.
>
> **—Ezra Pound**

THE PERSUASIVE POWER OF SOCIAL IMAGERY

"A picture is worth a thousand words." That saying is so much a part of our shared consciousness that it loses meaning. But nonetheless, the aphorism contains a universal truth. If you want to change my mind, tell me a story. If you want the job done faster, show me a picture.

Images, in their own way, tell stories. Imagery can impart richly elaborated social information digestible in the blink of an eye. This has been true from the first times images appeared in the context of culture. The paintings on the walls of caves such as those at Lascaux, France, tell stories. In turn, modern archeologists study these paintings to learn about their creators, and these explorations become a kind of archeological version of media literacy.

Images have been used as propaganda. For example, an image of the heiress Patty Hearst holding a gun in a bank robbery orchestrated by the so-called

Symbionese Liberation Army convinced the public that she was a terrorist. Those who were convinced by the photo ignored the fact that the young Hearst had been kidnapped and locked in a dark closet and that it was more likely that she complied with her kidnappers due to the use of force or to Stockholm Syndrome, a known psychological reaction to being held hostage. This is the way people commonly make attributions based on imagery. When we see a person doing a behavior we attribute the behavior to the person's own personality and individual will. This is called *correspondence bias* or the fundamental *attribution error* (Gilbert & Malone, 1995; Jones & Harris, 1967) and is a foundational concept of the discipline of social psychology.

More recently, research has revealed that watching one's own avatar (a digital twin) exercise increases the odds that a person will exercise in real life (Fox & Bailenson, 2009). Bailenson and colleagues call this imitation of one's digital doppelganger the *Proteus effect*. This Proteus effect has an even stronger influence than reward or punishment on exercising behavior.

This avatar research is similar to a study by Gilbert, Pelham, and Krull (1988; Study 2) in which participants were told they would watch other students read either a proabortion or antiabortion speech and then were asked to judge the speaker's real attitude. Participants ignored the obvious situational constraint (being assigned to the "pro" or "anti" condition) and instead believed that the attitude corresponded to the person (correspondence bias). In other words, if we see a person doing it, we believe the behavior reflects the person's personality or free choice. In the avatar research, this extends even to attributions about oneself. The internal thinking presumably goes something like this: I see myself exercising. I must be the sort of person who exercises. I will exercise. Given that the rewards and punishments in the Fox and Bailenson study were watching your avatar lose or gain weight, respectively, it is rather astonishing that the effect of viewing self-imagery outweighed the effect of reward or punishment on exercising behavior. We must conclude that, under a variety of powerful circumstances, seeing is believing.

According to cultivation theory, "[media are] the source of the most broadly shared images and messages in history" (Gerbner, Gross, Morgan, Signorielli, & Shanahan, 2002). In spite of this generally accepted sentiment, media psychology does not currently have a theory of media influence that focuses specifically on the influence of social media imagery on psychological outcomes. Certainly, there exists a media effects literature that illustrates how media can influence attitudes, feelings, and behaviors (Wyer & Adaval, 2004). For example, a sizeable media violence effects literature suggests that exposure to aggressive media leads to aggressive behaviors, thoughts, and feelings (Anderson et al., 2003). And, certainly, there exists social psychological theory that posits how media can influence and persuade us through avenues such as transportation into narrative worlds (Gerrig, 1993; Carpenter & Green, this volume; Green & Brock, 2000).

The transportation theory literature has focused primarily on written narrative (Gerrig, 1993; Green & Brock, 2000). The media violence literature, the largest media effects literature, has focused primarily on visual media (Anderson et al., 2003; Comstock & Powers, this volume). But even in this exploration of highly visual media, the major theoretical attention has been given to psychological mechanisms involved in processing and reacting to media (Buckley & Anderson, 2006; Bushman & Anderson, 2002). Humanities-oriented research, in areas like visual and cultural studies, has paid perhaps the greatest attention to the image per se (Dikovitskaya, 2005; Sturken & Cartwright, 2009), but using methods and approaches that are different from those used in communications and psychology research, which is a barrier to their integration into the existing media psychology literature. These humanities-oriented approaches remain informative to media psychology nonetheless. For instance, visual and cultural studies approaches have addressed the question of how the image and the written narrative differ, which is an important step in the process of understanding their individual influence (Dikovitskaya, 2005).

This paper frames a theoretical approach to the persuasive power of social imagery in the media, from a social psychology perspective. Using the term "social imagery" to indicate still and moving pictures involving social content such as social interactions and demographics, we make the argument that social imagery in the media is a form of social storytelling and that telling visual stories about people can and does influence attitudes, feelings, and behavior toward others from those social groups. We review research evidence that supports this argument. We call this the theory of media imagery and social learning (MISL).

THEORETICAL FRAMEWORK

At its most basic level MISL posits that media depictions of social groups (e.g., women or minorities) cause changes in our behaviors, thoughts, feelings, and attitudes about those groups. We posit that there are aspects of visual depictions that tend to move the viewer away from prejudice and discrimination and aspects of visual depiction that tend to move the viewer toward prejudice and discrimination toward the depicted group. Fundamental to the social learning process, we argue that when it comes to digesting social information from visual imagery in the media, seeing is believing. In other words, fictional representations are not processed as such, but seeing the social characterization present in visual imagery, the viewer does not differentiate between what is fact and what is fiction, what is real, and what is fantasy.

This is true for fictional narrative (Green, Garst, & Brock, 2004), but there may be an even stronger effect for imagery. When one reads a fictional narrative, one way that a person adds to the narrative is by visualizing characters, scenes, and other elements of the story "in the mind's eye" (Green & Brock, 2004). Indeed, this is a primary way "imagery" is discussed in the media psychology and communications literatures. With visual imagery in fictional media, the images are presented to the viewer. The perceiver may edit or add to the visual imagery, but much of the imagery is constructed and crafted by others. Slusher and Anderson (1987) demonstrated that people do not understand the difference between their own self-generated mental imagery about stereotypical groups doing stereotypical things and those images they have actually seen in real life. We believe this failure of reality monitoring applies to situations in which people fail to differentiate between media imagery of social characters and people they have seen in real life. Thus, seeing a stereotypical image of a person in the media is treated as a lesson or a confirmation of a previously held stereotype.

What are some reasons social imagery is persuasive? One reason is that, as stated earlier, seeing is believing. The argument has been made about written fictional narrative that the reader first accepts the narrative as true and then may adjust her beliefs later for multiple reasons (Green & Brock, 2004; Green & Dill, in press). This process is very much like the general social psychological process of attribution for others' behavior called the correspondence bias (Gilbert & Malone, 1995; Gilbert et al., 1988). For social imagery, we first accept what we see as true, making a dispositional attribution for the behavior of the people we see, for example. We only correct for the initial dispositional attribution if we are motivated and able (Gilbert et al., 1988).

Holland (2007, 2009) argues that because we seek a pleasurable state of flow through entertainment media, it is not enough to say we willingly suspend our disbelief when transported by mediated stories, but that we accept as true what we see. As the authors of transportation theory have argued (Green & Brock, 2004), we are persuaded by fictional narrative in part due to low elaborative scrutiny. Consumers of media overestimate the fact–fiction or fantasy–reality distinction, often believing consciously that something that is "just entertainment" does not change their real world behaviors, thoughts, feelings, or attitudes (Brenick, Henning, Killen, O'Connor, & Collins, 2007; Dill, 2009; Green & Brock, 2004). This disconnect between conscious statements about media persuasion and evidence of media persuasion certainly suggests that the persuasion happens outside of conscious awareness and remains there, even after active conscious processing. We believe this is because the adaptive unconscious, as elaborated by Wilson (2002), first judges visual images based on lower-level survival needs. Elaborative processes such as the correction phase of the attribution process happen later, if at all, through conscious mechanisms. For our purposes, this may mean, for example, that witnessing a fictional depiction of a stereotypical Black man, we first accept the characterization through the lens of the adaptive unconscious, which seeks to protect us and to react in support of our survival. This primary goal is not socially conscious, but instinctual and self-protective.

Furthermore, when we see impossible or improbable events occur in media imagery, we also accept them as true rather uncritically. For example, we accept that Spider-Man can swing from building to building using spider webs he shoots from his wrists (Holland, 2009). We also accept less fantastic social messaging, such as the idea that skinny models can indulge regularly in high-calorie food without gaining weight (Dill, 2009).

In the research examples that follow, we will concentrate on three areas: video games, music videos, and advertisements. Games are routinely defended as being just entertainment by gamers (Brenick et al., 2007), executives (Subcommittee on Commerce, Trade and Consumer Protection, 2007), and the general public ("Poll Says Games Are Safe," 1999). Music videos are understudied from an aggression perspective, in spite of being sometimes questioned for their pornographic depictions of sexuality (Strasburger & Wilson, 2002). Finally, advertisements are something that everyone, regardless of age, is exposed to, with some estimates as high as exposure to 37,000 ads per year (Bretl & Cantor, 1988), and extensive studies have shown the commonality of degradation of women and minorities in ads (Kilbourne & Pipher, 2000). All three of these types of media are repetitive in nature (games are played across multiple sessions, ads and videos are rerun regularly), and offer reinforcement (Dill & Dill, 1998; Gentile & Gentile, 2008), making them ideal teachers.

One of the reasons that we feel MISL is a useful addition to the field is that people often have a skewed perception of the psychology of media influence. For the sake of example, let's say that view could be encapsulated as "Don't let your child watch people shoot people or he will go shoot people." In other words, people tend to understand the effects of violent media as direct, immediate, and extreme (Gentile & Anderson, 2003; Potter, 2003). At the same time, a sizeable portion of the public rejects almost entirely the notion that media violence exposure causes any changes in aggressive behaviors (Huesmann, 2005, 2010; Poll: Do games cause violence? 2010). Some of the top theorists in the field have written about these myths and misunderstandings of media violence and there is plenty of research that debunks these myths (Anderson & Gentile, 2005; Gentile, Saleem, & Anderson, 2007; Huesmann, 2005, 2010; Potter, 2003). At the same time, another sizeable portion of the public does believe that media violence causes aggression (*Los Angeles Times*, 2010). Part of the confusion is probably caused by a misapplication of the journalistic value of presenting two sides of the story, which results in the notion that there are two equal groups of research and researchers who simply disagree about media violence effects (Sacks, Bushman, & Anderson, in press; Bushman & Anderson, 2002). We believe that another asset of the MISL theory is that it concentrates on more subtle, long-term examples of everyday aggression, which may make media effects easier for the public to understand.

Media depictions of social groups can vary widely both within and between different genres. However, many common depictions can be broadly sorted into two categories of "admirable" and "contemptible." Admirable images are those that portray a member of a social group as an individual worthy of respect either through their own actions or through affiliation with a respected social unit (e.g., the military or motherhood), as an autonomous person, or as someone who possesses characteristics valued by society (e.g., intelligence, physical attractiveness, friendliness). Contemptible images are those that portray a member of social group as degraded, dangerous, objectified (not an autonomous being but rather an object for the viewer's pleasure), or simply reliant on a stock stereotype about that social group as opposed to possessing the full range of human traits and capabilities. Note that what we're calling admirable and contemptible image categories map onto what is referred to in the stereotype content model as warmth and competence, respectively. This application to the stereotype content model (Cuddy, Fiske, & Glick, 2007) will be discussed in detail later.

When exposed to admirable portrayals of a particular social group, we hypothesize that people will make more positive judgments about members of that particular social group and will engage in more prosocial (i.e., helpful) behavior and less aggressive behavior toward members of that group. When exposed to contemptible portrayals of a particular social group, we hypothesize people will make more negative judgments about members of that particular social group and will engage in more aggressive behavior and less prosocial behavior toward members of that group.

It is critical to note at this point that these depictions will be filtered through the viewer's perceptual lens. MISL explicitly states that endorsement of the labels "admirable" or "contemptible" is not necessary for these types of images to elicit the predicted effects. For example, our data (Dill & Burgess, 2011) showing that students who viewed "admirable" political images of then–presidential candidate Obama were from a region that is uniformly conservative. Yet those who viewed positive images of Black professionals showed increased likelihood of endorsing an unrelated Black political candidate, compared to those who had seen positive images of White professionals. Therefore, we argue that, while perceptions will certainly vary about the admirability or contemptibility of any given person, it is the portrayal of the person as either admirable or contemptible that matters most. For example, whereas college students might agree that the woman in Figure 8.1 is admirably attractive, her portrayal as a sex object can lead to negative outcomes such as increased tolerance in men of the sexual harassment of women (Dill, Brown, & Collins, 2008).

In terms of persuasion, it is important to note here that the robust Third-Person Effect (Davison, 1983, 1996) demonstrates that people tend to believe others are more likely to be influenced by media than they are. And even more important for present purposes is the reverse third-person effect, which demonstrates that people believe they personally are more persuaded by positive media and less persuaded by negative media content (Douglas, Sutton, & Stathi, 2010).

FIGURE 8.1
Example of a sexualized, objectified female video game character. Screen shot of "Tina" from the *Dead or Alive Xtreme Beach Volleyball* series.

As Wyer and Adaval (2004) note, we tend to see common media characterizations as normative. For instance, to the degree that television depicts affluence, we believe affluence is normative and therefore are distressed if we lack affluence (O'Guinn & Shrum, 1997). The positive implication for this in terms of social stereotyping is that positive depictions can have a good influence on our understanding of real people from the same social groups (Dill, 2009; Wyer & Adaval, 2004). This is related to the availability heuristic. In this case, if we see many positive examples from a particular social group (Christians, grandmothers) then we generalize that this is because more positive examples exist in the world. On the other hand, if we see a preponderance of negative examples young Black men as criminals on television shows like *Cops*), then we extrapolate that this negative characterization describes the social group generally.

Another goal we have with this model of media imagery and social learning is to unite theories of prejudice and theories of aggression. As with other research areas, the prejudice and aggression literatures tend to be divided into what Potter (2009) calls "scholarly neighborhoods," with, to our way of thinking, not enough visits between neighbors. Specifically, we hypothesized that when media perpetuate social biases, this results in derogation of and aggression toward the derogated group. This derogation may take many forms. The harm inflicted is often subtle and long term such as unequal pay and promotion or sexual harassment in the workplace. In terms of uniting prejudice and aggression research, one can take the cognitive, affective, and behavioral routes described in the general aggression model (Bushman & Anderson, 2002) and dovetail them with the stereotype content model (Cuddy et al., 2007). By joining the two, you have the social psychology of aggression joined with the social psychology of stereotyping, prejudice, and discrimination.

It was important that our model explicitly address both positive and negative media effects and posit them as coexisting. Although this is hardly a surprising notion to most scientists, too often the public and press take a reductionistic view that media are either good or bad for you (Dill, 2009). Taking an integrative approach to the social bias, aggression, and prosocial literatures, then, we can see that portrayals in the media can translate into real harm or real help toward members of those groups.

Furthermore, theories of stereotyping, prejudice, and discrimination can align with theories of aggression to explain the coercion and power elements behind aggression toward women and minorities. As Jost and Kay (2005, p. 498) explain: "There is an aura of presumed consensus that often surrounds racial and other group attitudes, and this perceived social environment serves to maintain and increase prejudice." Mass media images pervade our culture, subtly infusing social biases into the public consciousness, often without our direct awareness. On the flip side, by relating literature on the positive components of stereotypes (e.g., the model minority, see Cuddy et al., 2007) with the prosocial literature, we can explain how positive media imagery can result in increased fairness toward and tolerance of social minorities. Our behaviors, thoughts, and feelings toward members of groups that are stereotyped by the mass media are influenced at an unconscious level. Even though we may not consciously hold the stereotype, we may unconsciously act upon it, for better or worse.

Finally, we must discuss the issue that media images themselves do not actually physically or directly harm women and minorities—the people who digest the messages and act on them carry out the harm (including the women and minorities themselves). More distally, those who create media bear responsibility for the harm as well. The extent to which media producers and creators are intentional in creating the harm is a question that merits a thorough analysis, but is not the purview of this chapter or theory.

MEDIA RESEARCH ON THE DEROGATION OF WOMEN AND MINORITIES

According to the most recent information from the US Census Bureau, (http://quickfacts.census.gov/qfd/states/00000.html), about 80% of US citizens are White, 15% Hispanic, 13% Black, and 4% Asian, and about 50% of the population are women. Statistics such as these are useful in assessing whether women and minorities are given adequate representation in the media. Representation, in and of itself, is a form of respect. Beyond representation, we can analyze the types of stories and characterizations of women and minorities that appear in the media.

Derogation of women is an aggressive act designed to lower the status of women and to elevate men to the top of the status hierarchy. This derogation is often socially transmitted through media. For example, stereotyped characterizations of women in the media often portray them as secondary to men or as sexual objects for men's pleasure. Figure 8.2, an image from the video game *Saint's Row*, is a rather blatant example of this type of derogation and subjugation. We each have done work independently illustrating that this portrayal is typical of women who, in video games, are most frequently portrayed as sexually objectified accessories, while (White) men are portrayed as valiant heroes here to save the day (Burgess, Stermer & Burgess, 2007; Dill & Thill, 2007). Burgess et al. (2007) analyzed 225 best-selling video games' covers. The authors found that from the perspectives of both frequency and type of portrayal, women were consistently derogated. For example, male characters were five times more frequently depicted as primary characters (central to the action) and four times more likely to be ancillary characters. Among the ancillary characters, the infrequent females were significantly more likely to be portrayed in physically exaggerated ways as compared to their more frequent male counterparts. It is important to note that this physical exaggeration for females typically involved sexual objectification, however irrelevant these attributes may be to the action of the game. This sexualization of the female ancillary characters was far more common than physical exaggeration of the male characters (large muscles and hyper-masculinity), in spite of the potential usefulness of physical strength in regards to the action of the game.

Dill and Thill (2007) analyzed images in gaming magazines. They intentionally chose the largest image on each page as the image most likely

FIGURE 8.2
An image from the video game *Saint's Row 2*.

to attract attention even from casual perusal of the magazine. These are a particularly important investigations because research has shown that exposure to visual imagery and the associated stereotypes in that imagery automatically activates consistent behavior (Bargh & Chartrand, 1999). The images in the video game magazines were as stereotype-laden as the covers were: In every possible comparison, the female characters were portrayed more stereotypically than the males. Women were consistently more likely than men to be sexualized, scantily clad, sex-role stereotyped and, when aggressive, sexualized. Even more importantly, Dill and Thill (2007, Study 2) showed that even youth who are not avid gamers are aware of these common characterizations. These two representative works demonstrated that through the medium of video games a derogatory image of women is not only consistently being transmitted to children and young adults, but that they are aware of this.

However aware young adults are about the presence of stereotyped images, and however aware social psychologists may be of the influence of stereotyped images, as Bargh and Chartrand (1999) have discussed, people generally remain resistant to the notion that these images have any impact on us. Brenick et al. (2007) surveyed young adults regarding the sex stereotypes in video games. Whereas women were generally less accepting than men, there was general consensus that the images were just entertainment and as such unlikely to have any serious consequences.

Dill et al. (2008) illustrated just how serious the consequences of this imagery can be. They showed college students either screen shots of typical male and female video game characters (hypermuscular or sexually objectified, respectively) or photographs of male and female US senators. The students then read a true scenario in which a male professor sexually harasses a female student. In assessing the professor's guilt, men exposed to the video game imagery rated him as less guilty and deserving of less punishment. Additionally, men who reported more violent video game exposure indicated greater tolerance for sexual harassment. Dill et al.'s work (2008) was one of the first studies to illustrate the extent to which these negative portrayals of women can persuade people to think differently about aggression toward women.

Recently, video games have released even more disturbing images of women in a series of advertisements for the game *Hitman: Blood Money* (Eidos Interactive, www.hitmanbloodmoney.com). In several of these ads, beautiful women are portrayed as brutally murdered. The women in the images are beautiful, busty, and arrayed in erotic positions—if one can get past the single bullet hole in the head or the toaster in the bubble bath. As images like this are not limited to those who play the game (with an "M" rating, this would theoretically be limited to those 17 and older) by virtue of being in the advertisements, one can't help but wonder what impact this has on young people's attitudes about sexuality and violence. When erotic violence is marketed as fun-and-games, is it any surprise that researchers have found that the more game exposure one has, the more there is an associated increase in acceptance of rape myths (Dill et al., 2008)?

Media Research on Derogation of Minorities

Across the modern media era, the depiction of African Americans has changed, but it has also been marked by underrepresentation and by specific characterizations. Some of the common stereotypes of Blacks projected in the media include the image of Blacks as harmless or comical, as violent, or a combination of the two (Berkowitz, 2008; Burgess, Dill, Stermer, Burgess, & Brown, 2011; Holtzman, 2000; Leonard, 2003; Wilson, Gutierrez, & Chao, 2003). It is interesting in and of itself that these extreme positions have been presented—the Black man as harmless, smiling, and comical, and the Black man as dangerous and violent. Happily, especially on television and movies, more complex roles have appeared over time for Black characters. Sadly, in video games, blatant racial characterizations are typical (Burgess et al., in press; Leonard, 2003). Hispanics have also been underrepresented in the media and depicted as poor and uneducated and as buffoons (Holtzman, 2000; Wilson et al., 2003). Other minorities such as Asians and Native Americans have been relatively invisible. Interestingly, though, Asians have also been depicted as the "model" minority. Of course, all of these racial depictions take place in the context of a world view that suggests Whiteness is normal and dominant (Holtzman, 2000). Furthermore, young, White maleness is hegemonic and women—especially minority women—are stereotyped as victims (Holtzman, 2000; Jhally, 1994).

There is a surprising dearth of research on the portrayal of minorities in video games. The small amount of scholarship that does exist in this area, as noted above, suggests that racial stereotypes in video games tend to be blatant and quite negative. Burgess, Dill, & Stermer (2008, Study 1) conducted two extensive content analyses that explored the way race is portrayed among popular video game characters. In the top-selling video game magazines, minority characters—especially minority women—were underrepresented, often to the point of invisibility. Under-representation is another form of marginalization. Black and Hispanic men were significantly more likely to be aggressive than White and Asian men. Looking more deeply into the portrayal of aggression, Whites were significantly more likely than minorities to be depicted as soldiers. In fact, although about 33% of the U.S. armed forces are minorities (Department of Defense, 2002), not a single minority was depicted in military action, while 8% of the White male characters were portrayed as soldiers. Furthermore, in fighting scenes, significantly more White males than minority male characters wore protective armor.

A second content analysis of video game covers (Burgess et al., 2008; Study 2) revealed similarly blatant racial stereotypes. Black men were grossly overrepresented as thugs (perpetrators of illegal aggression absent any clear and present danger), and were seldom depicted as engaging in justified aggression, unlike White men. These characterizations reinforce the stereotype of Black men as the dangerous minority. Further support of this notion comes from the finding that Black men were also more likely than White men to be portrayed using guns, including using extreme guns, as characterized by their excessive size or firepower.

What are the effects of this type of prejudicial characterization—especially of Black men—in video games? In an experiment (Burgess et al., 2011, Study 3), students viewed game action featuring either Black or

White video game characters who were either violent or nonviolent. Then they were asked to identify violent and nonviolent stimuli. Results showed that regardless of the violence level of the video game, participants identified violent stimuli faster after seeing a Black male video game character. Also regardless of the violence level of the game, participants identified nonviolent stimuli faster after viewing a White male video game character. Thus, these results indicate that Black male video game characters, regardless of the violent content of the game, elicit behavior that is consistent with stereotypes of Black men as violent.

At the same time as we were working on these content analyses revealing such derogatory portrayals of minorities in video games, particularly Black men, Barack Obama was making his historic, and eventually successful, run for the office of president of the United States. We were intrigued by the dichotomous portrayal of race in the media. Here was the first Black man in the history of the United States being portrayed as a worthy contender for the highest office of the land: articulate, thoughtful, and intelligent. Yet, our research on video games' portrayal of race was yielding a very different portrayal: Men of color were routinely portrayed as social menaces, violent thugs with large guns, or aggressive athletes who were certainly not valued for their thoughtful intelligence, but rather for their brute force (Dill & Burgess, 2008). It was this juxtaposition that led us to ask, do the media portrayals of a social group, either as admirable or contemptible, alter peoples' perceptions of (and attitudes toward) that group generally?

To test this proposition, we exposed college students to either respectful images of Black and White male US politicians or screen shots of typically contemptible Black and White male video game characters. The political images were simply photographs of contemporary or historic American politicians in recognizable political situations (e.g., then presidential candidate Barack Obama addressing a large crowd or former President Lyndon Johnson meeting with Martin Luther King Jr. in the Oval Office). The game images were screen shots of typical Black and White video game characters such as "CJ" from *Grand Theft Auto: San Andreas*; the game characters were not portrayed as actively engaged in violent behavior, but rather posed with their accoutrements of violence (Dill & Burgess, 2008).

The students were told we were studying their memory for game imagery, and while we waited for the images to be stored in long-term memory we needed them to participate in an unrelated study for a (fictitious) colleague investigating web-page efficacy for political candidates. They saw a web page for a candidate for the House of Representatives and the candidate varied randomly between groups as either a Black or a White man. Students who saw the game images portraying Black men as contemptible rated the unrelated Black candidate as less favorable, less likable, and less capable. However, students who viewed the political images portraying Black men as admirable rated the unrelated Black candidate as more favorable, more likable, and more capable (Dill & Burgess, 2008).

OTHER TIES TO SOCIAL PSYCHOLOGICAL THEORY

Outside of media theory, MISL is grounded in other social psychological theory. One very important theory for understanding media imagery and social learning is the work of Glick, Fiske, Cuddy, and colleagues on ambivalent sexism and the BIAS (behaviors from intergroup affect and stereotype) map. Media images, either admirable or contemptible, are filtered through Cuddy et al.'s (2007) BIAS map. Admirable images can be classified as high in warmth and competence while the contemptible images can be classified as low in warmth and competence. These different media constructions should yield different psychological responses.

Coercive behavior theory (Tedeschi & Felson, 1994) is another foundational social theory. Coercive behavior theory frames aggression as a social influence behavior. Other than harm, the goals of aggression include coercion, power, dominance, and impression management. Stereotypes and prejudices, as noted above, are known collectively as *social biases*, with any negative action that results referred to as *discrimination*. In the literature on social biases, social dominance is also discussed as a motive. For example, social biases and discrimination can be fueled in part by a desire for downward social comparison—to win out over another person or group. Maass and colleagues (Maass, Cadinu, Guarnieri, & Grasselli, 2003) showed that male college students were more likely to sexually harass females who expressed beliefs in the equality of men and women, particularly if their masculinity had been threatened. Similarly, men are more likely to harass independent and feminist women (Berndahl, 2007). A recent meta-analysis showed a consistent relationship across a variety of studies between stereotypical male dominance and sexual aggression (Murnen, Wright, & Kaluzny, 2007).

In this chapter, we argue that social bias, as perpetuated by negative media imagery, can be seen as a persuasive tool that can be used to promote social dominance of one group over another. For example, one may derogate a woman or minority in order to "put her in her place." We apply our theory to derogatory imagery in the mass media, though the same theoretical reasoning applies to a variety of domains. Thus, the underlying theories come together to explain the use of mass media imagery as persuasive degradation of group members and to support aggression against members of the targeted group; ultimately, the effect of the media's derogation and aggression is to promote and/or preserve the differential social status.

Realistic Conflict Theory

Realistic conflict theory (Sherif, 1966) predicts that as competition for resources increases, derogation and aggression should also increase. This is because it is to each competing group's advantage to remove the threat to the resources, therefore increasing their own welfare. As women entered the workforce, particularly the professional workforce (as opposed to support and service staff positions—historically and, currently, largely dominated by women), the media has increased the derogation of women in a number of ways. One of the more striking changes in female imagery in the last 30 years is in the portrayal of the ideal body (Voracek & Fisher, 2002). The ideal female, as portrayed by models, centerfolds, Miss Americas, and so forth, has not only become significantly taller than the average woman, but has also become increasingly, and dangerously, thin (Kilbourne, 2010). It is certainly reasonable to question how thin models fit into a model of media derogation and its facilitation of aggression against women. One proposed mechanism of harm is the notion that media ideals distract women by concentrating their energy on so-called beautification and also by damaging women's self esteem (Kilbourne & Pipher, 2000; Wolf, 2002).

The most obvious criticism of body presentation in the media is the effect "curvaceously thin" (Harrison, 2003) women have on women's body image. Certainly, scores of studies have demonstrated that exposure to these images decreases women's satisfaction with their own bodies (e.g., Knauss, Paxton & Alsaker, 2007). But additional work has indicated that women are increasingly willing to both normalize and endorse extreme and dangerous methods (e.g., liposuction, purging, etc.) for achieving this ideal (Posavac, Posavac, & Posavac, 1998; Cusumano & Thompson, 1997).

Internalization of the thin ideal and endorsement of extreme measures is certainly not aggression in the typical sense. However, Naomi Wolf (2002) was the first to suggest that this portrayal of an unattainable ideal, and its subsequent consumption of women's energies and resources, was a socially acceptable way to restrain women. This analysis of media portrayals of the thin ideal closely mirrors the realistic conflict theory. If women are dismissed for failing to achieve the unachievable, resources need not be shared.

This reluctance to share resources, and its physical justification, was powerfully demonstrated in the landmark sex discrimination case of *Price Waterhouse vs. Hopkins* (1989). Ann Hopkins, the demonstrated top earner in the prestigious accounting firm of Price Waterhouse, was denied promotion to partner as the single woman in her promotion class of 88 candidates. Solo status research has demonstrated that when a solo member of a distinctive social group (e.g., one woman among 87 men) is judged, the member is more likely to be judged along stereotypic lines (Taylor, Fiske, Etcoff, & Ruderman, 1978). The evaluators at Price Waterhouse demonstrated this adherence to a physical ideal by suggesting that Ann Hopkins might have been more successful had she worn more makeup, changed her clothing style, and had her hair professionally styled. The Supreme Court's decision in Hopkins' favor dismissed this adherence to a physical ideal as nothing more than the dangerous results of stereotypes (Fiske, Bersoff, Borgida, Beaux, & Heilman, 1991).

The world of advertising not only presents women with an increasingly unattainable physical ideal, but it also routinely portrays women as unintelligent, shallow, and fixated on appearances—in short as "bimbos" (Kilbourne, 2010). Davies, Spencer, Quinn, and Gerhardstein (2002) explored the effect of television commercials that portrayed women as bimbos. They found that these types of portrayals had two distinctive effects on women. First (Study 2), after exposure to these kinds of advertisements, women actively avoided quantitative items in favor of verbal items on a mixed-item test. Additionally, when the women did attempt the quantitative items, they performed significantly worse than those women who had not viewed these advertisements. Second (Study 3), women who were exposed to these images rated careers involving quantitative skills as significantly less desirable than fields that were less threatening (i.e., requiring more verbal skills as opposed to math skills). These are instances of stereotype threat, the idea that exposure to social stereotypes influences members of the stereotyped group to conform to the negative assumptions of others (Steele, Spencer, & Aronson, 2002). In 2005, Harvard University president Lawrence Summers publicly speculated that women might be innately inferior to men at math (Bombardieri, 2005). While Summers drew a significant amount of attention to the issue of which factors are most significant in explaining the relative lack of women faculty in math-related fields, Davies et al.'s work raises a more complicated issue. By portraying women as bimbos, advertising sends a derogatory message to women that they can't and shouldn't pursue fields requiring these quantitative skills. Regardless of whether women would choose faculty positions in mathematics and related fields, knowledge of mathematics is required for many well-paying professional jobs (e.g., accounting, management, business, etc.).

Davies et al. (2005) followed this research with an investigation of women's leadership aspirations as a function of exposure to these bimbo ads. Female college students were exposed to either the bimbo ads or a series of neutral ads and then asked to choose a role in a problem solving–group. The roles available included the leader (from whom strong interpersonal and communication skills were explicitly required, avoiding any negative quantitative stereotypes), or a subordinate position labeled as a "problem solver." Problem solvers were described as team players with excellent communications skills. The nature of the leader's authority was clearly presented, avoiding the possibility that those who chose to be problem solvers didn't realize they were choosing subordinate positions. Following exposure to the bimbo ads, but not the neutral ads, women consistently chose the subordinate position, thus demonstrating that exposure to the stereotypical images had undermined the women's aspirational goals.

Davies and his colleagues (2002, 2005) have convincingly demonstrated that derogatory presentations of women in the media actively discourage women from choosing traditionally male-dominated paths, be they educational or occupational. These derogatory portrayals not only discourage the women from seeking the resources of more valuable educations and occupations, but by actively derogating the outgroup (i.e., women), the ads thereby facilitate the lack of professional resource sharing that Sherif's realistic conflict theory (Sherif, 1966) predicts.

Researchers have also investigated aggression resulting from media degradation. For example, Kenrick, Guiterres, and Goldberg (1989) demonstrated that realistic conflict also impacts professional as well as interpersonal relationships from the perspective of respect/affection and time.

Kenrick and colleagues showed that following exposure to sexually objectified centerfolds, men reported loving their own wives less. They also found that male college students expressed increased dissatisfaction with their (nonmarital) relationships after exposure to objectified attractive women (Kenrick et al., 1994). Kenrick, Neuberg, Zierk, and Krones (1994) also found that attractive women with dominant positions posed no threat to men's perceptions of their relationships, but depictions of attractive women of low dominance (i.e., objectified) decreased men's satisfaction with their relationships. Taken together, this research illustrates that body presentation does have real, damaging effects on women, both professionally and personally.

Kenrick and colleagues' work illustrates that derogatory images in the media decreases men's satisfaction with their partners. Does this decreased satisfaction in turn decrease men's support for the women in their lives, and their willingness to share in their mutual responsibilities? In a world of two-income couples, one of the most desired resources is time. If a relationship is marred by exposure to degraded images of women, does this in turn influence how willing male partners are to treat their wives with respect and make decisions that support women and families?

Recent research by Ward and her colleagues suggests that it does (Ward, Merriwether, & Caruthers, 2006). They investigated the relationship between traditional gender ideologies, media consumption, and attitudes toward breastfeeding. They found that traditional gender ideologies were driven in large part by frequency of media consumption and that these ideologies fueled concerns that breastfeeding would interfere with their sexual relationships. This is some of the first research to illustrate that these objectified images of women are associated with decreased support for women and the healthy use of her body as nature intended. Although Ward et al. are in no way arguing that the images cause men to discourage breastfeeding, they are making the point that the objectified images of women's bodies can make it difficult for men to see women as anything other than their own personal playthings. Additionally, women themselves seem to see their bodies as more for men's entertainment than anything else (Morse, 1989). This view is further supported by the ever-increasing rates of surgical breast augmentation; although it may make breasts sexier, it is associated with difficulties breastfeeding, difficulties diagnosing breast cancer, and decreased sensation—arguably all harmful to women.

Hegemonic Masculinity Theory and Ambivalent Sexism Theory

As explained above, theories like Sherif's realistic conflict theory (Sherif, 1966) propose that competition over resources causes people to derogate the out-group and to favor the in-group with everything ranging from material resources to friendship. Hegemonic masculinity theory (Connell, 1987) and ambivalent sexism theory (Glick & Fiske, 1996; Glick, Fiske, et al., 2004) also propose that sexist stereotypes preserve male hegemony and dominance. A sociological approach to sexism, Connell's (1987) hegemonic masculinity theory posits that masculinity is at the top of the social hierarchy and femininity is subordinate. Media perpetuate myths about femininity that are degrading in order to communicate the inferiority of women to men. Media representations, therefore, are a social force to degrade the status of women.

Ward and her colleagues have conducted research consistent with hegemonic masculinity theory using music videos. Music videos have been soundly criticized not only for their pornographic depictions of sexuality, but for the portrayal of women as little more than objectified bodies (or even just body parts), available for men's enjoyment as opposed to part of a real person with her own thoughts and desires (Jhally, 2007). Ward, Hansborough, and Walker (2005) conducted one the most thorough examinations of music videos' influence on adolescents' views about sexual stereotypes and sexual roles. With both experimental and correlational data, Ward et al. demonstrated that as exposure to the sexually stereotyped music videos increased, so too did teens' endorsement of sexual stereotypes and traditional sexual roles. Ward et al.'s work bears out the predictions of hegemonic masculinity theory. First, music videos do not reflect reality as we generally know it. While the sexual exploits of rich and famous men such as Wilt Chamberlain and his alleged 10,000 partners (see the Wilt Chamberlain Theory at www. urbandictionary.com) do occasionally mirror the world seen in music videos, this is presumably not the norm. Rather, music videos represent a virtual reality in which women are clearly subordinate and exist, seemingly, only to pleasure men. If this were confined to the small screen it might remain simply distasteful, but Ward and her colleagues (see also Johnson, Adams, Ashburn, & Reed, 1995) have convincingly demonstrated that regular viewing of this artificial world promotes acceptance of these very sexist notions in real teens.

Ward et al.'s (2005) work demonstrates fulfillment of hegemonic masculinity theory's darkest prediction: that this alternate worldview is presented to shape a desired reality of superior men and subordinate women. By aggressively degrading women in a fictional world of entertainment, music videos are effectively harming and degrading women in the real world through increased endorsement of stereotyped sex roles.

In addition to Ward et al.'s data, Jhally (2007) describes various real-word examples of how this material influences men and women. In his film *DreamWorlds 3*, Jhally shows the footage of two episodes of gangs of men assaulting women at a parade in NYC and a Mardi Gras festival in Seattle. These two episodes are a horrifying "live" version of what is regularly depicted in music videos: women being groped, slapped, sprayed with alcohol, fondled, and so on. The chilling difference, of course, between reality and the videos is the reaction of the women: In music videos women are always portrayed as enjoying the attention, yet the women in real life demonstrated nothing but terror. Although this is a dramatic example, it may be so extreme that many people fail to see the relevance to themselves (e.g., "I've watched tons of videos and I've never assaulted a woman"). Jhally (2007) addresses this by emphasizing that more than violence and degradation, the videos are promoting ideologies that have men in dominant positions over submissive, oversexed women who exist merely to pleasure men, and that these ideologies in turn lead to the harm of real women.

Ward et al. (2006) presented data that supported the two-step model Jhally (2007) proposes. First, men who have frequent media use, particularly those who identify with the characters, have more traditional gender ideologies. These traditional gender ideologies, as measured by Ward and her colleagues, primarily dealt with perceptions of women's sexuality and bodies. Men with more traditional ideologies viewed a women's body as less a tool for her pleasure and more an object for a man's pleasure; this is particularly pronounced for views about the breasts, which traditionally are seen as providing sexual pleasure for men as opposed to providing nourishment for an infant. This two-step model was supported by Ward et al.'s data: Men who viewed more media and identified with it more had more traditional views of women's sexuality and bodies (particularly breasts), and those ideologies in turn were associated with less support for breastfeeding in their partners and more belief that breastfeeding would interfere with sexual relations. Whereas most people can accurately claim that they have watched videos and never assaulted a woman, MISL theory predicts, and is supported by Ward's data, that viewing these aggressively degrading images is associated with more hegemonic attitudes about women.

According to Glick and colleagues' ambivalent sexism theory (Glick et al., 2004), there are mixed feelings about both men and women. Men are stereotyped as "bad but bold," and women as "wonderful but weak." However, women are subordinate to men because traditionally male characteristics are more valued in general. In countries around the world where the "bad but bold" stereotype was most pronounced, women had lower financial and social status than men. According to system justification theory (Jost, Banaji, & Nosek, 2004) women may actually buy into their own lower status because, ironically, the derogated group can find comfort in their own inequality. Justifying the status quo can actually lower victims' distress, and experts believe people are motivated to justify the existing social order. This counterintuitive desire to support group inequalities may be part of the reason that women and minorities are not as outspoken as they could be about their negative portrayal in the media.

The case of domestic violence of men against their female partners is an especially compelling example of how dominance and control are part of the constellation of aggression—both physical and nonphysical. In his book *Coercive Control*, Evan Stark (2007) emphasizes that the public understanding of domestic violence is one that focuses almost exclusively on physical violence. Stark maintains that domestic violence often is a broader pattern of behavior where the key factor is the abuser's control over the victim's life. For example, many abusive men dominate their partners by degrading them (e.g., insulting their physical appearance and convincing them that no one else wants them as a partner) and lowering their self-esteem. They also control their partners' access to transportation, communication, and education. They even exert detailed control of their partners' behavior such as eating, sleeping, and other everyday activities. For example, one man limited how many sheets of toilet paper his wife was allowed to use per day (Stark, 2007). When men, who are supposed to be on the top of the social hierarchy, have issues with self-esteem, they may degrade their partners in order to underline their own social superiority as men. Media imagery that belittles women feeds this destructive cycle.

Additionally, ambivalent sexism theory and MISL together predict a variety of common aggressive behaviors, such as the psychological control

seen in domestic violence. It is important to review the details of ambivalent sexism theory. Glick and Fiske (1996) proposed that sexism toward
women is composed of both the more traditional "women are inferior"
type of sexism and the more nuanced "women are wonderful" views of
women. The antiwoman sexism is encapsulated in hostile sexism—comprised of agreement with statements such as "Many women are actually
seeking special favors, such as hiring policies that favor them over men,
under the guise of asking for 'equality.'" or "Many women get a kick out
of teasing men by seeming sexually available and then refusing male
advances." The "women are wonderful" view is encapsulated by benevolent sexism—comprised of agreement with such statements as "Women
should be cherished and protected by men," or "Men should be willing
to sacrifice their own well-being in order to provide financially for the
women in their lives."

Ambivalent sexism theory, since its publication in 1996, has been measured in more than 19 nations, with more than 15,000 participants, and
both hostile and benevolent sexism have been found to measure valid
and distinct types of attitudes toward women (Glick & Fiske, 2001). MISL
predicts that these two types of sexism are reflected in different media
images, and that these types of media images serve different purposes.
First, benevolent sexism, with its view of women as nurturing, domestic,
and dependent on men, promotes women as wives and mothers, and as
such necessarily removed from the decision-making positions of power.
Second, hostile sexism, with its view of women's aggressive sexuality and
prickly feminism, portrays women as unreasonably demanding a fair cut
of the resource pie as well as the freedom to reject men's sexual advances
as they choose.

MISL predicts that the benevolent images will be held up as positive
portrayals of women, and viewed, therefore, as harmless. For example,
June Cleaver and Carol Brady, as well as the more modern crop of Disney
princesses, represent the ideals of benevolent sexism: women who strive
for nothing more than being married and happily sacrificing all for
home and family. While there is nothing inherently wrong with marriage and motherhood, these images do persuade women. Rudman and
Heppen (2003) found that romantic fantasies involving chivalrous res-
cue by Prince Charming were negatively related to women's desire for
educational achievement, high-status jobs, and group leadership. It is
critical to note that these implicit romantic fantasies were not consciously

endorsed. In other words, women did not expect to be rescued by Prince Charming. But, the more a woman implicitly endorsed a chivalrous view of romance, the more negatively this impacted her educational and occupational goals.

The hostile parallel was demonstrated by Sibley and Wilson (2004). They had university men read a scenario about a woman who modeled either a positive sexual subtype (chaste and modest) or a negative sexual subtype (a sexually active woman who had multiple partners, yet felt free to decline a man's sexual advances). Consistent with ambivalent sexism theory, men who read about the negatively portrayed women responded with higher levels of hostile sexism (and higher levels of benevolent sexism to the positive subtype). Sexual freedom in women is thus viewed as threatening and in need of aggressive male control. This is observed in Dill et al.'s (2008) finding that the more exposure men have to video games (and the sexualized women within them), the more they endorse views of sexuality that punish women for sexual freedom.

In sum, MISL incorporates ambivalent sexism theory, as well as other social psychological theories, and applies it to media. Benevolent sexism, with its restraint of women on their pure and sexually innocent pedestal, is every bit as limiting as hostile sexism with its advocated punishment of aggressive (sexually or otherwise) and demanding women. The media perpetuates this limiting of women through both benevolent and hostile images. The benevolent images have peaked in the portrayal of the celebrity mom who happily gushes about how much more fulfilling motherhood is than any career, even the career that garnered her celebrity status in the first place (see Douglas & Michaels, 2004). The hostile images perhaps were best illustrated in Demi Moore's performance as the sexually harassing predator in *Disclosure*. Aside from the less likely situation of a female boss sexually harassing a male employee, this character embodied the essence of what a hostile sexist fears most: a woman who is sexually active and powerful, but refuses to submit to male authority. These sexual and aggressive women are common images in video games. Dill et al. (2008) demonstrated exactly what MISL predicts: that these images lead to men minimizing the seriousness of sexual harassment and reporting increased sympathy for the perpetrator, presumably as payback for her violation of traditional sex roles.

Also relevant to MISL theory is the literature on pornography and other sexual media and violence against women. Research demonstrates that watching sexual violence desensitizes viewers to it (e.g., Linz, Donnerstein, & Penrod, 1988; Strasburger & Wilson, 2002). Exposure to violent pornography in which the victim responded positively to a rape—thus supporting the rape myth that women secretly enjoy rape—caused nonprovoked males to exhibit increased violence to an unrelated woman (Donnerstein & Berkowitz, 1981). Furthermore, men exposed to film scenes that sexually degrade and sexually objectify women are more likely to endorse rape myths than those who only see control scenes (Milburn, Mather, & Conrad, 2000). These studies indicate that viewing sexually aggressive media influences violence against women. Another relevant concern is that there may be parallels between the aggressive pornography and other media. For example, in media such as video games, a mix of sexuality and aggression in female characters has become much more commonplace over the last decade (Dill & Thill, 2007). MISL predicts that these characterizations may cause similar negative effects (e.g., Dill et al., 2008) to that of more traditional aggressive pornography.

SUMMARY AND CONCLUSIONS

Media images that degrade members of certain groups such as women and minorities support a social hierarchy that in turn supports violence against members of these groups. In proposing MISL theory, we call for future work that more explicitly integrates the social bias and aggression literatures. We intentionally used the phrase "Toward a Theory of Media Imagery and Social Learning" in our title because we recognize this is a theory in its infancy. We look forward to future work that elaborates on the theory and makes it more precise.

Our reasoning is that derogatory media portrayals beget derogation in real life. This derogation can take many forms including sexual harassment in the school and workplace and greater tolerance of violence (Dill et al., 2008; Looby, 2001). We believe this theory has clear advantages for media violence researchers in that it concentrates on types of harm that are not usually associated with common misunderstandings of media violence effects—such as the ideas that media violence exposure results in immediate, extreme, direct, observable acts of physical violence. Since discrimination takes many forms—often forms that are long-term and subtle, such as sex and race discrimination in the workplace and sexual harassment—one advantage of our approach is that it may be more readily understood by the public.

In closing, we address an obvious concern and area for discussion in the consideration of media influence on the broadly defined violence against women and minorities that we have proposed: the issue of intentionality on the part of the media. We feel it is important to clarify that we, in no way, imagine a group of White men in a board room cackling and fiendishly plotting to keep women and minorities in their place with their clever media portrayals. However, there is enough research demonstrating that these portrayals do influence behavior: from judgments about what is sexual harassment, and endorsement of rape myths, to women's own judgments about the suitability of various educational and occupational options. The growing body of research unequivocally supports the hypothesis that exposure to these types of portrayals *causes* increased aggression, however it is defined.

When media executives are questioned about their responsibility in these matters, they routinely claim that "censoring" their products would be a violation of their first amendment rights (Subcommittee on Commerce, Trade and Consumer Protection, 2007). As Americans, this is taken extremely seriously, both by the courts and private citizens, and as a society we have so far been reluctant to forbid the media from all but the most heinous portrayals (e.g., airing an execution live). As social scientists aware of the impact of stereotyping, we pose the following question: Is it not our responsibility to advocate curbing the most damaging portrayals, thereby protecting American citizens' most basic right to "life, liberty, and the pursuit of happiness"?

REFERENCES

Anderson, C. A., Berkowitz, L., Donnerstein, E., Huesmann, L. R., Johnson, J. D., Linz, D., et al. (2003). The influence of media violence on youth. *Psychological Science in the Public Interest, 4*(3), 81–110.

Bargh, J. A., & Chartrand, T. L. (1999). The unbearable automaticity of being. *American Psychologist,* 54, 462–479.

Berndahl, J. (2007). Sexual harassment of uppity women. *Journal of Applied Psychology, 92,* 425–437.

Berkowitz, L. (2008). On the consideration of automatic as well as controlled psychological processes in aggression. *Aggressive Behavior, 34*(2), 117–129.

Bombardieri, M. (2005, January 19). *Harvard women's group rips Summers.* Retrieved April 21, 2008 from http://www.boston.com/news/education/higher/articles/2005/01/19/harvard_womens_group_rips_summers

Brenick, A., Henning, A., Killen, M., O'Connor, A., & Collins, M. (2007). Social evaluations of stereotypic images in videogames: Unfair, legitimate, or "just entertainment"? *Youth & Society 38*(4), 395–419.

Bretl, D. J., & Cantor, J. (1988). The portrayal of men and women in US television commercials: A recent content analysis and trends over 15 years. *Sex Roles, 18*, 595–609.

Brockmyer, J. H., Fox, C. M., Curtiss, K. A., McBroom, E., Burkhart, K. M., & Pidruzny, J. N. (2009). The development of the game engagement questionnaire: A measure of engagement in video game-playing. *Journal of Experimental Social Psychology, 45*, 624–634.

Burgess, M. C. R., Dill, K. E., & Stermer, P. (2008). The prevalence and consequences of the portrayal of race in video games. Presented at the annual meeting of the Association for Psychological Science, Chicago, IL.

Burgess, M. C. R., Dill, K. E., Stermer, S. P., Burgess, S. R., & Brown, B. P. (2011). Playing with prejudice: The prevalence and consequences of racial stereotypes in videogames. *Media Psychology, 14*, 289–311.

Burgess, M. C. R., Stermer, S. P., & Burgess, S. R. (2007). Sex, lies, and videogames: The portrayal of male and female characters on videogame covers. *Sex Roles, 57*, 419–433.

Bushman, B. J., & Anderson, C. A. (2002). Violent video games and hostile expectations: A test of the general aggression model. *Personality and Social Psychology Bulletin, 28*, 1679–1686.

Connell, R. W. (1987). *Gender and power.* Stanford, CA: Stanford University Press.

Cuddy, A. C., Fiske, S. T., & Glick, P. (2007). The BIAS map: Behaviors from intergroup affect and stereotypes. *Journal of Personality and Social Psychology, 92*(4), 631–648. doi: 10.1037/0022-3514.92.4.631

Cusumano, D. L., & Thompson, J. K. (1997). Body image and body shape ideals in magazines: Exposure, awareness and internalization. *Sex Roles, 37* (9/10), 701–721.

Davies, P. G., Spencer, S. J., & Steele, C. M. (2005). Clearing the air: Identity safety moderates the effects of stereotype threat on women's leadership aspirations. *Journal of Personality and Social Psychology, 88*, 276–287.

Davies, P. G., Spencer, S. J., Quinn, D. M., & Gerhardstein, R. (2002). Consuming images: How television commercials that elicit stereotype threat can restrain women academically and professionally. *Personality and Social Psychology Bulletin, 28*, 1615–1628.

Davison, W. P. (1983). The third-person effect in communication. *Public Opinion Quarterly, 47*, 1–15.

Davison, W. P. (1996). The third-person effect revisited. *International Journal of Public Opinion Research, 8*(2), 113–119.

Department of Defense. (2002). Population representation in the military services. Retrieved September 26, 2007 from http://www.defenselink.mil/prhome/poprep2002/summary/summary.htm

Dikovitskaya, M. (2005). *Visual culture: The study of the visual after the cultural turn.* Cambridge, MA: MIT Press.

Dill, K. E. (2009). *How fantasy becomes reality: Seeing through media influence.* New York: Oxford University Press.

Dill, K.E., & Burgess, M. C. R. (in preparation). Priming differing media visions of Black masculinity influences judgments of others: An exemplar approach.

Dill, K. E., Brown, B. P., & Collins, M. A. (2008). Effects of exposure to sex-stereotyped video game characters on tolerance of sexual harassment. *Journal of Experimental Social Psychology 44*, 1402–1408.

Dill, K. E., & Burgess, M. C. R. (2008, October). *Media images as positive and negative exemplars of race: Evoking Obama or videogame characters changes outcomes for black men.* Presented at the 30th annual conference of the Society of Southeastern Social Psychologists, Furman University, Greenville, SC.

Dill, K. E., & Dill, J. C. (1998). Video game violence: A review of the empirical literature. *Aggression and Violent Behavior, 3*(4), 407–428.

Dill, K. E., & Thill, K. P. (2007). Video game characters and the socialization of gender roles: Young people's perceptions mirror sexist media depiction. *Sex Roles, 57*, 851–865.

Donnerstein, E., & Berkowitz, L. (1981). Victim reactions in aggressive erotic films as a factor in violence against women. *Journal of Personality and Social Psychology, 41*, 710–724.

Douglas, K. M., Sutton, R. M., & Stathi, S. (2010). Why I am less persuaded than you: People's intuitive understanding of the psychology of persuasion. *Social Influence, 5*, 133–148.

Douglas, S. J., & Michaels, M. W. (2004). *The Mommy myth: The idealization of motherhood and how it has undermined all women.* New York: Free Press.

Fiske, S. T., Bersoff, D. N., Borgida, E., Deaux, K., & Heilman, M. E. (1991). Social science research on trial: Use of sex stereotyping research in Price Waterhouse v. Hopkins. *American Psychologist, 46*, 1049–1060.

Fox, J., & Bailenson, J. N. (2009). Virtual self-modeling: The effects of vicarious reinforcement and identification on exericise behaviors. *Media Psychology, 12*, 1–25.

Gentile, D., & Anderson, C. (2003). Violent video games: The newest media violence hazard. In D. Gentile (Ed.), *Media violence and children* (pp. 131–152). Westport, CT: Praeger.

Gentile, D. A., & Gentile, J. R. (2008). Violent video games as exemplary teachers: A conceptual analysis. *Journal of Youth and Adolescence, 37*, 127–141.

Gentile, D. A., Saleem, M., & Anderson, C. A. (2007). Public policy and the effects of media violence on children. *Journal of Social Issues and Policy Review, 1*, 15–61.

Gerbner, G., Gross, L., Morgan, M., Signorielli, N., Shanahan, J., Bryant, J., & Zillmann, D. (2002). Growing up with television: Cultivation processes. In J. Bryant & D. Zillmann (Eds.), *Media effects: Advances in theory and research, 2nd edition* (pp. 43–67). Mahwah, NJ: Lawrence Erlbaum Associates Publishers.

Gerrig, R. J. (1993). *Experiencing narrative worlds.* New Haven, CT: Yale University Press.

Gilbert, D. T., & Malone, P. S. (1995). The correspondence bias. *Psychological Bulletin, 117*, 21–38.

Gilbert, D. T., Pelham, B. W., & Krull, D. S. (1988). On cognitive busyness: When person perceivers meet persons perceived. *Journal of Personality and Social Psychology, 54*, 733–740.

Glick, P., & Fiske, S. T. (1996). The ambivalent sexism inventory: Differentiating hostile and benevolent sexism. *Journal of Personality and Social Psychology, 70*, 491–512.

Glick, P., & Fiske, S. T. (2001). An ambivalent alliance: Hostile and benevolent sexism a complementary justifications for gender inequality. *Amercian Psychologist, 56*, 109–118.

Glick, P., Fiske, S. T., Masser, B., Manganelli, A. M., Huang, L., Castro, Y. R. et al. (2004). Bad but bold: Ambivalent attitudes toward men predict gender inequality in 16 nations. *Journal of Personality and Social Psychology, 86*, 713–728.

Grabmeier, J. (2010). *Does video game violence harm teens? New study weighs the evidence.* Retrieved April 28, 2011 from http://researchnews.osu.edu/archive/vidviollaw.htm.

Green, M. C., & Brock, T. C. (2000). The role of transportation in the persuasiveness of public narratives. *Journal of Personality and Social Psychology, 79*, 701–721.

Green, M. C., & Brock, T. C. (2004). In the mind's eye: Transportation-imagery model of narrative persuasion. In M. C. Green, J. J. Strange, & T. C. Brock (Eds.), *Narrative impact: Social and cognitive foundations.* Psychology Press: London, England.

Green, M. C., & Dill, K. E. (under contract). Fact, fiction and media persuasion. In K. E. Dill (Ed.), *The Oxford handbook of media psychology.* New York: Oxford University Press.

Green, M. C., Garst, J., & Brock, T. C. (2004). The power of fiction: Determinants and boundaries. In L. J. Shrum (Ed.), *The psychology of entertainment media: Blurring the lines between entertainment and persuasion* (pp. 161–176). Mahwah, NJ: Lawrence Erlbaum Associates.

Harrison, K. (2003). Television viewers ideal proportions: The case of the curvaceously thin woman. *Sex Roles, 48*(5/6), 255–264.

Holland, N. N. (2007). Literature and happiness. *PSYART.*

Holland, N. N. (2009). *Literature and the brain.* Gainesville, FL: PSYART Foundation.

Holland, N. N. (2009, July 24). Why don't we doubt Spider-Man's existence? This is your brain on culture. *Psychology Today.* Retrieved March 11, 2011 from http://www.psychologytoday.com/blog/is-your-brain-culture/200907/why-dont-we-doubt-spider-mans-existence-1

Holtzman, L. (2000). *Media messages: What film, television and popular music teach us about race, class, gender and sexual orientation.* New York: M.E. Sharpe.

Huesmann, L. R. (2005). Imitation and the effects of observing media violence on behavior. In S. Hurley & N. Chater (Eds.), *Perspectives on imitation: From neuroscience to social science, volume 2: Imitation, human development, and culture* (pp. 257–266). Cambridge, MA: MIT Press.

Huesmann, L. R. (2010). Nailing the coffin shut on doubts that violent video games stimulate aggression: Comment on Anderson et al. (2010) (Vol. 136, pp. 179–181).

Hurley, S. (2004). Imitation, media violence, and freedom of speech. *Philosophical Studies, 117*, 165–218.

Jhally, S. (executive producer and director). (1994). *The killing screens: Media and the culture of violence.* [Video]. (Available from the Media Education Foundation, http://www.mediaed.org/).

Jhally, S. (executive producer and director). (2007). *Dream worlds 3: Desire, sex, and power in music videos.* [Video]. (Available from the Media Education Foundation, http://www.mediaed.org/).

Johnson, J. D., Adams, M. S., Ashburn, L., & Reed, R. (1995). Differential gender effects on exposure to rap music on African-American adolescents' acceptance of teen dating violence. *Sex Roles, 33*, 597–606.

Jones, E. E., & Harris, V. (1967). The attribution of attitudes. *Journal of Experimental Social Psychology, 3*, 1–24.

Jost, J. T., Banaji, M., & Nosek, B. A. (2004). A decade of system justification theory: Accumulated evidence of conscious and unconscious bolstering of the status quo. *Political Psychology, 25*, 881–919.

Jost, J. T., & Kay, A. C. (2005). Exposure to benevolent sexism and complementary gender stereotypes: Consequences for specific and diffuse forms of system justification. *Journal of Personality and Social Psychology, 3,* 498–509.

Kenrick, D. T., Gutierres, S. E., & Goldberg, L. L. (1989). Influence of popular erotica on judgments of strangers and mates. *Journal of Experimental Social Psychology, 25*(2), 159–167.

Kenrick, D. T., Neuberg, S. L., Zierk, K., & Krones, J. M. (1994). Evolution and social cognition: Contrast effects as a function of sex, dominance, and physical attractiveness. *Personality and Social Psychology Bulletin, 20*(2), 210–217.

Kilbourne, J. (2010). Killing Us Softly 4 [videorecording]. Sut Jhally.

Kilbourne, J., & Pipher, M. (2000). *Can't buy my love.* New York: Free Press.

Leonard, D. (2003). "Live in your world, play in ours": Race, videogames, and consuming the other. *Studies in Media & Information Literacy Education, 3*(4), Article 41. Retrieved July 24, 2007 from http://www.utpjournals.com/simile/issue12/Leonardfulltext.html

Linz, D. G., Donnerstein, E., & Penrod, S. (1988). Effects of long-term exposure to violent and sexually degrading depictions of women. *Journal of Personality and Social Psychology, 55,* 758–768.

Looby, E. J. (2001). The violence of sexual harassment: Physical, emotional, and economic victimization. In D. S. Sandhu (Ed.), *Faces of violence: Psychological correlates, concepts, and intervention strategies* (pp. 229–249). Hauppauge, NY: Nova Science.

Maass, A., Cadinu, M., Guarnieri, G., & Grasselli, A. (2003). Sexual harassment under social identity threat: The computer harassment paradigm. *Journal of Personality and Social Psychology, 85,* 853–870.

Morse, J. (1989). "Euch, those are for your husband!" Examination of cultural values and assumptions associated with breast-feeding. *Health Care for Women International, 11,* 223–232.

Murnen, S. K., Wright, C., & Kaluzny, G. (2007). If boys will be boys, then girls will be victims? A meta-analytic review of the research that relates masculine ideology to sexual aggression. *Sex Roles, 46,* 359–375.

O'Guinn, T. C., & Shrum, L. J. (1997). The role of television in the construction of consumer reality. *Journal of Consumer Research, 23,* 278–294.

Poll says games are safe. (1999, May 24). Retrieved Feb. 1, 2000 from http://pc.ign.com/articles/068/068231p1.html

Poll: Do games cause violence? (2010). Retrieved April 28, 2011 from http://www.escapistmagazine.com/forums/read/18.181950-Poll-Do-video-games-cause-violence?page=2

Posavac, H. D., Posavac, S. S., & Posavac, E. J. (1998). Exposure to media images of female attractiveness and concern with body weight among young women. *Sex Roles, 38*(3/4), 187–201.

Potter, W. J. (2003). *The eleven myths of media violence.* Thousand Oaks, CA: Sage.

Potter, W. J. (2009). *Arguing for a general framework for mass media scholarship.* Thousand Oaks, CA: Sage.

PTC. (2011). Facts and TV statistics: "It's just harmless entertainment" Oh really? Retrieved from http://www.parentstv.org/ptc/facts/mediafacts.asp

Rudman, L. A., & Heppen, J. B. (2003). Implicit romantic fantasies and women's interest in personal power: A glass slipper effect? *Personality and Social Psychology Bulletin, 29,* 1357–1370.

Sacks, D. P., Bushman, B. J., & Anderson, C. A. (2011). Do violent video games harm children? Comparing the scientific amicus curiae "experts" in Brown v. Entertainment Merchants Association. *Northwestern University Law Review, 106*, 1–12.

Sherif, M. (1966). *In common predicament: Social psychology of intergroup conflict and cooperation.* Boston: Houghton Mifflin.

Sibley, C. G., & Wilson, M. S. (2004). Differentiating hostile and benevolent sexist attitudes toward positive and negative sexual female subtypes. *Sex Roles, 51*, 687–696.

Slusher, M. P., & Anderson, C. A. (1987). When reality monitoring fails: The role of imagination in stereotype maintenance. *Journal of Personality & Social Psychology, 52*, 653–662.

Stark, E. (2007). *Coercive control.* New York: Oxford.

Steele, C. M., Spencer, S. J., & Aronson, J. (2002). Contending with group image: The psychology of stereotype and social identity threat. In M. P. Zanna (Ed.), *Advances in experimental social psychology, 34* (pp. 379–440). San Diego, CA: Academic Press.

Strasburger, V. C., & Wilson, B. J. (2002). *Children, adolescents and the media.* Thousand Oaks, CA: Sage.

Sturken, M., & Cartwright, L. (2009). *Practices of looking: An introduction to visual culture.* New York: Oxford University Press.

Subcommittee on Commerce, Trade, and Consumer Protection (2007, September 25). *From Imus to industry: The business of stereotyopes and degrading images.* Retreived March 20, 2008 from http://energycommerce.house.gov/cmte_mtgs/110-ctcp-hrg.092507.Imus.to.Industry.shtml

Taylor, S. E., Fiske, S. T., Etcoff, N. L., & Ruderman, A. J. (1978). Categorical and contextual bases of person memory and stereotyping. *Journal of Personality and Social Psychology, 36*, 778–793.

Tedeschi J. T., & Felson, R. B. (1994). *Violence, aggression, & coercive actions.* Washington, DC: American Psychological Association.

Voracek, M., & Fisher, M. (2002). Shapely centrefolds? Temporal change in body measures: Trend analysis. *British Medical Journal, 325* (7378), 1447–1448. doi: 10.1136/bmj.325.73.78.1447

Ward, L. M., Hansborough, E., & Walker, E. (2005). Contributions of music video exposure to black adolescents gender and sexual schemas. *Journal of Adolescent Research, 20*(2), 143–166.

Ward, L. M., Merriwether, A., & Caruthers, A. (2006). Breasts are for men: Media, masculinity ideologies, and men's beliefs about women's bodies. *Sex Roles, 55*, 703–714.

Wilson, C. C., Gutierrez, F., & Chao, L. M. (2003). *Racism, sexism, and the media: The rise of class communication in multicultural America* (3rd ed.). Thousand Oaks, CA: Sage.

Wilson, T. D. (2002). *Strangers to ourselves: Discovering the adaptive unconscious.* Cambridge, MA: Harvard University Press.

Wolf, N. (2002). *The beauty myth: How images are used against women.* New York: Perennial.

Wyer, R. S., & Adaval, R. (2004). Pictures, words, and media influence: The interactive effects of verbal and nonverbal information on memory and judgments. In L. J. Shrum (Ed.), *The psychology of entertainment media: Blurring the lines between entertainment and persuasion* (pp. 137–159). Mahwah, NJ: Lawrence Erlbaum Associates.

9

Alcohol Messages in Television Series: Content and Effects

Cristel Antonia Russell
American University
Washington, DC

Dale W. Russell
Uniformed Services University
Bethesda, Maryland

Problems associated with alcohol consumption are on the rise; the World Health Organization estimates that alcohol consumption results in approximately 2.5 million fatalities annually as well as over 69 million disability-adjusted life years (i.e., the number of years lost due to poor health, disability, or early death; World Health Organization, 2010). In the United States alone, alcohol consumption is directly responsible for 23,199 deaths annually (Xu, Kochanek, Murphy, & Tejada-Vera, 2010), including 12,700 vehicle fatalities (Yi, Williams, & Hilton, 2005) and 1,574,000 hospital admissions annually (Chen, Yi, & Hilton, 2005). There are many other negative externalities (e.g., lost productivity, prevention programs and healthcare expenditures) related to alcohol consumption.

This chapter draws from a program of research funded by the National Institute on Alcohol Abuse and Alcoholism (NIAAA), an institute of the National Institutes of Health, which has been the lead U.S. federal agency responsible for scientific research on alcohol and its effects for nearly 40 years. Thus, one of the goals of the NIAAA is to research factors that affect, positively or negatively, alcohol consumption, including the factors that shape people's attitudes and beliefs about drinking. The aim of this program of research is to document the nature and impact of alcohol messages embedded in the content of television series. Television programs provide vivid insights into the lifestyles of influential and often aspirational characters (Diener, 1993; Russell, Norman, & Heckler, 2004). These depictions often involve showing characters' eating and drinking, which may affect the viewers' own lifestyles and consumption behaviors (Avery & Ferraro, 2000; O'Guinn & Shrum, 1997). Consumers garner a substantial amount of knowledge (nonfactual and factual) through television series, including health-related behavioral information (Beck, Huang, Pollard, & Johnson, 2003; Gerbner, 1995). This method of knowledge acquisition can become an issue when the information presented or lifestyles depicted do not accurately reflect reality or when behaviors displayed are not recommended (Way, 1984). For instance, studies have demonstrated that viewers who spend more time consuming mass media hold beliefs that are less supportive of good health and nutrition (Avery, Mathios, Shanahan, & Bisogni, 1997; Signorielli, 1993).

The presence of alcohol messages in program content has generated societal concern given the potential of television series to influence audience behaviors. Portrayals of alcohol in the media have been linked to the development and maintenance of beliefs about and attitudes toward alcohol. For example, several studies have found that young people who are more exposed to positive alcohol portrayals and advertising have more favorable beliefs about drinking and are more likely to consume alcohol (Grube & Wallack, 1994; Snyder, Milici, Slater, Sun, & Strizhakova, 2006; Stacy, Pearce, Zogg, Unger, & Dent, 2004). Alcohol portrayals in the content of television programs also serve to reinforce existing alcoholic behaviors. For instance, research has shown that exposing people with high alcohol dependence to a television program with alcohol scenes makes it more difficult for them to resist the urge to drink heavily (Sobell, Sobell, Toneatto, & Leo, 1993).

We begin by reviewing findings from content analyses of prime time television series to document the characteristics of alcohol messages contained therein, and in particular, to distinguish between those messages that portray alcohol positively and those that portray alcohol negatively. Next, we review empirical evidence regarding how these embedded alcohol messages are processed and the impact they have on audiences' alcohol beliefs and attitudes. Finally, based on the growing body of knowledge in this area, we review implications for public health and public policy, in particular with regard to young audiences, who are especially susceptible to alcohol messages.

FACTORS AFFECTING THE PRESENCE OF
ALCOHOL MESSAGES IN TELEVISION SERIES

There are many forces driving the inclusion of alcohol messages in the stories or on the sets of television programs. One is product placement. Product placement is a marketing practice in which companies pay for inclusion of their products in films and television programs (Balasubramanian, 1994; Russell, 1998), is a frequent practice for the alcohol industry. In fact, alcohol is one of the most actively placed product categories in Hollywood television programs and movies (Russell and Belch, 2005). A major content analysis found that alcohol placements occurred at least once in 181 television series during the 1997–98 season and in 233 movies (Federal Trade Commission, 1999).

A competing and more recent trend is the use of television programs, along with other entertainment media, as platforms for educating viewers about risky behaviors, including alcohol abuse. The use of comingled entertainment–education techniques is becoming more common to tackle especially difficult issues such as sexual behavior or gender issues targeting especially vulnerable audiences (Pechmann & Wang, 2008; Singhal & Rogers, 2002). There is common consensus that television series have much educational potential, and indeed entertainment–education collaborative efforts between public health organizations and the television industry has resulted in the intermingling of health-related information in varying social contexts (Fox, 2005). A number of studies have shown that embedded health messages can influence viewers' attitudes and beliefs in areas such as emergency contraception (Folb, 2000) and AIDS prevention (Kennedy, O'Leary, Beck, Pollard, & Simpson, 2004), and these placements are perceived as more practical than overt persuasive attempts such as public service announcements. As a case in point, an episode of the popular program *Friends* that contained a storyline about condom failure and a resulting pregnancy increased viewers' perceptions of risks associated with condom use (Collins, Elliott, Berry, Kanouse, & Hunter, 2003).

Of course, television producers and writers are not always guided by marketers or education–entertainment efforts when developing storylines and creating sets. In a content analysis of sex portrayals in the television series *Sex and the City*, Jensen and Jensen (2007) found that the series' writers incorporated a number of important health issues (e.g., smoking, cancer, and sexual health) into the storylines of many episodes. However, although the series earned a number of awards for treatments of health issues, researchers have also identified missed opportunities for conveying realistic and useful messages, such as those focusing on the central breast cancer narrative included in one of the episodes (Gray, 2007).

In most cases, artistic freedom prevails and products such as cars, home furnishings, or food and drinks are used, first and foremost, to depict scenes as realistic and life-like (Russell & Belch, 2005) and to serve as "psycho-cultural" cues for the audience to construct meanings about characters and groups (Avery & Ferraro, 2000; Hirschman, Scott, & Wells, 1998; Sherry, 1995; Solomon & Greenberg, 1993). The term "word-of-author advertising" actually captures the fact that writers of screenplays, novels, or television dramas incorporate consumption references and brands in the texts of their works because of their desire to reflect real life (Friedman, 1985).

In sum, three major factors influence alcohol messages depicted in television series, as depicted in Figure 9.1. They are color-coded, with green depicting product placement efforts that result in more positive messages (messages that communicate positive consequences of drinking alcohol; i.e., pro-alcohol) and red depicting education–entertainment (a.k.a. edutainment) practices that result in more negative messages (messages that communicate negative consequences of using/drinking alcohol [i.e.,

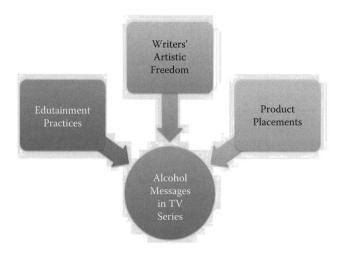

FIGURE 9.1
Forces affecting alcohol messages in TV series.

anti-alcohol]). This color scheme will be used throughout the chapter and figures to link forces to alcohol messages' nature and then to the ways audiences process them.

THE NATURE OF EMBEDDED ALCOHOL MESSAGES IN TELEVISION SERIES

Portrayals of drinking and alcohol product placements abound in television series, and to the extreme in many of the current young audience favorites such as *Skins* and *Jersey Shore*, which depict heavy alcohol consumption as a favorable norm (Christensen, Henriksen, & Roberts, 2000; Mathios, Avery, Bisogni, & Shanahan, 1998; Russell & Stern, 2006). In the absence of a stringent regulatory framework, it is important to actively monitor the content of television programs in order to provide an accurate and thorough assessment of how alcohol is portrayed in television programs. To this end, and as part of a program of research funded by the NIAAA, 18 top-rated prime-time television series from the 2004–2005 season were analyzed for alcohol-related content. The sample consisted of 144 unique episodes, eight from each of the series. The sample spanned genres and included five situation comedies (sitcoms), one cartoon, and twelve dramas (see Table 9.1).

Content Analysis Procedures

Content analysis is widely used in analyzing media productions, and has proven especially useful in understanding consumer behavior and informing public policy research (Avery et al., 1997; Avery & Ferraro, 2000; Bang & Reece, 2003; Berelson, 1971; Kelly, Slater, Karan, & Hunn, 2000; Kolbe & Burnett, 1991). We used content analysis to systematically code alcohol messages depicted in television programming.

In the first step of our content analysis, we coded alcohol messages based on their modality of presentation (visual and auditory) and their level of plot connection (Russell, 2002). Alcohol messages were further coded both at the instance level and at the episode level. Coding procedures and measures were based on protocols utilized in previous alcohol content analyses (Avery et al., 1997; Pendleton, Smith, & Roberts, 1991;

TABLE 9.1

Sample of Prime-Time Television Series Investigated

Program Genre (Length)	Series Name (Season)
Drama, action/crime (1 hour)	*CSI* (S5)
	CSI: Miami (S3)
	CSI: New York (S1)
	Law & Order (S15)
	Law & Order: Special Victims Unit (S6)
	NYPD Blue (S12)
Drama, soap (1 hour)	*7th Heaven* (S9)
	Desperate Housewives (S1)
	The O.C. (S2)
Drama (1 hour)	*Everwood* (S3)
	E.R. (S11)
	The West Wing (S6)
Situation comedy (30 minutes)	*Everybody Loves Raymond* (S9)
	Joey (S1)
	That 70s Show (S7)
	Two and Half Men (S2)
	Will & Grace (S7)
	The Simpsons (S16)

Note: Program genres based on categorizations provided by CNET Networks Entertainment.

Wallack, Grube, Madden, & Breed, 1990; Story & Faulkner, 1990) with some minor variations. In order to accurately measure visual alcohol displays, any depiction that was visually presented for three continuous seconds was coded.

In the second step of the content analysis, we computed the overall scores at the episode level by counting the number of auditory references and by summing the amount of time alcohol appeared for each beverage category and each setting. The connection of alcohol to the plot of the episode was measured at the end of the episode. The level of plot connection captures the degree to which alcohol contributes to the advancement of the main or the subplot patterns. The overall valence of the alcohol message was also assessed at the end of each episode, guided by the literature on positive and negative alcohol expectancies (Grube & Agostinelli, 1999). This approach categorizes the consequences of consuming alcohol into positive ones (e.g., having a good time without consequences) and negative ones (e.g., getting a hangover). Previous research has found that these two dimensions should be assessed independently (Grube, Chen, Madden, & Morgan, 1995; Grube & Agostinelli, 1999) because they represent dual messages.

Content Analysis Findings

Our analyses revealed that alcohol was present in at least one episode of every program coded. Alcohol was consumed 58.6% of the time it was portrayed and consumption was more frequently depicted when it was in the foreground (77.5% of the time) than when it was in the background (14.2% of the time). Another important finding was that characters under the legal drinking age in the United States (i.e., under 21 years of age) were present 21.1% of the time when alcohol was depicted, and actual consumption was depicted in half (50.0%) of the instances involving these underaged characters.

To take into account the different lengths of the programs, rates per hour were computed for each visual and auditory measure. The rate of total amount of visual exposure significantly differed by program: In some programs, the majority of the visual alcohol depictions are of the background type. In *Everybody Loves Raymond*, for example, alcohol was visually present in every episode and was in the background 78.9% of the time (a wine rack always in Raymond's kitchen). In contrast, only one episode of *7th Heaven* included visual depictions of alcohol but the visual display was more prominent (wine glasses on tables in a restaurant scene).

Alcohol messages were also analyzed based on the visual, auditory, and plot connection dimensions, and compared across genres and programs. Situation comedies displayed overwhelmingly more alcohol than any other genre, with an average rate of 6:56 visual depictions per hour. Soaps have an opposite pattern, with a rate of 2:37 per hour but including only 0:12 depictions of background per hour. Several situation comedies stand out as having a relatively large rate of alcohol visual exposure per hour: *Two and a Half Men* (13:53 per hour), *Will & Grace* (11:24 per hour), and *Joey* (6:11 per hour). At the high end of the alcohol portrayals spectrum is *Two and a Half Men,* where an average 22-minute episode contains over 5 minutes of visual depictions of alcohol, including 2:26 of actual alcohol consumption inside the home. The main character, Charlie Harper (actor Charlie Sheen), consumes alcohol, of all types, in nearly every setting (i.e., home, bar, restaurant, etc.).

In contrast to previous analyses, however, messages about alcohol are found to be, on the whole, more negative than positive (Christensen et al., 2000). The valence of the alcohol message is directly related to the way that message is communicated. An overall more negative message about alcohol relates to verbal discussions that affect the plot of the episodes whereas an overall more positive message is related to visual depictions of the background type. In particular, whenever alcohol is central to the plot of an episode, it tends to be associated with negative elements such as a crime, addiction, or lowered job performance. Overall, messages associating alcohol with positive consequences (i.e., having fun or partying hard) are primarily communicated visually in the background. Therefore, prime-time television series convey both positive and negative messages about alcohol and, while the central alcohol message is more often negative, the secondary message is usually positive.

The case of the teen drama *The O.C.* is especially telling. Each episode averages almost four minutes of alcohol visual depictions and over four verbal references to alcohol per episode. Furthermore, almost all of the episodes contained positive messages about alcohol (i.e., fun parties, relaxation, social events, etc.). Positive messages were primarily conveyed visually using low plot/background visual depictions. However, negative messages (i.e., drunken driving, addiction, death, etc.) were mainly presented through discourse and highly tied to the episode's plot. Overall, the alcohol messages are often mixed, with overt antialcohol messages stemming mainly from auditory discussions that are connected to the plot, and covert pro-alcohol messages more often being visual and of the background type. Figure 9.2 graphically shows how these dimensions relate to each other.

Implications of Content Analysis Findings

The different ways in which positive and negative alcohol messages are communicated in television programs suggest differences in their impact on the audience. The more central negative messages should invoke semantic processing (Roberts, Cowen, & MacDonald, 1996) and be more easily recalled (Craik & Lockhart, 1972), whereas the more subtle positive messages may be less noticeable but could still influence audiences via low-effort processing (Russell, 2002). Furthermore, the finding that alcohol depictions in youth-oriented series like *The O.C.* are

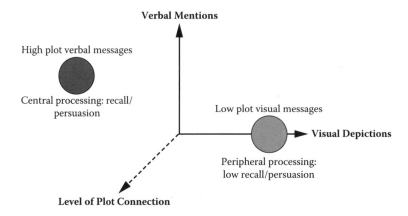

FIGURE 9.2
Nature of alcohol messages in TV series.

often associated with aspirational underage drinkers is important given the likelihood for young viewers to treat television characters as referent others and emulate their behaviors. Previous research has shown that parasocial referents who are associated with certain consumption patterns such as smoking can impact viewers' attitudes and intentions, especially if they identify with them (Pechmann & Wang, 2008). Therefore, it is likely that as viewers become more connected to the characters in the series, the attitudes and behaviors depicted by these characters will have even more impact on their own opinions and behaviors. The proposed processes are depicted visually in Figure 9.3. Research on the response side, presented next, can illuminate some of the key findings concerning audience effects.

EFFECTS OF EMBEDDED MESSAGES ON AUDIENCES

Another component of the research program involved testing how viewers perceive the positive and negative alcohol messages embedded in television series, and in turn how those perceptions relate to their own drinking attitudes and beliefs. In particular, several studies were conducted to test the proposed model depicted in Figure 9.3. One central component of the proposed model involves connectedness, which refers

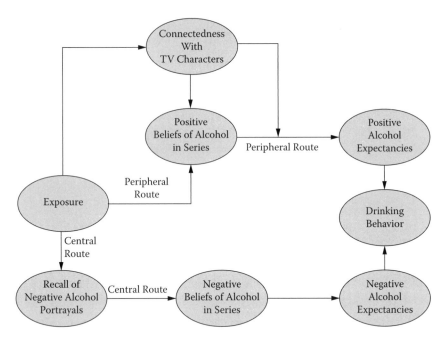

FIGURE 9.3
Effects of exposure and connectedness to TV series on alcohol beliefs.

to the intensity of the relationships viewers develop with programs and the characters in those programs in a parasocial television environment (Russell & Puto, 1999). Research has demonstrated that the relationships viewers develop with television characters drive the viewers' own consumption experiences and beliefs about consumption (Russell & Puto, 1999; Russell & Stern, 2006), and that connectedness affecting the processing of program-related information occurs above and beyond mere exposure to and involvement with the program (Russell et al., 2004). This section focuses on the central findings from research conducted with audiences of youth-oriented programs to test the ways in which they process embedded alcohol messages and to assess the role of connectedness in these processes.

Methodological Procedures

A series of studies were conducted with young viewers of television series with alcohol messages embedded therein to assess their recall and perceptions of the alcohol messages in the series and test the relationships to their real-life alcohol attitudes and beliefs. The survey instruments included questions about the participants' experience of watching the series in question: overall exposure, attitude toward the program, involvement with the program, and connectedness with the program (Russell et al., 2004). Participants were then asked to provide their perceptions of the alcohol portrayals in the program. They were first asked to describe up to 10 instances of alcohol having been depicted in the program. They then indicated the extent to which they felt that alcohol was linked to each of eight positive and eight negative outcomes in the series, a measure commonly used in alcohol research (Grube et al., 1995).

The instruments concluded with a series of questions assessing the respondents' general beliefs and normative perceptions regarding alcohol consumption. The alcohol expectancies measure asked respondents to indicate how likely it is that each of eight positive and eight negative consequences would happen to them personally if they were to drink three or four whole drinks of alcohol (Grube et al., 1995). Lastly, the respondents' own alcohol consumption was measured by asking them to report how often, in the past 30 days, they had one or more whole drinks, on how many days they felt drunk, and on how many days they had five or more whole drinks in a row (the definition of binge drinking).

Differences in Processing Positive and Negative Alcohol Messages

Recalled alcohol events were coded based on whether they were positive (e.g., Seth's parents drinking to loosen themselves up before sex), negative (e.g., drunk Seth throwing up everywhere and rolling over the hood of his parents' car), or neutral (e.g., Seth's dad meeting prospective clients in a bar). In *The O.C.* studies, where viewers listed an average of 5.2 instances of alcohol, more negative messages were recalled (3.2). These findings suggest that negative alcohol messages are processed more centrally. The number of recalled instances of alcohol in the series, as well as viewers' estimates of the prevalence of alcohol, were also affected by overall amount of exposure to the series. Thus, increased exposure to the program leads to increased estimates of prevalence and recall of negative alcohol instances, regardless of viewers' levels of connectedness. These findings are consistent with the salience of the negative alcohol messages in *The O.C.* and with previous research showing that the amount of exposure to a program affects general estimates of the prevalence of alcohol in that program (O'Guinn & Shrum, 1997).

An analysis was also conducted to determine whether viewers also perceived the message about alcohol in the program to be associated with negative or positive outcomes and what variables predict these perceptions. Only overall exposure was significantly related to the negative perceptions. These perceptions in turn are also related to viewers' beliefs about the negative consequences of alcohol in real life. However, a different pattern emerged for positive perceptions: Those were affected only by viewers' levels of connectedness. The more connected viewers were to the program, the more they perceived that alcohol is associated with positive outcomes such as feeling happy, having fun, or having an easier time expressing one's feelings. Whereas reception of the salient negative messages about alcohol increased with exposure to the program, reception of the subtle positive messages about alcohol in *The O.C.* increased with connectedness.

The Impact of Audience Connectedness

The studies conducted within this research program provide evidence that that viewers' level of connectedness to a television series plays a major role in the impact of embedded alcohol messages. Connectedness has been shown to not only affect how viewers process alcohol messages in television programs, as described in the above section, but to also affect how these messages are integrated into the viewers' own beliefs and attitudes about drinking. As a result of the strong relationships viewers enjoy with the characters in the program, highly connected viewers are more likely to internalize the messages contained within it. Highly connected viewers are also more likely to mold characteristics of their own life after what they see in the program (Pechmann & Wang, 2008; Russell & Puto, 1999). Thus, viewers who feel strongly connected are more impacted by the alcohol messages in terms of their own opinions about drinking and attitudes toward drinkers than are viewers who are weakly connected. Connected viewers are also especially receptive to the subtle positive messages.

These results are especially evident in studies of young viewers of *The O.C.* The subtle positive messages (depicted in Figures 9.2 and 9.3 in green) are processed differently and follow different routes of recall and persuasion than the salient negative ones (depicted in red). The negative alcohol messages are more readily recalled. Moreover, the reception of those messages, as evidenced by recall and estimates of prevalence and perceptions, is a function of the amount of exposure to the series. However, there is also evidence that the subtle pro-alcohol messages that are not explicitly recalled are primarily related to highly connected viewers' alcohol beliefs and attitudes. The more connected viewers are, the more they associate alcohol with positive outcomes, not only within the program, but in real life as well. Overall, this program of research shows that, whereas the amount of exposure to a program is related to viewers' general estimates of the prevalence of alcohol in the program, connectedness is the best predictor of the impact of these alcohol messages on viewers' beliefs about alcohol in real life. Connectedness thus reflects greater receptiveness to the latent positive message communicated about alcohol.

Additional Effects of Audience Connectedness: The Impact of Warnings

This program of research has identified another key role of connectedness: its moderating effect on the impact of warnings placed before television episodes to alter the processing and persuasive effect of embedded alcohol messages. Forewarning is known to produce resistance to persuasive attempts, as evidenced by less attitude change in the direction intended by the communication (Petty & Cacioppo, 1977; Wood & Quinn, 2003). Forewarning increases counterarguments during the presentation of the persuasive communication, thus undermining its persuasive power (Fukada, 1986), allowing individuals to access persuasion knowledge and counterarguments in response to the message (Friestad & Wright, 1995). However, warnings may not be effective if viewers are distracted (Campbell & Kirmani, 2000; Petty, Wells, & Brock, 1976). Distraction from the warning is especially relevant to the processing of messages embedded within television programs. In particular, high levels of connectedness, which reflect engagement with the characters and transportation in the story, may preempt viewers from treating the embedded alcohol messages as persuasive attempts. Such interference inhibits viewers' ability to develop counterarguments and thus the effect of the warning is lost (Romero, Agnew, & Insko, 1996).

To test these interactive effects, we conducted an experiment based on a 2 (connectedness level) X 3 (warning: none, before or after the episode) design (Russell & Russell, 2008). Connectedness was measured and the timing of the warnings was manipulated to appear either before or after the episode. The stimulus in this study was an episode of *Two and a Half Men* that included alcohol product placements. All participants were informed that the purpose of the study was to examine perceptions of the realism of television programs and that they would watch a sitcom episode and then respond to questions about aspects of the show that might influence their perceptions. This was the only information provided in the control condition. In the other conditions, participants read additional instructions either just before or just after the episode (timing manipulation) stating that "Sometimes marketers and advertisers persuade television producers to have the characters communicate specific messages about their products because, for them, it is a good way to advertise their products." All instructions concluded with "You may notice such messages in the episode" if the warning preceded the episode or "You may have noticed such messages in the episode" if the warning followed the episode.

One-hundred and fifty young adults viewed the episode and completed a questionnaire concerning their attitude toward the episode, involvement with the program, and connectedness with the program. Next, alcohol expectancies, the main dependent variables, were measured (Grube et al., 1995), followed by control and demographic variables.

Here, our analyses revealed a significant interaction between the connectedness level and the timing of the warning. This interaction is depicted in Figure 9.4, with connectedness scores split at the median, for illustrative purposes. As the figure indicates, pre-warning decreased the positivity of alcohol attitudes but only for the low-connected viewers (3.57 versus 4.10 in the control condition). For the highly connected viewers, the opposite effect was observed, with even more positive attitudes (4.33) in the pre-warning condition than in the control condition (4.18). The post-warning had no effect on alcohol attitudes.

The study provides evidence that warning viewers about embedded messages in the content of a television series can impact their alcohol attitudes, but that this effect occurs primarily for low-connected viewers, and only when a warning is placed before the episode. Highly connected viewers, who have developed parasocial relationships with the television

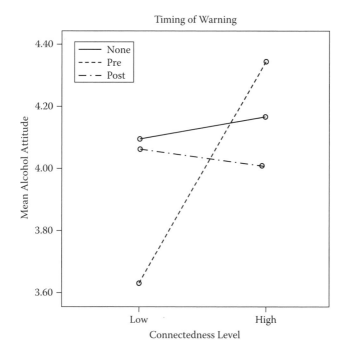

FIGURE 9.4
Impact of warnings on alcohol attitudes as a function of connectedness level.

characters, are not affected by the warnings. In fact, in the study just discussed, not only were highly connected viewers resistant to the warnings in general, but in the pre-warning condition, they demonstrated a reactance effect (Brehm, 1972), with even more positive attitudes than in the no-warning condition. As such, it is important to note the potential for forewarning messages to have the opposite effect on viewers' beliefs than is intended.

DISCUSSION AND IMPLICATIONS

Television series have been and continue to be mass conduits for disseminating messages directed at promoting but also preventing alcohol use (Russell & Russell, 2009). Given the ubiquity of product placements, with one estimate approximating their use in 75% of prime-time television programming (Consoli, 2004), NIAAA is keen to assess the nature and impact of embedded alcohol messages. This chapter has highlighted the fact that there are many countervailing forces at play. The alcohol industry strives to achieve an ongoing flow of customers, the entertainment world wants to preserve its creative freedom rights, and governmental and other health organizations try to reduce alcohol abuse. As these forces pull in opposite directions to satisfy their own agendas, they can generate counteracting "pro" and "anti" messages within the media that compete for audiences' attention and interest and ultimately yield mixed or counteracting effects on attitudes, beliefs, and behaviors regarding alcohol use.

There are important public policy implications for this research. Research has found that the earlier in life alcohol consumption begins, the more likely an individual is to experience future chronic problems with both alcohol and illicit drug abuse, as well as medical problems associated with their usage (Grant & Dawson, 1998). The Surgeon General believes that, because of their immense influence over media productions, entertainment and alcohol companies have a moral responsibility to limit not only alcohol advertisements but also alcohol depictions to younger audiences. To this end, the Surgeon General recommends that television programs avoid excessive alcohol portrayals, not glamorize underage drinking in any respect, convey more balanced and realistic depictions of excessive alcohol consumption, and most importantly, take research of this nature into consideration when developing media and advertising products (USDHHS, 2007).

Limiting exposure to positive portrayals of alcohol is an important component of prevention campaigns and, although efforts have been made to reduce television alcohol advertisements, little has been done to abate alcohol depictions contained in television programming (Jernigan, Ostroff, & Ross, 2005).

Another strategy proposed by public health advocates is to display content warning messages to prompt viewers about the presence of alcohol messages in television programs (Commercial Alert, 2008). However, our program of research shows that highly connected viewers are not only resistant to warnings about pro-alcohol messages in a television episode but that they even become more positive toward alcohol (Russell & Russell, 2008). Therefore, advocates of message warnings should be conscious of the differential impact of forewarning on high- and low-connected viewers. A forewarning about alcohol product placements in a television program, as advocated by Commercial Alert, may effectively reduce the effect of those placements among low-connected viewers, but it will also increase the placements' impact on highly connected viewers.

This research contributes to the growing body of evidence that messages contained within television programming influence consumers' health-related attitudes, beliefs, and behaviors, especially among younger viewers. Television programs continue to be important agents of socialization (O'Guinn & Shrum, 1997), and young people consume a great deal of them. The findings of how embedded alcohol messages are processed by audiences have implications beyond this context, and future research could incorporate them to study the processing of messages about other health issues depicted on television, such as nutrition or smoking.

AUTHOR NOTES

This research was supported by National Institute on Alcohol Abuse and Alcoholism grant R21AA014897. The content is solely the responsibility of the authors and does not necessarily represent the official views of the National Institute on Alcohol Abuse and Alcoholism or the National Institutes of Health. The opinions or assertions contained herein are the private ones of authors and not to be construed as official or reflecting the views of the DoD or the USUHS.

REFERENCES

Avery, R. J., & Ferraro, R. (2000). Verisimilitude or advertising? Brand appearances on prime-time television. *The Journal of Consumer Affairs, 34*(2), 217–227.

Avery, R. J., Mathios, A., Shanahan, J., & Bisogni, C. (1997). Food and nutrition messages communicated through prime-time television. *Journal of Public Policy & Marketing, 16*(2), 217–227.

Balasubramanian, S. K. (1994). Beyond advertising and publicity: Hybrid messages and public policy issues. *Journal of Advertising, 23*(4), 29–46.

Bang, H. K., & Reece, B. B. (2003). Minorities in children's television commercials: New, improved, and stereotyped. *The Journal of Consumer Affairs, 37*(1), 42–67.

Beck, V., Huang, G. C., Pollard, W. E., & Johnson, T. J. (2003). TV drama viewers and health information. Paper presented at the *American Public Health Association 131st Annual Meeting and Exposition*, San Francisco, CA.

Berelson, B. (1971). *Content analysis in communication research*. Glencoe, IL: Free Press.

Brehm, J. W. (1972). *Responses to loss of freedom: A theory of psychological reactance*. Morristown, NJ: General Learning Press.

Campbell, M. C., & Kirmani, A. (2000). Consumers' use of persuasion knowledge: The effects of accessibility and cognitive capacity on perceptions of an influence agent. *Journal of Consumer Research, 27*(June), 69–83.

Chen, C. M., Yi, H., & Hilton, M. E. (2005). *Trends in alcohol-related morbidity among short-stay community hospital discharges, United States, 1979–2003*. Bethesda, MD: National Institute on Alcohol Abuse and Alcoholism.

Christensen, P. G., Henriksen, L., & Roberts, D. F. (2000). *Substance use in popular prime-time television*. Washington, DC: Office of National Drug Control Policy.

Collins, R. L., Elliott, M. N., Berry, S. H., Kanouse, D. E., & Hunter, S. B. (2003). Entertainment television as a healthy sex educator: The impact of condom-efficacy information in an episode of *Friends*. *Pediatrics, 112*, 1115–1121.

Commercial Alert. (2008). Retrieved from www.commercial alert.org.

Consoli, J. (2004). Running in place(ment). *Brandweek, 45*(28), 4–6.

Craik, F. I. M., & Lockhart, R. S. (1972). Levels of processing: A framework for memory research. *Journal of Verbal Learning and Verbal Behavior, 11*(6), 671–684.

Diener, B. J. (1993). The frequency and context of alcohol and tobacco cues in daytime soap opera programs: Fall 1986 and Fall 1991. *Journal of Public Policy & Marketing, 12*(2), 252–258.

Federal Trade Commission. (1999). *Self-regulation in the alcohol industry: A Federal Trade Commission report to Congress*. Retrieved from http://www.ftc.gov/reports

Folb, K. L. (2000). Don't touch that dial! TV as a—what!?—positive influence. *Sexuality Information and Education Council of the United States Report, 28*(5), 16–18.

Fox, S. (2005). *CDC award: Writers and producers gather to address the role of women in daytime dramas*. Retrieved from http://www.soapsummit.org/cdcaward.htm

Friedman, M. (1985). The changing language of a consumer society: Brand name usage in popular American novels in the postwar era. *Journal of Consumer Research, 11*, 927–938.

Friestad, M., & Wright, P. (1995). Persuasion knowledge: Lay people's and researchers' beliefs about the psychology of advertising. *Journal of Consumer Research, 22*(June), 62–74.

Fukada, H. (1986). Psychological processes mediating persuasion-inhibiting effect of forewarning in fear-arousing communication. *Psychological Reports, 58*(1), 87–90.

Gerbner, G. (1995). Alcohol in American culture. In S. E. Martin (Ed.), *The effects of the mass media on the use and abuse of alcohol* (pp. 3–29). Bethesda, MD: National Institute on Alcohol Abuse and Alcoholism.

Grant, B. F., & Dawson, D. A. (1998). Age at onset of alcohol use and its association with DSM-IV drug abuse and dependence: Results from the national longitudinal alcohol epidemiologic survey. *Journal of Substance Abuse, 10*(2), 163–173.

Gray, J. (2007). Interpersonal communication and the illness experience in the *Sex and the City* breast cancer narrative. *Communications Quarterly, 55*(4), 397–414.

Grube, J. W., & Agostinelli, G. E. (1999). Perceived consequences and adolescent drinking: Nonlinear and interactive models of alcohol expectancies. *Psychology of Addictive Behaviors 13*, 303–312.

Grube, J. W., Chen, M., Madden, P., & Morgan, M. (1995). Predicting adolescent drinking from alcohol expectancy values: A comparison of additive, interactive, and nonlinear models. *Journal of Applied Social Psychology, 25*(10), 839–857.

Grube, J. W., & Wallack, L. (1994). Television beer advertising and drinking knowledge, beliefs, and intentions among schoolchildren. *American Journal of Public Health, 84*, 254–259.

Hirschman, E. C., Scott, L., & Wells, W. D. (1998). A model of product discourse: Linking consumer practice to cultural texts. *Journal of Advertising, 27*(Spring), 33–50.

Jensen, R. E., & Jensen, J. D. (2007). Entertainment media and sexual health: A content analysis of sexual talk, behavior, and risks in a popular television series. *Sex Roles, 56*, 275–284.

Jernigan, D. H., Ostroff, J., & Ross, C. (2005). Alcohol advertising and youth: A measured approach. *Journal of Public Health Policy, 26*(3), 312–325.

Kelly, K. J., Slater, M. D., Karan, D., & Hunn, L. (2000). The use of human models and cartoon characters in magazine advertisements for cigarettes, beer, and nonalcoholic beverages. *Journal of Public Policy & Marketing, 19*(Fall), 189–200.

Kennedy, M. G., O'Leary, A., Beck, V., Pollard, K., & Simpson, P. (2004). Increases in calls to the CDC National STD and AIDS Hotline following AIDS-related episodes in a soap opera. *Journal of Communication, 54*(June), 287–301.

Kolbe, R. H., & Burnett, M. S. (1991). Content-analysis research: An examination of applications with directives for improving research reliability and objectivity. *Journal of Consumer Research, 18*(September), 243–250.

Mathios, A., Avery, R. J., Bisogni, C., & Shanahan, J. (1998). Alcohol portrayal on prime-time television: Manifest and latent messages. *Journal of Studies on Alcohol, 59*, 305–310.

O'Guinn, T. C., & Shrum, L.J. (1997). The role of television in the construction of consumer reality. *Journal of Consumer Research, 23*(March), 278–294.

Pechmann, C., & Wang, L. (2008). *An experimental investigation of an entertainment education television episode about adolescent smoking: Reference group and identification effects.* Retrieved from http://www.gsb.stanford.edu/FACSEMINARS/pdfs/2006_01-25_Pechmann.pdf

Pendleton, L. L., Smith, C. C., & Roberts, J. L. (1991). Drinking on television—A content analysis of recent alcohol portrayal. *British Journal of Addiction, 86*(6), 769–774.

Petty, R. E., & Cacioppo, J. T. (1977). Forewarning, cognitive responding, and resistance to persuasion. *Journal of Personality and Social Psychology, 35*, 645–655.

Petty, R. E., Wells, G. L., & Brock, T. C. (1976). Distraction can enhance or reduce yielding to propaganda: Thought disruption versus effort justification. *Journal of Personality and Social Psychology, 34*, 874–884.

Roberts, D. S. L., Cowen, P. S., & MacDonald, B. E. (1996). Effects of narrative structure and emotional content on cognitive and evaluative responses to film and text. *Empirical Studies of the Arts, 14*(1), 33–47.

Romero, A. A., Agnew, C. R., & Insko, C. A. (1996). The cognitive mediation hypothesis revisited: An empirical response to methodological and theoretical criticism. *Personality and Social Psychology Bulletin, 22*, 651–665.

Russell, C. A. (1998). Toward a framework of product placement: Theoretical propositions. In J. W. Alba & J. W. Hutchinson (Eds.), *Advances in consumer research* (Vol. 25, pp. 357–362). Duluth, MN: Association for Consumer Research.

Russell, C. A. (2002). Investigating the effectiveness of product placements in television shows: The role of modality and plot connection congruence on brand memory and attitude. *Journal of Consumer Research, 29*(December), 306–318.

Russell, C. A., & Belch, M. (2005). A managerial investigation into the product placement industry. *Journal of Advertising Research, 45*(1), 73–92.

Russell, C. A., Norman, A. T., & Heckler, S. E. (2004). The consumption of television programming: Development and validation of the connectedness scale. *Journal of Consumer Research, 31*(1), 150–161.

Russell, C. A., & Puto, C. P. (1999). Rethinking television audience measures: An exploration into the construct of audience connectedness. *Marketing Letters, 10*(4), 393–407.

Russell, C. A., & Russell, D. W. (2009). Alcohol messages in prime-time television series. *Journal of Consumer Affairs, 43*(1), 108–128.

Russell, C. A., Russell, D. W., & Grube, J.W. (2009). Nature and impact of alcohol messages in a youth-oriented television series. *Journal of Advertising, 38*(3), 97–111.

Russell, C. A., & Stern, B. (2006). Consumers, characters, and products: A balance model of sitcom product placement effects. *Journal of Advertising, 35*(1), 7–18.

Russell, D. W., & Russell, C. A. (2008). Embedded alcohol messages in television series: The interactive effect of warnings and audience connectedness on viewers' alcohol beliefs. *Journal of Studies on Alcohol and Drugs, 69*(May), 459–467.

Sherry, J. F. (1995). Bottomless cup, plug-in drug: A telethnography of coffee. *Visual Anthropology, 7*, 351–370.

Signorielli, N. (1993). *Mass media images and impact on health: A sourcebook*. Westport, CT: Greenwood Press.

Singhal, A., & Rogers, E. M. (2002). A theoretical agenda for entertainment-education. *Communication Theory, 12*(2), 117–135.

Snyder, L. B., Milici, F. F., Slater, M., Sun, H., & Strizhakova, Y. (2006). Effects of alcohol advertising exposure on drinking among youth. *Archives of Pediatrics & Adolescent Medicine, 160*(1), 18–24.

Sobell, L. C., Sobell, M. B., Toneatto, T., & Leo, G. I. (1993). Severely dependent alcohol abusers may be vulnerable to alcohol cues in television programs. *Journal of Studies on Alcohol, 54*, 85–91.

Solomon, M. R., & Greenberg, L. (1993). Setting the stage: Collective selection in the stylistic context of commercials. *Journal of Advertising, 22*(March), 11–24.

Stacy, A. W., Pearce, S. G., Zogg, J. B., Unger, J., & Dent, C. W. (2004). A nonverbal test of naturalistic memory for alcohol commercials. *Psychology & Marketing, 21*(4), 295–322.

Story, M., & Faulkner, P. (1990). The prime time diet: A content analysis of eating behavior and food messages in television program content and commercials. *American Journal of Public Health, 80*(6), 738–740.

USDHHS. (2007). *The Surgeon General's call to action to prevent and reduce underage drinking*. Rockville, MD: Office of the Surgeon General.

Wallack, L., Grube, J. W., Madden, P. A., & Breed, W. (1990). Portrayals of alcohol on prime-time television. *Journal of Studies on Alcohol and Drugs, 51*, 428–437.

Way, W. L. (1984). Using content analysis to examine consumer behaviors portrayed on television: A pilot study in a consumer education context. *The Journal of Consumer Affairs, 18*(1), 79–92.

Wood, W., & Quinn, J. M. (2003). Forewarned and forearmed? Two meta-analytic syntheses of forewarnings of influence appeals. *Psychology Bulletin, 129*, 119–138.

World Health Organization. (2010). *ATLAS on substance use: Resources for the prevention and treatment of substance use disorders.* Paris, France: World Health Organization Press.

Xu, J., Kochanek, K. D., Murphy, S. L., & Tejada-Vera, B. (2010). *Deaths: Final data for 2007.* National Vital Statistics Reports, *58*(19). Retrieved from http://www.cdc.gov/nchs/data/nvsr/nvsr58/nvsr58_19.pdf

Yi, H., Williams, G. D., & Hilton, M. E. (2005). *Surveillance report #71: Trends in alcohol-related fatal traffic crashes, United States, 1977–2003.* Rockville, MD: National Institute on Alcohol Abuse and Alcoholism.

10

Selling Beauty: The Hidden Cost to Women's Self-Worth, Relationships, and Behavior

Erin J. Strahan
Wilfrid Laurier University
Ontario, Canada

Vanessa M. Buote
Wilfrid Laurier University
Ontario, Canada

Anne E. Wilson
Wilfrid Laurier University
Ontario, Canada

INTRODUCTION

Imagine a teenage girl is watching television, and an advertisement for Covergirl appears. Covergirl spokesmodel Taylor Swift introduces a new line of cosmetics, promising that the foundation would provide "a flawless finish," and indeed her skin appears to be smooth and free of imperfections. She is pictured in light, wispy fabrics walking through sheer curtains, and her body and slim silhouette are featured in the ad at least as frequently as is her face and skin. The ad closes as Swift says, "Goodbye heaviness, hello easy breezy beautiful Covergirl" (www.covergirl.com). Swift is attractive and appealing in the ad and the teen girl thinks to herself that she might want to try this new line of makeup. The intended effect of this commercial is to get the viewer to purchase the new cosmetics. It may even work. But, are there other unintended effects of watching a commercial like this?

In this chapter, we discuss research that explores the impact of viewing idealized images, particularly on women. When people turn on the television, they are seeking entertainment. They don't tune in for the advertisements, and they don't give much thought to the peripheral effects that the shows or the commercials could have on them. But both advertisements and entertainment media send some clear, consistent messages about standards of beauty that go beyond the explicit purpose of the programming. In this chapter, we look at effects that go beyond persuasion and entertainment, and even beyond the well-established body dissatisfaction effects found in the literature (Groesz, Levine, & Murnen, 2002). We will begin by discussing the evidence that exposure to idealized images can affect body image and appearance self-appraisals. Next, we go beyond these findings to describe research that our lab has conducted examining how exposure to idealized images influences not only women's appearance self-appraisals, but also has broader implications for identity, behavior, and social relationships. Specifically, we argue (and provide evidence) that media messages strongly link women's appearance with their social acceptance and value. Given that people care deeply about their social inclusion (Leary & Baumeister, 2000), the link between appearance standards and social acceptance can be especially threatening to women, particularly since most women cannot measure up to these standards. Throughout the chapter we present evidence that concerns about social acceptance and rejection are an important consequence of exposure to idealized media images. First, we discuss how idealized images affect women's contingencies of self-worth (the degree to which they base their self-worth on appearance) and, in turn, their concern with others' perceptions. Next, we describe how idealized images can lead women to activate rejection concerns, which can then lead them to engage in restrained eating behavior. Finally, we focus directly on the social consequences of media ideals, demonstrating that idealized images can threaten feelings of social worth and thereby decrease women's willingness to engage in social contact.

DOES BEAUTY SELL?

Researchers have long been interested in studying the impact of using attractive communicators to enhance persuasion. In one of the first studies on the topic, Chaiken (1979) found clear support that physically attractive communicators were more persuasive than unattractive communicators. There are a number of mechanisms that may help to account for how attractiveness influences persuasion. For instance, attractive communicators may be more socially confident or have other personality qualities that influence persuasiveness (Chaiken, 1979). However, attractive communicators may also be perceived as warmer, more confident, or more likeable, even in the absence of real differences, due to the "what is beautiful is good" stereotype (Dion, Berscheid, & Walster, 1972). In addition, research on the elaboration likelihood model of persuasion suggests that people often use the physical appearance of the communicator as a peripheral cue to persuasion. When people are not motivated to process the message carefully, they are more persuaded when an appeal is delivered by an attractive source than an unattractive one (Petty, Cacioppo, & Schumann, 1983).

Consumer behavior research suggests that a model's physical attractiveness has a positive effect on consumers' attitude toward the product, their willingness to buy the product, and their actual purchasing behavior (Caballero & Solomon, 1984; Kahle & Homer, 1985). Although research suggests that the effectiveness of an attractive model is partly dependent on the type of product being sold, Bower and Landreth (2001) have demonstrated that highly attractive models are more effective than models of average attractiveness at selling appearance-related products (e.g., lipstick, earrings). Thus, it seems clear that attractive communicators can be used to enhance persuasion. However, researchers and theorists have also pointed to the side effects of this cultural and media emphasis on unattainable standards of beauty (Wolf, 1991). In the present chapter, we will explore some of the side effects—that go far beyond the intended persuasion effects—of exposing women to culturally idealized images.

SOCIOCULTURAL NORMS FOR IDEAL APPEARANCE

In North America, people place a lot of value on physical appearance. They expend a lot of time, energy, and money pursuing appearance goals. For example, estimates indicate that Americans spend at least 8 billion dollars annually on cosmetics alone (UNDP, 1998). Fashion, weight loss, hair care, and cosmetic surgery are all comparably thriving industries. Staying on top of these pursuits can be stressful and time-consuming and can even involve significant health risks (Leary, Tchividjian, & Kraxberger, 1994). Theorists have proposed that sociocultural norms for ideal appearance play a significant role in society's concentration on beauty and attaining the perfect body. In his sociocultural norm theory (Thompson, Heinberg, Altabe, & Tantleff-Dunn, 1999), Thompson suggests that social and cultural factors have a great deal of influence on the attitudes people hold toward their body. Through these social and cultural forces, individuals internalize the ideal and strive to attain it. However, because this ideal is largely unattainable, internalization of the ideal can result in body dissatisfaction.

The media in particular has been strongly criticized for generating and disseminating a sociocultural ideal for beauty that is simply too thin for the average woman to attain. For example, the average American woman is 5 ft. 4 in. tall and weighs 140 pounds. The average model, on the other hand is 5 ft. 11 in. tall and weighs 117 pounds (National Eating Disorders Association, 2002). The average woman's body mass index (BMI) falls within the "normal" range, whereas the average model falls into the underweight category, which puts them at risk for many serious health outcomes. Researchers also find that fashion models are thinner than 98% of American women (Smolak, 1996) and that the cultural ideal of beauty has shown an increase in thinness over time (Wiseman, Gray, Mosimann, & Ahrens, 1992), but the average North American woman is actually getting heavier over time (Spitzer, Henderson, & Zivian, 1999). Clearly, the media portrays a cultural ideal for beauty that is both impossible and unhealthy for the average woman to try to attain.

CONTENT OF MEDIA IMAGES

Our research team has conducted research that examines the content of media images directed at men and women in Western society. Although there is considerable agreement in the literature that cultural standards for women's appearance are too high (Fallon, 1990; Kilbourne, 1994; Wolf, 1991), much of the classic research investigating the content of media images was conducted a decade or more ago (Silverstein, Perdue, Peterson, & Kelly, 1986; Wiseman et al., 1992). In addition, in recent years researchers have become increasingly interested in cultural standards for men's appearance. For example, researchers have found that images of men in men's magazines have become increasingly leaner and more muscular over the past 30 years (Law & Labre, 2002; Leit, Pope, & Gray, 2001). However, we suspected that, although cultural ideals for appearance certainly exist for both genders, women were likely to still be encountering a greater number of idealized images than were men.

To examine cultural portrayals of both men and women in the media, we conducted a series of coding studies to elucidate the content of media images directed at men and women (Buote, Wilson, Strahan, Gazzola, & Papps, 2011). In this research we sampled traditional archival sources (e.g., magazines, television), but also took a more novel approach by sending coders out to a variety of locations reflecting a young adult's "typical day" (e.g., to restaurants, shopping malls, laundromats, etc.) to investigate the frequency of actual encounters with culturally idealized images. This allowed us, in part, to address typical exposure to these images and messages whether or not a person sought out traditional sources (like reading magazines or watching television). Even without trying, the average young adult is exposed to frequent idealized images simply by walking through campus, going to restaurants and bars, going grocery shopping and to the mall, and even going to public restrooms.

Through these various sources, we found that media images of women were far more homogeneous than media images of men. Proportionally, the majority of female images encountered in daily life fit the rigid ideal (i.e., they were tall, thin, young, and very attractive). In contrast, although idealized images of men certainly were present, the images of men that were encountered were heterogeneous (varying in attractiveness, age, and body type), and these images contained far more "average" male bodies. We also found that culturally idealized images of women were encountered far more frequently in absolute numbers than images of men. Corresponding with our content analysis of media sources, we also found that both women and men were aware of the discrepancy in media representations. Both genders reported more frequently encountering images of idealized women than men in daily life. Hence, these studies support the often-made claim that women are "bombarded" with culturally idealized images.

In the present chapter, we will focus primarily on the impact of these images on women. Although we acknowledge that men may also be influenced by idealized images in the media (Strahan, Wilson, Cressman, & Buote, 2006), the research just mentioned suggests that idealized images still target women more pervasively than men, and that women are more at risk for negative effects of such exposure (Fallon & Rozin, 1985). Indeed, in one experimental study, we exposed both men and women to the types of same-sex images women saw on a "typical day" (rigid, homogenous, idealized) or the types of same-sex images men saw on a "typical day" (flexible, varied, and more often "average") and found that both genders were only affected by the kind of bombardment women usually face—that is, a very stringent, inflexible appearance norm (Buote et al., 2011). This finding suggests that, although both women and men can be affected by idealized media images, when considering real-world advertising and media, the effects on women are still likely to be stronger and more pervasive.

IDEALIZED IMAGES INFLUENCE SELF-WORTH CONTINGENCIES, BODY DISSATISFACTION, AND CONCERN WITH OTHERS' PERCEPTIONS

In the first set of studies, we review research on the impact of culturally idealized images on women's contingencies of self-worth, body satisfaction, and their concern with others' perceptions (Strahan et al., 2008). Before this research was conducted, it was fairly well-established that women exposed to idealized images felt more dissatisfied with their bodies than women exposed to neutral images (Groesz et al., 2002). Researchers had also identified two mediators of this effect: thin-ideal internalization and social comparison processes. For example, Stice, Schupak-Neuberg, Shaw, and Stein (1994) found that the extent to which women had internalized the thin ideal mediated the relation between media exposure and body satisfaction. Additionally, Tiggemann and McGill (2004) demonstrated that the number of social comparisons women made after exposure to idealized images partially mediated the effect of these images on body dissatisfaction and negative mood.

We investigated an additional mechanism through which media images affected women's body dissatisfaction (Strahan et al., 2008). We tested whether exposure to idealized images would affect women's self-image by increasing the extent to which women base their self-worth on weight and appearance. Theorists and researchers have long recognized that failures and successes in personally valued domains determine self-worth far more than outcomes in less important arenas (James, 1890/1950; Kernis, 2003). Indeed, Crocker and Wolfe's (2001) Contingencies of Self-Worth Scale measures individual differences in people's tendency to base their self-worth on domains including academic achievement, moral virtue, family's acceptance, and appearance. Crocker and her colleagues theorize that external contingencies of self-worth, such as basing one's worth on appearance, put people at risk for negative outcomes because they lead people to look to others for validation. For example, Sanchez and Crocker (2005) found that individuals who wanted to resemble their gender's ideal appearance reported greater external contingencies of self-esteem, which led to lower global self-esteem and more eating disorder symptomatology.

We expected that women exposed to idealized images would base their self-worth more strongly on weight and appearance, which in turn would lead them to feel more dissatisfied with their bodies and more concerned with others' perceptions of them (Strahan et al., 2008). The direct effects we proposed are consistent with past research. As previously stated, a meta-analysis of previous research demonstrated that exposure to idealized images most typically lead women to feel dissatisfied with their bodies (Groesz et al., 2002). Additionally, Fredrickson and Roberts' (1997) body objectification theory contends that women are socialized to take a third-person perspective on their own bodies, and that media depictions of women as objects lead them to feel self-conscious and to habitually monitor their outward appearance. Fredrickson and Roberts argue that media depictions of women as objects contribute to women's feelings of objectification. We suggest that ideal images in the media that highlight these sociocultural norms may lead women to worry about whether they are thin or attractive enough in the eyes of others, and more generally, may lead women to feel concerned about how other people view them.

To test these predictions, we brought female participants into the lab for a study ostensibly on long-term memory. Participants were told that their long-term memory for a series of commercials would be tested. This cover story was used to ensure that participants would attend to the commercials while obscuring the study's true purpose. This procedure reduces the chances that participants' responses are due to demand characteristics, and keeps participants from "thinking too much" about the purpose of the study. Arguably, people often view advertisements in passing and rarely devote their full attention to evaluating the advertisement's content itself. No one turns on the television specifically to watch commercials, and rarely do they stop to think carefully or critically about the content of the commercials they see. By making the task "about" something else (a memory test), the researchers aimed to mimic the same kind of relatively peripheral processing of media images that occurs in real-world settings.

Participants were randomly assigned to watch either neutral commercials (containing no images of people) or culturally idealized commercials. The culturally idealized commercials contained images of thin and beautiful women. After watching the commercials, participants were asked to take a break before their long-term memory was assessed. During this break they filled out a booklet of measures to assess their appearance-contingent self-worth (i.e., how strongly they based their self-worth on weight and appearance), their body dissatisfaction, and their concern with others' perceptions. Consistent with our predictions, we found that women who were exposed to idealized images based their self-worth more strongly on weight and appearance than women exposed to neutral images. We also found support for the direct effects: Women exposed to idealized images were more dissatisfied with their bodies and more concerned with others' perceptions. Most importantly, we found support for our mediation model. Exposure to culturally idealized images led women to base their self-worth more strongly on their appearance, which in turn led them to feel less satisfied with their bodies and more concerned with others' opinions.

In a follow-up study, we delivered an intervention to adolescent participants in several local schools that challenged sociocultural norms for ideal appearance. Each activity in the intervention was specifically designed to challenge the sociocultural norm for idealized appearance. The research assistants who delivered the intervention highlighted the ways in which idealized images were unrealistic and altered by expert stylists, makeup artists, lighting specialists, and digital enhancements. The intervention also challenged the idea that idealized images depicted in the media were attainable, appropriate, or healthy to strive for, and debunked the notion that people needed to meet these appearance standards to be accepted in society. To rule out the possibility that the results could be attributed to the fact that participants in the intervention group received special attention or treatment, a control group was included. This control group received an intervention on the benefits of volunteering that was matched in length and format to the experimental intervention. In order to reduce demand characteristics, the researchers waited one week before collecting the dependent measures, had a different set of research assistants collect the measures, and used a cover story to disguise the true purpose of the data collection session. The results showed that the intervention designed to challenge the sociocultural norms for ideal appearance alleviated adolescent girls' vulnerability to the effects of sociocultural standards of appearance. When female adolescents received the intervention that challenged the norms, they based their self-worth *less* strongly on appearance, leading to increased body satisfaction and decreased concern with others' perceptions.

These studies identified appearance-contingent self-worth as a previously uninvestigated mechanism that helps account for the relation between exposure to idealized images and outcomes such as body dissatisfaction and concern with others' perceptions. It is important to note that this research does not imply a critique of previous process models (i.e., thin-ideal internalization and social comparison processes), nor does it supersede these models. These previous process models make very significant contributions to the literature's comprehension about the psychology of body image. Our studies add to this understanding and focus on broader self and relational implications of exposure to idealized images (Strahan et al., 2008). Not only do idealized media images influence women's beliefs about their appearance, but they also have the power to affect where they derive their feelings of self-worth and how much they are concerned with other people's perceptions of them.

One of the most important findings from these studies is the strong causal link between exposure to culturally idealized images and appearance-contingent self-worth. This finding has important implications for women: When women are exposed to these idealized images, appearance becomes a larger basis of their self-worth. Given that most women cannot meet the standards set by these ideal images, basing their self-esteem more strongly on weight and appearance is inherently threatening. In the studies just described, simply viewing culturally idealized images reinforced women's belief that they should measure their self-worth by their appearance. The finding that women value their appearance more after being exposed to threatening ideal images is rather paradoxical, given that, generally, research suggests that people prefer to base their self-esteem upon things that boost their self-image, not crush it. Past research demonstrates that people will typically devalue or disidentify with a domain when faced with threatening information about the self in that domain. For instance, when people are reminded of a negative in-group stereotype, they attempt to disidentify with the stereotyped dimension to protect their selfesteem (e.g., Major, Spencer, Schmader, Wolfe, & Crocker, 1998; Steele, 1997). Alternatively, when faced with a threatening social comparison, people may attempt to protect themselves by reducing the self-relevance of that comparison dimension (Tesser & Campbell, 1980). Our findings suggest a dramatic exception to this general rule. When women were presented with images of the unattainable cultural ideal, they did not disidentify; instead, they actually cared *more* about their weight and appearance despite the threat these ideals present to the self.

These findings suggest that when women are exposed to idealized images, there are clear implications for the self: Women base their self-worth more strongly on weight and appearance and are more dissatisfied with their bodies. But, these findings also suggest that the impact of culturally idealized images extends beyond the self. Women exposed to idealized images are more concerned about relational acceptance and how other people view them. These findings relate to Leary and Baumeister's work on sociometer theory (Leary & Baumeister, 2000). Sociometer Theory proposes that the purpose of self-esteem is to monitor a person's level of social acceptance (Leary & Baumeister, 2000). When social cues point to possible rejection, the monitor alerts the individual by eliciting emotional distress and low self-esteem. On the other hand, when an individual experiences a high level of acceptance, the monitor reflects high self-esteem.

Leary and Baumeister (2000) also argue that most people desire and strive for high levels of relational value. Perceived relational value is defined as the extent to which people believe that others accept, value, and consider them to be important. The more warmly accepted people feel, the more positively they evaluate their perceived relational value, which in turn leads to increased positive affect and increased self-esteem (Leary, 2004). Although people can be valued for many qualities across multiple dimensions, we propose that women's appraisals of their weight and appearance are inordinately important predictors of perceived relational value. We suggest that sociocultural norms communicated in the media equate attractiveness with acceptance to a far greater degree for women than for men, and that these messages influence women's expectations about relational acceptance. These norms send the message that women need to be thin and beautiful to be happy and to be accepted by other people in their lives (Thompson et al., 1999). Thus, we argue that when women feel unhappy with their appearance, their confidence that they are loved and accepted by others may decline. The findings from this first set of studies support this theorizing: Women who were exposed to culturally idealized images were more concerned about their social acceptance and worth in the eyes of others.

It is worth noting that this link between appearance and social value has important implications for women. Even though some women internalize the norms for ideal appearance more than others do (Thompson et al., 1999), research has demonstrated that women often believe that *others* buy into sociocultural norms for ideal appearance even more than they do themselves. For example, Milkie (1999) found that even though high school girls viewed media images as "unrealistic," they were still harmed by them because they believed that other people in their culture (particularly boys) valued these images and judged them on the basis of these images. Consequently, even women who do not personally accept the norms can still feel pressure to strive for the ideal body because they perceive that other people endorse these appearance standards (Milkie, 1999; Park, 2005).

IDEALIZED IMAGES INFLUENCE WOMEN'S EATING BEHAVIOR

In the previous set of studies, we demonstrated that exposure to culturally idealized images led women to base their self-worth more strongly on weight and appearance, which, in turn, led to decreased body satisfaction and increased concern with others' perceptions. In the next series of studies, we discuss research that examines the impact of idealized images on women's concerns about interpersonal rejection and their eating behavior (Strahan, Spencer, & Zanna, 2007). Idealized media images convey the message that thinness and beauty are strongly valued in society (Stice, 1998; Thompson, 1992; Thompson et al., 1999). Thus, we reasoned that when presented with these idealized images, women may feel compelled to limit the amount of food that they eat (to attain a thinner body). Therefore, we expected that women exposed to idealized images would consume less food than women exposed to neutral images. In the first study, we had female participants come to the lab, ostensibly for a long-term memory study. Participants were told that their long-term memory for a series of commercials would be tested. Like in the studies described previously, participants were randomly assigned to watch either neutral commercials (containing no images of people) or commercials depicting culturally idealized women. After watching the commercials, participants were asked to take a break before their long-term memory was assessed. During this break, they were asked to taste and rate a variety of foods, supposedly for an unrelated study. Participants were told to eat as much of the food as they liked to make their evaluations, and were left alone to do the taste tests. Bowls of food were weighed before and after the experiment, so participants were unaware that the quantity of food intake was being assessed. As expected, we found that women who viewed the culturally idealized commercials ate significantly less food than women who viewed the neutral commercials.

To determine whether activation of an association between weight and interpersonal acceptance could account for the effect of exposure to thin images on eating behavior, we conducted a second study (Strahan et al., 2007). In this study, female participants followed the same procedures as the participants in the first study, except that in between viewing the commercials and performing the taste test, participants completed a computer task designed to assess whether they believed that weight and interpersonal rejection are associated. In the computer task, participants were primed with words related to heaviness and unattractiveness and then the authors measured how these words influenced participants' activation of interpersonal rejection. We predicted that women exposed to culturally idealized images would be more likely to activate an association between weight and rejection and that this activation would in turn predict eating behavior. This is exactly what we found. The main effect from the first study was replicated: Women who viewed the culturally idealized commercials ate less food than women who viewed the neutral commercials. Moreover, the researchers found support for their process model. Exposure to culturally idealized images led women to activate an association between heaviness and interpersonal rejection. The more this association was activated, the less participants ate in the taste test. In other words, worries about interpersonal rejection on the basis of weight caused women to restrict their eating in order to get thinner.

These findings provide additional support for theorizing on the link between exposure to idealized images and women's relational acceptance. Women exposed to culturally idealized images activated an association between weight and interpersonal rejection, which was not activated for women exposed to neutral images. Other researchers have demonstrated that viewing idealized images leads women to activate "thin thoughts," and the more these thoughts are activated, the less satisfied women are with their bodies (Brown & Dittmar, 2005; Hargreaves & Tiggemann, 2002). Our findings support the growing literature that suggests that culturally idealized images lead women to activate appearance-related schemata that, once activated, have an impact on how women feel about their appearance. We also extend these findings by demonstrating that weight and relational acceptance may be automatically associated for women, and that idealized images can activate this threatening cognitive association.

The findings from our studies examining restrained eating have important health implications for women. These studies demonstrate that women exposed to culturally idealized images ate less food than women exposed to neutral images. Restrained eating has been linked to binge eating (Polivy & Herman, 1985) and eating disorder symptomatology (Heatherton & Polivy, 1992). Furthermore, theorists have suggested that women who chronically restrain their eating might develop eating disorders (Heatherton & Polivy, 1992). The research we have reviewed offers an interesting account of how culturally idealized images frequently seen in the media may play a role in the development of eating disorders (Stice & Shaw, 1994; Stice et al., 1994). Frequent exposure to idealized images may lead women to frequently restrain their eating. This frequent restraint may eventually lead to eating disorders such as anorexia nervosa or bulimia.

Our warnings against the dangers of restrained eating may raise the question of whether restraining eating is necessarily a bad thing, especially in the context of rising obesity in North American society. The question of how to achieve a healthy lifestyle and healthy body weight is a large and complex topic beyond the scope of this chapter. However, it is important to emphasize one point. Patterns of restrained eating and dieting are not likely to serve those health goals. Research suggests that restrained eating is an ineffective way to maintain a healthy body weight (Polivy & Herman, 2002). Not only do dieters rarely succeed in their weight loss goals (Heatherton, Mahamedi, Striepe, Field, & Keel, 1997), but their repeated attempts and failures to lose weight lead to a cycle of false hope and self-blame that is damaging to dieters' psychological well-being (Polivy & Herman, 2002).

IDEALIZED IMAGES INFLUENCE WOMEN'S FEELINGS OF SOCIAL WORTH AND DESIRE FOR SOCIAL CONTACT

In our final set of studies, we investigated the impact of idealized images on women's feelings of social worth and desire for social contact. Participants viewed magazine advertisements containing either culturally idealized images or neutral images (which contained no people) (Buote, Wilson, & Strahan, 2011). Then, they filled out a booklet of measures to assess their self-perceived physical attractiveness, their perceived relational value (i.e., how valued they felt by the important people in their lives), and their desire for social contact. Participants indicated their desire for social contact by rating how much they would like to engage in a variety of activities. These activities ranged from activities they would do while alone in a secluded or private environment (e.g., read a book, nap) to public situations with a lot of social contact (e.g., meet new people, go to a party). First, we expected that participants exposed to culturally idealized images would have lower perceived relational value than participants exposed to neutral images. In other words, seeing idealized images would lead them to feel less accepted, loved, and valued in their interpersonal relationships with peers, significant others, and in society generally. Moreover, we expected that lowered feelings of relational value would, in turn, influence the type of social contact they would like to engage in. Specifically, we expected that participants who perceived that their relational value had dropped would want to be alone or would want to seek out contact only via electronic means. We expected this because we argue that when a person feels that their perceived relational value is vulnerable or has decreased, a conflict takes place within the person. On one hand, an individual might be strongly motivated to seek reassurance of their perceived relational value (Leary, 2001; Maner, DeWall, Baumeister, & Schaller, 2007; Smart Richman & Leary, 2009). On the other hand, seeking out reassurance from another individual, especially an unknown individual, allows for the potential of further rejection and a possible further decrease in perceived relational value.

To protect their vulnerable perceived relational value, we expected that participants exposed to culturally idealized images would avoid social situations that have the potential to further harm perceived relational value (e.g., meeting new people) and that they would also be motivated to be alone. However, we also suggested that people may be motivated to seek out another individual to reaffirm their perceived relational value. Keeping in mind that the appearance threat would be maintained, we suggested that participants would be more likely to seek another person through electronic means, in which they could not be seen.

We found support for our hypotheses. Participants who viewed the culturally idealized images reported more unfavorable self-appraisals of physical appearance (than did those exposed to neutral images), which led to decreased perceived relational value, and subsequently, decreased desire to engage in social situations with unknown others, a greater desire for seclusion, and a greater desire for electronic contact with a friend. Interestingly, after exposure to these culturally idealized images (and the subsequent drops in self-perceptions of attractiveness and perceived relational value), participants reported an increased desire to engage in activities in which they were both alone and secluded, but not in activities in which they were alone but in public (and thus could be seen by others). These findings suggest that being alone but potentially visible to others did not provide enough assurance that their perceived relational value would not be further threatened. Notably, threatened participants did appear to want to seek out social support, but not if it involved face-to-face contact (e.g., meeting a friend for coffee). They only reported a greater desire for social contact through electronic contact. It appears that exposure to culturally idealized images may have acted as a barrier to initiating social contact, inhibiting participants from seeking out others in face-to-face contexts. If they felt insecure about their physical appearance as a result of exposure to idealized images, they may have worried that seeing others—even close others—in person could involve the risk of interpersonal rejection.

These findings highlight another relational consequence women face when exposed to idealized images. After exposure to idealized images, participants' social worth dropped, and they wanted to avoid face-to-face social contact with others. To protect their vulnerable perceived relational value, participants wanted to seclude themselves and remain entirely alone. The implications of these findings are quite serious. Lack of social interaction has been linked to a number of negative outcomes, such as loneliness and sadness (Buckley, Winkel, & Leary, 2004; Leary, Koch, & Hechenbleikner, 2001; Leary, Twenge, & Quinlivan, 2006). Furthermore, although isolating oneself to ensure that one's social worth does not drop further might be adaptive in the short-term, avoiding social contact in the long-term could lead to chronically low levels of perceived relational value, which is seriously damaging to a person's fulfillment of the need to belong.

CONCLUDING REMARKS

The research described in this chapter clearly demonstrates that the impact of viewing advertisements containing idealized images extends far beyond the intended persuasion effects of these advertisements. In the first series of studies, we showed that women exposed to idealized images based their self-worth more strongly on weight and appearance, which in turn led them to feel more dissatisfied with their bodies and more concerned with other people's perceptions of them. The second series of studies demonstrated that exposure to idealized images led women to activate an association between weight and interpersonal rejection, and the more this association was activated, the more women restrained their eating. In the final set of studies, we showed that exposure to idealized images led to a drop in feelings of social worth, which in turn led to a decreased desire for social contact. These findings show that culturally idealized images have a direct impact on the self (i.e., they influence women's contingencies of self-worth, body dissatisfaction, and eating behavior), but that their impact also extends beyond the self. Idealized images also have relational consequences for women: They make women feel more concerned about interpersonal rejection, and they affect their feelings of social worth and their desire for social contact.

It is also important to note that although the findings highlighted in this chapter are not the intended effects of media advertising, they may nonetheless lead women to purchase more products. In fact, the dichotomy of "intended" and "unintended" effects of advertisements may be somewhat too black and white. Although the effects described in this chapter go beyond persuading buyers to like and purchase a product, they may still contribute to the product's success indirectly via the advertisements' influence on women's identity. Recall the advertisement mentioned at the beginning of this chapter. As a spokesmodel for Covergirl, Taylor Swift is communicating a message about the product (foundation makeup). The intended goal is to sell the product—to persuade consumers to positively evaluate the brand of foundation being presented, which is described as especially light and natural. In the ad, Swift promotes (albeit somewhat unrealistically) the features of the product (a "flawless" finish). Her own skin does appear flawless. Of course, the behind-the-scenes assistance of a host of makeup artists, lighting crew, and photography experts are not shown in the final commercial. All of these features of the advertisement do likely help to persuade the viewer to evaluate the product more favorably.

However, in light of the research described in this chapter, we suggest that the teen girl viewing this ad may also base her self-esteem to a greater extent on her weight and appearance, feel worse about her appearance, worry more about how others view her, and start thinking about going on a crash diet. These represent some of the unintended effects of this commercial. Moreover, some of the commercial's features may function to exacerbate these side effects. Recall that the commercial spends considerable time focusing on images of Swift's slim figure (rather than her face), even though her body is unrelated to the product being sold. Finally, recall that Swift closes the ad with the slogan "Goodbye heaviness, hello easy breezy beautiful Covergirl." It is worth noting that one of the words in this slogan is "easy," implying that attaining these standards of perfection is not only a worthy goal, but an attainable, even easy goal, provided one uses the right products.

All in all, this single advertisement may cause women to feel insecure about their weight and appearance, while causing them to care more about appearance as a basis of self-worth. They may worry about whether friends, family, and romantic partners really value them, and fear putting themselves at risk in social situations. At the very moment women feel badly about themselves and their perceived relational value, the ads then offer salvation: By purchasing this product, these standards of beauty are attainable. Easy, even!

The findings from this chapter demonstrate that when women view an advertisement containing idealized images, they base their self-worth more strongly on weight and appearance, which should lead them to spend more time, energy, and money on enhancing their appearance. In addition, these images lead women to feel more dissatisfied with their bodies, and by making women feel that they do not measure up to beauty standards, should also lead women to put more effort into enhancing their beauty. One way to try to achieve this is by purchasing more products that promise to help them attain these ideals. Women may be even more desperate to buy any product promising improvement if they feel their social value and relationships are at risk. Advertisements often imply— either indirectly by presenting their audience with a model's perfection, or more directly with slogans like, "Maybe she's born with it, maybe it's Maybelline"—that their products are the key to attaining a beautiful, thin, impossible ideal. Of course, unless regular women happen to have precisely the right genes, be the right age and body type, *and* are lucky enough to have a team of experts enhancing their day-to-day appearance, chances are that advertised products will not produce the promised changes in appearance. Hence, every product bought and tried, and every failed attempt, can contribute to women's feelings that they have not measured up to the standards for beauty sold in the media.

REFERENCES

Bower, A. B., & Landreth, S. (2001). Is beauty best? Highly normative versus normally attractive models in advertising. *Journal of Advertising, 30,* 1–12.

Brown, A., & Dittmar, H. (2005). Think "thin" and feel bad: The role of appearance schema activation, attention level, and thin-ideal internalization for young women's responses to ultra-thin media ideals. *Journal of Social and Clinical Psychology. Special Issue: Body image and eating disorders: Sociocultural pressures and perceptions, 24,* 1088–1113.

Buckley, K. E., Winkel, R. E., & Leary, M. R. (2004). Reactions to acceptance and rejection: Effects of level and sequence of relational evaluation. *Journal of Experimental Social Psychology, 40,* 14–28.

Buote, V. M., Wilson, A. E., & Strahan, E. J. (2011). *To seek or to avoid? How an appearance threat impacts desire for social contact.* Poster presented at the annual convention of the Society for Personality and Social Psychology, Texas, February 2011.

Buote, V. M., Wilson, A. E., Strahan, E. J., Gazzola, S. B., & Papps, F. (in press). Setting the bar: Divergent sociocultural norms for women's and men's ideal appearance in real-world contexts. *Body Image.* Retrieved from http://www.sciencedirect.com/science/article/pii/s1740144511000672#FCANote

Caballero, M.J., & Solomon, P. J. (1984). Effects of model attractiveness on sales response. *Journal of Advertising, 13,* 17–23.

Chaiken, S. E. (1979). Communicator physical attractiveness and persuasion. *Journal of Personality and Social Psychology, 37,* 1387–1397.

Crocker, J., & Wolf, C. T. (2001). Continqencies of self-worth. *Psychological Review*, 108, 593–623.

Dion, K. K., Berscheid, E., & Walster, E. (1972). What is beautiful is good. *Journal of Personality and Social Psychology, 24*, 285–290.

Fallon, A. (1990). Culture in the mirror: Sociocultural determinants of body image. In T. Cash & T. Pruzinsky (Eds.), *Body images: Development deviance and change* (pp. 80–109). New York: Guilford.

Fallon, A. E., & Rozin, P. (1985). Sex differences in perceptions of desirable body shape. *Journal of Abnormal Psychology, 94*, 102–105.

Fredrickson, B. L., & Roberts, T. (1997). Objectification theory: Toward understanding women's lived experiences and mental health risks. *Psychology of Women Quarterly, 21*, 173–206.

Groesz, L. M., Levine, M. P., & Murnen, S. K. (2002). The effect of experimental presentation of thin media images on body satisfaction: A meta-analytic review. *International Journal of Eating Disorders, 31*, 1–16.

Hargreaves, D., & Tiggemann, M. (2002). The effect of television commercials on mood and body dissatisfaction: The role of appearance-schema activation. *Journal of Social and Clinical Psychology, 21*, 287–308.

Heatherton, T. F., Mahamedi, F., Striepe, M., Field, A. E., & Keel, P. (1997). A 10-year longitudinal study of body weight, dieting, and eating disorder symptoms. *Journal of Abnormal Psychology, 106*, 117–125.

Heatherton, T. F., & Polivy, J. (1992). Chronic dieting and eating disorders: A spiral model. In J. H. Crowther, D. L. Tennenbaum, et al. (Eds.), *The etiology of bulimia nervosa: The individual and familial context. Series in applied psychology: Social issues and questions* (pp. 133–155). Washington, DC: Hemisphere Publishing Corp.

James, W. (1950). *The principles of psychology*. New York: Dover.

Kahle, L. R., & Homer, P. M. (1985). Physical attractiveness of the celebrity endorser: A social adaptation perspective. *Journal of Consumer Research, 11*, 954–961.

Kernis, M. H. (2003). Toward a conceptualization of optimal self-esteem. *Psychological Inquiry*, 14(1), 1–26.

Kilbourne, J. (1994). Still killing us softly: Advertising and the obsession with thinness. In P. Fallon, M. A. Katzman, & S. C. Wooley (Eds.), *Feminist perspectives on eating disorders* (pp. 395–418). New York: The Guilford Press.

Law, C. L., & Labre, M. P. (2002). Cultural standards of attractiveness: A thirty-year look at changes in male images in magazines. *Journalism and Mass Communication Quarterly, 79*, 697–711.

Leary, M. R. (2001). Toward a conceptualization of interpersonal rejection. In M. R. Leary (Ed.), *Interpersonal rejection* (pp. 1–20). New York: Oxford University Press.

Leary, M. R. (2004). The sociometer, self-esteem, and the regulation of interpersonal behavior. In R. F. Baumeister & K. D. Vohs (Eds.), *Handbook of self-regulation: Research, theory, and applications* (pp. 373–391). New York: Guilford Press.

Leary, M. R., & Baumeister, R. F. (2000). The nature and function of self-esteem: Sociometer theory. In M. P. Zanna (Ed.), *Advances in experimental social psychology* (Vol. 32, pp. 1–62). San Diego, CA: Academic Press.

Leary, M. R., Koch, E.J., & Hechenbleikner, N. R. (2001). Emotional responses to interpersonal rejection. In M.R. Leary (Ed.), *Interpersonal rejection* (pp. 145–166). New York: Oxford University Press.

Leary, M. R., Tchividjian, L. R., & Kraxberger, B. E. (1994). Self-presentation can be hazardous to your health: Impression management and health risk. *Health Psychology, 13,* 461–470.

Leary, M. R., Twenge, J. M., & Quinlivan, E. (2006). Interpersonal rejection as a determinant of anger and aggression. *Personality and Social Psychology Review, 10,* 111–132.

Leit, A. R., Pope, H. G., & Gray, J. J. (2001). Cultural expectations of muscularity in men: The evolution of Playgirl centerfolds. *International Journal of Eating Disorders, 29,* 90–93.

Major, B., Spencer, S., Schmader, T., Wolfe, W., & Crocker, J. (1998). Coping with negative stereotypes about intellectual performance: The role of psychological disengagement. *Personality and Social Psychology Bulletin, 24,* 34–50.

Maner, J. K., DeWall, C. N., Baumeister, R. F., & Schaller, M. (2007). Does social exclusion motivate interpersonal reconnection? Resolving the "porcupine problem." *Journal of Personality and Social Psychology, 92,* 42–55.

Milkie, M. A. (1999). Social comparisons, reflected appraisals, and mass media: The impact of pervasive beauty images on black and white girls' self-concepts. *Social Psychology Quarterly, 62,* 190–210.

National Eating Disorders Association. (2002). http://www.nationaleatingdisorders.org/nedaDir/files/documents/handouts/Stats.pdf

Park, S. (2005). The influence of presumed media influence on women's desire to be thin. *Communication Research, 32,* 594–614.

Petty, R. E., Cacioppo, J. T., & Schumann, D. (1983). Central and peripheral routes to advertising effectiveness: The moderating role of involvement. *Journal of Consumer Research, 10,* 135–146.

Polivy, J., & Herman, C. P. (1985). Dieting and binging: A causal analysis. *American Psychologist, 40,* 193–201.

Polivy, J., & Herman, C. P. (2002). If at first you don't succeed: False hopes of self-change. *American Psychologist, 57,* 677–689.

Sanchez, D. T., & Crocker, J. (2005). How investment in gender ideals affects well-being: The role of external contingencies of self-worth. *Psychology of Women Quarterly, 29,* 63–77.

Silverstein, B., Perdue, L., Peterson, B., & Kelly, E. (1986). The role of the mass media in promoting a thin standard of bodily attractiveness for women. *Sex Roles, 14,* 519–532.

Smart Richman, L., & Leary, M. (2009). Reactions to discrimination, stigmatization, ostracism, and other forms of interpersonal rejection: A multi-motive model. *Psychological Review, 116,* 365–383.

Smolak, L. (1996). Methodological implications of a developmental psychopathology approach to the study of eating problems. In L. Smolak, M. P. Levine, (Eds.), *The developmental psychopathology of eating disorders: Implications for research, prevention, and treatment* (pp. 31–55). Mahwah, NJ: Lawrence Erlbaum Associates, Inc.

Spitzer, B. L., Henderson, K. A., & Zivian, M. T. (1999). Gender differences in population versus media body sizes. *Sex Roles, 40,* 545–565.

Steele, C. M. (1997). A threat in the air: How stereotypes shape intellectual identity and performance. *American Psychologist, 52,* 613–629.

Stice, E. (1998). Modeling of eating pathology and social reinforcement of the thin-ideal predict onset of bulimic symptoms. *Behavior Research and Therapy, 36,* 931–944.

Stice, E., Schupak-Neuberg, E., Shaw, H. E., & Stein, R. I. (1994). Relation of media exposure to eating disorder symptomatology: An examination of mediating mechanisms. *Journal of Abnormal Psychology, 103,* 836–840.

Stice, E., & Shaw, H. E. (1994). Adverse effects of the media portrayed thin-ideal on women and linkages to bulimic symptomatology. *Journal of Social and Clinical Psychology, 13,* 288–308.

Strahan, E. J., Lafrance, A., Wilson, A. E., Ethier, N., Spencer, S. J., & Zanna, M. P. (2008). Victoria's dirty secret: How sociocultural norms influence adolescent girls and women. *Personality and Social Psychology Bulletin, 34,* 288–301.

Strahan, E. J., Spencer, S. J., & Zanna, M. P. (2007). Don't take another bite: How sociocultural norms for appearance affect women's eating behavior. *Body Image, 4,* 331–342.

Strahan, E. J., Wilson, A. E., Cressman, K. E., & Buote, V. M. (2006). Comparing to perfection: How cultural norms for appearance affect social comparisons and self-image. *Body Image, 3,* 211–227.

Tesser, A., & Campbell, J. L. (1980). Self-definition: The impact of the relative performance and similarity of others. *Social Psychology Quarterly, 43,* 341–346.

Thompson, J. K. (1992). Body image: Extent of disturbance, associated features, theoretical models, assessment methodologies, intervention strategies, and a proposal for a new DSM-IV diagnostic category-Body image disorder. In M. Hersen, R. M. Eisler, & P. M. Miller (Eds.), *Progress in behavior modification, 28* (pp. 3–54). Sycamore, IL: Sycamore.

Thompson, J. K., Heinberg, L. J., Altabe, M., & Tantleff-Dunn, S. (1999). *Exacting beauty: Theory, assessment, and treatment of body image disturbance.* Washington, DC: American Psychological Association.

Tiggemann, M., & McGill, B. (2004). The role of social comparison in the effect of magazine advertisements on women's mood and body dissatisfaction. *Journal of Social and Clinical Psychology. Special Issue: Body Image and Eating Disorders, 23,* 23–44.

U.N. Development Programme (UNDP). (1998). *Human development report 1998.* New York: Oxford University Press.

Wiseman, C. V., Gray, J., Mosimann, J. E., & Ahrens, A. H. (1992). Cultural expectations of thinness in women: An update. *International Journal of Eating Disorders, 11,* 85–89.

Wolf, N. (1991). *The Beauty Myth.* Toronto: Vintage Books.

11

Learning Aggression Through the Media: Comparing Psychological and Communication Approaches

Julia A. Maier
Saint Francis University
Loretto, Pennslyvania

Douglas A. Gentile
Iowa State University
Ames, Iowa

Access to images and ideas of violence permeate the media. A question asked by many is whether this exposure has any effect on our actual behavior. Hundreds of studies have been conducted to address this very concern and found that aggressive media can increase viewers' aggressive thoughts, feelings, and behaviors (e.g., Anderson et al., 2003; Gentile, 2003). Despite resting on a strong foundation of theoretical and empirical support, this area of research is often considered controversial. As individuals, we look at ourselves and our peers, we make note of the movies we watch or the games we play, but may fail to see any of these predicted increases in thoughts, feelings, and behaviors. One reason for this supposed disconnect is there are many levels of analysis from which one can investigate, such as at individual, group, or societal levels. The research methods, the variables considered, and the conclusions reached can be different depending on the perspective taken, and this can lead to results that appear to be difficult to reconcile but are not inherently contradictory.

The psychological research on the effects of media violence is predominately focused on passive learning, meaning exposure to violent media has an effect regardless if the person intends to learn or not.

Psychological approaches have generated many valuable learning theories that have been used to predict how viewing violence can result in average increases in thoughts, feelings, and behaviors for groups of people. Whether imitating someone else's aggressive behavior, or having been repeatedly shown that aggression can be an effective solution to a problem, some form of learning is occurring. If conducted carefully, this type of research is very valuable for documenting causal effects of media violence. Nonetheless, we know that not every individual in the violence-viewing group of a given study increased in aggression, even though the group average does tend to increase. Therefore, there may be something important to study at the individual level.

In contrast to the psychological literature on media violence, the communication literature offers the perspective of the "active viewer" and the manner in which motivations can lead to different outcomes. Studies may demonstrate that individual viewers have different goals for viewing a particular media product and take away different meanings from it. If conducted carefully, this type of research is very valuable for demonstrating how individuals' uses of media can moderate the effects that the media have. Nonetheless, although individuals may differ in their responses to a specific media product, this does not invalidate the overall effect at the broader, group-average level that many psychological studies focus on. Therefore, gains in understanding the effects of violent media may be made through interdisciplinary approaches that utilize the strengths from both psychological and communication studies.

The goal of this chapter is to describe how approaches based in psychology and communication studies can complement each other and lead to a richer understanding of how media can influence viewers. We will describe an integrative psychological theory of learning and how it may be applied to learning from the media. We will then describe a perspective that a communication theory of media can offer and how it applies to learning from the media. Finally, as an example of the value of crossing these disciplinary boundaries, we will describe a study that blends elements from psychological and communication studies to address somewhat different questions than are usually answered within either discipline.

PSYCHOLOGICAL THEORY: GENERAL LEARNING MODEL

A great deal is known about how humans can learn. Over the past century, hundreds of studies have tested and verified several specific psychological learning mechanisms. These theories have generally been developed independently of each other, come out of different areas of psychology, and focus on different types of learning. This is valuable as it allows researchers to design a program of related studies and gain detailed information about how and when learning occurs. It is limiting, however, in that it means that the connections between types of learning are not easily addressed because we have developed several domain-specific learning theories that each address only one part of the bigger picture.

The General Learning Model that we describe here is an attempt to integrate each of the domain-specific aspects into one meta-model. This model has been described at a lower level of detail previously (Buckley & Anderson, 2006; Gentile et al., 2009; Swing, Gentile, & Anderson, 2008), and may allow for the generation of new testable hypotheses as links between different levels of analysis are explicated. The call for an integrated model is also warranted because the human brain is integrated. Each area or module of the brain, while optimized for certain tasks, works with the others for efficient learning. The brain has evolved to be able to learn through multiple methods, while still being an integrated whole. Finally, an integrated model allows for us to see how different learning processes build upon and can support each other.

The first component of the General Learning Model is the proposition that to learn there must be some sort of input of information (Figure 11.1). These inputs come from both the person learning and the situation around them. This is a basic proposition of nearly all psychology, not simply learning, for that matter. The interaction between personal qualities, such as attitudes, beliefs, and behavior tendencies, and situational factors, or stimuli in environment, as the basis for behavior was even quantified as a mathematical equation by Kurt Lewin (1936). What we learn and how we learn it is the result of the stimuli presented to us from the environment, combined with our own personality and biological mechanisms for learning them.

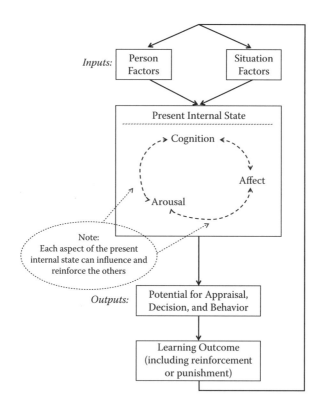

FIGURE 11.1
Short-term processes in the General Learning Model (simplified view).

The second proposition of the General Learning Model is that nearly all learning theories address how interacting with environmental information can result in learning. This is reflected by the present internal state component of the model. Once the information is detected, it must be stored and organized in some way that constitutes learning. Depending on the type of learning, these inputs can affect our cognitions, our affect, or our arousal; different domain-specific mechanisms address what is affected and how. Note that there is an important distinction between learning and performance. Learning often occurs without an immediate behavioral performance that would demonstrate that learning has occurred.

Whether we are interested in how people learn basic facts about the world from watching the 6 o'clock news, how we learn about new products and develop an opinion about them, or, relevant to the current chapter, how people can learn aggression from the media, the General Learning

Model utilizes what we know about learning from a multitude of areas to understand these processes. Following are some examples of important learning theories from various areas of psychology, such as neurology, behaviorism, perception, and cognition. The descriptions exemplify how different each theory is, yet each theory is represented by some component of the General Learning Model.

The Mechanisms of Learning

Learning can be examined at multiple levels of analysis, even solely within the brain. At the individual synapse level, Bliss and Lomo (1973) discovered that after simple repetition of a stimulus, the synapse changed to be more receptive to the stimulus. They called this *long-term potentiation*, meaning that the potential that a neuron would fire given the presentation of the stimulus has increased, and that this is a long-term change in the synapse. At the structural level, several different brain structures have been implicated in different types of learning and memory. For example, the amygdala (a part of the brain in the limbic system) is involved in attending to and learning about the emotional aspect of experiences, whereas the hippocampus is involved in attending to cognitive aspects of experiences. At a network level, the different systems of the brain work together to learn multiple aspects at once and to associate them together.

There is, unfortunately, no simple way to understand how the brain circuitry relates to different types of learning and memory. In general, the brain does not have a single structure or area that corresponds directly to each type of learning. Learning can happen in almost all regions of the brain. Some types of learning happen within specific systems, and others connect multiple systems. For example, habituation learning (described in the next section) seems to happen within whatever perceptual system is being used (e.g., vision, auditory), whereas when viewing words, some areas of the brain attend to the shape of the words and other areas attend to the conceptual meaning of them. For our purposes here, however, the important thing is to recognize that although neural mechanisms support the psychological mechanisms of learning, they are not simply isomorphic. Furthermore, understanding the multiple levels of organization in the brain can help to understand complexities of what is learned (e.g., attitudes have both a conceptual and an emotional component, and each is learned within different brain structures linked in broad network systems).

The Processes of Learning

Perceptual Learning

Each of our sense organs has evolved to be able to detect information that exists in the environment. That is, the "stimuli" that we can perceive are not random, but are structured by the laws of physics in such a way that they are useful for organisms to detect. For example, light bounces off of surfaces in precisely lawful ways, and this reflected light fills the space around an observer in a highly structured way. Eyes have evolved to be able to detect energies at certain frequencies (which we see as colors), because this information is useful for our survival. We have thus evolved to be able to detect the affordances around us, which is a functional level of learning. We can learn to detect what surfaces we can walk on, sit on, swim in, pick up, etc. We come prepared by evolution to be ready to learn how to get around and act in the world. There are two types of what could be called perceptual learning—habituation and discrimination.

Habituation is learning to tell that something is recognizable. It is perhaps the easiest type of learning to demonstrate, and can be shown even in very young babies. Simply show a baby a picture of a person repeatedly and measure looking time; looking time will begin to decrease after only about three presentations of the picture, thus demonstrating that the baby has learned enough about what the picture looks like to recognize that it is the same picture when it is put up another time. All that is needed for habituation learning is single or repeated exposure to a stimulus. In fact, even a single exposure that is too fast to be consciously noticed can be learned and can change behavior (e.g. Bridger, 1961; Colombo & Mitchell, 2009).

Discrimination is learning to tell that two or more things are not the same. An example is learning to tell different red wines apart. If one is not experienced with wines, one might not be able to tell the difference between a cabernet and a shiraz. In fact, telling the taster what the name of each is will not help; they will not be able to learn which name goes with which wine until after they can tell them apart. Discrimination learning also only needs repeated exposures to happen. It usually helps if the repeated exposures provide an opportunity for comparison. If one only tries one wine at a time, it will take longer to learn to discriminate. Discrimination learning also does not need any type of reinforcement, although reinforcement can sometimes speed up the process.

The distinction between habituation and discrimination also demonstrates a feature of learning—that we can learn to generalize from a specific learning. Consider, for example, young children who often call all four-legged animals "doggie," demonstrating that they have learned that four legs is a salient feature. Only later do they learn to discriminate that the word *doggie* does not also apply to cats—that more than just four legs matters. This example is not an entirely accurate representation, however, because word learning is a different learning process (but does still rest on discrimination learning). Furthermore, even babies can learn to generalize from specific instances to broader categories. For example, infants shown a series of photographs of stuffed animals will demonstrate habituation to a novel stuffed animal photograph, but not a novel photograph of a rattle (Younger & Cohen, 1985). These learning processes do not require language or higher cognition (although they can benefit from it), but can occur simply from repetition with something. Once you can recognize something (habituation) or can discriminate it as different from other things, then you can learn to associate it with different things and consequences. That is, it is necessary to be able to discriminate something *before* association learning can occur with it.

Association Learning

Classical Conditioning

Classical conditioning (Pavlov, 1927) rests on two foundations of the brain—that some responses to the environment are automatic, and that the brain can learn to connect (associate) multiple stimuli and responses. In the classic example, when a dog is given food, it always salivates. This is an automatic physiological response that cannot be consciously controlled. Therefore, the food is an unconditioned stimulus (US) and the salivating is an unconditioned response (UR). That is, they are "unconditioned," meaning that they did not require conditioning or training. If a neutral unrelated thing (like a bell or a light) immediately precedes the presentation of the US, it can become "conditioned" such that the dog learns that the bell signals food and then begins to salivate to the bell alone. Once this has happened, the bell is no longer a neutral stimulus but has become a conditioned stimulus (CS), and the salivating to it has become a conditioned response (CR).

Once learned, more can be learned than this simple single association of stimulus and response. For example, we will tend to generalize our initial learning to other similar stimuli. If dogs learned to salivate to the sound of a bell ringing at the pitch of C, they will often salivate to a bell at the pitch of B as well. In the classic "Little Albert" study of conditioned fear (Watson & Rayner, 1920), the baby Albert was conditioned to fear the sight of a white rat by pairing a loud noise with it (babies are startled and scared by sudden loud noises). After conditioning, Albert also cried at the sight of a white rabbit and even a white Santa Claus beard. In addition, one can chain these types of conditionings (known as higher-order conditioning). For example, after being conditioned to salivate to a bell, we can precede the bell with a light, and the dog will learn to salivate to the light as much as it did to the bell.

Not all types of things can be learned in this way. Classical conditioning rests on automatic responses, so if the initial behavior is not reflexive, then learning cannot happen through this process. Furthermore, even if we do start with an automatic response, there are some things that cannot be learned easily in combination with it. For example, when humans or other animals ingest food and later become sick, they often learn to associate the taste of that food with illness and will avoid it (even if the food wasn't what made them sick). Similarly, rats given blue-colored water will not learn to associate the color with illness, whereas they will learn to associate the color with an electric shock (Garcia & Ervin, 1968). This makes evolutionary sense, as our sense of taste evolved to help us seek foods that were healthful, whereas our sense of sight evolved to help us for many other reasons. Thus, although classical conditioning is powerful, it is limited in many ways.

Operant Conditioning

Most human associative learning is not related to reflex behaviors, but instead to learning from the consequences of behaviors under voluntary control. Also known as instrumental conditioning, humans (and other animals) try behaviors and learn from whether the consequences are reinforcing or punishing (Thorndike, 1905; Skinner, 1938). Behaviors that are reinforced become more likely to be repeated in the future, whereas behaviors that are punished become less likely to be repeated. Reinforcement can be positive (by providing something desired) or negative (by removing something unpleasant), as can punishment (positive:

providing something unpleasant; negative: removing something desired). In an evolutionary sense, behaviors become selected, as they are subject to the pressures of the environment. Those behaviors that provide benefit (real or perceived) get stronger, and those that do not get selected against.

Much of the time in the real world, however, reinforcements or punishments do not reliably or immediately follow the behavior. Ironically, this can strengthen learning. How reinforcements are "scheduled" can affect both the speed of learning and the resistance to extinction. When reinforcement is given reliably (fixed) after a certain amount of time or after a certain number of behaviors have been performed, learning tends to be fast, but it can be extinguished fairly quickly. If, for example, we paid you $10 every time you did a somersault, you would probably do several. If we stopped paying you, you would quickly stop doing them. In contrast, when reinforcement is more random (variable), either after some unknown amount of time or an unknown number of behaviors, initial learning is slower, but it is highly resistant to extinction. Gambling on slot machines is a good example, where one performs the behavior (put coin in, pull lever/push button) multiple times, with the hope that one of these times it will pay off. Winning once will often make people play much longer and lose much more money than if they never won.

Observational Learning

Humans are able to learn even without trying behaviors themselves, but simply by seeing others do things. Humans are not the only animals able to do this, of course. For example, young chimpanzees can learn how to "fish" for termites by watching older chimpanzees do it. Humans, however, are so good at it that we can learn even by watching people we do not know on television. In a classic experiment, Bandura, Ross, & Ross (1963) showed preschool children an adult woman modeling several novel aggressive acts toward a doll on a television screen. The children were then allowed to play in a room with several toys, including the toys that were modeled in the aggressive acts. Children spontaneously imitated the acts that they had seen. In a follow-up experiment, Bandura & Kupers (1964) had the adult model either praised or punished in the television show. When the model had been punished, children did not spontaneously imitate the aggressive acts. When the model was rewarded, children did. Therefore we can learn not only from observing others' actions, but can also learn from the consequences of others' actions. Perhaps even more interesting, however, was that the children learned the novel actions in all cases, but only spontaneously imitated when the model was either rewarded or had no consequences. Although the children who had seen the model punished did not spontaneously imitate, they were able to demonstrate the behaviors when asked to. This demonstrates how learning can clearly occur even when there is no immediately observable change in behavior and why distinguishing between learning and performance is important.

Cognitive Learning

Human communication also allows for learning that is devoid of the need to act. Your reading this chapter gives you a chance to learn concepts or to connect them in new ways. Thus, humans can learn by associating cognitive concepts together, by creating new mental representations of concepts, by creating cognitive maps of spatial arrangements, etc. These do not need to be reinforced to be learned, although reinforcement can often make learning occur faster.

Declarative conceptual information is often described as being linked in associative networks of related concepts. Thus, the concept of "bird" is probably closely related to the concept of "sparrow," but less closely related to the concept of "ostrich," and even less to the concept of "dinosaur." As we learn, however, that birds are the modern descendants of dinosaurs, we can reorganize our associations between different concepts. Although neural networks are generally assumed to be semantic in nature, concepts can also be linked with feelings related to those concepts.

Emotional Learning

Emotional learning and memory is connected to cognitive learning and memory, but it is also a distinct form (Eichenbaum, 2008). The brain has circuits designed specifically to attend to the emotional importance of situations, such as the amygdala. These brain circuits support our feelings and expressions of emotions, our learning about the emotional aspects of experiences, and also can change what is learned. In brief, there are three major outputs of the amygdala. In response to seeing something (a fight, for example), one neural response pathway travels to the cerebral cortex to support our conscious awareness of our feelings.

A second pathway travels to other memory systems (e.g., striatum and hippocampus), which can influence what is attended to and therefore what is learned. A third pathway controls our bodily responses, such as hormone release and the autonomic nervous system (e.g., the "fight or flight" response).

One implication is that emotion plays an important role in attention and vigilance. Not only does it moderate attention and memories, but we can remember emotional aspects of experiences and concepts. A second implication is that when we have an emotional response (especially one that releases the hormones epinephrine and cortisol), memory is enhanced. One study demonstrated this effect with media, by randomly assigning participants to view either 12 emotionally arousing film clips or 12 emotionally neutral film clips while undergoing brain scans (Cahill et al., 1996). The amygdala and related areas were more active during the arousing film clips, and memory for those clips was better 3 weeks later than for the neutral film clips. Importantly, the amount of amygdala activation predicted performance on the memory task for the emotionally arousing film clips, but not for the neutral film clips.

The Content of Learning

The strengths of an integrative approach to learning emerge when we try to consider what can be learned through these various learning processes. In order to have successful and meaningful outcomes for learning, it quickly becomes apparent that we must utilize different types of knowledge that were perhaps acquired through multiple processes. At a psychological level, there are many ways that learning and memory can be understood. We do not suggest that the following list is comprehensive, but it is illustrative. Memory is often described as being either declarative or procedural, but this underestimates what can be learned, which can be declarative, procedural, perceptual, emotional, or some combination of these.

At a perceptual level, we can become sensitized to types of information. For example, it is important to separate male from female chickens shortly after hatching, but it is very difficult to tell the difference between them by sight. Although most people initially cannot tell the difference, they can learn to with years of practice, but even then the experts do not really know on what they are basing their judgment. One classic study demonstrated that there is information in the cloacal region of chicks that can be perceived through training, bringing novices up to almost expert levels (Biederman & Shiffrar, 1987).

At a cognitive level, we not only learn conceptual information like the meanings of words, but also how concepts fit together at different levels of organization. Networks of related concepts are referred to as schemas; for example, our "bird" schema can consist of those characteristics that classify something as a bird (e.g., feathers, wings, beak) and even exemplars or prototypes of the category (e.g., robin). Concepts that are more strongly related would have the strongest connections in the network, such that bird–robin would be stronger than bird–kiwi (Collins & Loftus, 1975). In addition to basic category-related schemas, information can also be organized to direct behavior, known as *scripts* (such as knowing what the sequence of events is at a restaurant; Fiske & Taylor, 1991).

Many cognitive concepts also have emotional components associated with them. For example, attitudes and stereotypes are based not only on cognitive "facts" about situations or types of people, but also on our feelings about them. Thus, as we learn that there can be differences in cultures or groups of people, we often tie those differences to our feelings or preferences for them. At an emotional level, the "Little Albert" study demonstrates that fears can be conditioned by experiences; a great deal of advertising works on this principle as well, by continually pairing attractive models with their products, for example. Furthermore, repeated opportunities to experience or practice certain feeling states can lead to them becoming solidified into traits. This is similar to how cognitive or behavior habits can become personality traits.

The Moderators of Learning

When presented with a new situation, we have an opportunity to learn, but not everyone will learn from it, and those who do may learn different things from it. This is because several factors moderate what gets attended to initially, how it interacts with prior knowledge, and how the brain encodes and retains information. As with our discussion of the content of learning, the following is merely an illustrative sample of moderators of learning and not intended to be comprehensive.

Emotion

Emotional states can increase vigilance, change what is attended to, and change the neurochemistry to influence memory retention. In a classic study, Kleinsmith and Kaplan (1963) had participants learn words in pairs, a type of cognitive learning task called paired-associate learning. Some of the words were emotionally laden words, such as kiss, rape, and money, whereas others were neutral. At immediate recall, neutral words were remembered better than emotional words. When tested a week later, however, participants recalled the emotional words better than the neutral words. Therefore, emotions can moderate what is learned and recalled in ways that may not be immediately straightforward.

Stress

If the emotion is stressful, hormones are released in response to the stressful event. These include many of the same hormones that enhance memory, such as epinephrine and cortisol. If the stress is too severe or prolonged, however, it can disrupt the retention of memory (Newcomer, et al., 1999).

Level of Processing

When learning, how the material is analyzed can change the amount that is learned. For example, when studying a list of words, those who attended to surface characteristics (whether the words were in capital or lowercase letters) learned the words much more poorly than those who attended to the meaning of the words (Craik & Tulving, 1975).

Practice Schedule

Learning tends to get better with more time practicing, but how the time is distributed can change how well something is learned. This is sometimes referred to as the distinction between *massed* and *distributed* practice, where massed practice is spending a lot of time all at once and distributed practice is practicing a little at a time over multiple sessions. It turns out that distributed practice is better for learning (Gentile & Gentile, 2008; Robinson, 1921). Furthermore, the amount of delay between initial learning and rehearsal can influence ultimate retention, with several studies demonstrating that increasing the time between study episodes often enhances memory (sometimes referred to as the "spacing" effect or "lag" effect). Although there is no single optimal delay for all types of learning (and the optimal lag can change across time as one rehearses), one set of studies suggests that it may fit an inverted-U function, with performance increasing up to several days of delay and then falling off as the lag increases to several months (Cepeda et al., 2009).

Proactive and Retroactive Interference

During learning, the new information being learned interacts both with what is already known and what happens after. That is, other information can interfere with learning. Previously known information can change how new information is attended to and encoded, known as proactive interference (Underwood, 1957). Furthermore, retroactive interference impedes the learning and retrieval of previously learned material due to information that was learned after it (Baddeley & Dale, 1966).

Context

As can be seen above, we can learn many things through many processes simultaneously. Therefore, it should not be surprising that the context in which we learn something can affect how well it is remembered. A classic study demonstrated this with underwater divers learning lists of words either while underwater or on land (Godden & Baddeley, 1975). Memory for the lists was better when tested in the same context that the words were learned—that is, if they had initially studied the list underwater, they recalled more words when tested underwater than when tested on land. Therefore, cues that we might assume are irrelevant to what is being learned may also be learned and influence memory.

State

Similar to context-dependent learning and memory, one's mental or emotional state can influence learning and memory. In one study, participants studied lists of words that included positive, neutral, or negative words. They were then induced to feel happy or sad moods. Following this mood manipulation, participants were asked to recall the words. Participants remembered more words with meanings that matched their moods than words that did not (Teasdale & Russell, 1983).

Sleep

Sleep appears to be essential for the consolidation of certain types of learning—most specifically for perceptual and motor learning. For example, in a perceptual training study, participants were taught to identify letters in their visual periphery that were then covered by other letters (Stickgold, Whidbee, Schirmer, Patel, & Hobson, 2000). When tested the following day, those who had slept with the most REM-level sleep showed the greatest improvements in learning. The evidence for the role of sleep in the consolidation of cognitive learning is less clear, however (Siegel, 2001).

Consolidation Disruptors

Beyond disrupting sleep, several other variables can disrupt the consolidation of learning. These include drugs, alcohol, electroconvulsive shocks, or distracter tasks (Dudai, 2004).

Transfer of Learning

Once something has been learned, it can usually be remembered in a situation similar to how it was learned (e.g., state- or context-dependent learning). In education, this is seen through tests in classes. The gold standard, however, to which educators aspire is *transfer*. That is, can what is learned in one context be recalled and applied in a novel context? For example, it is not particularly useful for children to learn math if they cannot transfer that knowledge to know if they have enough money to purchase something. Although transfer has historically been difficult to demonstrate with cognitive knowledge gained in school, it is less difficult to demonstrate with other types of learning, such as attitudes and stereotypes, which may generalize to novel situations very well (e.g., Das & Nanda, 1963; Gim & Yoon, 1998).

It has been long recognized that some specific elements are required to be similar in order to transfer what is learned in one context to another (e.g., Thorndike & Woodworth, 1901). Nonetheless, modern theorists have attempted to categorize the multiple dimensions on which transfer can occur, from nearly identical domains/contexts (near transfer) to those which are highly dissimilar (far transfer). Barnett & Ceci (2002), in particular, have elucidated a thoughtful taxonomy for considering the dimensions of transfer. They describe two broad dimensions, *content* and *context*, that need to be defined to understand the type of transfer desired. The content dimension includes the skill that is learned (e.g., procedural or broad principle), the type of performance change (e.g., speed or accuracy), and the memory demands of the learned material. The context dimension includes the knowledge domains across which transfer is desired, the physical context, the temporal context, the functional context, the social context, and the modality of learning and testing. For our purposes, however, what is of interest is understanding that the real power of learning rests in its ability to be applied outside of the original learning context and its power to shape later behaviors, especially if the later situation has some similar features or primes concepts that were originally learned together.

General Learning Model

The General Learning Model has value as a metatheory precisely because it defines the multiple levels at which learning can occur and how they can work independently or influence each other, rather than focusing only on one or two mechanisms or processes. Furthermore, it incorporates both short-term and long-term processes. Using learning aggression from the media as an example, we can describe how the General Learning Model incorporates the multiple domain-specific theories and allows for a more complex description of the parallel learning processes at work.

The short-term process is shown in Figure 11.1, where both the personal and situational variables can influence the learning encounter. People bring their genetics, history, prior knowledge, schemas, intelligence level, expectations, feelings, and state to the encounter, whereas situational variables include the specific content of interest (violent content, for example), contextual factors, distractions, and so forth. When one watches violent media, these influence one's present internal state. The script elements can prime cognitions related to aggressive concepts, thereby reinforcing them through repetition. Violence is often physiologically and emotionally arousing, which can direct and increase attention, while also increasing stress hormones, which can improve learning. Furthermore, because we often watch media violence as a form of entertainment that can include other enjoyable experiences (such as eating snack food or watching a favorite actor), we are classically conditioning ourselves to like violence and to find it entertaining rather than being disgusted by it (a more natural reaction to viewing violence). Following from operant conditioning, because we like feeling the adrenaline rush of excitement, this further reinforces the aggressive cognitions that are primed. Finally, because one way we learn is by observing others, we will learn the attitudes and behaviors of the characters and often are able to imitate them after the show (such as by repeating characters' catch phrases).

With repeated exposure, we would predict a different level of effects. Figure 11.2 demonstrates the perceptual, cognitive, and emotional constructs that are likely to be influenced by repeated learning trials. Perceptual constructs include perceptual schemas, such as vigilance for enemies and hostile attribution biases. For example, with repeated exposure to violent media, one begins to interpret daily events as being more hostile (Gentile, Coyne, & Walsh, 2010). Cognitive constructs include beliefs, such as whether people believe aggression is normal (Huesmann & Guerra, 1997), and scripts, such as expecting that the most typical response to being provoked should be to retaliate (Anderson & Carnagey, 2004). Because many thoughts get linked with emotions during learning, these also may be influenced, such as attitudes about the acceptability of using aggression (Anderson et al., 2003), or stereotypes about what types of people are more likely to be aggressive (for example, blacks are often portrayed as much more aggressive than they are in reality; Dixon & Linz, 2000).

Additionally, emotional responses can be affected by media violence. Some studies, for example, have demonstrated that people can become desensitized to aggression (Carnagey, Anderson, & Bushman, 2007). Others have demonstrated increases in trait anger (Bushman & Huesmann, 2006), that is, the tendency to react with anger easily. Furthermore, repeated exposure to violent media links the concept of violence with feelings of excitement and fun, such that these emotions become conditioned responses to further exposures of media violence (near transfer) and perhaps real-world aggression (far transfer). Ultimately, all of these learned

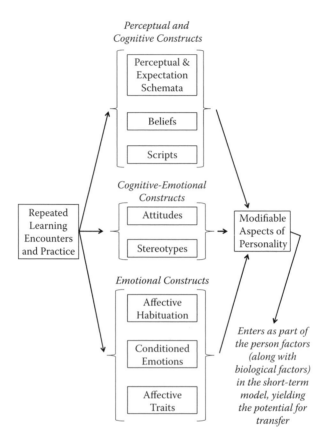

FIGURE 11.2
Long-term processes in the General Learning Model.

habits of perception, cognition, and emotion, aggressive or otherwise, come together with the person's genetic and prior dispositions to form what is typically thought of as *personality characteristics*—the tendency for a person to react in patterned or regular ways to situations. At this point, most of the specific lessons learned from the media have become generalized as attitudes, beliefs, scripts, etc., and can therefore transfer to novel situations in the person's life.

The General Leaning Model demonstrates that there are many routes to learning, some of which occur in parallel simultaneously. Therefore, the acquisition of aggressive thoughts, feelings, behaviors, and even modifiable personality tendencies from violent media should not be as surprising as some may believe. It may be that people react strongly against this idea because they feel that psychological theories are too deterministic, but the fact that we learn so easily from every experience we have should not be controversial. Although we can certainly engage in practices that can increase our learning, such as repetition or distributed practice, preventing learning from happening at all is much more difficult, if not impossible, given that many of these processes occur automatically and without any specific intention to learn. Many studies on violent media effects have even emphasized this very point, showing that people can have increases in aggressive behavior even when simply in the same environment as an aggressive stimulus, such as a photograph of a weapon left on a table (Berkowitz & LePage, 1967). What is missing from this picture, however, is the influence of the learner's motivations and any active role he or she can play in a learning encounter with the media.

Communication Theory: Uses and Gratifications

In contrast to the psychological methods described earlier, with the intention to understand processes and outcomes, the Uses and Gratifications Theory within communications began as more of an ecological field with its goal of understanding why people engaged in different forms of media-related behavior (Katz & Lazarsfeld, 1955). As the theory developed through the years, however, the scientific rigor increased and methods were used to try to predict viewers' choices and satisfaction, such as with television channels (Dobos, 1992). Throughout its development, though, the central theme of the Uses and Gratifications Theory has been on the role of the audience (Windahl, 1981).

According to the Uses and Gratifications Theory, people have a variety of needs that influence their media-viewing behaviors, including needs for relatedness, identification, information, and escaping from reality (Blumler, 1979; Blumler & Katz, 1974; Katz, Blumler, & Gurevitch, 1973). How a person chooses to fulfill these may influence both the selection of media content, as well as the level of processing applied. Besides picking which movies to watch, for example, viewers might also choose which type of scenes they will attend to during the movie. Some may be more excited by violence and thus pay closer attention to these scenes, whereas others may be more interested in the relationship-oriented storyline. Additionally, some people may choose to process the images and dialogues on a relatively surface level in order to simply follow the plot, thus requiring the use of fewer cognitive resources (Lang, 2000). Others may choose to process these on a deeper level to get at the underlying messages, by looking for symbolism or thinking about themes, for instance, and would thus use more cognitive resources in the process (Lang, 2000). Others may not consciously think about all the ideas presented but will become emotionally involved, by allowing themselves to empathize with the characters to discern meaning and thus activate schemas (Lang, 2000; Miall, 1989). At present, the manner in which the viewer processes the media is not typically considered in psychological media violence studies, and such research may simply suggest that viewing style does not matter; everyone would be at risk for an increase in aggressive behavior.

Although the Uses and Gratifications Theory emphasizes the role of the active audience member, the above examples demonstrate that simply because an individual can play an active role when viewing the media, there is no guarantee that he or she always will (Rubin, 1984). The amount of activity can certainly vary depending on the type of communication setting or point in the communication process; furthermore, activity of the viewer can also differ on type instead of simply amount. This variance of both quantitative and qualitative factors of activity has led to many theoretical models of active viewing (Ruggiero, 2000). For example, dependency theory posits two factors that determine a reliance on the media for information: the satisfaction of needs by the media and the stability of society. How many needs are satisfied by a given source will certainly increase an individual's dependence on that source. As for social stability, the theory states that when there are times of social change or conflict, one's reliance on the media for information increases (DeFleur & Ball-Rokeach, 1982).

When considering how we learn from the media, particularly nondeclarative knowledge types of learning such as learning aggressive scripts and conditioned emotions, factors pertaining to active viewing become important moderators of learning. Two such factors of the "active" audience member would be choosing the type of information to attend to and how deeply to process that information. Let us consider, for example, a movie-going audience member. A movie contains, on average, 2 hours' worth of auditory and visual stimuli that are organized to create plots, symbolism, storylines, themes, and messages. Additionally, in the case of violent movies, there are also a number of nonviolent scenes, as well as storylines, themes, or messages that may be unrelated to aggression altogether. This allows for a number of concepts to which the viewer can attend. Furthermore, the viewer may intend to watch a movie without much mental effort and engage in a rather low level of processing, or this movie may be one in which the viewer intends to be involved and think about the content, thus engaging in a higher level of processing.

What one focuses on (attention) and how one thinks about it (processing) are closely related because one must pay attention to something in order to process it on a deeper level. In the movie setting, however, it is possible to attend to one type of scene for plot-related information, but not process it on a meaningful level. This makes it important to consider attention and level of processing separately. The interaction that needs to be considered is how thinking deeply or not thinking deeply about either aggressive or nonaggressive concepts may have different effects on the subsequent accessibility of aggressive cognitions.

Differences in attention and level of processing allow for a number of situations worth considering in the media violence discussion. If the viewer is focused on the nonviolent aspects of the movie, do the violent scenes still have the same impact? Does thinking about the movie during viewing change the magnitude of the media effects? And how do these two factors interact? In particular, how does a deeper processing of nonviolent themes compare to a general "surface-level" processing of the movie? Despite the thorough investigation of moderating variables on learning and the effects of media violence, little research has considered these differences in "viewing style" as something that could influence the magnitude of the media effects of aggression. What the viewer attends to in the media and how deeply they process it are two cognitive viewing-style factors that can influence learning, both of which need more research for a better understanding of media violence effects.

Interdisciplinary Research

The questions of attention and processing can be addressed by either communication or psychological research. The Uses and Gratifications Theory of communication allows for the consideration of viewers' motivations and their influence on what is attended to and how it is processed. Learning theories of psychology offer insight into the mechanisms through which the viewer retains what is attended to and processed. By integrating these approaches, however, perhaps we can develop a more complete picture of how people learn from the media and the role individual motivations can play.

A study designed to test the hypothesis that the media violence effect could be moderated by viewing styles effectively combined the assumptions from both the psychological and communication disciplines. Previous research in the area of media effects on aggression has had a foundation in social cognitive learning, where the acquisition of knowledge comes from associating concepts together in a mental semantic network (Anderson, 1997; Lindsay & Anderson, 2000). Once these networks have been created, repeated exposures serve to strengthen them. Furthermore, activating one of these concepts in the network, such as by seeing a weapon or an act of violence, will cause the entire network to become activated through a process called *spreading activation* (Collins & Loftus, 1975). It is this activation of the entire network that is believed to lead to a short-term increase in aggressive thoughts, feelings, or behaviors.

Uses and Gratifications Theory, from communication, provides an important consideration in this learning model. As the General Learning Model demonstrates, both situation and person factors are important for a given learning trial. The media provides the situational information, but the person's individual motivations for viewing the media should also play a role in what is learned. By considering these individual "viewing styles" in a typical psychological paradigm studying these effects, we are able to consider many important parts of the General Learning Model combined with the Uses and Gratifications approach at one time.

The goals of the study described here were to determine if, and how, the motivations of viewers would moderate the effects of violent media on subsequent aggressive thoughts. Previous research has established that, on average, viewers will have more aggressive thoughts after watching a violent movie clip (Anderson, 1997; Bushman 1995). Based on Uses and Gratifications Theory, it was hypothesized that this effect would be different for participants based on their viewing style.

Design

Introductory psychology students at a large Midwestern university were recruited to participate in this study. Every participant watched a full-length R-rated movie, *Witness* (Feldman, Bombyk, & Weir, 1985), starring Harrison Ford and Kelly McGillis, and completed a lexical decision task. The movie was selected for the numerous violent and nonviolent scenes it contains, as well as themes that contrasted with the violent storyline, such as community and romance. Viewing the entire movie allowed participants to become involved in either the corrupt cop/murder investigation storyline, which incorporated a lot of violent scenes as that plotline developed, or the romantic storyline as the good cop fell in love with an Amish woman and became accepted by the Amish community.

The accessibility of aggressive cognitions was measured using a lexical decision task (Neely, 1991). This task was developed as a way to measure the accessibility of cognitions using reaction time data. Theoretically, if a given semantic network is activated, participants should respond more quickly to concepts included in that network, compared to concepts that are semantically unrelated. For the task itself, participants are shown a group of letters and must make only a decision regarding if the letters create a real English word. Participants make this decision more quickly for concepts that are already accessible in their mind. For example, after shown the word "doctor," participants classify "nurse" as a word more quickly than "butter" because of the semantic relatedness between the first two words.

The lexical decision task consisted of 96 target trials: 24 aggression-related words, 24 movie-related words, 24 control words, and 24 nonwords. Words were chosen for this task using the word and nonword generators on the English Lexicon Project website (Balota et al., 2007). A list was created of words similar in average reaction time, letter length, and frequency of use in English. From this list, 24 words were chosen that were aggression-related and 24 that were unrelated to aggression or the movie. Finally, 24 words were chosen that were relationship- or journey-related, scene-specific words, and Amish culture-related words. The nonwords were selected from a nonword-generated list with similar length and average reaction time.

Active Viewing

To evaluate if active viewing moderates the increase of aggressive cognitions after viewing violent media, both attention, the storyline attended to, and processing the level of thought about the film were considered. Attention was not manipulated, but following the film, participants were asked to identify and describe the scene they considered most striking—scenes that stood out or were particularly memorable. This method has previously been used in literary studies to measure readers' reactions to stories (Kuiken et al., 2004). These responses were evaluated to determine the type of scene participants attended to and one of three codes were assigned: orthogonal, mix, or aggressive. Both the actual content of the scene and the focus of the participants' discussion were considered in coding. No presence of aggression in either the scene or the discussion yielded an "orthogonal rating," whereas presence in both the scene and discussion yielded an "aggressive" rating. A "mix" rating was assigned when aggression was present in either the scene or the discussion, but not both.

A manipulation was used to simulate differences in levels of processing. Participants were randomly assigned to one of three conditions: surface, depth, and control. In the surface condition, prior to watching the film, participants were instructed to pretend they were watching the film as a way to relax and not have to think. The emphasis on relaxing and not thinking much about the film was intended to induce participants to a surface level of processing, engaging just enough to follow the plot. The depth condition incorporated instructions to pay attention to deeper themes or messages in the film. These instructions specifically stated there was more to a film than the basic plot, and encouraged participants to look beyond the surface. Participants in the control condition received no instruction on how to watch the film and completed the lexical decision task prior to watching the film, whereas participants in the other two conditions completed the lexical decision task after watching the film.

Hypothesis I—Concept Activation

As previous studies on violent media effects have used separate violent and nonviolent movie clips (e.g. Bushman, 1995), whereas the current study used a full-length movie with both violent and nonviolent images, the first goal was to replicate past findings that exposure to specific images would result in an increase in the accessibility of related thoughts. Specifically it was hypothesized that participants in the experimental conditions (those who completed the dependent measure *after* watching the movie) would identify both aggression and movie concepts as words faster than control words, whereas participants in the control condition would not (who completed the dependent measure *before* watching the movie).

To test this, each individual participant's average reaction times for aggressive words and movie words were subtracted from their average reaction time for the control words to create an indexed aggression score and

TABLE 11.1

Mean Aggressive and Movie Scores by Condition

	Condition	N	Mean	Std. Deviation
Aggression score	Surface	72	9.4146	44.52193
	Depth	66	10.9875	50.39522
	Control	60	−1.3555	45.62401
Movie score	Surface	72	15.3656	40.25912
	Depth	66	15.2692	45.74242
	Control	60	5.7612	40.16824

Note: Means represent the difference in reaction times between control words and aggressive/movie-related words. Positive scores indicate an average faster reaction time to target words than control words.

indexed movie score (see Table 11.1). A t-test was conducted for each indexed score to determine if it was a statistically different zero because a score of zero would indicate the same reaction time as for control words. For participants in the surface condition, results indicated that the mean aggression score was marginally significantly different from zero, $t(71) = 1.794$, $p = .077$, and the mean movie score was significantly different from zero, $t(71) = 3.239$, $p = .002$. Similarly, for the depth condition, the mean aggression score was also marginally significantly different from zero, $t(65) = 1.771$, $p = .081$, and the mean movie score was significant different from zero, $t(65) = 2.712$, $p = .009$. For the control condition, neither the mean aggression score nor the mean movie score were significantly different from zero.

These results support the hypothesis that concepts related to aggression and other movie-related themes were activated in viewers of the film because participants did respond faster to these words than unrelated control words. Additionally, the participants who completed the word task before watching the movie did not respond any differently to the aggression- or movie-related words. Given support for our initial hypothesis, the second and third hypothesis look specifically at the active viewer variables of attention and level of processing.

Hypothesis II—Role of Attention

In general, learning theories tend to explain learning as an experience where any exposure will activate concepts in a semantic network regardless of whether the person is aware of the stimuli. The weapons effect is a strong example of this mechanism, where the mere presence of the image of a weapon is enough to elicit aggression (Berkowitz & LePage, 1967). The second hypothesis of this study, however, was more in line with communications theories of the role of the active viewer and that attention to particular types of information can moderate the activation of concepts in the semantic network. Specifically, we hypothesized that participants who attended to nonaggressive scenes would respond faster to movie-related words than to aggression-related words, and the opposite was expected for those who attended to aggressive scenes.

To test this hypothesis, the average movie score for each participant was subtracted from their average aggression score to create a difference score. A negative difference score indicates the participant responded faster to movie-related words than aggression words. A one-way ANOVA was conducted for type-of-scene with the difference score as the dependent variable, and the test was significant, $F(2,135) = 3.9$, $p = .023$; however, it was not in the expected direction. Looking at the mean difference scores, we see that participants who chose an aggressive scene responded faster to movie words than aggressive words, $M = -13.51$, $SD = 36.63$; whereas participants who chose an orthogonal scene responded slightly faster for aggression words, $M = 6.45$, $SD = 37.94$ (See Figure 11.3). Pair-wise comparisons revealed that these two groups were significantly different from each other, $t(101.19) = 2.775$, $p = .007$. Those participants whose response yielded a mixed coding were in the middle, not being significantly different from those who chose an orthogonal nor those who chose an aggressive scene.

These results clearly are in the opposite direction of the hypothesized effect, with those attending to aggressive scenes responding more quickly to the movie-related words than the aggressive words, and vice versa. There are many possible explanations for why this may have occurred that need to be explored in future research. One explanation focuses on the instructions participants were given, being asked to describe the scene they found to be "the most striking." They were further instructed, "This could be either your favorite scene or one that you just found particularly memorable." The first scene chosen may have been particularly striking because it was different from everything else the participant was attending to during the movie. For instance, if the participant spent the movie attending to the romantic relationship between the two main characters,

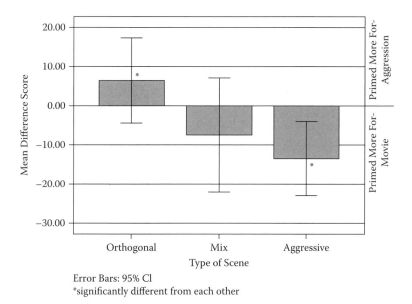

FIGURE 11.3
Mean difference score by type of scene.

they may have found one of the aggressive scenes striking because it was so different from that on which they had focused. Similarly, if the participant was invested in the aggressive storyline, a nonaggressive scene that focused on community building and social support could have been striking because it was in such contrast to the violence.

In this case, the type of scene classification could be an indicator of the types of concepts they were not paying attention to for the majority of the movie. If this interpretation is correct, the opposite direction of the results could then be interpreted as supporting the hypothesis. If participants initially chose an orthogonal scene because it was different from the aggression they had been paying attention to, then the results showed they were more likely to respond the quickest to aggression words. Similarly, if the participants initially chose an aggressive scene as most striking because they had been attending to one of the nonviolent storylines, then the results showed they were more likely to have movie words activated. Regardless of the reason for why the results were opposite of our initial expectations, the results still demonstrate that the way in which individuals approached viewing the movie changed the extent to which aggressive cognitions were primed.

Hypothesis III—Role of Processing

Although the previous hypothesis was not supported in the direction predicted, results do show that attention does matter. The final factor to consider in the role of the active viewer is how deeply the information they attend to is processed. Again, participants in this study were instructed to watch the movie with a particular level of processing: a surface level where they were told to just relax and not think, and a depth level where they were told to think about themes and messages in the film beyond the basic plot.

Following previous research on depth of processing (Lang, 2000), it was expected that deeper processing of particular information would lead to greater activation of these concepts. It was hypothesized, therefore, that there would be a polarization of the type-of-scene effect for participants in the depth condition. Without knowing that the test of Hypothesis II would reveal the opposite pattern as expected, we had originally predicted that participants in the depth condition who selected an aggressive scene would respond faster to aggressive words than similar participants in the surface condition, with a comparable pattern for participants who selected an orthogonal scene.

To test this hypothesis, a 2(condition) X 3(type-of-scene) ANOVA was conducted for the difference score. The interaction was not significant, $F(2,132) = 1.775$, $p = .173$, but there was a main effect for type of scene, $F(2,132) = 4.460$, $p = .013$. Despite the interaction being nonsignificant, the depth condition did appear to pull the effect toward the extremes, suggesting a trend for the depth condition to polarize the difference score (Figure 11.4). Post-hoc pair-wise comparisons revealed the only scores significantly different from each other were for those participants in the depth condition who selected an orthogonal scene, $M = 14.192$, $SD = 45.15$, compared to those who selected an aggressive scene, $M = -21.36$, $SD = 45.00$, $t(43.68) = 2.672$, $p = .011$. These results, although not statistically supporting the hypothesis, do offer a trend in the expected direction, suggesting more power or clearer operational definitions are needed in future research.

CONCLUSION

The current study was a demonstration of research based on both psychological and communication theories, specifically investigating how

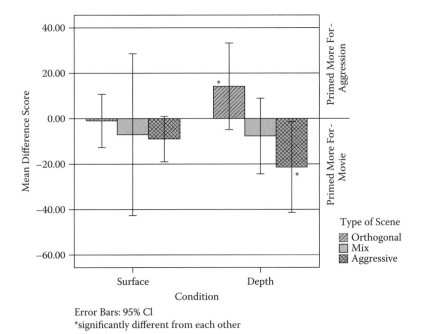

FIGURE 11.4
Mean difference score by type of scene and condition.

attention and level of processing may affect the magnitude of semantic priming of aggressive cognitions. Although some of the hypotheses tested were not significant in this sample, a few effects emerged that supported the theories. Specifically, both the aggressive and nonaggressive content of the movie was learned, as measured by the semantic priming task. Furthermore, the data supported the hypothesis that the viewer's motivations (i.e., viewing for meaning rather than to relax) could potentially increase the magnitude of the learning effects.

More research is needed in the area of cognitive viewing styles, particularly in the development of a more precise operational definition. Furthermore, the role of the active viewer is an important one in understanding a viewer's experience with the media. Although the level of processing and attention are important considerations for how a person may engage with the media, there may be many other important active viewer factors explored in the area of Uses and Gratifications Theory that may offer a more appropriate construct through which to define viewing styles, such as the types of needs viewers use the media to satisfy (Blumler

& Katz, 1974). Additionally, even though the study presented here only utilized a portion of the General Learning Model to understand violent media effects on aggressive cognitions, there are several other levels of learning that can be explored.

It is our contention that incorporating both psychological and communication approaches to media effects can offer valuable insights beyond the scope of either by themselves. The General Learning Model is able to bring to the communications research an integrative approach to understanding normative processes by which viewers can learn from and be affected by the media, and also describes the mechanisms through which the effects occur. The Uses and Gratifications Theory is able to bring to the psychological research the importance of considering the active role of viewers and the important moderating effects that individuals' motivations, goals, and needs can have on what and how they learn from the media. Together, these approaches can lead to a more complete understanding of the roles and effects of the media in our lives.

REFERENCES

Anderson, C. A. (1997). Effects of violent movies and trait hostility on hostile feelings and aggressive thoughts. *Aggressive Behavior, 23,* 161–178.

Anderson, C. A., Berkowitz, L., Donnerstein, E., Huesmann, L. R., Johnson, J., Linz, D., et al. (2003). The influence of media violence on youth. *Psychological Science in the Public Interest, 4,* 81–110.

Anderson, C. A., & Carnagey, N. L. (2004). Violent evil and the general aggression model. In A. Miller (Ed.), *The social psychology of good and evil* (pp. 168–192). New York: Guilford Publications.

Baddeley, A. D., & Dale, H. C. (1966). The effect of semantic similarity on retroactive interference in long- and short-term memory. *Journal of Learning & Verbal Behavior, 5,* 417–420.

Balota, D. A., Yap, M. J., Cortese, M. J., Hutchison, K. A., Kessler, B., Loftis, B., et al. (2007). The English lexicon project. *Behavior Research, 39,* 445–459.

Bandura, A., & Kupers, C. J. (1964). Transmission of patterns of self-reinforcement through modeling. *Journal of Abnormal and Social Psychology, 69,* 1–9.

Bandura, A., Ross, D., & Ross, S. A. (1963). Imitation of film-mediated aggressive models. *Journal of Abnormal and Social Psychology, 66,* 3–11.

Barnett, S. M., & Ceci, S. J. (2002). When and where do we apply what we learn? A taxonomy for far transfer. *Psychological Bulletin, 128,* 612–637.

Berkowitz, L., & LePage, A. (1967). Weapons as aggression-eliciting stimuli. *Journal of Personality and Social Psychology, 7,* 202–207.

Biederman, I., & Shiffrar, M. M. (1987). Sexing day-old chicks: A case study and expert systems analysis of a difficult perceptual learning task. *Journal of Experimental Psychology: Learning, Memory, and Cognition, 13,* 640–645.

Bliss, T. V. P., & Lomo, T. (1973). Long-lasting potentiation of synaptic transmission in the dentate area of the anesthetized rabbit following stimulation of the perforant path. *Journal of Physiology (London), 232,* 331–356.

Blumler, J. G. (1979). The role of theory in uses and gratifications studies. *Communication Research, 6,* 9–36.

Blumler, J. G., & Katz, E. (1974). *The uses of mass communications.* Beverly Hills CA: Sage Publications.

Bridger, W. H. (1961). Sensory habituation and discrimination in the human neonate. *The American Journal of Psychiatry, 117,* 991–996.

Buckley, K. E., & Anderson, C. A. (2006). A theoretical model of the effects and consequences of playing video games. In P. Vorderer & J. Bryant (Eds.), *Playing video games: Motives, responses, and consequences* (pp. 363–378). Mahwah, NJ: Lawrence Earlbaum Associates.

Bushman, B. J. (1995). Moderating role of trait aggressiveness in the effects of violent media on aggression. *Journal of Personality and Social Psychology, 69,* 950–960.

Bushman, B. J., & Huesmann, L. R. (2006). Short-term and long-term effects of violent media on aggression in children and adults. *Archives of Pediatrics & Adolescent Medicine, 160,* 348–352.

Cahill, L., Haier, R. J., Fallon, J., Alkire, M. T., Tang, C., Keator, D., et al. (1996). Amygdala activity at encoding correlated with long-term free recall of emotional information. *Proceedings of the National Academy of Science, 93,* 8016–8021.

Carnagey, N. L., Anderson, C. A., & Bushman, B. J. (2007). The effect of video game violence on physiological desensitization to real-life violence. *Journal of Experimental Social Psychology, 43,* 489–496.

Cepeda, N., Coburn, N., Rohrer, D., Wixted, J. T., Mozer, M., & Pashler, H. (2009). Optimizing distributed practice: Theoretical analysis and practical implications. *Experimental Psychology, 56,* 236–246. doi: 10.1027/1618-3169.56.4.236.

Collins, A. M., & Loftus, E. F. (1975). A spreading-activation theory of semantic processing. *Psychological Review, 82,* 407–428.

Colombo, J., & Mitchell, D. W. (2009). Infant visual habituation. *Neurobiology of Learning and Memory, 92,* 225–234.

Craik, F. I. M., & Tulving, E. (1975). Depth of processing and the retention of words in episodic memory. *Journal of Experimental Psychology: General, 104,* 268–294.

Das, J. P., & Nanda, P. C. (1963). Mediated transfer of attitudes. *Journal of Abnormal and Social Psychology, 66,* 12–16.

DeFleur, M. L., & Ball-Rokeach, S. (1982). *Theories of mass communication* (4th ed.). New York: Longman.

Dixon, T. L., & Linz, D. (2000). Overrepresentation and underrepresentation of African Americans and Latinos as lawbreakers on television news. *Journal of Communication, 50,* 131–154.

Dobos, J. (1992). Gratification models of satisfaction and choice of communication channels in organizations. *Communication Research, 19,* 29–51.

Dudai, Y. (2004). The neurobiology of consolidations, or how stable is the engram? *Annual Review of Psychology, 55,* 51–86.

Eichenbaum, H. (2008). *Learning & memory.* New York: W. W. Norton Company.

Feldman, E. S., Bombyk, D. (Producer), & Weir, P. (Director). (1985). *Witness* [Motion Picture]. United States: Paramount Pictures.

Fiske, S. T., & Taylor, S. E. (1991). *Social cognition.* New York: McGraw-Hill.

Garcia, J., & Ervin, F. R. (1968). Gustatory-visceral and telereceptor-cutaneous conditioning-adaptation in internal and external milieus. *Communications in Behavioral Biology Part A, 1,* 389–415.

Gentile, D. A. (Ed.). (2003). *Media violence and children.* Westport, CT: Praeger Publishing.

Gentile, D. A., Coyne, S., & Walsh, D. A. (2010). Media violence, physical aggression, and relational aggression in school age children: A short-term longitudinal study. *Aggressive Behavior,* n/a. doi: 10.1002/ab.20380.

Gentile, D. A., & Gentile, J. R. (2008). Violent video games as exemplary teachers: A conceptual analysis. *Journal of Youth and Adolescence, 37,* 127–141.

Gentile, D. A., Anderson, C. A., Yukawa, S., Saleem, M., Ming, L. K., Shibuya, A., et al. (2009). The effects of prosocial video games on prosocial behaviors: International evidence from correlational, longitudinal, and experimental studies. *Personality and Social Psychology Bulletin, 35,* 752–763.

Gim, W. S., & Yoon, S. G. (1998). Effects of ad exposures and types of ads on the relationship between attitude toward the ad and brand attitudes: Salient attribute hypothesis vs. affect transfer hypothesis. *Korean Journal of Industrial and Organizational Psychology, 11,* 21–38.

Godden, D., & Baddeley, A. D. (1975). Context-dependent memory in two natural environments: On land and under water. *British Journal of Psychology, 66,* 325–331.

Huesmann, L. R., & Guerra, N. G. (1997). Normative beliefs and the development of aggressive behavior. *Journal of Personality and Social Psychology, 72,* 1–12.

Katz, E., Blumler, J. G., & Gurevitch, M. (1973). Uses and gratifications research. *Public Opinion Quarterly, 37,* 509–523.

Katz, E., & Lazarsfeld, P. F. (1955). *Personal influence: The part played by people in the flow of mass communications.* Glencoe, IL: Free Press.

Kleinsmith, L. J., & Kaplan, S. (1963). Paired associate learning as a function of arousal and interpolated interval. *Journal of Experimental Psychology, 65,* 190–193.

Kuiken, D., Phillips, L., Gregus, M., Miall, D. S., Verbitsky, M., & Tonkonogy, A. (2004). Locating self-modifying feelings within literary reading. *Discourse Processes, 38,* 267–286.

Lang, A. (2000). The limited capacity model of mediated message processing. *Journal of Communication, 50,* 46–70.

Lewin, K. (1936). *Principles of topological psychology.* New York: McGraw-Hill.

Lindsay, J. J., & Anderson, C. A. (2000). From antecedent conditions to violent actions: A general affective aggression model. *Personality and Social Psychology Bulletin, 26,* 533–547.

Miall, D. S. (1989). Beyond the schema given: Affective comprehension of literary narratives. *Cognition and Emotion, 3,* 55–78.

Neely, J. H. (1991). Semantic priming effects in visual word recognition: A selective review of current findings and theories. In D. Besner & G. Humphreys (Eds.), *Basic processes in reading: Visual word recognition* (pp. 264–336). Hillsdale, N J: Lawrence Erlbaum Associates.

Newcomer, J. W., Selke, G., Melson, A. K., Hershey, T., Craft, S., Richards, K., et al. (1999). Decreased memory performance in healthy humans induced by stress-level cortisol treatment. *Archives of General Psychiatry, 56,* 527–533.

Pavlov, I. P. (1927). *Conditioned reflexes: An investigation of the physiological activity of the cerebral cortex.* Oxford, England: Oxford University Press.

Robinson, E. S. (1921). The relative efficiencies of distributed and concentrated study in memorizing. *Journal of Experimental Psychology, 4,* 327–343.

Rubin, A. M. (1984). Ritualized and instrumental television viewing. *Journal of Communication, 34,* 67–77.

Ruggiero, T. E. (2000). Uses and gratifications in the 21st century. *Mass Communication & Society, 3,* 3–37.

Siegel, J. M. (2001). The REM sleep–memory consolidation hypothesis. *Science, 294,* 1058–1063.

Skinner, B. F. (1938). *The behavior of organisms: An experimental analysis.* Oxford, England: Appleton-Century.

Stickgold, R., Whidbee, O., Schirmer, B., Patel, & Hobson, J. A. (2000). Visual discrimination task improvement: A multi-step process occurring during sleep. *Journal of Cognitive Neuroscience, 12,* 246–254.

Swing, E. L., Gentile, D. A., & Anderson, C. A. (2008). Learning processes and violent video games. In R. E. Ferdig (Ed.), *Handbook of research on effective electronic gaming in education* (pp. 876–892). Hershey, PA: Information Science Reference.

Teasdale, J. D., & Russell, M. L. (1983). Differential effects of induced mood on the recall of positive, negative, and neutral words. *British Journal of Clinical Psychology, 22,* 163–171.

Thorndike, E. L. (1905). *The elements of psychology.* New York: A. G. Seiler.

Thorndike, E. L., & Woodworth, R. S. (1901). Influence of improvement in one mental function upon the efficiency of other functions. *Psychological Review, 8,* 247–267, 384–395, 553–564.

Underwood, B. J. (1957). Interference and forgetting. *Psychological Review, 64,* 49–60.

Watson, J. B., & Rayner, R. (1920). Conditioned emotional reactions. *Journal of Experimental Psychology, 3,* 1–14.

Windahl, S. (1981). Uses and gratifications at the crossroads. *Mass Communications Review Yearbook, 2,* 174–185.

Younger, B. A., & Cohen, L. B. (1985). How infants form categories. In G. H. Bower (Ed.), *The psychology of learning and motivation* (Vol. 19, pp. 211–248). Orlando, FL: Academic Press.

12

Paths From Television Violence to Aggression: Reinterpreting the Evidence*

George Comstock
Syracuse University
Syracuse, New York

Jack Powers
Ithaca College
Ithaca, New York

Entertainment provides at least three gratifications: a respite from the anxieties and pressures of everyday life; the opportunity to compare oneself and one's possessions with the demeanor, behavior, and possessions of others; and a means of keeping up with what is transpiring in the world. These gratifications have been particularly well documented in the case of television (Comstock & Scharrer, 1999; Comstock & Scharrer, 2007), where a variety of measures of stress and interpersonal conflict predict greater affinity for, or consumption of, television; where viewers tend to watch more attentively those on the screen like themselves in gender, age, or ethnicity (which would make comparisons more meaningful); where there is a common belief that something can be learned from all types of programming; and where keeping abreast embraces both events in the world at large and the varied portrayals and depictions offered by the medium in news, sports, and entertainment programming. There are also less positive consequences of attending to entertainment, with one of the most investigated

* This is a revised version of the chapter as it originally appeared in Comstock, G. (2004). Paths from television violence to aggression: Reinterpreting the evidence. In L.J. Shrum, (Ed.), *The psychology of entertainment media: Blurring the lines between entertainment and persuasion.* Mahwah, NJ: Lawrence Erlbaum Associates, with only a few revisions.

by the social and behavioral sciences being the facilitation of aggressive and antisocial behavior by violent television and film portrayals (for a good overview and meticulous critique, see Kirsh, 2006).

The empirical evidence on the influence of violent television entertainment on aggression often has been interpreted as supporting the view that attitudes serve as the link between exposure to violent programs and behavior. The evidence, in fact, gives equal support to the hypothesis that the link is the availability of genres of behavior in the minds of viewers—that is, the readiness by which they may be retrieved—rather than dispositions toward behavior.

From this latter perspective, television violence is processed by young viewers in a manner similar to advertising within the elaboration likelihood model (Cacioppo & Petty, 1985; Petty & Cacioppo, 1990). The factors that seemingly promote favorable evaluations of aggressive behavior instead govern the salience of such behavior. Violent portrayals operate like television commercials, which most of the time, because they are low in persuasive argumentation, affect consumers by maintaining the salience of particular brands among purchase options (Comstock & Scharrer, 1999).

The research on television violence and aggressive and antisocial behavior has been voluminous but generally assigned to a sphere of scientific endeavor quite distinct from consumer psychology. This is more a product of an inclination to honor the apparent boundaries of paradigms than it is one of distinctiveness among theory-based explanations. In fact, it is a quick and comfortable journey that leads face-to-face with consumer psychology if one travels the backward loop from Bandura's (1986) social cognitive theory to the health belief model (Becker, 1974). The health belief model was derived from social learning theory, an earlier version of what Bandura now calls *social cognitive theory*. The health belief model argues that behavior related to health—such as food preferences, cigarette and alcohol consumption, seat belt use, and cancer examinations—can be changed by manipulating beliefs about personal risk, the availability of effective means of risk reduction, and the ease of access to and social acceptability of these means of risk reduction. It has been the conceptual model for such large-scale federally financed interventions as the Stanford cardiovascular field experiments (Farquhar et al., 1977, 1990), in which persuasive campaigns, using the mass media and counseling by physicians, were employed to encourage individuals to behave in ways that would reduce the risk of cardiovascular mishap.

Social cognitive theory, of course, is the underpinning for much of the experimental research on young children's increased aggressiveness as a consequence of exposure to violent portrayals (e.g., Bandura, Ross, & Ross, 1963a, 1963b). The health belief model makes it clear that social cognition is a theory of persuasion, although one that emphasizes behavior, modeling of that behavior by attractive persons, relevance achieved through attributes of the portrayal that encourage identification, and, in its application to the area of television violence and aggression, persuasion that is unintended. Thus, the connection between consumer psychology and television violence is not limited to the frequent consumption of media content that is a vehicle for commercials, but extends to the fundamentals of theory, and specifically in the present case, the analogy provided by the peripheral or heuristic path of dual-processing theories such as the ELM.

THE MOST USEFUL GATEWAY

At this point in time, the most useful gateway to the evidence on television violence and aggressive and antisocial behavior is through meta-analyses (Comstock & Scharrer, 2003). Meta-analysis estimates the magnitude of the relationships among variables. These estimates become the best available—in terms of reliability and validity—because they are based on the pooling of data from all qualifying studies that can be found, although various individual studies may have characteristics that merit particular attention.

The role of meta-analysis, and its appeal, is aptly conveyed by the title of Morton Hunt's (1997) account of its development and uses, *How Science Takes Stock*. It has become an important tool for drawing inferences when several and often many empirical studies exist on the same topic. The essence of meta-analysis is the estimating of the size of the relationship between two variables. There usually is an exhaustive search for unpublished as well as published studies to address the "file drawer" problem—published studies alone may result in an overestimate of the magnitude of a relationship because those showing larger, statistically significant outcomes are more likely to be published (Rosenthal, 1979). In turn, studies can be scored on various dimensions for quality and for ecological validity (conditions that parallel everyday life) so that the analysis eventually can focus on the studies that have the strongest claims for generalizing beyond their particular sets of data.

In meta-analysis jargon, the goal is to estimate the *effect size*—the magnitude of the association between two variables. Despite this language, there is nothing about meta-analysis that ensures that the independent variable contributes to or in any way is causally related to the dependent variable. This is an inference that is left to the analyst.

The benefit of meta-analysis is the use of all retrievable data to estimate the magnitude of a relationship, the greater reliability and validity that result from the enlarged *N*, and the ability to code studies for any and every conceivable attribute so that the analyst can focus on those with particular characteristics or qualities. For example, in the case of violent television portrayals and aggressive or antisocial behavior, the analyst could isolate those experiments where a portrayal of justified aggression was the treatment and compare the effect size for the dependent variable with effect sizes for other treatments. The estimate based on several experiments would have greater reliability and validity than the estimate from the original 1963 experiment by Berkowitz and Rawlings (assuming, of course, that the additional experiments are equivalent as a group in quality and ecological validity to the original).

In effect, studies are treated analogously to respondents in a survey. The basic calculation is:

$$\text{Mean } t - \text{Mean } c$$

$$\text{Effect size} = \text{ESD}$$

Where t = treatment, c = control, and *ESD* = estimate of the standard deviation. Because the standard deviation represents the same proportion of cases for all normal distributions, this produces an effect size that can be pooled with others for an aggregate estimate. The formula obviously fits only experimental designs, but procedures have been developed to estimate the equivalent for surveys and other designs. In addition, procedures also have been developed to estimate the statistical significance of any effect size and to calculate fail-safe numbers, which are the number of additional outcomes with null results that would be necessary to reduce the obtained estimate to null. Thus, meta-analysis in its current form makes it possible for the confidence of the analyst to rest not only on the magnitude of the effect size but also on the estimated probability that an outcome is attributable to sampling variability and the estimated quantity of null results that would have to be uncovered to overturn an observed effect size.

Nevertheless, meta-analysis is not a substitute for interpretation. The fretful analyst, among other things, must decide whether the outcomes of experiments are generalizable to everyday circumstances and whether positive correlations between two variables in survey data represent the operation of a third variable or causation, as well as the direction of causation. Kirsh (2006) provides an excellent review of the many issues that must be resolved.

In the case of television and film violence and aggressive and antisocial behavior, interpretation is confronted with a large array of data—eight quantitative aggregations of study outcomes. The most comprehensive (Paik & Comstock, 1994) presents almost 1,150 instances in which an effect size was calculated. Furthermore, the outcomes of individual studies sometimes may supply information that clearly adds to, extends, and qualitatively enriches what is represented in a meta-analysis. As a result, meta-analysis should not be thought of as a means by which all scientific questions are answered but as a source of particularly reliable and valid estimates of the relationships among variables that may be importantly augmented or qualified by the outcomes of particular studies. In the present instance, the meta-analytic data lead to a number of conclusions thoroughly supported by empirical evidence. In addition, the examination of the outcomes of a particularly compelling study leads to a surprise that suggests a revision in theory.

Andison (1977), in a pioneering effort, simply categorized the outcomes of 67 experiments and surveys as to the direction and size of the relationship between violence viewing and aggressive or antisocial behavior. Hearold (1986) was the first to apply the now widely accepted meta-analytic paradigm in which the standard deviation is the criterion for assessing the magnitude of the relationship between variables to the literature on media and behavior. A student of Eugene Glass at the University of Colorado (who is credited with developing meta-analysis in the 1970s in an attempt to quantitatively discredit H. I. Eysenck's claims that psychotherapy was ineffective) examined more than 1,000 relationships (drawn from 168 separate studies) between exposure to anti- and prosocial portrayals and anti- and prosocial behavior.* Wood, Wong, and Cachere (1991) examined 23 experiments in a nd out of the laboratory in which the dependent variable was "unconstrained interpersonal aggression" among children and teenagers. Allen, D'Alessio, and Brezgel (1995) aggregated the data from

---

* The meta-analytic paradigm made its first public appearance in the 1976 presidential address by Glass (1976) at the annual meeting of the American Educational Research Association in San Francisco. This justifiably places him foremost among the pioneers of the method. However, at about the same time, Robert Rosenthal at Harvard was at work on a similar scheme (Rosenthal & Rubin, 1978). Neither knew of what the other was doing (Hunt, 1997), an example of the frequently simultaneous innovation of independent investigators.

33 laboratory-type experiments in which the independent variable was exposure to sexually explicit video or film portrayals, and the dependent variable was aggression. Hogben (1998) confined himself to 56 coefficients drawn from studies measuring everyday viewing but included a wide array of aggression-related responses, including, in addition to aggressive or antisocial behavior, hostile attitudes, personality variables, and, in one case (Cairns, Hunter, & Herring, 1980), the content of imagined news stories. Bushman and Anderson (2001) tracked the viewing and behavior correlations in experimental and nonexperimental designs in 5-year intervals over a 25-year period. Savage and Yancey (2008) focus on 26 samples where the outcome measure qualified as criminal conduct or analogous to such behavior. Paik and Comstock (1994), in a comprehensive updating of Hearold's assessment of the relationship between exposure to television violence and aggressive and antisocial behavior, included 82 new studies for a total of 217 that produced 1,142 coefficients between the independent and dependent variables.

Paik and Comstock (1994) focused on the most substantial portion of the Hearold (1986) meta-analysis. Hearold examined all possible combinations of antisocial and prosocial portrayals and behavior, including the effect size between exposure to prosocial portrayals and antisocial behavior and the effect size between exposure to antisocial portrayals and prosocial behavior (although the data on these pairings expectedly was not voluminous). However, she did not include erotica or pornographic portrayals among the independent variables, and she included among her antisocial dependent variables such outcomes as stereotyping, passivity, and feelings of powerlessness. Aggressive portrayals and behavior nevertheless made up the largest number of independent and dependent variables. Paik and Comstock confined themselves to aggressive portrayals and outcomes, except for including erotic and pornographic portrayals among their independent variables. Thus, they updated the major portion of Hearold's analysis and extended it in terms of coverage by including erotica and pornographic portrayals and in terms of method by including estimates of statistical significance and fail-safe numbers.

These data represent the behavior of many thousands of persons ranging in age from preschool to adulthood, an assortment of independent and dependent variables, and a variety of research methods. For example, Paik and Comstock (1994) included the full range of ages, a variety of types of programming, nine categories of behavior, and laboratory-type experiments, field experiments, time series, and surveys. These are all typically positive features of meta-analyses that, as surveys of a literature, take on the characteristics of the area of inquiry in contrast to the more limited (and limiting) attributes of a single study.

These analyses irrefutably confirm that there is a positive correlation between exposure to violent television and movie portrayals and engagement in aggressive or antisocial behavior. This holds for the data from experiments and for the data from surveys. Seven of the quantitative aggregations of data clearly can be invoked on behalf of this outcome, including the four not confined to a narrow focus on particular measures of exposure or quite specific outcomes (such as unconstrained interpersonal aggression)—the initial pioneering efforts by Andison (1977), Hearold (1986), Bushman and Anderson (2001), and Paik and Comstock (1994). Savage and Yancey (2008) insist they are an exception, yet their summary coefficient for longitudinal data is positive and statistically significant. However, interpretation quickly strides to center stage because this pattern is not very informative about the processes responsible for the relationship. Experiments unambiguously document causation within their circumstances, but it is a matter of judgment whether their outcomes can be generalized to other circumstances; positive correlation coefficients within surveys document association in everyday life but by themselves are insufficient to infer causation (Cook & Campbell, 1979).

INTERPRETING THE EVIDENCE

The case for causation is quite strong. It rests on two factors readily observable in the meta-analyses. The first is the consistency of the outcomes for the experimental designs, where the positive effect sizes are quite robust ($r = .40$ in Paik & Comstock, 1994). Statistical significance is readily achieved (p exceeds four digits in Paik & Comstock), and failsafe numbers are huge (over 700,000 in Paik & Comstock). The second is the confirmation by the survey designs that the condition necessary to infer causation in everyday life exists: a positive correlation between everyday violence viewing and everyday aggressive or antisocial behavior. This is to say that a correlation outside the laboratory exists that stoutly resists explanation other than by some causal contribution of viewing to behavior. Furthermore, these survey designs have effect sizes that are more modest but respectable (r = .19 in Paik & Comstock), while statistical significance and fail-safe numbers (the quantity of null findings necessary to reduce a coefficient to statistical insignificance) remain impressive. Thus, the experiments provide evidence of causation within their limited circumstances, and the surveys confirm that this relationship is generalizable beyond those circumstances. This is essentially the argument offered by Anderson et al. (2003) of the review in *Psychological Science in the Public Interest*, the journal devoted to arbitrating controversial issues that have been addressed by social psychology.

Evidence for the reverse hypothesis (Belson, 1978), though superficially promising, is particularly disappointing. This is the proposition that the positive correlation is explained by the seeking out of violent entertainment by those prone to aggressiveness. Admittedly, there are some sets of data in which aggressiveness predicts subsequent violence viewing, although the literature is quite mixed as to the regularity or pervasiveness of such an outcome (Comstock & Scharrer, 2007). In fact, the analysis that supplies some of the strongest evidence against the reverse hypothesis also provides some data consistent with it. The difficulty is that the reverse hypothesis fails woefully as a complete explanation for the correlation.

The most convincing evidence comes from the reanalysis by Kang (1990) of the NBC panel data on elementary school children (Milavsky, Kessler, Stipp, & Rubens, 1982).* This repeated-measures surveying of the same sample over a 3.5-year period permitted the calculation of coefficients representing earlier viewing and later behavior or earlier behavior and later viewing, leading to inferences about which was affecting the other. Kang found eight statistically significant coefficients for a viewing-to-behavior effect but only four for a behavior-to-viewing effect, out of a total of 15 pairings of earlier and later measurement. Moreover, there was only one instance of reciprocal association (viewing-predicted behavior and behavior-predicted viewing within the same span of time). These data are wholly inconsistent with the reverse hypothesis as a comprehensive explanation.

---

* The NBC panel study involved the collection of data from elementary and high school samples over a 3.5-year period in two cities, one in the Midwest and one in the Southwest. There were 6 points of data collection, which led to 15 wave pairs of earlier and later measurement (I-II, I-III, I-IV, etc.). The focus was on earlier television violence exposure and later aggressive behavior. The lag time between measurements varied from 3 months to more than 3 years. The elementary school N for the shortest period was 497 and for the longest period, 112, with attribution reducing the *N* as the time lags became longer.

The behavior variable in the NBC data was interpersonal aggression—hitting, fighting, stealing, name calling. Belson (1978), in his survey of about 1,600 London teenage men, extends the dismissal of the reverse hypothesis to seriously harmful behavior. He statistically manipulated his data so that he could compare directly the plausibility of the direct and the reverse hypothesis. He concluded that there was no support for the reverse hypothesis and strong support for the direct hypothesis that violence viewing increased the committing of seriously harmful acts (such as attempted rape, false report of a bomb threat, and use of a tire iron, razor, knife, or gun in a fight) among a subsample with a high propensity for delinquent behavior (p. 390, Table 12.13).

The impression given by Bandura and colleagues (Bandura et al., 1963a, 1963b) and often repeated in textbooks, on the basis of early experiments with nursery school children, is that boys are more likely to be affected than girls. Meta-analysis demurs. Girls as well as boys appear to be affected. In Paik and Comstock (1994), effect sizes are similar for boys and girls in survey data. Only in experiments are effect sizes clearly greater for boys than girls. Whether this false impression is attributable to entertainment history (aggressive females on the screen are now more frequent), social change (childrearing is probably now somewhat more accepting of the expression of aggression by girls), norms (the Stanford nursery school surely was a campground of gender role convention), or the preponderance of boys as subjects in the experiments (they outnumber girls by about 6 to 1) is a matter of speculation. What is not speculation is that meta-analysis has supplied a corrective. Meta-analysis also leads to the conclusion that effects do not diminish with age, although they are largest among the very young. In Paik and Comstock, effect sizes displayed an upward shift among those of college age, although otherwise there was a modest decline from preschool to adulthood with increasing age. Thus, it is not justified to conclude that the effects of television violence on aggressive and antisocial behavior are limited to the very young, or that they decline as cognitive ability increases to understand what is transpiring on the screen, to separate fantasy from reality, and to make distinctions between stirring acts and devious motives. Again, this is a pattern that becomes more readily recognizable in meta-analyses because single studies typically are quite restrictive in the range of ages included.

The experiments that began to accumulate in 1963 with the work of Bandura, Berkowitz, and their colleagues (Bandura et al., 1963a, 1963b;

Berkowitz & Rawlings, 1963) drew attention to the possibility that exposure to violent portrayals increased aggressive and antisocial behavior. However, they also were rather starkly limited to immediate effects. Surveys began to address the possibility of effects over time by attempting to represent earlier viewing in the measure of exposure (McLeod, Atkin, & Chaffee, 1972a, 1972b). Eron and Lefkowitz and colleagues (Lefkowitz, Eron, Walder, & Huesmann, 1972, 1977), meanwhile, reported a statistically significant correlation between violence viewing at about age 8 years and aggressive behavior a decade later, after controlling for aggression in the earlier time period (and, thus, its correlates, including any otherwise unmeasured causes of the behavior) as part of the 1972 U. S. Surgeon General's inquiry into television violence. This was the beginning of the production of data sets that seemingly show an effect over time. An example is Johnson and colleagues (Johnson, Cohen, Smailes, Kasen, & Brook, 2002), who report statistically significant correlations between television viewing at age 14 years and aggressive and antisocial behavior at ages 16 and 22 years. Here, too, the reverse hypothesis encounters the usual inhospitality among the data with the pattern about the same for those both high and low initially in aggressive and antisocial behavior. However, the clearest documentation of effects over time occurs in the NBC panel data, where it is possible to distinguish between longitudinal effects and cumulative effects.

NBC's original analysis by Milavsky et al. (1982) found that there were two instances in which effects increased with the passage of time. In one case, the coefficients among the elementary school sample became larger as the number of months between measurements increased, with the largest clustered among the five coefficients representing the longest time spans. In the other, the coefficients among the same elementary school sample became somewhat larger when there were no statistical controls for the influence of earlier viewing, implying that there was an aggregative influence of violence viewing. Two reanalyses of the NBC panel data provide further evidence of effects over time. Cook, Kendzierski, and Thomas (1983) concluded that there was evidence of increasing coefficients with the passage of time among both the elementary school sample and the teenage sample and for several different measures of aggressive and antisocial behavior. Kang (1990) found that five of his statistically significant eight viewing-to-behavior coefficients were clustered among the longest time spans, whereas three of his four behavior-to-viewing coefficients were clustered among the shortest time span. These analyses suggest that there are longitudinal effects and cumulative effects. The former probably represents the influence of earlier viewing on behavior and has become newly relevant or newly within the range of the individual. The data also indicate that influence accumulates. Thus, the data support the development interpretation that earlier viewing establishes traits that will persist and perhaps become even more pronounced while confining the reverse hypothesis largely to the short term (Anderson et al., 2003; Eron & Huesmann, 1987).

Milavsky and colleagues (Milavsky et al., 1982) seized on socioeconomic status as a possible explanation for positive coefficients in their panel data. They argued that the substantial representation of young people from households low in socioeconomic status led to samples where television viewing—thus, exposure to violent portrayals—and aggressive behavior would be correlated. Alas, socioeconomic status proves inadequate to producing the required artifact. Socioeconomic status consistently has been judged as unable to fully explain positive associations between violence viewing and aggressive and antisocial behavior (Belson, 1978; Chaffee, 1972; Comstock & Scharrer, 1999, 2007). Furthermore, in the case of their data, Cook et al. (1983) teased out a truly embarrassing rejoinder—the pattern that held for the males of increasing coefficients as time spans increased, alleged by Milavsky and colleagues as an artifact of socioeconomic status, was duplicated among middle-class girls.

The recorded effects are not trivial in seriousness or size. The effect sizes in Paik and Comstock (1994) for interpersonal aggression, the category of behavior for which the evidence is the strongest because it has been examined more often than any other type of antisocial behavior, are in the medium range by Cohen's (1988) frequently employed criteria (Rosenthal, Rosnow, & Rubin, 2000). Interpersonal aggression includes hitting, fighting, name calling, and stealing, and ordinarily would constitute an experience that most victims would prefer to avoid. Other seriously harmful or criminal outcomes have much smaller effect sizes but they are statistically significant and represent the infliction of greater harm than merely hitting, fighting, name calling, or stealing. The Belson data (Belson, 1978) provide a particularly striking example of a nontrivial outcome. He found in his London sample of teenage males that the viewing of violent television entertainment predicted the committing of significantly more seriously hurtful (and decidedly criminal) acts than were committed by those like them in every of measured respect (other than the greater viewing of violence), and there was evidence that this could not be attributed to the reverse hypothesis. Similarly, Johnson and colleagues (2002) found that greater television viewing (which would imply greater exposure to violent portrayals) at an earlier age predicted more frequent assaults or physical fights resulting in injury among 16- and 22-year-old males. However, the plausibility of the reverse hypothesis was diminished (as pointed out earlier) by the occurrence of the same pattern for those scoring lower as well as higher in aggressiveness at the earlier time period.

Taking advantage of the Federal Communication Commission's (FCC) television station license freeze in the late 1940s and early 1950s to conduct a quasi-experimental time series with switching replications (Cook & Campbell, 1979), a group led by the methodologist Thomas Cook (Hennigan et al., 1982) found consistent evidence across two different samples (cities and states) and at two points in time (early and late introduction of television) that television's introduction was followed by a significant rise in larceny theft. This is an outcome that had two distinct interpretations: that it should be attributed to relative deprivation accelerated by the materialistic emphases of the medium (Hennigan et al., 1982) and that it represents emulation of television's antisocial emphases in a manner that apprehension would be unlikely and sanctions modest (Comstock, 1991).

In the Paik and Comstock (1994) meta-analysis, coefficients were mostly in the medium range (by Cohen's criteria) for simulated aggressive behavior (such as aggressive inclination measured by questionnaire or performance on an aggression machine) and minor aggression (such as violence done to an object or physical aggression against a person that would fall under the law's radar), although sometimes they were in the large range. The coefficients were smaller when illegal activities were the dependent variable and became progressively smaller as the seriousness of the offense increased. Even so, criminal violence against a person achieved statistical significance and scored a fail-safe number just shy of 3,000.

Paik and Comstock (1994) divided outcomes into three categories: simulated aggression, minor aggressive behavior, and illegal activities. In effect, they created a scale of increasing social consequence in terms of the validity of the dependent variable. The first included use of an aggression machine and self-report of aggressive inclination, play with aggressive toys, and miscellaneous simulated aggressive behavior. The second included physical aggression against an object, verbal aggression, and physical aggression against a person below the threshold of serious harm. The third included burglary, grand theft, and seriously harmful violence against a person. Self-report of aggressive inclination was largely represented by responses indicating what the individual would do in hypothetical situations. Thus, it was analogous to the expression of a norm, value, or attitude—a disposition—rather than an intention to behave in the future in a particular way in a specific situation.

The issue of the possible triviality of the effect sizes for television violence viewing and aggressive and antisocial behavior is addressed somewhat differently by Bushman and Anderson (2001). They compiled a catalogue of effect sizes to compare with the effect size for all observations in the Paik and Comstock (1994) meta analysis (Figure 2). The $r = .31$ for media violence and aggression compares favorably in terms of magnitude with those for such pairings as passive smoking and lung cancer, calcium intake and bone mass, and homework and academic achievement. In their own meta-analysis, Bushman and Anderson found stable, statistically significant correlations for experimental designs from 1975 to 2000, and for the ecologically most valid data, the nonexperimental designs representing real-life aggression or antisocial behavior, Bushman and Anderson found statistically significant correlations that have increased in magnitude over the past 25 years. In contrast, in a parallel content analysis of major news media, they uncovered a decline in the frequency that reports linked television and film violence with an undesirable behavioral outcome (they record a sizable negative correlation of $r = -.68$ between average effect sizes and the ratings of news reports for their fealty to the scientific evidence at 5-year intervals—for a total of six data points between 1975 and 2000). They conclude, with considerable exasperation at the performance of the news media, that "regardless of preference for experimental or nonexperimental methods, it has been decades since one could reasonably claim that there is little reason for concern about media violence effects" (p. 485).

Finally, based on Paik and Comstock (1994), the U. S. Surgeon General's report on youth violence (U. S. Department of Health and Human Services, 2001) identifies greater exposure to television violence between the ages of 6 and 11 years as an early risk factor for the committing of criminal violence equivalent to a felony between the ages of 15 and 18 years (Box 4.1).

The effect size (*r* = .13) was categorized as falling into the small range. However, about three fourths of the near 20 factors identified as posing early risks for later violence also fell into the small category. Savage and Yancey (2008) cast themselves as dissenting in regard to a relationship between exposure to media violence and serious misbehavior, but in fact their data are quite compatible with those of Paik and Comstock—a very small, statistically significant positive effect size (although they put their emphasis on the possibility of an overestimate).

Young people are particularly vulnerable to the influence of television and film violence when they have attributes that predict greater exposure to violent portrayals or greater likelihood of engaging in aggressive or antisocial behavior (Comstock & Scharrer, 1999; U. S. Department of Health and Human Services, 2001). Five such attributes are low socio-economic status, rigid or indifferent parenting, unsatisfactory social relationships, low psychological well-being, and predisposition for antisocial behavior. Exposure to television and to television violence is inversely associated with socioeconomic status (Comstock & Scharrer, 1999; Thornton & Voigt, 1984). When parent–child communication is open and constructive (in contrast with families where communication is rigid, many topics are avoided, differences in opinion are discouraged, and orders rather than explanations by parents are the rule), there typically is less television viewing by children and less exposure to violent television entertainment (Chaffee, McLeod, & Atkin, 1971; McLeod, Atkin, & Chaffee, 1972b).

In addition, a variety of delinquent behavior is inversely associated with parental interest in the whereabouts of children and teenagers (Thornton & Voigt, 1984). Psychological discomfort and social conflicts predict greater exposure to television; those under stress, lonely, anxious, in negative moods, or in conflict with others apparently find the medium a satisfying escape and thus score high in viewing or attraction to television (Anderson, Collins, Schmitt, & Jacobvitz, 1996; Canary & Spitzberg, 1993; Comstock & Scharrer, 1999; Kubey & Csikszentmihalyi, 1990; Maccoby, 1954; Potts & Sanchez, 1994).

Furthermore, it is clear that the predisposed—those scoring higher in antisocial behavior or possessing attributes that are correlates of antisocial behavior—are most likely to be affected. Surveys (Belson, 1978; Robinson & Bachman, 1972), experiments (Josephson, 1987; Celozzi, Kazelskis, & Gutsch, 1981), and a meta-analysis (Paik, 1991) all record associations that are greater among or limited to the predisposed. We doubt that it is a necessary condition because results are so consistent for general populations in surveys and experiments, but, if it is, then it is also very widespread. Thus, television violence is most likely to add to the burdens of those who already face considerable challenge in coping with everyday life, and this becomes particularly clear when it is acknowledged that the kind of behavior likely to be increased by violent portrayals is also the kind likely to lead to conflicts with others and clashes with the law.

Two independent analyses concur that among the independent variables responsible for effects on aggression one of the most powerful is violent erotica. Both Paik and Comstock (1994), who examined erotic as well as violent portrayals, and Allen, D'Alessio, and Brezgel (1995), who examined only erotic portrayals, although proceeding somewhat differently (as is usually the case in these matters) and producing somewhat different effect sizes (as would be expected), report effect sizes for violent erotica that are among the highest recorded.

The data also provide an important contribution to the debate over whether it is the sex (Weaver, 1991) or the violence (Donnerstein, Linz, & Penrod, 1987) that is responsible. Effect sizes for violent erotica are consistently higher than they are for erotica without violence. However, coefficients for erotica without violence are consistently positive. When Allen and colleagues (Allen et al., 1995), following the schema developed by the Attorney General's Commission on Pornography (1986), divided their independent variables into portrayals of nudity without sex, erotica (sex without violence), and violent erotica, they found for the first an inverse effect size and for the latter two positive and increasing effect sizes. The answer, then, is that it is both the sex and the violence, with the two creating a powerful joint stimulus.

Meta-analysis in this instance also raises an unresolved question: How is the pattern explained? The dual outcomes for sex and violence would seem to favor arousal (rising with eroticism and violence) and aggressive cues (at a maximum here with violent erotica). However, the findings by Allen and colleagues (Allen et al., 1995) that throughout the meta-analysis self-reported arousal was inversely (if modestly) correlated with aggression precludes quick embrace of such an inference (although with additional data—the number of cases was undeniably small—it may prove to be the explanation). This leaves aggressive cues, which may be stimulated by the sexuality of erotica but at a much lower level than when combined with explicit violence directed against a female (as would be the case with violent erotica).

The data bestow considerable confidence that the patterns observed are not the products of methodologically inferior or ecologically questionable undertakings. In neither the early meta-analysis of Hearold (1986) nor the more recent one by Paik and Comstock (1994) does the introduction of measures of study quality and ecological validity alter conclusions, with one noteworthy exception. Hearold found that when she confined her analysis to the studies scoring high in methodological quality (which would give the data particular credibility) the outcomes were symmetrical for antisocial and prosocial portrayals. Antisocial portrayals were associated with a positive effect size for antisocial behavior and a negative effect size for prosocial behavior. Prosocial portrayals were associated with a positive effect size for prosocial behavior and a negative effect size for antisocial behavior. One clear implication is the imposition of a double jeopardy by violent children's programming: greater likelihood of antisocial behavior and lesser likelihood of prosocial behavior by the young viewer.

Hearold (1986) also examined another design element—the matching in experiments of treatment and outcome variables. These experiments involved pure modeling, with the outcomes undeterred by the requirement that the subjects generalize from one situation to another. She found that this design element doubled effect sizes for both antisocial and prosocial behavior. There are two implications. One is that commercial entertainment has less effect than might otherwise be the case because it often fails to match the situations in which viewers find themselves. The other is that experiments with these characteristics should not be taken as offering an effect size likely to be duplicated in everyday life, except when portrayal and behavioral options exactly match.

REINTERPRETATION

Often, exposure to violent portrayals has been a predictor of an attitudinal disposition favorable to aggressive or antisocial behavior, and, often, these outcomes have occurred in experimental designs. As a consequence, exposure in these cases can be said to be the cause of the disposition. For example, in the Paik and Comstock (1994) meta-analysis, a substantial number of the outcomes categorized under the rubric "aggressive intent" (r = .33, medium magnitude by Cohen's criteria) consisted of responses indicating what the individual would do in hypothetical situations. Such measures represent attitudes or dispositions rather than clear-cut intentions in regard to concrete circumstances. Thus, meta-analysis (and the many individual studies encompassed) provides evidence of a causal link between violence viewing and dispositions. Nevertheless, there is little direct evidence that dispositions are a necessary link between the exposure to violent portrayals and aggressive or antisocial behavior.

There is a data set that addresses this issue and possesses attributes that give it unusual credibility. Belson's (1978) sample of London male teenagers was very large (about 1,600) and is the only probability sample in the literature (as a result, it has the inferential nicety of clearly representing a larger population). Belson's measurement was meticulous and statistical analysis assiduous. The respondents were personally interviewed by a conservatively attired male in a clinical setting. Boys were given false names to emphasize the confidentiality of the investigation, and the names were used throughout to encourage forthright responses. The interviews were unusually lengthy—about 3.5 hours. This is the equivalent of almost 1,000 days of interviewing, an apt reflection of the scale of this enterprise. When it came to aggressive and antisocial behavior, they were asked to indicate whether, within the past 6 months, they had committed an act printed on a card by placing the card in a location clearly designated as representing "Yes," "No," or "Not sure." The intent was to reduce guile resulting from shame or embarrassment by eliminating the need for the respondent to speak about what he had done. The interviewer then engaged in forceful probes in regard to a "Not sure" and the frequency with which a confessed act had been committed. The subsequent labeling of these acts as to their seriousness was based on the rating of adult judges. Thus, the aggressive and antisocial outcome measures were sensitive, probing, and rooted in normative social judgments and presumably minimized both guile and conformity to interviewer expectancies, and the data have a strong claim to representing real-world patterns.

Among the variables included in the Belson (1978) survey were a number of items representing attitudinal dispositions—norms, values, and beliefs. He included them as possible outcomes associated with exposure to violent television entertainment. Belson obtained direct measures of four dispositions—antisocial attitudes, approval of violence, hostile personality traits, and willingness to commit violence. Reliability was high, each with multi-item scales with 10 or more items. None of these outcomes was predicted by the viewing of violent television entertainment. Thus, there was no evidence of a dispositional link between viewing and behavior.

Nevertheless, much of the research that has been central in the investigation of the relationship between exposure to television and film violence and aggressive and antisocial behavior would seem to assign a central place to attitudes, norms, and values. Both Bandura's (1986) social cognition and Berkowitz's (1984, 1990) neoassociationism give considerable weight to the categorizing of acts according to their effectiveness, social approval, and appropriateness for the circumstances. Both theories hold that portrayals with these characteristics are more likely to influence behavior. Such categorizing would seemingly depend on cognitive processes whose terminal state would be a disposition. The conclusion of Eron and Huesmann (1987), in interpreting a positive correlation in survey data between childhood violence viewing and adult aggressiveness, is representative of many others writing on television violence and antisocial behavior:

> It is not claimed that the specific programs these adults viewed when they were 8 years old still had a direct effect on their behavior. However, the continued viewing of these programs probably contributed to the development of certain attitudes and norms of behavior and taught these youngsters ways of solving interpersonal problems that remained with them over the years. (p. 196)

Interpretation thus faces a quandary. The Belson (1978) survey provides strong evidence that attitudes, norms, and values are not invariably a link in real life in the causal chain between exposure and behavior. Numerous experiments also provide convincing evidence that aggression and antisocial behavior are increased when certain factors are present that would seem to operate through cognitive processes—portrayals that depict behavior as effective, socially approved, and appropriate for the viewer, as well as circumstances that place the viewer in the market for some behavioral guidance. These are the contingencies that Comstock and Scharrer (2007) refer to as efficacy, normativeness, pertinence, and susceptibility. They represent, respectively, the degree to which a portrayed behavior is perceived as effective, as evidenced by reward or, for those intrinsically pleasurable, lack of punishment; as socially accepted, approved, or conventional; relevant to the viewer, such as a perpetrator of the same age or gender or a victim resembling a potential real-life target; and the degree to which the viewer is motivated or rendered vulnerable to being affected by the portrayal.

Susceptibility is a factor that has been found often to play a role in the influence of communication. In the case of aggressive or antisocial behavior, it is typically represented by frustration or provocation and in experiments often induced by the rude or insulting behavior of the experimenter. However, it also has been found to operate in other contexts. For example, in the Stanford cardiovascular experiment (Farquhar et al., 1977, 1990), those who scored higher in risk proneness were more influenced by persuasive appeals intended to reduce behavior that contributed to cardiovascular disorder, and in the area of agenda setting (Comstock & Scharrer, 1999) those scoring higher in the need for orientation are more likely to be influenced by the emphases of media coverage in regard to the issues and topics they perceive as important. In each of these three instances, the influence of messages is somewhat contingent on individual motives, needs, and interests.

The Belson (1978) data clearly falsify the hypothesis that certain attitudes and norms (to use the phrasing of Eron and Huesmann, 1987) are a necessary link in the causal chain. The interpretation that conforms to both sets of evidence is that these factors promote the incorporation and accessibility of the portrayed behavior. The function of these factors is to govern the salience of classes or genres of behavior in the repertoire of the individual. Efficacy, normativeness, pertinence, and susceptibility would act as gatekeepers.

From this perspective, observation, and attitudes, norms, and values often act as competitors rather than the coconspirators they are usually taken for. Attitudes, norms, and values may remain stable while the likelihood of a change in behavior increases or decreases. Good people (at least, those with constructive thoughts) may behave badly without any sign of a change in expressed dispositions. This lowers the predictive power of attitudes, norms, and values, which have a notoriously weak resistance to the demands of situational circumstances (Eagly & Chaiken, 1993; Terry & Hogg, 2000) and heightens the predictive power of observation. Efficacy, normativeness, pertinence, and susceptibility become conditions that enhance the availability and salience and not necessarily attitudinal dispositions.

This revision of theory addresses two nagging puzzles. One is the quite frequent occasion when attitudes, norms, and values, and behavior part ways. The other is the similarly frequent occasion when the enormity of an act seems beyond a contribution by the media. The revision asserts that there are routes to behavior other than through dispositions and that the role of the media may be confined to gatekeeping.

The data support the view that one route by which entertainment affects behavior is analogous to peripheral processing in the elaboration likelihood model. Accessibility or salience is a key element. However, it would be premature to conclude that this is the sole route by which behavioral effects occur. Attitudes, norms, and values surely sometimes play a role. One would occur when these cognitive dispositions and accessibility coincide, which would increase the likelihood of an effect; this would be a special case of susceptibility in operation. Another is when thoughtful motivation enters, such as Bandura's (1986) famous example of a well-contrived (and financially successful) airline bomb extortion attempt following the televising of a movie depicting such a caper. This analysis obviously fits quite well with the general aggression model (GAM) proposed by Anderson and Bushman (2002), where cognitive processes may have an influence but are not a necessary element, and the role of shifts in salience as an influence on behavior as emphasized by Dijksterhuis and Bargh (2001). The present analysis, however, addresses the specific question of whether attitudes, norms, and values—that is, cognitive elements—are a necessary part (as much research suggests) of any causal chain where exposure to violent portrayals predicts aggressive or antisocial behavior (as in the Belson data), and the conclusion is that they are not.

The Belson (1978) data do not support a role for direct effects of attitudes, norms, and values. However, they are consistent with a role for cognitive dispositions through effects on accessibility and salience. In addition, there remains the possibility that attitudes, norms, and values held by others may create an environment more or less favorable to model behavior made accessible or salient by the media. Thus, attitudes, norms, and values remain important concepts for explaining the effects of violent portrayals on aggressive and antisocial behavior, although they are not a necessary mediating link between exposure and behavior.

We conclude with three points:

1. The case for television viewing and real-life aggression is strong.
2. Attitudes are not a necessary condition to behave aggressively (that is, it is possible to behave aggressively based on exposure to violent media without necessarily forming aggressive attitudes).
3. There is strong support for the rival hypothesis that entertainment media sometimes affect behavior, based on the elements of accessibility and salience (but that attitudes, norms, and values sometimes play a role).

REFERENCES

Allen, M., D'Alessio, D., & Brezgel, K. (1995). A meta-analysis summarizing the effects of pornography II: Aggression after exposure. *Human Communication Research, 22*(2), 258–283.

Anderson, C. A., Berkowitz, L., Donnerstein, E., Huesmann, L. R., Johnson, J. D., Linz, D. et al. (2003). The influence of media violence on youth. *Psychological Science in the Public Interest, 4*(3), 81–110.

Anderson, C. A., & Bushman, B. J. (2002). Human aggression. *Annual Review of Psychology, 5*, 27–51.

Anderson, D. R., Collins, P. A., Schmitt, K. L., & Jacobvitz, R. S. (1996). Stressful life events and television viewing. *Communication Research, 23*(3), 243–260.

Andison, F. S. (1977). TV violence and viewer aggression: A cumulation of study results. *Public Opinion Quarterly, 41*(3), 314–331.

Attorney General's Commission on Pornography. (1986). *Final report.* Washington, DC: Government Printing Office.

Bandura, A. (1986). *Social foundations of thought and action: A social cognitive theory.* Englewood Cliffs, NJ: Prentice Hall.

Bandura, A., Ross, D., & Ross, S. A. (1963a). Imitation of film-mediated aggressive models. *Journal of Abnormal and Social Psychology, 66*(1), 3–11.

Bandura, A., Ross, D., & Ross, S. A. (1963b). Vicarious reinforcement and imitative learning. *Journal of Abnormal and Social Psychology, 67*(6), 601–607.

Becker, M. H. (Ed.). (1974). The health belief model and personal health behavior. *Health Educator Monographs, 2*(4), 324–473.

Belson, W. A. (1978). *Television violence and the adolescent boy.* Westmead, UK: Saxon House.

Berkowitz, L. (1984). Some effects of thoughts on anti- and prosocial influences of media events: A cognitive-neoassociationistic analysis. *Psychological Bulletin, 95*(3), 410–427.

Berkowitz, L. (1990). On the formation and regulation of anger and aggression: A cognitive neoassociationistic analysis. *American Psychologist, 45*(4), 494–503.

Berkowitz, L., & Rawlings, E. (1963). Effects of film violence on inhibitions against subsequent aggression. *Journal of Abnormal and Social Psychology, 66*(5), 405–412.

Bushman, B. J., & Anderson, C. A. (2001). Media violence and the American public: Scientific facts versus media misinformation. *American Psychologist, 56*(6–7), 477–489.

Cacioppo, J. T., & Petty, R. E. (1985). Central and peripheral routes to persuasion: The role of message repetition. In L. F. Alwitt & A. A. Mitchell (Eds.), *Psychological processes and advertising effects: Theory, research, and applications* (pp. 91–111). Hillsdale, NJ: Lawrence Erlbaum Associates.

Cairns, E., Hunter, D., & Herring, L. (1980). Young children's awareness of violence in Northern Ireland: The influence of Northern Irish television in Scotland and Northern Ireland. *British Journal of Social and Clinical Psychology, 19,* 3–6.

Canary, D. J., & Spitzberg, B. H. (1993). Loneliness and media gratification. *Communication Research, 20*(6), 800–821.

Celozzi, M. J., II, Kazelskis, R., & Gutsch, K. U. (1981). The relationship between viewing televised violence in ice hockey and subsequent levels of personal aggression. *Journal of Sport Behavior, 4*(4), 157–162.

Chaffee, S. H. (1972). Television and adolescent aggressiveness (overview). In G. A. Comstock & E. A. Rubinstein (Eds.), *Television and social behavior: Television and adolescent aggressiveness* (Vol. 3, pp. 1–34). Washington, DC: US Government Printing Office.

Chaffee, S. H., McLeod, J. M., & Atkin, C. K. (1971). Parental influences on adolescent media use. *American Behavioral Scientist, 14,* 323–340.

Cohen, E. E. (1988). *Children's television commercialization survey.* Washington, DC: National Association of Broadcasters.

Comstock, G. (1991). *Television and the American child.* San Diego, CA: Academic Press.

Comstock, G., & Scharrer, E. (1999). *Television: What's on, who's watching, and what it means.* San Diego, CA: Academic Press.

Comstock, G., & Scharrer, E. (2003). Meta-analyzing the controversy over television violence and aggression. In D. A. Gentil (Ed.), *Media violence and children* (pp. 205–206). Westport, CT: Praeger.

Comstock, G., & Scharrer, E. (2007). *Media and the American child.* San Diego, CA: Academic Press.

Cook, T. D., & Campbell, D. T. (1979). *Quasi-experimentation: Design and analysis issues for field settings.* Chicago: Houghton Mifflin.

Cook, T. D., Kendzierski, D. A., & Thomas, S. A. (1983). The implicit assumptions of television research: An analysis of the 1982 NIMH report on television and behavior. *Public Opinion Quarterly, 47*(2), 161–201.

Dijksterhuis, A., & Bargh, J. A. (2001). The perception-behavior expressway: Automatic effects of social perception on social behavior. In M. P. Zanna (Ed.), *Advances in experimental social psychology* (Vol. 33, pp. 1–40). San Diego, CA: Academic Press.

Donnerstein, E., Linz, D., & Penrod, S. (1987). *The question of pornography: Research findings and policy implications.* New York: Free Press.

Eagly, A. H., & Chaiken, S. (1993). *The psychology of attitudes.* Orlando, FL: Harcourt.

Eron, L. D., & Huesmann, L. R. (1987). Television as a source of maltreatment of children. *School Psychology Review, 16*(2), 195–202.

Farquhar, J. W., Fortmann, S. P., Flora, J. A., Taylor, C. B., Haskell, W. L., Williams, P. T. et al. (1990). Effects of communitywide education on cardiovascular disease risk factors: The Stanford Five-City Project. *Journal of the American Medical Association, 264*(3), 359–365.

Farquhar, J. W., Maccoby, N., Wood, P. D., Alexander, J. K., Breitrose, H., Brown, B. W., Jr. et al. (1977). Community education for cardiovascular health. *Lancet, 1,* 1192–1195.

Glass, G. V. (1976). Primary, secondary, and meta-analysis of research. *Educational Researcher, 5,* 3–8.

Hearold, S. (1986). A synthesis of 1043 effects of television on social behavior. In G. Comstock (Ed.), *Public communication and behavior* (Vol. 1, pp. 65–133). New York: Academic Press.

Hennigan, K. M., Heath, L., Wharton, J. D., Del Rosario, M. L., Cook, T. D., & Calder, B. J. (1982). Impact of the introduction of television on crime in the United States: Empirical findings and theoretical implications. *Journal of Personality and Social Psychology, 42*(3), 461–477.

Hogben, M. (1998). Factors moderating the effect of television aggression on viewer behavior. *Communication Research, 25,* 220–247.

Hunt, M. (1997). *How science takes stock.* New York: Russell Sage.

Johnson, J. G., Cohen, P., Smailes, E. M., Kasen, S., & Brook, J. S. (2002). Television viewing and aggressive behavior during adolescence and adulthood. *Science, 295,* 2468–2471.

Josephson, W. L. (1987). Television violence and children's aggression: Testing the priming, social script, and disinhibition predictions. *Journal of Personality and Social Psychology, 53*(5), 882–890.

Kang, N. (1990). *A critique and secondary analysis of the NBC study on television and aggression.* Unpublished doctoral dissertation, Syracuse University, Syracuse, NY.

Kirsh, S. J. (2006). *Children, adolescents, and media violence.* Thousand Oaks, CA: Sage.

Kubey, R., & Csikszentmihalyi, M. (1990). *Television and the quality of life: How viewing shapes everyday experience.* Hillsdale, NJ: Lawrence Erlbaum Associates.

Lefkowitz, M. M., Eron, L. D., Walder, L. O., & Huesmann, L. R. (1972). Television violence and child aggression: A follow-up study. In G. A. Comstock & E. A. Rubinstein (Eds.), *Television and social behavior: Vol. 3. Television and adolescent aggressiveness* (pp. 35–135). Washington, DC: U. S. Government Printing Office.

Lefkowitz, M. M., Eron, L. D., Walder, L. O., & Huesmann, L. R. (1977). *Growing up to be violent: A longitudinal study of the development of aggression.* Elmsford, NY: Pergamon.

Maccoby, E. E. (1954). Why do children watch television? *Public Opinion Quarterly, 18*(3), 239–244.

McLeod, J. M., Atkin, C. K., & Chaffee, S. H. (1972a). Adolescents, parents, and television : Adolescent self-report measures from Maryland and Wisconsin samples. In G. A. Comstock & A. Rubinstein (Eds.), *Television and social behavior: Television and adolescent aggressiveness* (Vol. 3, pp. 173–238). Washington, DC: U.S. Government Printing Office.

McLeod, J. M., Atkin, C. K., & Chaffee, S. H. (1972b). Adolescents, parents, and television: Self-report and other-report measures from the Wisconsin sample. In G. A. Comstock & E. Rubinstein (Eds.), *Television and social behavior: Television and adolescent aggressiveness,* (Vol. 3, pp. 239–313). Washington, DC: U.S. Government Printing Office.

Milavsky, J. R., Kessler, R., Stipp, H. H., & Rubens, W. S. (1982). *Television and aggression: A panel study.* New York: Academic Press.

Paik, H., (1991). *The effects of television violence on aggressive behavior: A meta-analysis.* Unpublished doctoral dissertation, Syracuse University, Syracuse, NY.

Paik, H., & Comstock, G. (1994). The effects of television violence on antisocial behavior: A meta-analysis. *Communication Research, 21*(4), 516–546.

Petty, R. E., & Cacioppo, J. T. (1990). Involvement and persuasion: Tradition vs. integration. *Psychological Bulletin, 107*(3), 367–374.

Potts, R., & Sanchez, D. (1994). Television viewing and depression: No news is good news. *Journal of Broadcasting and Electronic Media, 38*(1), 79–90.

Robinson, J. P., & Bachman, J. G. (1972). Television viewing habits and aggression. In G. Comstock & E. A. Rubinstein (Eds.), *Television and social behavior: Television and adolescent aggressiveness* (Vol. 3, pp. 372–382). Washington, DC: US Government Printing Office.

Rosenthal, R. (1979). The "file drawer problem" and tolerance for null results. *Psychological Bulletin, 86,* 638–641.

Rosenthal, R., Rosnow, R. L., & Rubin, D. B. (2000). *Contrasts and effect sizes in behavioral research: A correlational approach.* New York: Cambridge University Press.

Rosenthal, R., & Rubin, D. B. (1978). Interpersonal expectancy effects: The first 345 studies. *Behavioral and Brain Sciences, 5,* 377–386.

Savage, J., & Yancey, C. (2008). The effects of media violence exposure on criminal aggression: A meta-analysis. *Criminal Justice and Behavior, 35,* 772–791.

Terry, D. J., & Hogg, M. A. (Eds.). (2000). *Attitudes, behavior, and social context.* Mahwah, NJ: Lawrence Erlbaum Associates.

Thornton, W., & Voigt, L. (1984). Television and delinquency. *Youth and Society, 15*(4), 445–468.

U. S. Department of Health and Human Services. (2001). *Youth violence: A report of the Surgeon General.* Rockville, MD: U. S. Department of Health and Human Services, Centers for Disease Control and Prevention, National Center for Injury Prevention and Control, Substance Abuse Mental Health Services Administration, Center for Mental Health Services, National Institute Health, National Institute of Mental Health.

Weaver, J. (1991). Responding to erotica: Perceptual processes and dispositional implications. In J. Bryant & D. Zillmann (Eds.), *Responding to the screen: Reception and reaction processes* (pp. 329–354). Hillsdale, NJ: Lawrence Erlbaum Associates.

Wood, W., Wong, F., & Cachere, J. (1991). Effects of media violence on viewers' aggression in unconstrained social interaction. *Psychological Bulletin, 109*(3), 371–383.

Author Index

Subject Index

DATE DUE	RETURNED